THE RUSSIAN MILITARY TODAY AND TOMORROW: ESSAYS IN MEMORY OF MARY FITZGERALD

Stephen J. Blank

Richard Weitz

Editors

July 2010

The views expressed in this report are those of the authors and do not necessarily reflect the official policy or position of the Department of the Army, the Department of Defense, or the U.S. Government. Authors of Strategic Studies Institute (SSI) publications enjoy full academic freedom, provided they do not disclose classified information, jeopardize operations security, or misrepresent official U.S. policy. Such academic freedom empowers them to offer new and sometimes controversial perspectives in the interest of furthering debate on key issues. This report is cleared for public release; distribution is unlimited.

*****

*****

Comments pertaining to this report are invited and should be forwarded to: Director, Strategic Studies Institute, U.S. Army War College, 122 Forbes Ave, Carlisle, PA 17013-5244.

*****

CONTENTS

Dedication v
    Andrew Marshall

Introduction: Russian Military Studies:
A Call for Action 1
    Stephen J. Blank and Richard Weitz

1. "No Need to Threaten Us, We Are Frightened of Ourselves," Russia's Blueprint for a Police State, The New Security Strategy 19
    Stephen J. Blank

2. Is Military Reform in Russia for "Real"? Yes, But 151
    Dale R. Herspring

3. Operational Art and the Curious Narrative on the Russian Contribution: Presence and Absence Over the Last 2 Decades........................193
    Jacob W. Kipp

4. Russian Information Warfare Theory: The Consequences of August 2008 265
    Timothy L. Thomas

5. Russian Strategic Nuclear Forces and Arms Control: Déjà Vu All Over Again..........................301
    Daniel Goure

6. The Challenge of Understanding the Russian Navy...331
    Mikhail Tsypkin

7. Russian Military Challenges Toward
   Central-East Europe 359
   Joshua B. Spero

8. Russian-Chinese Security Relations:
   Constant and Changing 389
   Richard Weitz

Publications by Mary C. Fitzgerald......................455

About the Contributors..463

DEDICATION

Andrew Marshall

Mary Fitzgerald made many contributions to the national security field over the course of the years through her close reading of the writings of Soviet and Russian military officers. Particularly useful was her focus on those of Soviet military theorists who put forward forecasts of future warfare and the impact of technology on warfare. These Russian reviews deserved respect and study; Mary's work made this possible.

After the collapse of the Soviet Union, it became easier to meet with and talk with a number of these Soviet officers so as to explore more fully their thinking and the continuing development of their ideas about future warfare, and the likely direction of the military revolution they had begun writing about in the late 1970s. Organizing meetings with them was greatly aided by Mary because of the good relations she had developed with several of these officers, who liked her as a person and were flattered that she had been so careful a reader of their writings.

We are all in her debt.

INTRODUCTION

RUSSIAN MILITARY STUDIES: A CALL FOR ACTION

Stephen J. Blank
Richard Weitz

The essays in this volume represent both a memorial and an analytical call to action. We have brought these authors and their essays together in memory of our colleague, Mary Fitzgerald of the Hudson Institute, who passed away far too soon, on April 5, 2009. Mary was one of the most brilliant and vivacious practitioners of the study of the Russian and Chinese militaries, whose insights helped not just to put those fields of study on the map, but also to influence U.S. military thinking. Her work helped shed light on the concrete meaning of such terms as the "Revolution in Military Affairs" (RMA), as well as the profoundly original works of thinkers like Marshal Nikolai Ogarkov (1917-94), who was both Chief of the Soviet General Staff (1977-84) and an outstanding military thinker who coined that term.[1] As the Dedication by Andrew Marshall points out, the influence that terms like the RMA, and the concepts surrounding them that Ogarkov developed, influenced 20 years of U.S. and European thinking, from 1980-2000, about the conduct of war.

This achievement alone would suffice to merit lasting respect and admiration from her colleagues. All the authors here worked with or were influenced by Mary's contributions. But a memorial should be a living thing, not just a eulogy which is soon forgotten. In analytical terms, it is also a call to action, a continuing insistence that it is essential for the scholarly, professional, and policymaking communities not only to take into account Russian military developments, but also the military thinking that animates many of those developments. Just as Soviet military thinking was arguably the most profound of all military thinking during the interwar period of the 1920s and 1930s, so today we, both as scholars and professional actors, would benefit considerably from paying serious attention to the contemporary corpus of Russian thinking about warfare. Indeed, it can be argued that the U.S. military won one of its greatest victories in 1991 in Operation DESERT STORM precisely by assimilating and then operationalizing concepts laid out by Ogarkov and his contemporaries, as well as the "lost generation" of Soviet thinkers like Marshal Mikhail Tukhachevsky (1891-1937) and Colonel Alexander Svechin (1878-1938).[2] The serious study of current Russian thinking will benefit policymakers and military professionals alike, both on its own merits and by virtue of the ongoing importance of Russia as a strategic factor in world politics. Unfortunately, the study of this important subject is in danger of being buried along with one of its most gifted practitioners. Western interest in this field sharply declined after the fall of the Soviet Union and the end of the Cold War. To many, the issues and questions involved in this field, not to mention the effort connected with obtaining funding for such study, seemed to be irrelevant and not worth the time spent in doing so. Yet, recent events have shown that this approach is seriously misguided and involves major costs to the United States and its allies.

Of course, it is by now a truism to say that the Russo-Georgian war of 2008 demonstrated to all observers that "Russia was back," if they had not realized that before. But in fact, as Stephen Blank points out in Chapter 2, Russian military and political leaders well before then believed that Russia was at risk in both military and nonmilitary ways. Some went so far as to say that the country was, in effect, already in an information war against the West.[3] We often underestimate the impact of the Russian leadership's perception that Russia is intrinsically at risk, and in some sense under attack, from the West. That underestimation leads us astray, conceptually but also politically. It causes us to ignore some of the most vital and foundational issues in Russian defense policy, e.g., the relationship between the military and the civilian government and the importance of doctrinal statements and threat assessments.

Beyond that, this underestimation causes us to misperceive how Russian policymakers think about their country's security and about the nature of contemporary warfare. As Timothy Thomas points out in Chapter 4, the notion that Russia's leadership has of living through an ongoing and unending information war has been supplemented by original thinking regarding the nature of what such a war might look like and how it might be conducted, either by Russia or by its adversaries. Thomas reviews how information warfare (IW) issues are affecting Russian foreign, internal, and military policies. For the past decade, Russian diplomats have sought to secure resolutions and agreements supporting Moscow's position on the emerging international information environment. At home, the Russian government has adopted several policies design to enhance Russia's information security. Within the defense community, concerns about cyber warfare have shaped the evolution of Russian military theory, organization, and equipment for years. According to Thomas, the August 2008 Georgia War both underscored the growing role of information operations in Russian military policy and revealed several weaknesses, such as shortcomings with Russian command and control equipment, as well as precision-guided munitions, that Russian defense reformers are now striving to overcome. The boldness and originality of Russian thinking about IW, from which we might do well to profit, takes place in overlapping and simultaneously developing conceptual, strategic, and domestic political contexts. That conceptual context, for example, is embedded within Russia and Soviet history and those regimes' indigenous and often profound thinking about the nature of contemporary war.

Specifically, in Chapter 3 Jacob Kipp traces the development of the concept of operational art (*operativenoe iskusstvo*), which is a critical bridge to the translation of individual tactical operations into strategic-level campaigns that end in truly strategic rather than merely inconclusive tactical or even operational victories. The U.S. Army enriched its own thinking about this issue during the 1980s through a close study of Soviet military thought and practice regarding the operational art by its Training and Doctrine Command, the Combined Arms Command, and the Command and General Staff College. But then the end of the Cold War, and the Soviet adversary that sustained it, led the Army and other members of the defense community to lose interest in the operational art of warfare. Ironically, this diminished attention occurred at the very time when the value of the concept was evident in helping the U.S. military achieve its unprecedented operational success in Operation DESERT STORM and also when, thanks to the demise of Soviet censorship, much new and valuable material about Soviet military history, theory, and art was becoming available to interested scholars. Most defense intellectual capital during the past decades has been focused on post-conflict stabilization missions, counterterrorist operations, and most recently relearning how to fight protracted insurgencies. Yet, renewed study of the operational art would benefit the U.S. military—not just the Army—for arguably the kind of serious reflection that would then be generated might help us think our way out of the quandary of endless and inconclusive wars that we have stumbled into, in which successive tactical victories fail to achieve strategic success.[4]

Conceptually, there is a link between Kipp's tracing of the evolution of the term operational art and Thomas' chapter on IW because each chapter underlines the unceasing Russian imperative to think through what changes in contemporary war mean, and how Russia can avoid being trapped into protracted wars that have historically put its entire political system at stake. Indeed, since Ivan IV (Ivan the Terrible) launched his Livonian War in 1558, almost every prolonged or protracted war in Russian history has been accompanied by, and sometimes itself triggered, large-scale socio-political unrest that in many, though not all, cases shook the foundations of the political system and threatened to throw the country into a time of troubles (*Smuta*). No responsible Russian thinker, cognizant of this history, can therefore afford to overlook the implications of modern warfare even if, as Blank argues, today's leaders have re-embraced the Leninist notion of constant threats from abroad and within, seeing Russia through a perspective that embraces what the German philosopher Carl Schmitt called a presupposition of conflict.

Prominent military thinkers associated with the General Staff and the political leadership still embrace this vision.[5] However, it has proven exceedingly difficult, if not counterproductive and even dangerous, to try to rebuild the state, economy, and armed forces on this basis, for neither the state nor the economy can sustain the enormous military foundation needed to materialize this vision of modern war. Hence Russia confronts major strategic gaps. On the one hand, there is a gap between the threats assumed to be in existence (i.e., from the West), and the fact of a serious, stubborn, and long-term conflagration that has spread throughout the North Caucasus for years and shows no sign of burning out. Already by 2006, Russia had committed 250,000 troops, including Ministry of Interior Soldiers (VVMVD), to the interlinked insurgencies in this theater, but 3 years later the situation has worsened, mainly due to the continuing misrule and economic deprivation that marks Russian administration there.[6] This war threatens the foundations of Russia's territorial integrity. Russian strategists recognize the determination of the Islamic terrorists to realize their version of an independent Islamic state in the North Caucasus, a vision in which Russia has no part.[7]

This gap or disparity between threats that are emphasized at least in part for political reasons, and those that are actual is compounded by the second gap — namely the eternal disparity between Russia's vaulting ambitions in world affairs and the means at hand to realize that vision, a perennial dilemma for rulers going back to Ivan IV, if not even earlier. Thanks to this second gap, in modern times there has developed a tradition of rivalry between those who argue that Russia must, in whatever fashion, mobilize itself to meet these serious threats, and others who argue that

Russia's security must be based on an accurate, sober, and realistic appreciation of Russia's true capabilities and actual threats. This dilemma is built into the Russian political system and has never been fully or conclusively resolved. It continues to lie at the heart of the Russian Federation's contemporary strategic dilemmas.

Even though Russia won its war against Georgia, the Russian government and high command acknowledged that the military's performance was flawed during that campaign, indicating that the armed forces remain unprepared for 21st century warfare. They launched an unprecedented defense reform immediately after the conclusion of that war designed to address longstanding problems within the Russia military establishment. The current reform effort can trace it origins to at least 2005-06, if not even earlier in Vladimir Putin's presidency.[8] Nothing as systematic as this has been tried for years, either in the history of the Russian Federation or the Soviet Union.

In Chapter 2 Dale Herspring provides a comprehensive outline of the sweeping scope of this "reform of the armed forces," to give it its proper name in Russian (*Reform Vooruzhennykh Sil'*). The reform seeks to address four major problems confronting the Russian military: closing the technology gap with Western militaries; empowering lower-level officers to exercise authority; curtailing wasteful corruption; and making the military career more attractive to potential recruits. These problems became evident during the Georgian War, when Russian soldiers and officers were unprepared to fight effectively, Russian command and control arrangements functioned ineffectively, and shortages of vital equipment impeded operations. Under the leadership of Anatoly Serdyukov, Putin's surprise choice for Minister of Defense, the reformers have shed thousands of unneeded officers, consolidated military educational institutions and logistics support assets, and restructured command relationships.

Herspring points out that the reform effort is encountering stiff resistance, especially from the current generation of senior officers. Some of this opposition is motivated by a desire to avoid relinquishing the perks that come with senior officership. But another barrier is conceptual, since the reforms depart from the traditional framework of presuming that Russia's next war will be against the North Atlantic Treaty Organization (NATO). Instead, the current reforms implicitly acknowledge that Russia will most likely fight a campaign that resembles those waged by Israel against Hezbollah in 2006 or Hamas in 2008-09. Rather than fighting a tank heavy battle like World War II, the military will need a more flexible, smaller, and more agile and effective force. Another impediment to the reform's implementation is that Russia, especially under conditions of crisis, may not be able to afford the costs of implementing so sweeping a reform. These barriers may delay the reform's realization for a decade or more (i.e. until 2020). Even then, it may end up, like so many previous reform efforts, being only partially realized. In any case, here again the unresolved conflict between vision and capability will, in many different and unexpected ways, shape the outcome of what will clearly be a protracted political and economic struggle between rival groups within the armed forces and the political leadership.

Similarly, in Chapter 6 on the navy, Mikhail Tsypkin highlights as a central theme the clash between the vision of big power projection and a globally present fleet and the reality of a navy that can hardly afford to modernize its existing fleet. Tsypkin delineates the struggle between those who embrace an ambitious strategic vision and political mission, not to mention a military mission, for the navy, and those political and military opponents of that vision who insist on a navy tailored to what Russia- or the army which is by far the strongest service- can afford or will allow the navy to afford. This dilemma is not new. Stalin and his successors were gripped by the will of the wisp of the big navy or by its proponents. These issues came up for debate time and again, with the navy typically having to curtail its ambitions in the name of other priorities. In recent years, the navy has received several new small ships, greater political attention, and the important mission of enhancing Moscow's influence regarding Russia's weaker neighbors (such as against Georgia or Ukraine). It has also resumed global cruises to show the Russian flag on the world's oceans. Nonetheless, proposals to give the navy a new generation of aircraft carriers no longer appear to enjoy the support of a financially-constrained Russian government seemingly unable to resuscitate the country's chronically underfinanced shipbuilding industry. Although the decline in Russia's land-based strategic missile fleet is now offering the navy the opportunity to become the mainstay of the country's strategic deterrent, the failure to work of the Bulava submarine-launched ballistic missile (SLBM) despite some dozen tests might undermine the whole program. The new Borey class submarines that will represent the main combat weapon of the fleet and whose mission is clearly strategic deterrence, has been built to accommodate only that class of missile. If the missile does not work and the program has to be scrapped, then the navy will face a terrible dilemma as to its future. Both Tsypkin's and Herspring's chapters underscore how far the Russian military and government must travel if they are to maintain the great power status they so eagerly crave, and how daunting are the obstacles thrown up to this quest by a recalcitrant reality.

But Russia's difficulties in achieving its strategic vision by building effective instruments of military power do not end there. As Daniel Goure points out in Chapter 5 on nuclear weapons and arms control, Moscow has had to invest those weapons with pride of place because of the weakness of its conventional forces, as delineated by Herpsring and Tsypkin, and because of its fundamental presupposition of possible, perhaps probable, armed conflict with the West. Should a large-scale conventional conflict break out with either adversary, the Russian government would be hard-pressed to refrain from using nuclear weapons first in what Moscow would see as a retaliatory mode. Nuclear weapons—whether land, sea, or air-based—therefore become the priority weapons and strategic deterrence the priority mission of the Russian armed forces. Goure describes the many possible uses Russian military planners have ascribed to nuclear weapons, from overall strategic deterrence of a nuclear attack against Russia to "deescalating" conventional wars through demonstration effects, and even achieving battlefield victories through tactical nuclear use. He further notes that Russian military exercises and writings also depict nuclear weapons as "an all-purpose instrument" with which to address most of Russia's military security challenges of the 21st century.

Here again, as Goure and others have noted, practical considerations forcibly obtrude into defense planning because Moscow cannot afford to maintain a nuclear force as large as it did a generation ago. It must find ways to maintain deterrence, and if necessary fight, with a smaller, though higher quality strategic nuclear arsenal combined with an enormous stockpile of tactical nuclear weapons of uncertain quality (and uncertain safety and security). Not only does this dilemma lead the Russian government to look at maintaining nuclear forces despite the Obama administration's call for movement toward a nuclear-free world, but Russian leaders also insist on retaining a sizable deterrent as a condition of their security. Goure believes that the Russian government will at best accept modest reductions in its nuclear forces in any future bilateral strategic arms control agreement with the Obama administration; with ceilings no lower than that which Russia's aging nuclear forces would likely reach in any case through natural retirement. He further expects Russian negotiators in turn to seek major U.S. concessions that would constrain U.S. prompt global strike and ballistic missile defense capabilities, while leaving Russia's large tactical nuclear weapons stockpile unaffected. Goure urges U.S. policymakers to consider carefully whether the resulting package would represent a net improvement in U.S. security.

Yet, the practical value to Moscow of relying on nuclear weapons as a strategic cure-all can be questioned. If the foreseeable threats are of lower-level small wars like those in the North Caucasus, or a high-tech but brief conventional war like that in Georgia, can Moscow really threaten to use its nuclear weapons in a preventive or preemptive mode, or even in operational and tactical scenarios of local or conventional war, as it now seems to be suggesting?[9] Many observers would rightly question the credibility of such threats. Here again we see how the intractability of the practical context within which strategic, operational, and policy decisions must be made presents a series of unending puzzles and dilemmas for Russian rulers, not unlike those with which their Soviet predecessors had to grapple.

The enduring nature of the difficulties inherent in all of these three contexts—strategic, practical or domestic, and cognitive—is no less visible in the essays by Joshua Spero in Chapter 7 and Richard Weitz in Chapter 8, who look closely at Russia's strategic relations with Europe and China, respectively. In the case of Europe, we are clearly dealing with both the strategic and cognitive contexts, for some Russians have at least publicly committed to the idea that the West is simultaneously an adversary, even the main enemy (*Glavnyi Vrag*), but also a series of states that must be engaged and kept off balance to prevent their uniting politically and militarily against Russia. An integrated Europe under any provenance (European Union (EU), NATO, democracy, Bonapartism, Nazism, and everything in between) has historically been regarded as the greatest security threat to Russia. It is still seen this way by many Russians. According to Spero, the armed forces have developed a new mission—defending energy platforms. In addition, he argues that the government has had to show itself simultaneously open to cooperation, albeit on its terms, and hostile to anything that it thinks might reduce Russia's freedom of action as expressed in the phrase, "sovereign democracy." Many Russians see the West not just as a strategic military threat, but also a political one, since the Western commitment to democracy threatens Russia's ruling elite. Defense Minister Sergei Ivanov wrote in 2006 that Moscow regarded the main threat to its security as an attempt to change the constitutional order of any of the governments in the Commonwealth of Independent States (CIS), not just that of Russia.[10] Indeed, in a 2007 interview he revealed the elite's view of Western democracy by calling that phenomenon a "bardak," Russian for a particularly slovenly and chaotic brothel.[11]

Spero illustrates how this strategic and ideological clash complicates Russian-European relations; especially the irony of Russia's enduring ambivalence of wanting to be in Europe but not of Europe—to stand apart as an independent sovereign power. The author notes that, on the surface, Russia and Europe share several important security interests, especially regarding southwest Asia. Yet, Russian strategic thinking regarding its western neighbors is fixated on managing Eurasian energy challenges and preventing Ukraine or Georgia from joining NATO or the EU. Spero highlights how Russian policies have been able to keep Europeans divided by stoking energy security tensions among them and by playing on their diverging enthusiasm for extending European integration processes further eastward. He finds some evidence of possible Russian plans to use military force to ensure Russian control over Europe's vital east-west energy pipelines. Even more evident are Russian efforts to weaken NATO by preventing its further growth, attempting to decrease its paramount role in European security by creating a new regional security architecture more to Moscow's liking, and by trying to exploit the dependence of the alliance's contingents in Afghanistan on supply routes that traverse Russian territory. Spero notes that the latter effort could easily backfire since a return of Islamist extremists to power in Afghanistan would threaten Russian security as well as that of many other countries.

But is Russia then to affiliate with China? Richard Weitz examines both the affinities and factors making for distance in this relationship, which last year marked its 60th anniversary (Moscow established diplomatic relations with the People's Republic of China [PRC] in 1949.) Weitz argues that this relationship is a partnership but not an alliance, and that numerous differences will keep these two states apart even when they pursue parallel policies on several strategic issues, such as Iran and North Korea, or adopt joint declarations calling for an end to American global primacy and U.S. efforts to export democracy to countries whose authoritarian regimes tilt toward Moscow or Beijing. The Chinese government has shown no interest in accepting Russian invitations to join the nuclear arms reduction process, the Intermediate Nuclear Forces Treaty, or other hitherto bilateral Russian-American arms control processes inherited from the Cold War. Chinese officials have also declined to endorse Russia's dismemberment of Georgia and continue to encounter Russian efforts to constrain China's economic presence in Central Asia. Although Russia and China have jointly submitted a draft treaty designed to constrain U.S. military use of outer space, Russian strategists were not please by China's testing of an anti-satellite weapon in January 2007, breaking a 2-decade moratorium on such tests. Although there has been recent progress in breaking some of the deadlocks to the long-stalled energy commerce between Russia and China, the Russian defense industry is unhappy that China has sharply reduced its purchase of Russian arms in recent years, a development many Russians attribute to China's successful illegal copying of many of the defense items the PRC used to buy from Russia's military industrial complex. Blank has also pointed out that the Russian General Staff, wary of China's growing military power, looks very cautiously and carefully at Chinese military policy and behavior.[12]

Even though both sides claim that relations are at their highest point ever, few believe that it is a match made in heaven. Other scholars take a different, even alarmist, view of the potential for a genuine alliance against the United States.[13] But, however one interprets this crucial relationship for Russia and possibly for Asia, it is clear that the military and overall security stakes involved are of the highest magnitude. Ignoring Russian military perspectives here, as in other theaters, would gravely handicap Western security experts, both analytically and in policy terms.

Given the stakes involved in achieving a correct understanding of Russian and Chinese defense policies and military developments, the magnitude of Mary Fitzgerald's enlightening accomplishments in this regard becomes clear. But the problems we have outlined here were not unfamiliar to students of the Soviet Union. Indeed, they are enduring strategic issues for Russian policymakers as well as those who analyze or contribute to foreign policies towards the Russian military, despite the magnitude of the tremendous changes that have occurred since 1989 when the Soviet empire began to collapse. Even more important, Mary and her colleagues recognized that the issues outlined here are not just tasks relevant for the study of Russia. Addressing these strategic issues, and their underlying stakes, are essential tasks for creating an enduring structure of peace.

ENDNOTES - INTRODUCTION

1. Mary Fitzgerald, *Marshal Ogarkov on the Modern Theater Operations*, Alexandria, VA: Center for Naval Analysis, 1986; Mary Fitzgerald, *Marshal Ogarkov on Modern War: 1977-1985*, Alexandria, VA: Center for Naval Analysis, 1986; Mary Fitzgerald, *Marshal Ogarkov and the New Revolution in Soviet Military Affairs*, Alexandria, VA: Center for Naval Analysis, 1987, are only a few of the many works she wrote on these topics.

2. Stephen Blank, *The Soviet Military Views Operation DESERT STORM: A Preliminary Analysis*, Carlisle, PA: Strategic Studies Institute, U.S. Army War College, October 1991.

3. Apart from that chapter, he has outlined the implications of that stance in several articles: Stephen Blank, "Threats To and From Russia: a Reassessment," *Journal of Slavic Military Studies*, Vol. XXI, No. 3, Summer 2008, pp. 491-526; Stephen Blank, "Web War I: Is Europe's First Information War a New Kind of War?" *Comparative Strategy*, Vol. XXVII, No. 3, 2008, pp. 227-247.

4. Brigadier Justin Kelly and Dr. Michael James Brennan, *Alien: How Operational Art Devoured Strategy*, Carlisle, PA: Strategic Studies Institute, U.S. Army War College, 2009.

5. General M. A. Gareyev (Ret.), "Issues of Strategic Deterrence in Current Conditions," *Military Thought,* No. 2, 2009, pp. 1-9; Colonel I. A. Shapovalov, Colonel Ya. A. Zhaldybin, and Captain 1st Rank V. P. Starodubtsev, "Russia and Challenges of the 21st Century," *Military Thought*, No. 2, 2009, pp. 39-44; Colonel M. F. Vakkaus, "On the Military-Political Basis of the Methodology For Building Up and Employing the Russian Armed Forces," *Military Thought*, No. 2, 2009, pp. 129-136.

6. John B. Dunlop and Rajan Menon, "Chaos in the North Caucasus and Russia's Future," *Survival*, Vol. XLVIII, No. 2, Summer 2006, p. 110.

7. Gordon Hahn, *Russia's Islamic Threat*, New Haven, CT: Yale University Press, 2007.

8. Irina Isakova, *Russian Governance In the Twenty-First Century: Geo-Strategy, Geopolitics and New Governance*: London, UK: Routledge, 2005; Irina Isakova, *Russian Defense Reform: Current Trends*, Carlisle, PA: Strategic Studies Institute, U.S. Army War College, 2006.

9. "Interview With Russian Federation Security Council Secretary Nikolai Patrushev," Moscow, Russia, *Izvestiya*, in Russian, October, 14, 2009; *Open Source Center, Foreign Broadcast Information Service Central Eurasia* (henceforth *FBIS SOV*), October 14, 2009; David Novak, "Report: Russia To Allow Pre-Emptive Nukes," Associated Press, October 14, 2009.

10. Sergei Ivanov, "Russia Must Be Strong," *Wall Street Journal*, January 11, 2006, p. 14.

11. Transcript, Sergei Ivanov," *Financial Times*, April 18, 2007, available from *www.ft.com/cms/s/b7e458ea-ede1-11db-8584-000b5df10621.html*.

12. Stephen Blank,"Russia's Strategic Dilemmas in Asia," *Pacific Focus*, Vol. XXIII, No. 3, December, 2008, pp. 271-293.

13. David Kerr, "The Sino-Russian Partnership and U.S. Policy Toward North Korea, From Hegemony to Concert in Northeast Asia," *International Studies Quarterly*, Vol. XXXXIX, No. 3, September, 2005, pp. 411-437; Constantine C. Menges, *China: The Gathering Threat*, Nashville, TN: Nelson Current Publishers, 2005; Kim Yo'ng Hu'i, "The Relevance of Central Asia," Seoul, Korea, *JoongAng Ilbo Internet Version*, in English, July 11, 2005; *FBIS SOV*, July 11, 2005; Lyle Goldstein and Vitaly Kozyrev, "China, Japan and the Scramble for Siberia," *Survival*, Vol. XLVIII, No. 1, Spring 2006, pp. 175-176.

CHAPTER 1

"NO NEED TO THREATEN US, WE ARE FRIGHTENED OF OURSELVES," RUSSIA'S BLUEPRINT FOR A POLICE STATE, THE NEW SECURITY STRATEGY

Stephen J. Blank

INTRODUCTION

In May 2009 Russia published a long-awaited new national security strategy.[1] On its face, this document reads like a supremely self-assured and confident proclamation. But the deeper and longer one looks at it and at the debate preceding its adoption, a rather different, indeed much more anxious document and government emerge. Not only are fundamental issues unresolved, but also a strong debate over its issues and overall approach continues. Moreover, the debate preceding its adoption revealed many of the inherent defects of Russia's political structure. Meanwhile, the document itself and the debate leading to it are riddled with unresolved contradictions. These facts should not surprise us because such documents are always inherently political documents, and no society is immune from political contestation. However, the contradictions revealed in this process raise serious questions concerning the nature of the Russian policy process and Russia's national security strategy.

The concept of security still lacks a universally agreed upon definition. Therefore, it must necessarily be a contested concept among practical politicians who must deal with the concept in its tangible manifestations. Certainly this is true in Russia as elsewhere.

But certain conditions unique to Russia make these debates more important than may be the case in many other countries. Russian debates have continued for a long time because they have huge political repercussions, given the strength of the state and the global scope of its international and national activity. These debates are also important not only because they offer us a window into a very opaque political process, but also because—at least rhetorically—Russian elites attach great policy importance to such doctrinal documents.

Therefore, these debates possess more than academic significance. In Russian debates, whoever can define the nature and scope of security (i.e., what issues are to be "securitized" and then politically defined as well as the nature of the threat[s] to Russia) gains a large advantage over rivals in defining the state's policy and structure. He also obtains both the tangible and intangible political resources with which to enrich his constituents (and himself) and to execute missions. In political science terms, the debate and struggle over defining security and the security environment validates David Easton's claim that politics amounts to a struggle for the authoritative allocation of tangible and/or intangible values.

Russia's new security strategy and the supposedly forthcoming defense doctrine have had a long and difficult gestation. In 2002, 2005, 2006, and 2007, then President and current Prime Minister Vladimir Putin announced that there would be a new security concept and/or defense doctrine, only for the government to announce at the end of 2007 that neither document would be forthcoming anytime soon. Clearly many obstacles to announcing a new strategy had emerged. Indeed, in 2004 the Secretary of the Security Council,

Igor Ivanov, said that the council was working on a new national security concept.[2] However, in February 2005 Ivanov outlined a bleak picture of Russia's overall domestic and national security: "The leading academics of the Russian Academy of Sciences currently lack a common understanding of the methodology for shaping the national security strategy." Moreover, as Ivanov related, state institutions (not trusted by the citizenry) have not managed "to develop a mechanism for evaluating the condition of national security via a system of specific criteria."[3]

That no such strategy or concept appeared until 2009 signifies an unresolved and ongoing political struggle over its appearance and content. According to Vitaly Shlykov, Chairman of the Public Council under the Ministry of Defense, at the end of 2007 neither the General Staff nor the Ministry had the resources to prepare a defense doctrine, nor was the factual material submitted after years of work sufficient.[4] No reason is given for the fact that they apparently had an infusion of such resources in the 18 months since then. Neither was there an announcement of the assignment to them of such resources or of what those resources might be. Obviously Shlykov's explanation cries out for interpretation and probably concealed the real reason for delay (most probably unresolved policy debates). For example, it was silent about the role of the Security Council, which is nominally supposed to prepare these documents. Therefore, to obtain a better grasp of the dynamics of national security and national security policymaking in the Russian Federation, we must trace this struggle over the national security strategy and then analyze it. In so doing, we can discern at least the outlines, if not more, of the debate from events in 2008, if not earlier.

In fact, and despite the years of work on these documents and the repeated announcements by then Chief of Staff General Yuri N. Baluyevsky and others that the General Staff and the Ministry had finished their work and submitted it to the Security Council, Shlykov's announcement confirmed that no security strategy was possible, given the ongoing discord among the main players.[5] Indeed, Baluyevsky's January 2008 call for "a strategy of national security that would be fully observed by all government agencies, including the 'power departments'," betrayed his continuing frustration at the failure to arrive at such a determination, as well as the actual political stalemate then occuring.[6] In fact, one of the leading spokesmen for the General Staff and President of the Russian Academy of Military Sciences, Retired General M. A. Gareyev, represented the Academy and the General Staff's rejection of Ivanov's and the Duma's efforts to codify either a national security concept or relevant legislation. Gareyev claimed in June 2007 that a defense doctrine (largely drafted by his institute) would be ready by the end of 2007, and that while there were many debates that needed to be clarified and resolved in the process, The Russian Defense Act and the National Security blueprint (presumably that Ivanov was working on) "are of a lecture and unduly theoretical nature. Therefore their provisions are totally nonbinding."[7]

Gareyev thus revealed that his institution, which works for the General Staff, had essentially usurped the Security Council's role and work, and was trying to publish a defense doctrine in advance of the Council's overall National Security Strategy. This repeated the General Staff's 1999-2000 effort to do the same thing and enshrine itself rather than the government as the arbiter of both the assessment of threats to Russia and of the recommended policies to counter them.[8] The persistence of this attempt by the General Staff to usurp the government's role naturally put it in conflict with then Defense Minister Sergei Ivanov who at the time rejected the notion that a defense doctrine could precede the National Security Strategy. Indeed, Russian commentators wrote then that, "there is no unity of views on the content of the [military] reforms or of the doctrine. There is only a kind of ferment of minds and ambitions."[9] The struggle over sequencing the documents and determining both the threats to Russia and the policies to counter them, points to an unresolved and ongoing struggle of the General Staff to expand its discretion at the expense of the government and its civilian leaders. Thus, this issue identifies a hitherto underestimated example of an abiding and unsolved problem in Russian civil-military relations. Even though the General Staff has lost consistently for the last 5 years, it does not stop trying to impose its views upon the government.[10]

But this struggle points to another, even deeper problem. There still is no regularized, binding, and legally codified policymaking process or official consensus for defining security, threats, or any other defense policy that is established by law or regular institutions. Or if there are relevant laws, nobody pays them any serious attention. Rather, an ongoing and repetitive conflict takes place between the Ministry of Defense and the General Staff regardless of precedent or personalities. Given the absence of the rule of law in the government and state, it is hardly surprising that policymaking remains personalized, haphazard, fragmented, and subject to endless and often inconclusive struggles. Neither should we be surprised that the

Russian state is deficient in the means of conducting a true national strategy. After all, analysts like Dmitry Trenin of the Carnegie Endowment have publicly said that the Russian state still cannot conduct a true strategic policy and lacks the means for doing so.[11]

Since Russia is a government of men, not of laws, securitization, i.e., the definition of what constitutes national security and what issues must be subsumed in that definition, has occurred in Russia through a kind of incessant free for all among opaquely structured bureaucratic actors operating without any accountability or regard for anything other than winning the battle to influence the Tsar's (Putin's) thinking and actions, or of Putin enhancing his power and capability for actually executing his decrees. Alternatively the government, as numerous foreign and domestic analysts regularly charge, has long since been captured by elements that use it essentially as an instrument for the pursuit of private, departmental, or factional aims.[12] The formulation and implementation of security policy would fall under this rubric as the players struggle to maximize their personal and factional benefits at the expense of any coherent vision of the national interest. Consequently, there is no real concept of the national interest, let alone a coherent national strategy for security or anything else. Although Putin personally articulated a threat assessment and definition of security in 2006-07 through his speeches, statements, and press conferences, the government visibly lost the ability to do so through 2007. Possibly this is why the government lost that capability, or else Putin had to do it because nobody else could. Ultimately, then, threat assessment and the definition of what issues make up the composition of "national security" is or will be what Putin, or his successor, President

Dmitry Medvedev (or for that matter Nicholas II in his time), says it is. And as we shall see, Putin embraced the defense establishment and intelligence agencies' assessment, and this assessment has prevailed since 2006-07, even though it is a grossly exaggerated and patently self-serving assessment that also begins with a presumption of conflict and Russia's isolation.

Accordingly, the new national security strategy and a new defense doctrine became visible objects of intense political struggle long before 2008, and that struggle has continued into the present. Normally a national security strategy should precede both a defense and a foreign policy doctrine or concept. Instead, the foreign policy concept appeared in July 2008 and was followed in 2009 by the national security strategy.[13] Even if one argues that the foreign policy concept expressed the ideas and values of the subsequent national security strategy (as apparently is the case), this is an unusual procedure. Just as publishing a defense doctrine *avant la lettre* suggests an effort to impose a defense policy upon the government, so too does this suggest an attempt to impose a foreign policy even before the dust had settled on the debates over national security.[14] That clearly represents another sign of a covert and very opaque political struggle.

Thus, these political events and competing perspectives testify to the battle over the national security strategy and the defense doctrine. The latter still awaited release as of August 2009, but Russia's National Security Council received it for consideration in 2009.[15] However, we have been down this road before to no avail, so caution is warranted, especially in light of the tremendous struggle over a new defense reform at a time of protracted economic crisis.

STATE INCOHERENCE IN RUSSIA

By 2004, the debates over security and the nature of the threats confronting Russia had been joined. Thus the current debate has deep roots. In 2004, veteran Soviet retired general Stepan Tyushkevich wrote that Russia faced the following threats:
- The wish by some states and military coalitions—i.e., the United States and the North Atlantic Treaty Organization (NATO)—to dominate both world and regional politics, and supplanting the Organization for Security and Cooperation in Europe (OSCE) and the United Nations (UN) to use strong-arm methods to deal with disputed issues.
- Territorial claims to the Russian Federation by other states.
- The growing number and intensity of conflicts around Russian borders. (Since the only new wars after 2000 are the war instigated by Al-Qaeda on September 11, 2001 [9/11], which Russia supports, and Iraq. This is another example of the Russian argument that its borders really are the Soviet ones, for Iraq is quite far from the Russian Federation and was not even adjacent to the Union of Soviet Socialist Republics [USSR], but the standard argument was and is that the Middle East is a region adjacent to Russia. So we see here another example of the inability to come to terms with post-1991 trends). Beyond that point, Tyushkevich introduced an idea that has since moved to the heart of Russian national security discourse, namely that due to U.S. unilateralism and its harmful consequences, not only has the resort to war

become more likely as a solution to security issues in regions both near and allegedly near Russia, but also that the likelihood and scope of war in these areas is increasing, creating a greater danger of war involving or threatening to involve Russia.
- Tyushkevich then cited the retention of large nuclear potentials by leading world states like the United States and the proliferation of weapons of mass destruction (WMD) to states like India and Pakistan.
- Possible disruption of strategic stability by breaches of existing arms control treaties like the Anti-Ballistic Missile (ABM) Treaty, the buildup of forces near Russian borders, and the deployment of nuclear weapons on the territory of neighboring states.[16] Here we must point out that while the United States legally withdrew from the ABM Treaty, the buildups referred to by Tyushkevich, which have become a staple of Russian assertion, are utterly false. There has been neither a buildup of forces near Russia nor any deployment of nuclear weapons anywhere near Russia.

The constancy of such accusations is another example of the consistent and clearly deliberate disinformation of the Russian government by its military and intelligence agencies, a fundamental outgrowth of the failure to control these agencies after 1991 by civilian and democratic means. This second failure in civil-military relations has profound consequences for Russia's security. As Pavel Felgenhauer, a leading defense correspondent, reports,

Russia has a Prussian-style all-powerful General Staff that controls all the different armed services and is more or less independent of outside political constraints. Russian military intelligence—the GRU [*Glavnoye Razvedyvatel'noye Upravleniye*], as big in size as the former KGB [*Komitet gosudarstvennoi bezopasnosti* (Committee of State Security)] and spread over all continents—is an integral part of the General Staff. Through the GRU, the General Staff controls the supply of vital information to all other decision-makers in all matters concerning defense procurement, threat assessment, and so on. High-ranking former GRU officers have told me that in Soviet times the General Staff used the GRU to grossly, deliberately, and constantly mislead the Kremlin about the magnitude and gravity of the military threat posed by the West in order to help inflate military expenditure. There are serious indications that at present the same foul practice is continuing.[17]

- Tyushkevich then cited attempts by outside states to interfere in Russia's internal affairs by political, economic, and military pressure (e.g., as in Kosovo or Iraq).
- Only at the end of the list did he cite terrorism.[18]

After providing this assessment, he further stated, and this is entirely characteristic of the military's threat assessment, that "Against the background of a protracted economic crisis and a certain decline in Russian international influence, **military force is the real argument confirming the Russian Federation's stance as a world power and a guarantee of its territorial integrity and political independence**".[19] Indeed, the whole point of his article is that without the correct ideology and theoretical substantiation of contemporary threats, building a new army to meet them is impossible.[20] In other words, the General Staff's assessment, which this ultimately became, demands as its political corollary that the state and the economy be put at the service of the defense establishment, a view not far removed from what actually was the case in Soviet times.

Although the regime did not buy the latter part of his argument concerning military force as Russia's sole or primary factor confirming its status and independence, it did buy this threat assessment. As we shall see, subsequent assessments argue that the United States is bringing ever more military force and conflict closer to Russia's borders, which are very expansively defined, and that it is increasing military and especially nuclear pressure on Russia and even bringing nuclear weapons closer to Russia. Moreover, according to these assessments, attempts to interfere in Russia's internal life and that of its partners—i.e., to deny Russian suzerainty over the Commonwealth of Independent States (CIS)—is a well-thought-out deliberate policy by the United States, and that therefore Russia is facing an information war that justifies its resort to similar tactics. Terrorism was downgraded as a threat in the face of this Western onslaught.

Yet, the evidence for it is lacking. Even if NATO enlarges, its forces have not done so and, if anything, have shown their declining capability for and interest in war with Russia. Even the General Staff has admitted that 10 radars and interceptors in Poland and the Czech Republic cannot threaten Russia's deterrent for all their anger over missile defense. Nevertheless, the Russian military still considers NATO the enemy, and Deputy Commander in Chief of the Ground Forces

Lieutenant General Alexander Studenikin confirmed that NATO remains the main enemy and that most of Russia's exercises are directed against this traditional enemy.[21]

So it is clear that this is a politically manufactured threat assessment. For the military, it justifies big military spending on a big army, navy, and air force, not to mention nuclear weapons. While for the political elite, as many commentators have noticed, this assessment justifies an ongoing domestic concentration of power as well as the rhetoric and policy of neo-imperialism in the CIS. So because of its political utility to diverse audiences, it is hardly surprising that as time passed, this alarmist threat assessment became more pervasive, more expansive, and even more alarmist.

In 2005, writing about the Russian Far East (RFE), Viktor Ozerov, Chairman of the Federation Council Defense and Security Committee, outlined an updated threat assessment. Ozerov, however, emphasized that military strength is not the key determinant of national power in the system of international relations. Instead, he advanced a new idea that also would soon find favor and ratification in subsequent debates:

> The new geopolitics are based, as a rule, on the idea of "indirect wars" or "indirect influence." Overt military operations are being replaced by mechanisms of total regulation based on the concentration of financial-economic resources and information-psychological influence.[22]

Nevertheless, military threats were present and could still break out in the RFE. Indeed, he warned that Russia "could be susceptible to the impact of a most diverse spectrum of threat emanating both from external and internal sources here."[23] While the greatest military threat came from the armies of states close to Russia in the region (China, Japan, and the United States), the primary threats appear to have been internal ones from drug running, organized crime, illegal immigration, or economic ones like foreign creditors, the brain drain, etc. All of these are exacerbated by the ideology of double standards, propaganda, and a distortion of the Russian state's principles of democracy. That policy could also come to entail direct military intervention, but clearly is subsumed under the Russian understanding of information warfare (IW). In that understanding, IW in foreign hands represents a threat to the integrity of the state and government.[24]

However, Ozerov also identified domestic instability as a major internal factor, citing domestic social and economic instability, an undermining of the patriotic spirit and the absence of a clearly defined concept of the state's long-term interests, and thus an equivalent concept of the threats facing the state. Those symptoms lead to an inconsistent foreign policy and an equally unsustainable approach to the problems of military organization.[25] Clearly he was referring to Russia and demanding a much more rigorous security mobilization of the state and the society. Since then, he has advocated that national security doctrine actually incorporate the defense doctrine into itself, fusing the two documents into one and militarizing them at the same time, and also challenging the government's primacy in this sphere.[26]

By 2006, such formulations were becoming more rigorous as they pervaded the military press. In January, Baluyevsky further expanded this assessment. According to him, we are now seeing (i.e., in 2006) the predominance of the use of military force to resolve international problems, even ignoring norms and values of established international law and making military force a means of pursuing foreign policy.[27] Even though he credited Russian foreign policy with significantly reducing the threat of direct military aggression, he insisted that the armed forces be "maintained in a state that ensures the strategic deterrence of any potential adversary and supports every mission to localize new non-traditional threats."[28] Baluyevsky then proceeded to provide an assessment of the strategic environment and of threats to Russia that clearly built on Tyushkevich and Ozerov and added more substance to their claims. According to Baluyevsky, the geopolitical environment includes:

- An increase in the importance of the economic component of foreign policy for leading states, **"which results in expanding the sphere of requirements for military force to ensure the said economic interests"**[29];
- Attempts to ignore Russia's interests in the resolution of international security issues, to undermine its role as a center of gravity in a multipolar world;
- The intensification of a number of states' efforts to support disintegrative processes in Russia and the CIS, interfere in their internal affairs, and undermine Russia's economic independence.

Geostrategic conditions include:
- Consolidation of long-term foreign military presence and increased military potential in regions that are traditionally the focus of Russia's national interests;
- Unfinished delimitation of borders and establishment of state borders against a background

of expanding "zones of instability" in Russia's border territories that greatly complicate the combating of international organized crime, narcotics trafficking, illegal arms sales, and uncontrolled migration.[30] Here again, it should be noted that there is no evidence for this—certainly not of the United States or NATO supporting such manifestations—another example of inflated and phony threat assessments. Indeed, given Russian state support for the Russian mafia abroad and for such characters as the notorious arms seller Viktor Bout, one wonders where Baluyevsky got his evidence.

Even though he admitted that there was little chance of direct military aggression against Russia, he said new threats persist and in some areas even escalate. In other words, not content with listing the same threats as Ozerov and Tyushkevich, he added another key point in the burgeoning inflation of threats and securitization of domestic affairs, namely that Russia's security environment was deteriorating despite its recovery, and that threats involving the use of force were more likely even though there is no evidence to sustain that argument. Nonetheless, as we shall see, this line of argument has prevailed since then. Thus, even before leaks of a prospective new defense doctrine in 2007 that made clear the erasure of boundaries between internal and external security, i.e., the recognition of the comprehensive nature of security as in the West, authoritative Russian spokesmen were embracing this concept.[31] Yet the problem here, as with all efforts to conceptualize security in so comprehensive a manner, is that those conceptualizing security in this fashion are inevitably tempted to securitize everything

in domestic politics as threats. The process described here exemplifies this lamentable trend. Baluyevsky's list of threats clearly not only derives from, but also expands upon previous lists. Thus, in Baluyevsky's analysis the threats are:
- Persisting and potential centers of armed conflict in a number of former Soviet republics;
- Territorial claims against Russia, including the threat of political or coercive cession of Russian territories;
- Enlargement of hostile military blocs detrimental to Russia's security;
- Proliferation of equipment, technologies and components for WMD.

Internal threats comprise:
- Political extremism and secessionism aiming at disrupting the exercise of state power;
- Worn out industrial facilities that could lead to industrial and environmental accidents and catastrophes;
- International terrorism;
- Planning and execution of information and psychological operations against the Russian Federation.[32]

Thus, Baluyevsky not only expanded the scope of these threats, but also gave the military the right to comment on and argue for policy against internal threats. He duly added to the notion that Russia is under comprehensive internal and external threats to which the military must address itself and which demand a defense policy response. After publication of this article by Baluyevsky, the scope for threat assessments became both larger and more pervasive in the sense that he and others now adopted his line and developed it further. Indeed, he kept up the attack, continuing to define the threats to Russia in this way between 2006 and 2008.[33] Others, of course, followed his lead.

For example, the military journal *Voyenny Vestnik Yuga Rossii* (*The Military Herald of South Russia*) published in late 2006 an account of the tasks of the North Caucasus Military District's Personnel for 2007 that included a much more comprehensive threat assessment.[34] It, too, saw a world moving from an emphasis on military threats to a much more diversified palette of threats to Russia. Like innumerable other Russian publications, it postulated Russia's recovery from its crisis of the 1990s and that the U.S. drive for world leadership was meant not just to bring Russia and the former Soviet Union into its orbit, but also that Washington viewed Moscow as its principal geopolitical rival (a formulation that encourages Russian elites to think that the United States is Russia's principal rival). Accordingly, the contemporary military scene is characterized by a significant lowering of the threat of large-scale conventional war and nuclear war; the increased use of the military in peace operations; the emergence of new centers of economic power like Germany, China, and Japan; the expansion of potential crisis areas and the increased level of regional conflict in the area from the Balkans to Central Asia based on ethnicity, faith, and crime; terrorism; a renewed arms race with the danger of proliferation of WMD and other types of weapons; and NATO enlargement. Politically, we see increasing encroachment upon states' sovereignty, rising influence of multinational corporations, extremism based on religion, terrorism based on organized extremism, organized crime, etc.

Furthermore,

> Contemporary international military-political relations are characterized by a rigorous informational-psychological warfare that is aimed at undermining Russia's statehood and integrity. In this connection, daily attacks are made according to two criteria: the external and internal information environments, influence is being exerted on our country's population not by means of direct military interventions but by the adept exploitation of the national and religious contradictions within.[35]

Specific military threats confronting Russia are:
- The availability to countries of powerful groupings of armed forces and major arsenals of WMD;
- Attempts to establish monitoring over Russia's nuclear weapons;
- Foreign states' efforts to destroy the integrity of the Russian state by exploiting ethnic, religious, and other contradictions, and raising territorial claims against Russia, thus leading to the revision of interstate borders;
- Western efforts to undermine and restrain integration processes within the CIS;
- Exclusion of Russian interests from traditional areas like the Caucasus, Central Asia, and the Black and Caspian Seas;
- Weakening Russia's ties to Central and Eastern Europe and the Pacific East Asian region;
- Efforts to restrict Russia's presence on foreign markets;
- Lastly, he cited, "The informational-psychological influencing and infiltration of different spheres of the Russian Federation's vital activ-

ity, which may entail the disabling of the system and military administration and control."[36] Thus this threat of the Russian Federation being under information attack on a permanent basis entered into Russian thinking by 2006.[37]

As part of this debate, Gareyev offered a presentation in 2006 that strongly rejected the notion that security threats originate within Russia, and firmly stated that they all come from outside Russia.[38] So while he polemicized against the notion that IW represents a novelty in warfare, he accepted its newfound importance in contemporary war. Indeed, Gareyev advocated the creation of a,

> separate, independent directorate, as part of the Presidential Staff of the Russian government that would be entrusted with coordinating information activity on a countrywide level—from intellectual security, the development of a national idea and shaping Russia's favorable image abroad to countering all types of subversive activity, including the ideological support and organization of "color," "velvet", and other sorts of revolutions.[39]

It should be noted that much of this program has been put into active operation since then.

Thus, by 2006, it was clear that Moscow was looking at IW both as a threat and as an opportunity to wage the kinds of new wars its analysts were depicting even before it did so in Estonia in 2007. Deputy Premier and former Defense Minister Sergei Ivanov indicated Moscow's full awareness of the kinds of activity it was launching in Estonia and that it was a surrogate for a more classical military kind of operation.

> The development of information technology has resulted in information itself turning into a certain kind of weapon. It is a weapon that allows us to carry out would-be military actions in practically any theater of war and most importantly, without using military power. That is why we have to take all the necessary steps to develop, improve, and, if necessary – and it already seems to be necessary – develop new multipurpose automatic control systems, so that in the future we do not find ourselves left with nothing.[40]

Furthermore, leading Russian military figures like Baluyevsky and Gareyev openly discussed threats to Russia in which the country might suffer even a crushing defeat without a shot being fired.[41] Thus Gareyev stated that,

> The breakup of the Soviet Union and Yugoslavia, the parade of "color revolutions" in Georgia, Ukraine, and Kyrgyzstan, and so on show how principal threats exist objectively, assuming not so much military forms as direct or indirect forms of political, diplomatic, economic, and informational pressure, subversive activities, and interference in internal affairs. . . . The RF's [Russian Federation] security interests require not only that such threats be assessed, but also that effective measures of countering them be identified.[42]

In fact, Russian experts actually modeled this cyber attack against Estonia a year before it occurred.[43] By employing the tactics of the past and updating them to the instruments of the present, Russia today can wage an ongoing and long-term low-intensity conflict or political warfare against targeted states where the battleground is the cohesion of the targeted country's socio-political structure. In these kinds of wars, the target is the legitimacy, cohesion, and consensual basis of a society, if not the overall international order, not just soldiers on a battlefield.[44]

But beyond these points, these threat assessments, in advance of the new doctrine, not only formulated an all-encompassing definition of the scope of security and of threats to it, they identified the main enemy (i.e., the United States), the likely forms of attack, and, in keeping with the Leninist tradition behind this kind of thinking, identified a linked domestic and external enemy with calls for ever greater concentration of power and even militarization of the state. These trends illustrated another key development in the new security strategy that was already identified by 2007 in the debate leading up to its publication. Whereas the earlier doctrinal statements listed many of the same military threats but separated the nonmilitary ones from the military ones, the IW threat was a new one. As the Dutch analyst Colonel Marcel de Haas of the Royal Netherlands Air Force observed at the time:

> But the evolving international security situation shows that this division of threats and measures is becoming blurred. This prompts the conclusion that either the military doctrine should cover threats in all fields (that is, both military and non-military security threats), or the doctrine and the National Security Concept should be combined into one document, which might be called a defense doctrine or a security doctrine. The new military doctrine acknowledges that it's no longer justifiable to draw a line between internal and external security, or military and non-military threats and countermeasures. In general this should be appreciated. Like doctrine specialists in the West, their Russian counterparts now regard security as covering all areas and dimensions. This concept is behind the call for reinforcing the Security Council's status, as the body

that is supposed to ensure a multilateral, interagency response to internal and external security challenges.[45]

De Haas' analysis also pointed to the fact that it was at this time, 2006-07, that the strongest effort was made by Gareyev, Baluyevsky, and like minded actors to usurp the Security Council and publish a defense doctrine that followed along the lines of Tyushkevich's recommendations for a vastly enhanced defense effort rather than a national security strategy. Moreover, they sought a doctrine that would link internal and external security in ways that clearly enhanced the role of the General Staff as a director of Russia's overall security policy. They made this effort at the January 2007 conference of the Russian Academy of Military Sciences where Baluyevsky and Gareyev dominated the proceedings. At this meeting, Gareyev and Baluyevsky made a strong effort to take over the doctrine process on behalf of the General Staff. Baluyevsky again emphasized the growing threat from NATO enlargement and that it is (falsely we might add) involved with local conflicts near Russia's borders. Meanwhile, Gareyev emphasized the general threat to Russia's sovereignty and interests, politically based IW, the threat to energy security, and missile defenses. Both argued that the presence of large military powers and contingents near Russian borders created a threat of the start of armed conflicts all the way up to large-scale wars, particularly to Russia's South and East.[46] Gareyev, following Defense Minister Sergei Ivanov, called for a division of labors, i.e., spheres of influence between NATO and the Russian-led Collective Security Treaty Organization (CSTO).[47]

Gareyev also reiterated his call, based on his 2006 advocacy for a total reorganization of the state, to make the Minister of Defense the Deputy Commander in Chief even in peacetime.[48] Already in 2006 the General Staff's Academy of Military Science, led by Gareyev, had presented a comprehensive threat assessment embracing all those domains and the threat of information warfare and demanding a reorganization of the state whereby the Defense Minister would effectively become the President's Deputy Supreme Commander in both peacetime and wartime over a vastly strengthened government that would restore a Ministry of Defense Industry and prepare for Russia's comprehensive mobilization.[49] In other words, not only did the General Staff try to usurp the state's role in formulating the overall national security strategy, it also demanded a substantial conversion of the state into a permanently mobilized structure ready at all times for war, not unlike the Soviet precedent.

We see here how securitization and politicization of those processes, the attempt to use issues labeled as pertaining to security for directly political purposes and advantages, could easily run amok in Russian politics due to the failure to institute effective democratic controls over the government, armed forces, and special services (to use the Russian term). Here the crucial difference with the West is that this concept of security has been politicized to the point where threats are seen as ubiquitous, and has been used to produce the intellectual justification for further authoritarianism. And, as we shall see, the new national security strategy accepted this concept of security and the accompanying politicization and securitization processes linked to it.

As the debate progressed, in early 2008 Baluyevsky publicly fulminated against U.S. high-tech and nuclear threats to Russia, threatening even to add preventive nuclear strikes to Russia's proclaimed doctrine.[50]

Meanwhile, and virtually simultaneously, President Medvedev and civilian politicians like Finance Minister Alexei Kudrin and Anatoly Chubais, head of Russia's RAO UES Electricity firm, publicly complained that Russian foreign policy was unnecessarily alienating partners from whom Russia needs foreign investment and was both too costly in political terms and too risky.[51] These clashing statements in effect outlined the debate over the course and direction of Russian security policy.

From today's vantage point, however, it is clear who prevailed, at least until now. Despite these admonitions concerning Russia's economic vulnerability, the need for reform to include security policy, and the fact that severe economic crisis is crippling Russia's capabilities, Moscow's tough rhetoric and policies have, if anything, intensified, making it difficult to discern any sign of a qualitative change in policy. Indeed, even U.S. doves like former Ambassador to the Soviet Union Jack Matlock and Thomas Graham of the National Security Council during the George W. Bush administration complained that Russian policy remains "inflexible."[52] Meanwhile during 2006-08, Putin also took upon himself to outline a threat assessment in a series of major speeches (not just the Munich speech of 2007). Putin's litany of grievances in speeches going back to 2006 specified Russia's complaints in greater detail. Putin specifically charged that,

- America is a unipolar hegemon which conducts world affairs or aspires to do so in an undemocratic way (i.e., it does not take Russian interests into account).
- America has unilaterally gone to war in Iraq, disregarding the UN Charter and demonstrating an "unconstrained hyper use of force" that

is plunging the world into an abyss. It has therefore become impossible to find solutions to conflicts (in other words, American unilateralism actually makes it harder to end the wars in Iraq and Afghanistan— hardly an incontestable proposition). Because America seeks to decide all issues unilaterally to suit its own interests in disregard of others, "no one feels safe," and this policy stimulates an arms race and proliferation of WMD.

- Therefore we need a new structure of world politics, i.e., multipolarity and nonintervention in the affairs of others. Here Putin cited Russia's example of a peaceful transition to democracy! Of course, Russia hardly has a spotless record with regard to nonintervention, as Estonia, Moldova, Ukraine, and Georgia illustrate.
- Putin expressed concern that the Moscow Strategic Offensive Arms Reduction Treaty (SORT) of 2002 may be violated or at least undermined by America, which is holding back several hundred superfluous nuclear weapons for either political or military use. America is also creating new destabilizing high-tech weapons, including space weapons.
- Meanwhile, the Conventional Armed Forces in Europe (CFE) Treaty is not being ratified, even though Russian forces are leaving Georgia and only carrying out peacekeeping operations in Moldova. Similarly, U.S. bases are turning up "on our border" (here Putin revealed that, for him, the borders of Russia are, in fact, the old Soviet borders, since Russia no longer borders either Romania or Poland).
- America is also extending missile defenses to Central and Eastern Europe even though no

threat exists that would justify this. In regard to this program, Putin replied to a question at the Wehrkunde Conference in 2007 by saying that,

> The United States is actively developing and already strengthening an anti-missile defense system. Today this system is ineffective but we do not know exactly whether it will one day be effective. But in theory it is being created for that purpose. So hypothetically we recognize that when this moment arrives, the possible threat from our nuclear forces will be completely neutralized. Russia's present capabilities, that is. The balance of powers will be absolutely destroyed and one of the parties will benefit from the feeling of complete security. That means that its hands will be free not only in local but eventually also in global conflicts.[53]

Thus he has bought the General Staff's habit of thinking exclusively in terms of worst-case scenarios to justify a policy of threats and military buildup. Moreover, Baluyevsky and the General Staff all regularly argued that because there is allegedly no threat from Iran, these missile defenses can only be aimed at Russia and at threatening to neutralize its deterrent.[54] Possibly there may be private change in Russian thinking, though there is no public sign of it. Nevertheless, the role of the armed forces and intelligence services in promoting this expansive threat assessment is incontestable. As Secretary of Defense Gates (no stranger to the world of intelligence) recently observed,

> [Prime Minister Putin] basically dismissed the idea that the Iranians would have a missile that would have the range to reach much of Western Europe and much of Russia before 2020 or so. And he showed me a map that his intelligence guys had prepared. I told him he needed a new intelligence service. . . . The fact of the matter is, the Russians have come back to us and

acknowledged that we were right in terms of the nearness of the Iranian missile threat, and that they had been wrong. And so my hope is we can build on that.[55]

But Putin's listing of threats did not stop here. They further included:
- NATO expansion (the Russian term in opposition to the Western word enlargement) therefore bears no relationship to European security, but is an attempt to divide Europe and threaten Russia.
- America seeks to turn the OSCE into an anti-Russian organization, and individual governments, despite their so-called formal independence, are also using nongovernmental organizations (NGOs) for such purposes. Thus, revolutions in CIS countries are fomented from abroad, and elections there often are masquerades whereby the West intervenes in their internal affairs.[56] Obviously this view projects Russia's own politics and policies of interference in these elections (e.g., the $300 million it spent, and the efforts of Putin's "spin doctors" in Ukraine in 2004) onto Western governments and wholly dismisses the sovereign internal mainsprings of political action in those countries, another unconscious manifestation of the imperial mentality that grips Russian political thinking and action.

If we juxtapose Putin's assessment against the others presented here, the congruence, overlap, and even identity of these threat assessments becomes very clear. This 2006-09 debate is revealing in many other ways as well. It confirms that Russian discussions of security are no longer confined to defense, and that the meaning of the term security had been greatly amplified over the preceding generation as in the West and even China.[57] But that amplification has taken its own unique, even idiosyncratic, course. While Russia has followed Western examples in talking about common and comprehensive security and in thinking about its own security in those amplified terms, it also sees an enormous range of subjects as constituting the elements that comprise national security and considers them as fit subjects for state leadership if not control. In other words a process of securitization on a grand political scale has occurred even as defense issues no longer have sole pride of place in official Russian discourse. As Sergei Rogov, Director of the USA and Canada Institute, observed, "Over here, when the Russian Federation's Security Council was set up, we adopted an all-embracing definition of security that stipulated the security of the individual, society, and state from external and internal threats in all spheres of vital activity."[58]

And this process, in the absence of democratic reform to establish true democratic controls over the security sector, has allowed the military and the government to extend the securitization process, and allowed the military to concern itself with defining nonmilitary as well as military threats and argue for a role in policymaking towards them. Indeed, Felgengauer wrote that the military actively sought the right to use its forces, not the Ministry of Interior's Internal Troops (VVMVD), to quell domestic unrest should it break out.[59]

In other words, the military, by which we include the Ministry of the Interior (MVD) and the intelligence services, sought not just to securitize but also to politicize a wide range of issues, placing a wide range of both domestic and foreign policy issues on the agenda of the state or of leading political figures. To the extent that they were or are successful and the issue in question comes to be conceived of as referring to or posing a threat to the state, it has not only been politicized, but securitized, i.e., made a fixture of the state's security agenda and viewed mainly, if not exclusively, through that prism. Political actors who first politicize an issue as a threat to security and then securitize it, aim to persuade relevant audiences, in this case the political and military elite, that the issue in question poses an "existential threat to the country, either to its territory, the integrity of the state, its group identity, its environment, or its economic interests.[60]

Securitization thus denotes political actors' efforts, most often, though not exclusively, through speech or discourse, to take an issue out of normal politics and bring it into the realm of security. This process subordinates the issue to the competence of security organs, removes it from the public realm, substitutes secret bureaucratic decisions for open politics, and often contravenes human or civil rights.[61]

> The aim of a "securitizing move" is typically to enable "emergency measures" that can secure the survival of a referent object. If and when the content of the security "speech act" is acknowledged as legitimate by a (significant) "audience," the issue in question has become successfully "securitized." It has been moved out of the sphere of "normal politics" and into the sphere of "emergency politics"; where it can be dealt with in an urgent manner and with fewer formal and informal restrains.[62]

Actors make "securitizing moves" not just to place an item on the agenda, but also to claim that their agency alone has the capability either to define or resolve the problem or to implement the appropriate solution. In the Russian context, this all-encompassing securitization aimed not only to make the military the supreme arbiter of national defense, but also to provide an equally wide-ranging threat assessment based on the presupposition of enemies everywhere and pervasive threats to Russia's government, identity, territory, and economy. As we noted above, by 2006 the General Staff's Academy of Military Science, led by Gareyev, presented a comprehensive threat assessment embracing all those domains and the threat of IW that supposedly justified militarizing the entire state structure and making the Minister of Defense the Deputy Commander in Chief in both peacetime and wartime over a vastly strengthened government that would restore a Ministry of Defense Industry and prepare for Russia's comprehensive mobilization.[63]

This neo-Soviet securitizing move underscored the divergences of opinion among top military and political leaders and has continued without letup since then. The government adopted almost all of the assessment that Gareyev presented in 2006 but has consistently rejected his moves to militarize the country and enforce a mobilization economy. That is, it has refused to give the military control over the country or something close to it in peacetime, let alone in wartime. So while we have a threat assessment that presupposes conflict all around and even within Russia, the government either cannot or will not adopt policies that move completely in the direction of that logic. This result highlights the fact that the military (as defined here) is successful in embedding its threat perception among key elites only to the degree that they are receptive to it in advance, i.e., that it tallies with their ideas or with the government's success in systematically disseminating that perspective. In this respect, "The fate of securitizing moves is to a large degree determined by external factors such as their embeddedness, or lack thereof in social relations of power."[64]

As a result, we see a continuing incoherence in Russian policy. In 2006, for example, Defense Minister Sergei Ivanov, adopting the logic of all-encompassing and wide-ranging threats, said that the armed forces must be capable of operating in several regional and local conflicts simultaneously, a demand that is in no way possible unless one resorts to full-scale mobilization or the threat of nuclear war.[65] Clearly the military's threat assessment of 2006-08 that found its way into the new security strategy was embedded in the social relations of power as expressed in the state's takeover of control of military information and media and the central, or federal and regional instruments of media after 2000 that systematically fostered and disseminated a worldview based on this presupposition of conflicts and threats.[66] But there is no desire or perhaps capability to return completely to a Soviet mobilization state, hence the incoherence of Russian policy. Another way to state this is that despite its ambitions and the expansiveness of its threat perception, Russia cannot sustain either the magnitude of what its elites want to build or deal effectively with the real as opposed to notional threats confronting it. Caught between grandiose ends and perceived threats which are to some degree politically manufactured, Russia has not developed sufficient means to meet either existing or notional threats. Consequently its political and economic demands upon its own society and the world cannot be sustained, but it cannot desist from making those demands and thus creating a fundamentally untenable security situation in Eurasia.

An example of this unresolved contradiction relates to divisions even within the armed forces as to the nature of future wars. The threat assessment that has prevailed looks to wars with the United States and NATO, yet the current defense reform clearly points to an army capable of waging the smaller wars that prevail in our time and becoming more of an expeditionary force for Russia's and the CIS' peripheries. Anatoly Tsyganok, Head of the Center for Military Forecasting, expressed this concept of future war and of a defense for it in 2007, even as Gareyev and Baluyevsky were calling for something more traditional. Tsyganok argued that,

> We believe that in the 21st century, a guerilla war is more likely than a war launched by a modern army of, shall we say, the European or Asian type. . . . Therefore the arms and equipment must be prepared for that type of war. Unfortunately our military hardware that currently exists is last-century hardware.[67]

However, in the same article, Gareyev talked of the absolute priority of preparing the country as a whole for defense, determining the types of wars that Russia might fight and then proceeding to organize the armed forces and country accordingly. Gareyev, by forecasting the possibility of wars across much of the so-called spectrum of conflict, proposed something very different from Tsyganok's analysis. Indeed, this article reported that the draft defense doctrine was proposing to change the 2000 doctrine's statement that the development of the Armed Forces had to be carried out on the basis of Russia's economic potential to language indicating that the economy had to provide for the armed forces' development at any price, i.e., the Stalinist or Soviet answer to the problem.[68] As a sign of this debate, in 2007 Baluyevsky reported that each service was planning its own war, and that there had to be an integrated form of operational planning for the conduct of hostilities that might ensue.[69]

Indeed, this debate showed that, as of 2007-08 the government, while admittedly engrossed in taking ever more aspects of national security under its control, could not formulate or implement a coherent program attuned to the goal of enhancing national security under any definition. Baluyevsky's advocacy of "a strategy of national security that would be fully observed by all government agencies, including the 'power departments',"[70] underscored that institutional rivalry and obstruction. His remarks belied the carefully polished image of the Russian state under Putin as some kind of relentless, coherent juggernaut or machine (though its powers for striking fear are more than ample). Thus for all of the supposed advances made under Putin that allegedly unified policymaking, it turns out, not surprisingly to students of Russia's political folkways, that this was not the case and that policy division and internecine struggles were rampant. And in the light of Russian history those remarks highlighted the continuity of Putinism with Russia's past.

Certain conclusions suggest themselves. First, as noted above and in advance of the publication of the defense doctrine, it appears that despite Medvedev's elevation to the presidency, he, Kudrin, and Chubais lost the battle to define the threat assessment and the ensuing policy requirements dictated by that assessment to ensure Russian security. Second, the visible trend under Putin to securitize ever more areas of Russian socio-economic and political life continues to be in the ascendancy with significant consequences for both domestic and foreign policies. Third, this trend has led to an aggressive military campaign to seize the initiative in defining the threats confronting Russia and the policies it should therefore adopt. These policy conclusions preceded the Russo-Georgian war in August 2008, so they are not exclusively attributable to that war and its aftermath. Indeed, both the debate and the war can be traced to developments within the Russian policy process that go far beyond Moscow's problems with Tbilisi. At the same time, the importance of economics has reasserted itself with a vengeance not just in real life but in the national security strategy as well, making economic issues subject to greater securitization than before. As a result, Putin and now President Medvedev have presided over, if not championed, the further securitization of ever more areas of national policy. And this securitization process has allowed the military to take an aggressive posture on defining threats and recommended policy responses to them. Furthermore, President Medvedev (if not Putin) has consciously used the new strategy to try to impose coherence on the government and policy, a highly traditional Russian approach. And, of course, that self-conscious attempt to use this process and the new strategy for those purposes is another piece of evidence for the existence of a preceding tough political struggle.

THE NATIONAL SECURITY STRATEGY AND DOMESTIC POLITICS

Upon closer examination, it becomes clear that the new National Security Strategy was aimed first at a domestic audience for domestic political purposes, not the least of which was an authoritative ruling on threats to Russia and who will conduct the response to them. As we noted, while the military-intelligence bloc's assessment was largely accepted because it coincided with the political leadership's outlook, the response to that assessment proffered by the Siloviki was rejected in favor of a civilian-led program of action. Nevertheless, the net result is the securitization and politicization of ever more aspects of domestic politics. Consequently, the national security strategy serves primarily domestic political and strategic purposes, starting with the goal of imposing order upon this debate. Thus we see the following developments occurring with regard to Russia's overall national security policy.

- First, the status and stature of the Security Council, the body that is supposed to have coordinated the national security strategy and the defense doctrine, has been enhanced. The Security Council's authority has fluctuated widely, depending almost exclusively on who ran it, and it was used for political and military figures that had been removed from the active policy struggle. It exemplified the irregular, personalized world of Russian policymaking. Now the Council's Secretary, Nikolai Patrushev, former Director of the Federal Security Service (FSB), is to oversee the Council's coordinating role that covers all elements of the national security system and beyond that organs of state government, state organizations, and social organizations."[71] This looks like an effort to establish one supreme state organization above all others with the monitoring capability beloved of Russian leaders who, given the absence of regular legally defined institutions, have perennially suffered from a mania for creating institutions devoted to *control*—i.e., surveillance, monitoring of policy implementation and oversight—all to no avail. It is also another sign of the obsession with having a concentration of power in one supposedly centralized organ that will thus overcome all the defects of Russian governance. This is a long-standing but inherently unrealizable fantasy of Russian autocrats and officials.

Indeed, we have seen similar trends in the defense industrial sector indicating that Russia is reverting to an ever more Soviet or at least Tsarist-like defense industrial structure that will be even less transparent than before. This security strategy points to the diffusion of this mode of thinking throughout the government. In the case of the defense industry, this trend was visible by 2007. Conforming to the Russian tradition that an effort to root out inefficiencies and ineffectiveness often involves more centralization, that then entails the creation of ever more auditing and inspecting agencies to perform those regulatory functions summed up in *kontrol*, Deputy Prime Minister and head of the defense industry Sergei Ivanov had created by then what one writer called an audit pyramid under his supervision in the military industrial complex (MIC).[72] Such permanent monitoring is justified by the ideas that without it rampant corruption would ensue and, once again, that the market cannot be trusted.[73]

In this context, the new strategy introduced a new provision saying that all documents on domestic or foreign policy should be referred to the Security Council for review. The Council will be the body measuring progress by all concerned parties on implementing the new strategy, reporting annually to the President. This provision indicates the regime's intention of centralizing all of these *kontrol* functions in that body.[74]

- That intention, in turn leads to a second key point. With this document President Medvedev, if not Putin, has explicitly stated his intention to use the strategy and what he calls strategic planning as an instrument of control (in our sense of the word) to overcome the dominance of departmentalism and departmental priorities over national interest (the besetting vice of all Russian bureaucracy from time immemorial). This determination was proclaimed well before the document itself was released, indicating that this is a real priority for its authors if not President Medvedev and Putin. Thus Patrushev stated in December 2008 that, "On the whole, the country's leadership has already mapped out the first priority aspects of the national security strategy, which are the perfection of the political system, optimization of state governance and the enhancement of the state's defense and security capabilities."[75]

If this is the first priority (and we should take Patrushev at his word if we grasp his meaning), then obviously we are dealing with a highly dysfunctional government and policy process and a fundamentally insecure state. This lack of governmental coherence is pervasive. For instance, it is visible in the fact that while the Ministry of Defense is vigorously pushing a new and controversial reform, the Ministry of Foreign Affairs is generally acknowledged not to be the main source of foreign policy initiatives, while the Ministry of Trade and Development has long been disinclined to engage in independent thinking.[76] Since then, we have only had further confirmation of this fact. At the key meeting on the security strategy of March 24, 2009, the Security Council's Press Office reiterated Patrushev's point, "The strategy is aimed at increasing the quality of public administration and is intended to coordinate the efforts of the authorities and governmental and public organizations to protect Russia's national interests and to ensure, individual, public, and national security."[77]

- Third, the National Security Strategy is a fundamental, system-forming document, which is aimed at the enhancement of the quality of state control. It links together "the activities of the executive organs of the government and the state, corporative, and social organizations in the protection of the national interests of Russia and the provision of security for the individual, the public, and the state."[78] This document and the others surrounding it represent an attempt to silence debate and coordinate the state. For that reason, the strategy document is really part of a complex of different but interrelated state papers, and its classified agenda specifies actual numerical values for measuring the condition of security, formulating bases for strategic forecasting, and for foundation documents for implementing strategic goals through legislation.[79] Among these other documents are the Foreign Policy Concept, the forthcoming Defense Doctrine, The Long-Term Socio-Economic Development Concept of the Russian Federation to 2020, and even President Medvedev's speech to the Duma of November 5, 2008.[80]

Therefore it is not surprising that both analysts and officials like Patrushev state that the new strategy is an attempt to provide the basis for building a system of national interests and corresponding priorities and that it presupposes the preparation of predictive documents and statutory acts.[81] This is part of the state tradition that claims that doctrinal statements even possess juridical significance. As Patrushev told an interviewer, "Most importantly, it is aimed at improving the quality of state management and is designed to coordinate the activities of organs of state power and of the state and public organizations in defending Russia's national interests and ensuring the security of the individual, society, and the state."[82]

In this concern for systematizing the state and unifying it under a single centralized agency that is supposed to produce coherent policy and implementation, the new strategy extends some of the oldest aspirations of Russian rulers going back to Peter the Great. Russian rulers have almost to a man adopted the view that if they could formulate a document or policies that truly imbued the entire state system with a uniform view of its tasks and goals from top to bottom, they could achieve systematic government in the absence of the rule of law. Putin and President Medvedev, not to mention their subordinates, are clearly equally susceptible to this delusion, one that apparently remains entrenched in the official mind and ethos of Russia.[83] After all this is what the concept of a power vertical is all about.

For centuries Russian rulers have vainly tried to square the circle professing their desire for "regular government" while simultaneously refusing to accept the fact that incoherence and the absence of system are inherent in the nature of their power. Moreover, this incoherence guarantees their autocratic power. Therefore, any effort by them to preserve that power untouched only reinforces the inherent incoherence of the state, even as they vainly try to impose systematic government by autocratic methods. Certainly an overview of Putin's defense and institutional reforms underscores his aspiration to unify the so called "power vertical" into a single machine functioning to enhance the state's unity and interests and supposedly guarantee the people's rights even though there is no rule of law or challenge to autocracy.[84] Yet the very nature of the autocracy with its lack of the rule of law or legal limits on the president's (or tsar's or general secretary's) power inherently precludes the achievement of this goal. Consequently, the resulting reality is one of unending policy and personal rivalry behind and often in front of the scenes.

THE MILITARY THREAT ASSESSMENT-2008

The unending rivalry over the terms of the new strategy is visible in the Russian media. The fully elaborated military threat assessment associated with Baluyevsky was outlined by Gareyev at a special conference of the academy in January 2008 specifically intended to elaborate proposals for the new National Security Concept (as it was then called). Gareyev began by complaining about the dearth of competent organizations to work out such a draft, saying there was not one such competent institution in all of Russia.[85] In an openly and self-consciously ideological report, Gareyev then warned that,

> From the military-political viewpoint the NATO war against Yugoslavia ushered in, in essence, a new epoch not only in the military, but also in the universal history, the epoch of open military-force diktat.... Along with the growth of the dependence of its economy on the access to world markets and natural deposits the military-force component of the US policy will be systematically intensifying, including toward Russia owing to the specifics of its geographical position.[86]

Gareyev's assessment was clearly not a policy neutral one. Instead, it led to specific policy recommendations. Specifically, he called for new treaties to replace the Strategic Arms Reduction Treaty I (START I), limitations on U.S. missile defenses, and the preservation of restrictions on strategic offensive weapons (i.e., U.S. high-precision weapons that could be used to launch a strategic attack on Russia's nuclear weapons or command and control centers for them, in effect making conventional weapons strategic weapons according to the counting rules of that new arms control treaty). Likewise, Russia had to seek to ban the replacement of nuclear warheads with conventional precision warheads on land or sea-based ballistic missiles, and conduct a vigorous foreign policy with the support of the UN, NATO, OSCE, European Union (EU), China, India, and other states to overcome America's confrontational policy, "seeking wherever possible the adoption of international legal norms banning subversive activities against other states."[87] Since then every one of these policy prescriptions—as well as the strategy itself—has been accepted by the government and incorporated into Russia's posture in the current negotiations with the United States for a new treaty to reduce strategic arms.[88] He then proceeded to outline a comprehensive universal external and internal threat assessment that would have done justice to the General Staff in the USSR by the scope of ubiquitous threats to Russia that he discerned.[89]

Inasmuch as Gareyev's recommendations became Russia's exact foreign policy and arms control position, this debate's political ramifications were clear. Furthermore, the military and factions aligned to it have won the debate over defining the threats to Russia.[90] Certainly this approach has little or nothing in common with that of Kudrin and Chubais, not to mention President Medvedev's January 2008 speeches. Indeed, already in 2007, when speaking of missile defenses to the members of the G-8 press corps, Putin basically said that if the military calls it a threat, we agree with that assessment even though it is clear, as Secretary of Defense Gates told him, that he needs new intelligence analysts if he believes that those missile defenses threaten Russia and that Iran is not a threat.[91] Baluyevsky's and Gareyev's victory on this point is in no small measure an ironic one since the controversial defense reform that was inaugurated immediately after the Russo-Georgian war has been devised and implemented in the teeth of enormous and unceasing military opposition.[92] That defense reform, with its call for smaller, more professional and mobile armies, is based on a threat assessment that there will not be a major war against NATO but rather that military operations are most likely in and around the CIS on a smaller scale.[93] Indeed, Baluyevsky was sacked due to his opposition to that reform. Nevertheless, this threat assessment has reigned undisturbed until now despite the fact that it is at odds with the emerging force structure of the Russian Army. And it clearly is a self-serving assessment that reflects not just the folkways of Russia's historic bureaucratic organization but also the dangers inherent in the lack of democratic control over the military and intelligence agencies that allow them to go their own way with dangerous results as Felgenhauer noted above.[94]

Moreover, the contradictions embodied in the debate process remain, as of now, unresolved. The new strategy apparently downplays nuclear weapons, and, even more importantly, the defense reform presupposes the end of the need for the huge mass army that has historically been invoked as the only way to meet the expected NATO and/or U.S. attack. In other words, careful examination of the new strategy and the debate leading up to it betrays a split personality, particularly as regards the imminence and nature of threats to Russia.

What this episode also shows is that the military's victory on the nature of the threat and policy prescriptions to meet it was only possible to the degree that powerful civilian political actors accepted or agreed with its position. Where that is not the case, as in the defense reform, the military can only resort to obstruction, a tactic of dubious value, not least because it has nothing to offer but more of the same. Thus, the government professes to have bought the military's threat assessment but has launched a defense reform that points in an entirely different direction than would have been indicated by this acceptance. So it is not surprising that a vicious struggle is currently roiling the entire military establishment. That struggle is continuing, attesting to the failure to establish either regular government or democratic and truly civilian control over the armed forces. For instance, we are now told that in the forthcoming defense doctrine, there will be closed or classified sections, specifically those relating to the legal aspects of the army and navy's employment, including the use of nuclear weapons. Only the military-political sections will be publicized.[95] Then, in October 2009, Patrushev openly discussed the doctrine and its forthcoming nuclear provisions.[96] Apart from the fact that those provisions are highly dangerous in discussing options for a preventive or preemptive first use of nuclear weapons even in a local war, the contradiction between prior concealment and now public openness attests to the unresolved struggles over the doctrine as of October 2009. The earlier move towards concealment represents a hugely regressive step away from both democratic and civilian control, and although the General Staff claims it is only doing what is done in the United States and other Western countries, that is not the case (although there are classified annexes to key documents, they are often debated or discussed in the chambers of Congress).[97] But it represented both another attempt to create a kind of Chinese wall behind which the military can shelter itself free of any accountability to anyone, and a further step towards militarization of state policy along neo-Soviet lines. Thus the debate continues as before.

Meanwhile Gareyev's 2008 report not only cited the United States as the main threat, but also the problems caused by international terrorism and China's uncertain direction. He claimed (quite in opposition to the facts) that as U.S. dependence on access to world markets and reserves grows, so too does its proclivity for unilateral employment of military force. Obviously this is a classic vulgar Marxist-Leninist theory that shows just how antediluvian Russian strategic thinking remains. But it has become a central point of Russian threat assessment that found its way into the security strategy and even subsequent articles.[98] All of this occurs, of course, simultaneously with the creation of Russian thinkers' favorite hobbyhorse, a multipolar world, leading to intense "contradictions" in world politics, to use the Leninist term. Gareyev also attributed to America's leading theorists, Zbigniew Brzezinski and Henry Kissinger, the ambition to destroy Russia, another example of how blinkered this outlook is.[99]

U.S. intervention in the CIS and Central Asia and support for NATO enlargement to Georgia and Ukraine are most prominent in this threat assessment. Yet even so, because of nuclear weapons, a classical war against Russia is ruled out, although it may occur by other means, and the likelihood of local wars and conflicts increases. Whereas the main threat is Washington's goal of depriving Russia of its independence, interfering in its internal affairs and infringing on its economic and national interests, the targeting by various nuclear countries of Russia (including NATO, the United States, and China) constitutes the second group of threats. The third group of threats is the ambition of other countries (again read NATO and the United States) to continue the qualitative improvement of weapons towards achieving a dominant military-technical superiority as they approach Russia, and the use of information and information-psychological actions. The most dangerous of these threats are the separatist and terrorist threats directed against Russia's unity and integrity, which as a rule are incited from outside (a classic example of Russia's historic refusal to accept its responsibility for its own actions or what goes on in its territory or around its borders).

As a result, Russia must counter all these threats through its governmental and defense policies.[100] Gareyev's threat assessment and recommendations point to several key factors in this debate. First of all, much of this threat assessment is Soviet in origin and thus represents a carry-over of Soviet discourses into a wholly new world without any sense of their obsolescence, or of their quite visible falsity. This continuity pervades the security establishment.[101] Second, we see the recurrent obsession that Russia must again be a great power if it is to survive at all, i.e., an empire and world power and the corresponding paranoia that not only is it at the center of the United States' and other actors' strategic calculations, but that it is forever surrounded by threats on all sides and from within, notably from the threat of "color revolutions," which, it is taken for granted, are instigated from outside and which are a mortal threat, and accepted as such by the senor political leadership.[102]

Third, in keeping with this classical Leninist paranoia, threats are ubiquitous, and the internal and external threats are linked since they emanate from the same place. Even where other military writers, e.g., Anatoly Tsyganok, head of the Military Forecast Center, ascribe a different hierarchy of threats facing Russia, the list of threats seems enormous and ubiquitous.[103] This mentality fosters the securitization of virtually every aspect of state policy. Thus the military community presented—and still presents—a comprehensive and fully thought-out (even if reactionary) threat assessment, replete with policy recommendations, as its contribution to the ongoing debate over doctrine, policy, etc.[104]

SECURITIZATION UNDER PUTIN

Obviously any defense assessment is predisposed to focus on military threats, whatever their provenance. However, this current threat assessment represents some other key aspects of the ongoing debate that have developed over time. Under Putin's and Medvedev's presidencies, debates over Russian security have become, if anything, more acute, with attempts being made to securitize ever more aspects of domestic, defense, and foreign policy to justify state supervision over those domains.[105] Indeed, as in Gareyev's—and other less comprehensive—threat assessments, that securitization appears to display visible continuity from the Soviet period, suggesting an unreformed mindset regarding security. Thus, in regard to the Svalbard Archipelago (Spitzbergen) in the Arctic, Kristian Atland and Torbjorn Pedersen conclude that,

> There seems to be a high degree of *continuity* between Cold War and post-Cold War Russian interpretations of space-related activities on the Svalbard Archipelago. The current pattern of securitization is in reality not very different from the Cold War pattern and it seems fair to assume that the historic baggage of So-

viet/Russian mistrust and suspicion still serves as a "facilitating condition" for securitization (Italics in the original).[106]

In the case of Russia's overall national security concept and defense doctrine, as in the lesser case of a region like the Svalbard Archipelago, many of the securitizing actors like Gareyev held high positions in the Soviet period and are inclined to a Soviet, rather than Western, mindset. Moreover,

> ... the "audiences" that the "securitizing actors" were playing up to, such as the Russian Security council, the Foreign Ministry, and the Defense Ministry, shared many of their concerns. These 'audiences' were generally receptive to the calls for extraordinary measures on and around the archipelago at the time.[107]

The receptivity of these audiences to such enormous securitizing moves owes much to the unwillingness or inability of both the Yeltsin and Putin regimes to reform any or all of Russia's agencies concerned with national security policies. Indeed, Yeltsin started and Putin completed the process by which so many ex-KGB men have assumed key positions throughout the state for the first time in Russian history. The consequences of that dereliction are fully in evidence today.

This securitization process duly compounds the inherent contradictions of the policy process and the anti-liberal tendencies of Russian politics and is connected to the military mentality depicted above. Even if not all of these securitizing moves have succeeded, the scope of the effort, as well as its failures and successes, are noteworthy.[108] Indeed, as an examination of the new security strategy will show, this process has led to the securitization of whole areas of domestic policy that were hitherto excluded from the debate (e.g., culture and health). Now they too have been quite overtly securitized in an effort to impose the coordination referred to above.[109] Thus we see here the regime's ambition for a population that is, to use a German term of the Nazi period, *Gleischgeschaltet*, that is to say, coordinated around the state. We use this term advisedly, for this "coordination" reflected in Putin's policies and the new strategy are intrinsically anti-democratic and anti-liberal, aiming at the revival of a state power that is unfettered and unaccountable either to law or to other institutions. Undoubtedly, this securitization process has been essential to the implementation of this anti-democratic project, as it is instrumental in removing many areas of policy from public control or scrutiny and in politicizing others that normally might not be thought to fall within the realm or competence of the Russian power structures (*silovye struktury*). Moreover, it is continuing. For example, President Medvedev has called for a new law on defense that would supplement Clause 10 of the Federal Law On Defence with paragraph 21, specifying that in line with the generally accepted principles and provisions of international law, the Russian Federation's international treaties, and the Federal Law On Defence, Russian Armed Forces can be used in operations beyond Russia's borders for the following purposes:

- To counter an attack against Russian Armed Forces or other troops deployed beyond Russia's borders;
- To counter or prevent an aggression against another country;
- To protect Russian citizens abroad;

- To combat piracy and ensure safe passage of shipping.

The draft suggests that the Federal Law On Defence be supplemented with Clause 101, setting, in accordance with Russia's Constitution, the procedures for decisions on use of Russian Armed Forces beyond the country's borders.[110] At the same time the Deputy Chief of the General Staff, General Anatoly Nogovitsyn, announced on August 11 that,

> The new military *doctrine*, which is being drawn up under the guidance of the Russian Federation Security Council, will be different from the current text. It will consist of two parts—the public one, which will include mostly military-political aspects, and the classified one, where the issues of the right to use the army and navy, including the use of *nuclear* weapons as a strategic deterrent, will be clearly defined.[111]

Since the war in 2008 with Georgia occurred without any legislative sanction for military action and the new law will clearly bypass the Duma as well, we see here an ominous trend towards a minimization of any kind of civilian or democratic accountability in military defense, not to mention control over the most vital and profound issues of military defense.

These events merely represent the latest in a long series of events and trends reflecting both the securitization process and the escape from democratic control. For example, the hierarchy and politicians of the Orthodox Church increasingly invoke the spiritual security (*Dukhovnaya Bezopasnost*) of the nation and the threats to it.[112] Not surprisingly, this organization was thoroughly penetrated by the KGB under communism and remains wholly allied to the powers that be today as it seeks a status akin to that of the official state religion. Thus a double securitization has occurred, with religion being politicized and with its politics being intimately connected with the power structures. Similarly, the Russian Ministry of Emergency Situations has declared, without any official contradiction, that the possibility of an epidemic from avian flu represents a threat to Russia's national security, thus equating it to terrorism or nuclear arms races.[113] Here again public debate has been curtailed or at least limited by this securitizing move.

This also raises another point. Russian officials like to say that the major security documents like the new strategy arise out of the state's commitment to the security of individual citizens as well as the state. While avian flu undoubtedly threatens many individuals and communities, it hardly threatens the security of the state; yet is openly represented as doing so. This securitizing process therefore suggests that for Russian officialdom the individual only exists insofar as he serves the abstraction of the state, a long-standing Russian belief that grows out of the tradition of the service state. Since Putin has arguably restored key elements of that pre-modern service state, such mental gyrations and discourses are to be expected.[114] These examples would appear to validate the observations found in a 2006 study of Russian domestic politics, namely that,

> The securitization approach illuminates one of the overarching self-conceptualizations of the Putin government. If the Yeltsin regime defined itself in terms of democratization; then much that has been done since that time is defined in terms of security. Analysis of discourse, which is central to the methodological approach employed here, reveals repeatedly the power of the key signifier "security" and the frequency of its

adoption by the forces seeking hegemony within Russia's political elite.[115]

As we have seen from the discussion by Patrushev, statements by key analysts like Rogov, and President Medvedev's statements and policies, the regime aims to securitize ever more aspects of politics, subject them to centralized and unlimited official regulation based on their connection to officially defined canons of Russian security, remove them from active public debate, subordinate them to discourses and actions rationalized by security considerations, and/or take control of them by figures and institutions associated with the preservation of security (usually hard or military-police security). This does not mean that debate over security has ceased — far from it. Rather the debate has generally, though not always, been rendered opaque and occurs between or among bureaucratic factions which generally endeavor to hide their maneuvers and rationales from the public. This process is at best a mixed blessing and more often than not considerably worse. The securitization of ever more realms of politics creates many dangers for democratization and for state development — and these dangers are not confined to Russia. Neither is our concern here only that the *silovye struktury* are taking control of too much of Russian policy, though that certainly is the case.

As many observers warn, the extension of the term security to ever wider fields of non-military governmental operations and the desire to internationalize both the accompanying threat perceptions and responses to these perceptions brings about an undesirable threat inflation; these calls place ever greater pressures on governments to do and be more, even if they lack the resources for adequate responses to existing threats. In the Russian context where centralization of political controls is virtually an eternal mantra of policymakers, such demands can quickly become the basis for ever new expansions of state control at the expense of the public's self-rule. Moreover, such calls to action, though morally laudable, are intellectually incoherent and highly problematic.[116]

Consequently this securitization process entails risks for any state in regards to both democracy and state governing capacity. Two Canadian champions of the human security agenda are compelled to admit that,

> In a world where "security" seems to be overwhelming all other normative frameworks, to treat all these important issues as security concerns has actually come to cloud justifications for action and risks undermining important mechanisms of legal constraint.[117]

Similarly, this author has repeatedly argued that the failure to subject defense policy and the institutions responsible for it to authentic civilian democratic control creates a constant temptation for war either in Russia or around it. The record of five wars in and around Russia since 1991 (the coups of 1991 and 1993, two Chechen wars—in 1994-96 and since 1999—and the war with Georgia in 2008 that Russia instigated), not to mention Yeltsin's projected coups against elections in 1996, 1998, and 1999, all highlight the danger of this trend.[118]

The consequence of Russia's perennial threat inflation and devaluation of the concept of security are not long in coming. An unchecked process that securitizes ever more spheres of organized social life also generates an unending spiral of politicization that may make it harder to deal with these threats while corroding civil society and democratic politics. Every conceivable object of policy becomes a security question and thus overpoliticized, which in Russia means that it is then removed from public debate. Yet at the same time and paradoxically, but not surprisingly to any student of Russian institutional history, the effort to impose a uniform systematization of government inevitably breeds its own centrifugal forces that mock those aspirations in reality.

In Russia's case, this process has also helped undermine any effort at defense and/or security sector reform, or more precisely democratization, because it has allowed the power ministries the freedom to define security and postulate an ever growing series of threats to it without excessive contradiction from civilian authorities. Similarly they have been able to influence the authorities to adopt a kind of militarized view of the state with an emphasis on a quasi-military structure like the power vertical or an emphasis on an atavistic view of world politics, like that common to the Russian elite and as expressed by Gareyev and Baluyevsky. The virulent oppositon to the defense reform that we see now also embodies that point. If the ministries and affected bureaucracies can define the security environment without open challenges and secure official acceptance of that assessment, then fundamental areas of national security have been removed from public debate and scrutiny, leaving no alternative but opaque bureaucratic factionalism within a neo-Leninist culture of *kto kogo* (who does what to whom).

This securitization process in its military form in Russia assumes a particular kind of militarism that allows the regime to adopt and impose upon the public a quasi-military conception of the state as a kind of army in motion that is supposed to be the embodiment of machine-like obedience and concern for the national interest above any other consideration.[119] Second, under contemporary conditions it allows the power structures to seek their own autonomous sphere of decisionmaking accountable to nobody—not other ministries, not the legislature, possibly not even the ruler himself. This trend by the Siloviki to usurp civilian control was already quite evident by the end of Yeltsin's presidency where the Chief of Staff, General Anatoly Kvashnin, could launch an intervention in Kosovo without coordination from either the Ministry of Foreign Affairs or Defense because he had obtained presidential approval.[120] But this effort by these structures to monopolize the securitization process did not end here. Rather these kinds of actions reflected an ongoing and profound domestic crisis that neither Putin nor President Medvedev has really resolved.

Russia's securitization process is dangerous for other reasons too. Besides the efforts to militarize security definitions, inflate threat assessments so that political and military threats are conflated, and restrict democratic control over the relevant power structures, Russia's process entails several other risks. The process also puts the state at unintended risk because it tempts governments (not only in Russia) to overextend themselves and take on tasks for which they are ill-suited or which are beyond their capabilities. Arguably this is what happened to the Soviet Union, which defined itself as being in a state of perpetual conflict and thus under permanent threat both within and without from the "imperialist West." Thus the USSR was permanently organized as a war economy that ultimately could not compete either economically or militarily with its great rival.

In Russia's case these processes tempt the regime to believe that it can use force to solve internal or external problems with impunity and not reckon the costs of doing so. Thus Russia in 17 years has fought three wars and been vulnerable to coups in 1991, 1993, almost in 1996 and 1998, and again in 1999. So as we trace the securitization process under Putin, we should be asking ourselves if his regime is in danger of beginning to imitate its Soviet predecessor. Since Putin, and probably the elite, regard the collapse of the Soviet Union as the greatest geopolitical disaster of the 20th century, a discovery that Putin's regime has initiated a process that in key areas retraces the steps leading to that disaster would represent an enormous but ungratifying irony for Russia.

THE DEBATE ON THREATS TO SECURITY IN 2004-08

According to President Medvedev's website page on his signing of the new national security strategy, work on it began in 2004 to replace the 1997 national security concept, and drafting began on his instruction in June 2008.[121] This anodyne and reticent statement unintentionally reveals the kinds of struggle that took place. No mention is made here of the fact that Russia, under Putin, produced a national security strategy in 2000, something that all the players know. We do not know the reason for this silence, but it clearly indicates a major political struggle and apparently incensed Putin as reported below.[122] Second, it took four years to work on this, and the people involved could not even produce a draft. When President Medvedev finally decreed a draft, it took almost another year to produce. This is not the work of a confident, united government—quite the opposite.

What is clear is that by 2007 the Siloviki had gone far into the process of postulating their own threat assessment, the threat inflation that accompanied it, and the galloping process of securitization. To some degree, this descended from Putin's own speeches in 2006-07 that reflected his acceptance of their recommendations and their own contribution to those ongoing parallel processes.[123] Press accounts make clear that threat assessment was a big issue in 2007. In January 2007, i.e., before Putin's blistering speech to the Munich Security Conference in February 2007, Sergei Ivanov, then Minister of Defense, said that in respect of threats to Russian security, the Cold War was paradise compared to now because of its predictability and coherence.[124] Already by 2006, leaks had told the press that a strongly anti-U.S. and anti-NATO defense doctrine was in the offing, apparently prepared by Gareyev's Academy of Military Sciences and members of the Ministry of Defense (probably attached to the General Staff), though still no national security strategy had been proposed—a sign of continuing debate.[125]

But it was precisely these revelations that also produced signs of the bureaucratic strife over the security strategy and the defense doctrine. The 2006 reports had said the doctrine would soon be approved, but by early 2007, it was still hanging fire even though high-ranking officers had attended a January 2007 meeting where Gareyev and Baluyevsky outlined their views. It soon became clear that Ivanov opposed the whole idea. He told the Duma in February 2007, just before he was promoted to the position of Deputy Prime Minister and replaced by the current Minister Anatoly Serdyukov (apparently not in regard to this issue), that,

Our Military Doctrine exists and it is fairly new. It was adopted in 2001 when I was completing my work as the Secretary of the Security Council and was going into civilian service at the Defense Ministry. It contains some fundamental things, including terrorism, the threat of the spread of WMD, and internal conflicts. It is all there in the doctrine. I do not say that it is eternal, of course. Perhaps a new national security doctrine should be adopted. But if there is indeed a need for it, it should be passed first and then a military doctrine should be tailored to it because you cannot put the cart before the horse. I do not rule out that in several years we will need, if not a radically new military doctrine because the main things are already in the 2001 doctrine and the world has not changed all that much since then.[126]

Thus Sergei Ivanov seemingly contradicted his earlier statement about multiplying threats, and demonstrably displayed his antagonism to the idea of a new military doctrine and its stronger anti-Western threat assessment. His opposition apparently was telling because soon afterward the Security Council, then led by the former Foreign Minister Igor Ivanov, who was not a member of the Siloviki and had no relation to Sergei Ivanov, announced that it, together with other state departments, would prepare a new defense doctrine, even though it had no formal mandate for doing so as this work is usually the preserve of the Ministry of Defense and General Staff. It also suggested that the security strategy would precede a defense doctrine, rather than the other way around, even though the Council had been working since 2004 to prepare a new security strategy without success.[127] This suggests a clear effort to block this new strongly anti-Western doctrine and threat inflation, e.g., coming to see color revolutions as a form of political warfare induced by the West as part of a broader information campaign to destroy Russia without firing a shot.[128] Sergei Ivanov's remarks also point to a different hierarchy of threats, including terrorism, WMD, etc., on which basis cooperation with the West is much more possible, rather than the hard line state of siege represented by the forces for whom Gareyev speaks.

Thus Sergei's and Igor Ivanov's (they are not related) remarks add another line of debate to the question of threat assessment and priorities to meet them. Whereas Kudrin and Chubais, and seemingly President Medvedev, emphasized the need for economic development and progress, much as Putin did in his first years as President, and therefore the need for a policy that enhances economic links with the developed world, the two Ivanovs emphasized defense threats but threats for which a basis of cooperation with the West exists. The third line on this point, and the one that has prevailed until now, is the one that sees defense threats and internal threats and links them together in classic Leninist style. For these men (and perhaps women) the Western threat is both a political and a military one to undermine the integrity and legitimacy of their rule and with it Russia's great power status. That threat is buttressed by what they perceive as military-political threats, mainly by Washington, but also by NATO, to expand NATO and coerce Russia to surrender. Consequently, they have revived the Leninist threat paradigm that Russia is at risk from both internal and external enemies, and that they are one and the same set of forces (e.g., NGOs as spies). Naturally on this basis cooperation with the West is only possible on Khrushchevian-Brezhnevian terms of peaceful coexistence. On this basis, coexistence or cooperation can only be narrow on issues like arms control, and even here it will clearly be difficult because the United States will not simply roll over in the face of Russian obduracy and truculence.[129]

If our analysis of the differences in approach and threat assessment circa 2007-08 among key players in the security field is correct, then it makes sense to believe that—given these differences and the looming all-important issue of the succession to Putin which he refused to resolve until almost the last minute—the struggle around the strategy document and the ideas in it would have grown more intense during this period. This line of analysis might also help explain why the Foreign Policy Concept preceded the National Security Strategy. Since the former document is mainly a product of the Foreign Ministry, which is an executor, not an originator, of Russian foreign policy, it was to a considerable degree shielded from the struggles around defense issues at this time; and since Foreign Minister Lavrov has generally supported a tough line vis-à-vis the United States, that document could come out without materially affecting the interests and positions of the actors in the overall debate about national security.

In this context, it also is not surprising that the Siloviki in 2007 launched or intensified an ultimately successful campaign to oust Igor Ivanov from the Security Council as part of the general shuffle around the succession to Putin. Patrushev then replaced him, and has publicly charged the West not just with spying on Russia but on trying to split up Russia. He has also charged NGOs with being foreign spies or in their pay in order to influence Russia's domestic politics, a charge that has also resonated with Putin and suggests his affinities with the Siloviki faction.[130] Press commentary on Igor Ivanov's resignation also suggested that he had run afoul of one or more key factions in the government, and that therefore they may have sought to replace him with one of their own people.[131]

Western reports, based on Russian sources, of the supposedly forthcoming new defense doctrine in 2007 also saw it as an openly anti-Western one that marked a real point of departure from the already quite anti-Western defense doctrine of 2000. Even as a laborious discussion of the impending national security strategy worked its way through the executive and legislative bodies of Russia's regions and central government, Russian papers were leaking reports of the supposedly imminent defense doctrine. According to these reports, NATO was strengthening as a military bloc, allied forces were drawing closer to Russia, missile defense threatened Russia's nuclear capabilities, and cooperation with the West was minimal, if at all existent.

Meanwhile Russian documents and officials claim that wars are intensifying as a primary if not constant factor in achieving geopolitical aims, and are still likely to erupt over energy rivalries or environmental issues, but mainly as local conflicts. Even so, Russia must prepare for large-scale wars and even for nuclear threats given the advent of missile defenses in Central Europe. Threats to Russia came from Washington's determination to exercise world leadership and encroach upon "traditional areas of Russian presence," NATO's expansion, the alleged (though in fact nonexistent) buildup of powerful forces on Russia's borders, and continuous information campaigns against Russia. Therefore, Russia should form its own bloc like the CSTO and dominate the post-Soviet space exclusively.

These reports also indicated that the doctrine would drop terrorism as a threat and the opposition to military blocs so that Russia could organize the CSTO as it has relentlessly done since 2007. It also allegedly reduced Russia's reliance upon first strike and even preemptive nuclear strikes against the West because "the authors apparently believe that the armed forces can fight a regional conventional war against the US. Meanwhile they also want to prepare Russia to wage counter-insurgency wars as well."[132] However, more recent reports say that, in the latest version of the forthcoming defense doctrine,

> Russia has recognized for itself the right to the preventive employment of *nuclear* weapons should we be attacked by some military bloc (like NATO). It is hard to imagine that this could happen. Nonetheless, Moscow has, in having recorded this point, fairly warned Brussels of the action that could be taken in the event of aggression.[133]

Thus, it is unclear what the role of nuclear weapons will be, especially as that discussion will be classified, another example of the lack of democratic accountability and control.

Meanwhile the Siloviki also clearly invoked internal threats to the regime and demanded essentially a return to a full-time mobilization strategy:

> To prepare Russia for war, defense officials apparently agree on recommending that in wartime the Minister of Defense be made the deputy to the President (Commander-in Chief); that Russia establish an integrated air, air defense, and missile defense organization, and increase spending on nuclear weapons and air, air defense, and naval systems. Indeed, showing off their neo-Soviet outlook, the authors demand the economy provide for the military's growth "at any price."[134]

As this was the line being pushed while the succession struggle intensified, it is not surprising that no new doctrine was published and that Shlykov made his announcement cited above.[135] This was far too extreme and unaffordable a military strategy to adopt on the eve of a new presidency. And officials around President Medvedev presumably were not happy with it and sought to block its acceptance. Consequently, debate continued in 2008 as Gareyev's January article made clear.[136] That debate also criticized the previous doctrine of 2000. Notwithstanding the openly anti-American character of that earlier doctrine, Vladimir Lutovinov attacked it for relying too much on American thinking and went on to say that a new doctrine must uphold Russia's global great power status, freedom of maneuver in world politics, real national interests (supposedly the 2000 doctrine failed to do so), postulate the United States as the greatest threat, list his own set of threats, ensure the spiritual security of Russia's citizen, etc. Most tellingly he writes that,

> It is at last time for us to rid ourselves of the complex of fearing the state and the fear of encroaching upon the "free" and "democratic" individual. In both theory and practice it is not only the state that suffers from such a position, but society and the individual himself as well.[137]

Thus, the contemporary process of enlarging the definition of the attributes of security, in Russia's case, finds expression in threat inflation as was warned above, e.g., the call for spiritual security. This is precisely because the regime has failed to even try to rein in the *silovye struktury*, not just the army. Accordingly, leading Russian military figures like Baluyevsky and Gareyev have openly discussed internal threats to Russia in which the country might suffer even a crushing defeat without a shot being fired.[138] Gareyev stated that,

> The breakup of the Soviet Union and Yugoslavia, the parade of "color revolutions" in Georgia, Ukraine, and Kyrgyzstan, and so on show how principal threats exist objectively, assuming not so much military forms as direct or indirect forms of political, diplomatic, economic, and informational pressure, subversive activities, and interference in internal affairs. . . . The RF's [Russian Federation] security interests require not only that such threats be assessed, but also that effective measures of countering them be identified.[139]

Putin and the government, however, did not at first fully accept this perspective as subsequent policies showed. During 2000-02 he and the government strove particularly hard to define terrorism as the most immediate threat justifying Russian policy and to internationalize it as a global threat. As a recent assessment concludes,

> Official Russian discourse on the war in Chechnya has addressed three overarching threats in rationalizing the need for military intervention to the domestic and international audiences. These threats were, first, a multi-faceted security threat to both Russia and the world posed by Chechnya as a breeding ground for international terrorism; second, a threat to the integrity of borders and territories in Russia and abroad; and third, economic and physical threats to the civilian population in Chechnya.[140]

By doing so, Putin reined in the military's demand for power and budgetary outlays even as he redefined the hierarchy of threats, a process that facilitated his grasping the need to support America after the attacks on 9/11. But he did not exercise his option to demilitarize official (as opposed to academic) Russian thinking about security. Thus, he never convinced his elite of the need to reconceptualize threats to Russia and the contemporary strategic environment in less neo-Soviet ways. Instead, as we have seen, he came to embrace both the securitization process and much of the Silovye Struktury's threat asessment. So as terrorism faded with Russian success in Chechnya, there was no acceptable security or threat assessment available to the regime other than this vocabulary which has reasserted itself with a vengeance. Today, no other alternative view of security in general and of the particular threats facing Russia can be conceived of, let alone developed as a policy posture by the government machine even though this mode of thinking is throughly antiquated as we can see from our present vantage point. Perhaps the president alone can do so and then impose his view, but that would require a tremendous bureaucratic struggle and expenditure of scarce economic and political resources which Putin has clearly been loath to do.

Although Putin had regularly called for a new doctrine to meet the challenges of the post-9/11 strategic environment since 2002, the only document that appeared was the 2003 Defense Ministry's white paper that foreign observers then called an Ivanov doctrine after Defense Minister Sergei Ivanov.[141] It argued that the Russian forces must be ready for every sort of contingency from counter-terrorism to large-scale conventional theater war and even nuclear war.[142] Ivanov and the General Staff also argued that the forces can and must be able to handle two simultaneous regional or local wars.[143] This guidance also evidently followed Putin's direction that the armed forces must be able to wage any kind of contingency across this spectrum of conflict even though he apparently had ordered a shift in priorities from war against NATO to counterterrorist and localized actions in 2002-03.[144]

Through 2006, most published official and unofficial writing about the nature of threats to Russian security repeatdly stated that terrorism was the most immediate and urgent threat to Russia, that Russia had no plans to wage a war with NATO, i.e., a large-scale conventional or even nuclear war, and that Russia saw no visible threat from NATO or of this kind of war on the horizon.[145] Indeed, Putin, and Baluyevsky renounced the quest for nuclear and conventional parity with NATO and America, a quest whose abandonment was signified in the Moscow Treaty of Nuclear Weapons in 2002.[146] Yet, no new doctrine appeared. Indeed, in 2003, former Deputy Chief of Staff General (Ret.) V. L. Manilov, then First Deputy Chairman of the Federation Council Defense and Security Committee, admitted that the General Staff could not even categorize the threats then facing Russia. He told an interviewer,

> Let's take, for example, the possible development of the geopolitical and military-strategic situation around Russia. We don't even have precisely specified definitions of national interests and national security, and there isn't even the methodology itself of coming up with decisions concerning Russia's fate. But without this it's impossible to ensure the country's progressive development. -- It also should be noted that a systems analysis and the monitoring of the geostrategic situation around Russia requires the consolidation of all national resources and the involvement of state and public structures and organizations. At the same time, one has a clear sense of the shortage of intellectual potential in the centers where this problem should be handled in a qualified manner.[147]

Since Russian planners could not develop a truly credible hierarchy of threats or adequately define them or Russia's national interests, they inevitably came to see threats everywhere, while lacking the conceptual means for categorizing them coherently. Lacking a priority form of war or threat for which they must train, the troops had to perform traditional tasks and priority missions like defending Russia's territorial boundaries (i.e., Soviet territorial boundaries) preventing and deterring attacks on Russia, and maintaining strategic stability. They also had to participate directly in achieving Russia's economic and political interests and conduct peacetime operations, including UN or CIS sanctioned peace operations. Consequently, coherent planning and policymaking were still bedeviled by multiple threats that haunt senior military leaders. As Deputy Chief of Staff, Baluyevsky said in 2003,

> In order to conduct joint maneuvers [with NATO], you have to determine who your enemy actually is. **We still do not know** [bold by author]. After the Warsaw pact disappeared, there was confusion in the general staffs of the world's armies. But who was the enemy? Well, no enemy emerged. Therefore the first question is: Against whom will we fight? — But the campaign against terrorism does not require massive armies. And NATO's massive armies have not disappeared at all. No one says "We do not need divisions, we do not need ships, we do not need hundreds of thousands of aircraft and tanks". . . . The Russian military are accused of still thinking in World War II categories. Although we, incidentally realized long before the Americans that the mad race to produce thousands and thousands of nuclear warheads should be stopped![148]

This probably was the case until 2007-08 and helped precipitate the struggle that led up to the announcement that there would be no defense doctrine and presumably no security concept in 2008.[149] In other words, Russia's elite still could not articulate a consensus that gave political guidance and expression to its views as to what constituted security for Russia and the threats to it, let alone the means to defend against those threats and the resources that would be assigned to those tasks. Instead, because of the absence of any kind of regularized overall security policy, we have Putin's own personal threat assessment that has been articulated in a series of statments, speeches, etc., since 2006. This threat assessment is profoundly anti-Western, and, what is worse, discerns rising and multiple military threats issuing from the United States and NATO. Indeed, many of the references to a new doctrine, although it has not materialized, specify that the West would replace terrorism as the source of the main threat.[150]

In those speeches Putin has specifically submitted the threat assessment cited above.[151] Moreover, Baluyevsky and the General Staff all regularly argue that because there is allegedly no threat from Iran, U.S. missile defenses can only be aimed at Russia and at threatening to neutralize its deterrent.[152] For many reasons, this litany of threats makes for depressing reading.

> One of the most discouraging aspects of this litany of threats is that so many of them are utter fabrications. Putin's speeches and those of his subordinates reflect that they still have a woefully incomplete and distorted understanding of the West despite fifteen years of supposed democracy and freedom and are prone to

accept either the worst-case scenarios of Russian intelligence services and elites who are notorious for presenting distorted and utterly mendacious threat and policy assessments. Either that or they share a wholly cynical, materialistic, virtually exclusively self-referential, and misconceived notion of Western weakness, Russophobia, and disunity. To partisans of this mindset America does not count anymore as a partner because Iraq has distracted it and diverted its interest from Russia.[153]

Putin even complained that American politicians are invoking a nonexistent Russian threat to get more money for military campaigns in Iraq and Afghanistan. Putin's remarks represent a wholly fabricated analysis of Defense Secretary Gates' testimony to Congress, but signify that he wants to believe the worst about American intentions as does the General Staff and like-minded Russian political leaders.[154] For example, in his press conference before the annual G-8 conference in Heiligendam, Germany, in June 2007, Putin told reporters that Russia and the West were returning to the Cold War and added that,

> Of course, we will return to those times. And it is clear that if part of the United States' nuclear capability is situated in Europe and that our military experts consider that they represent a potential threat then we will have to take appropriate retaliatory steps. What steps? Of course we must have new targets in Europe. And determining precisely which means will be used to destroy the installations that our experts believe represent a potential threat for the Russian Federation is a matter of technology. Ballistic or cruise missiles or a completely new system. I repeat that it is a matter of technology.[155]

Similarly, despite dozens of statements and briefings to the contrary, Russian generals and politicians continue to insist that 10 missile defense radars and interceptors stationed in the Czech Republic and Poland represent a strategic threat to Russia and its nuclear deterrent, not because of what they are but because of what they might be, just as Putin said above.[156] Russia also charges that rotational deployments of no more than 5,000 army and air force troops in Bulgaria and Romania represent an imminent threat to deploy forces to the Caucasus.[157] Russian spokesmen view these new bases and potential new missions of U.S. and NATO forces, including missile defense and power projection into the Caucasus or Central Asia, as anti-Russian threats, especially as NATO has stated that it takes issues like pipeline security in the Caucasus and its members' energy security increasingly seriously.[158] Yet in fact U.S. "bases" in Romania and Bulgaria are nothing more than periodic rotational deployments of a small number of Army and Air Forces whose mission is primarily the training of the forces of their host countries. They are anything but a permanent base for strike forces into the CIS, and Moscow knows it.[159] Indeed, in 2004 Defense Minister Sergei Ivanov said that he understood the reasons behind the U.S. realignment of its forces and global basing structure, and did not find it alarming.[160]

In fact, Moscow neither faces an urgent or imminent strategic or military threat nor, in fact, does it claim to face one. Rather, the threat it perceives is psychological, one of influence and diminished status abroad. Thus, when Putin proposed in June 2007 that Washington share the Russian radar at Gabala, Azerbaijan, with it as a compromise, Putin's foreign policy envoy to the EU, Sergei Yastrzhembskiy, stated that,

"We consider this issue not a military question, but a political one."[161] The innumerable statements by Russian generals that their weapons could beat any missile defense confirm this point. So obviously there is, in fact, no military threat of the kind invoked by Russian officials— just alarm about America not respecting Russian interests. This gap between rhetoric and reality suggests not just a desire to ratchet up threat assessments for political and economic benefits for the military and political elites or a search for foreign policy gains, but also a deliberate mis- or disinformation of the leadership and the population as Felgenhauer suggests. But such discourses and perceptions have material policy consequences. Sergei Ivanov's call in December 2007 for nuclear parity between Russia and America repudiates past declarations, and was another signal of a major battle over force structures, budgetary allocations, and behind them threat assessments.[162]

At the same time these threat assessments reflect the idea of what numerous analysts have called Russia as the "besieged fortress," charging Washington with imperialism, launching an arms race, interfering in the domestic policies of CIS states including Russia, expanding NATO, unilateralism, disregard for international law when it comes to using force, and resorting to military threats against Russian interests, etc.[163] This wide-ranging threat perception also embraces Russia's domestic politics as well. Regime spokesmen, e.g., Vladislav Surkov, also openly state that Russia must take national control of all the key sectors of the economy, lest they be threatened by hostile foreign economic forces and so called "offshore aristocrats."[164] In other words, this threat perception links both internal and external threats in a seamless whole—as did Leninism and Russian thinking about information operations (IO) and information warfare (IF) — and represents the perception that Western democracy as such is a threat to Russia.[165] Therefore U.S. and Western military power, even if it is not actually a threat, is *a priori* perceived as such.

This point is crucial. Here we can also observe that this securitization process also represents a trap for Russia. For example, Julian Cooper has found that under Putin through 2007, state spending on domestic security has exceeded defense spending, testifying to the primacy of internal over external threats in actual policymaking, rhetoric to the contrary notwithstanding.[166] Indeed, the entire debate process leading up to the publication of the security strategy indicates that not only is the primary audience for this document a domestic one, it serves (like much of Russian security policy) like the wicked queen's mantra in *Snow White*, "mirror mirror on the wall, who's the fairest of them all?" This is a regime that must devote enormous effort to telling itself and its audience that it is as great a power and as important a player in world politics as it wants to be, because otherwise its authority and legitimacy will diminish.

Russian national security is therefore first and foremost a matter of regime security; a means by which the establishment, which knows that its power is illegitimate, can continue to gain ever more rents and power for itself. As we have shown, the new strategy openly admits this point in its concern for the quality of state performance. Empire (which is what the invocation of a great power status is all about) is, first of all, a domestic politics strategy to preserve the status quo and, second, an effort to persuade others that this kind of rule is good for them and represents a resurgent Russia. Indeed, Russia finds it difficult to sustain even its bottom line of an exclusive bloc in the CIS and claims that the West, not to mention the other states in the CIS who have their own agendas, will not let it do so.[167] Consequently—and this should not surprise us—Russian experience and overall security policy conforms to the pattern discernible in Asian and Third World states where security is primarily internal security and is recognized as such by all the leaders there. Observers have long ago noted this regression on Russia's part from what might be called the Second World (i.e., Europe) to the Third World. As Richard Sakwa wrote in 2003,

> In the past, Russia's messianism took the form of the espousal of Communism as an alternative route to modernity; today, one strand of Russian foreign policy casts the country as a victim of globalization, a Third Worldist perspective espousing multipolarity and resistance to American dominance. It should be noted that "multipolarism" reflects an "orientalist" strain in Russian foreign policy, promoted in particular by the Foreign Intelligence Service (SVR), headed between 1991 and 1996 by the specialist on the Middle East, the "orientalist" Primakov and then by another orientalist Vyacheskav Trubnikov. From this perspective, Russia appears to have achieved a transition from the Second to the Third World. Associated with this approach is Russia's implicit adoption of the "Asian values" agenda, where democracy and human rights are subordinated to developmental tasks and where priority is granted to order and discipline rather than to indiviudal liberty.[168]

These Asian and Third World countries simultaneously confront the exigencies of both domestic state-building, i.e., assuring the regime's internal security and defense against external threats without sufficient means, time, or resources to compete successfully with other more established states. Not surprisingly their primary concern becomes internal security and their continuation in power, hence the proliferation of multiple military forces, intelligence, and police forces in these countries—often enjoying more resources than do their regular armies—and their governments' recourse to rent-seeking, authoritarian, and clientilistic policies.[169]

These facts possess significant relevance for any discussion of security not only in the Third World, but clearly also for Russia where the security environment perceived by the government is one of "reversed anarchy" as described by Mikhail Alexiev and Bjorn Moeller. Moeller observes that,

> While in modernity the inside of a state was supposed to be orderly, thanks to the workings of the state as a Hobbesian "Leviathan," the outside remained anarchic. For many states in the third World, the opposite seems closer to reality —with fairly orderly relations to the outside in the form of diplomatic representations, but total anarchy within.[170]

Similarly, Amitav Acharya observes that,

> Unlike in the West, national security concepts in Asia are strongly influenced by concerns for regime survival. Hence, security policies in Asia are not so much about protection against external military threats, but against internal challenges. Moreover, the overwhelming proportion of conflicts in Asia fall into the intra-state category, meaning they reflect the structural weaknesses of the state, including a fundamental disjunction between its territorial and ethnic boundaries. Many of these conflicts have been shown to have

a spillover potential; hence the question of outside interference is an ever-present factor behind their escalation and containment. Against this backdrop, the principle of non-interference becomes vital to the security predicament of states. And a concept of security that challenges the unquestioned primacy of the state and its right to remain free from any form of external interference arouses suspicion and controversy.[171]

Indeed, for these states, and arguably even for transitional states like Russia, internal police forces enjoy greater state resources than do the regular armies, this being a key indicator of the primacy of internal security as a factor in defining the term national security.[172] In other words, for all the talk of great power recovery, Russia's security strategy continues to be dominated by the Third World paradigm of the primacy of internal threats. This posture reveals that Russia's regime knows that it is fundamentally illegitimate and therefore intrinsically insecure no matter what its accomplishments. As Dmitry Suslov, Deputy Research Director of the Moscow Based Council for Foreign and Defense Policy, stated, "The most important tasks and, at the same time, the most serious dangers are to be found inside the country — that means there's a need for modernization, a more effective system of state intervention, fighting corruption, and so on."[173] Yet, as has always been the historical case in Russia, every attempt at modernization further enmeshes the state in the contradictions of its own neo-Tsarist structure. Moreover, any attempt to do so strikes at the direct interests of the elite both in its rent-seeking and rent-granting postures and is thus a contradiction to the nature of a fundamentally anti-democratic state whose rulers are fully aware of their illegitimacy. This sense of illegitimacy also helps explain the lengths to which this elite will go to ensure its uncontested supremacy in Russian politics.

Nevertheless, despite the failure to reach a doctrine or national security concept in 2007-08, it appears that a corner was turned in 2008. Amid a sense of continuing crisis in the armed forces, inability to defend against a presumed U.S. military threat, lack of a satisfying doctrine and threat assessment, and a robust competition among different services for increased military funding, it was revealed on August 1, 2008, that a new defense doctrine was in the offing as well as a new security concept, the latter to be authored by Baluyevsky, who, after being basically forced to retire from the General Staff, was given the job of formulating these documents for the Security Council.[174]

The document referred to in August 2008 was a draft blueprint for the development of Russia's armed forces through 2030. It concluded:
- The United States will remain (until 2030) the only superpower and continue to exert a substantial influence on the general military-political situation.
- "Taking into account the continuity of Washington's foreign policy and its long-term military construction programs, we may surmise that the USA will regard military superiority as the most important precondition for the successful implementation of its foreign policy views."
- Since the U.S. military presence in all the regions of the world will continue, Washington and other NATO members during the period until 2030 will aim to react preventively to threats despite international law and seek international recognition of NATO as the sole organization with the right to use force on the

basis of its own governing body's decision, i.e., unilaterally bypassing the UN.
- Threats to Russia include proliferation of strategic nuclear forces, military operations by other countries that disregard international law, attempts to oust Russia from global and regional security organizations, breaching of arms control treaties, "a US course toward global leadership," and NATO enlargement in regions around Russia.[175]

Here we should note the continuation of the threat assessments presented by Gareyev from 2006-08 and by Putin in his speeches after 2006, indicating that these views had gained preeminence even before the war with Georgia that began a week later. Yet as of December 2009, this new defense doctrine remained unpublished, indicating continuing discord among top officials. It has been said that a draft would be completed in September 2009,[176] but too many deadlines had slipped to expect that this would happen as scheduled. As of October 2009, there was still no doctrine.

Meanwhile, the Russo-Georgian war revealed the glaring inadequacies of the armed forces that had already led Defense Minister Anatoly Serdyukov to begin a reform process to reshape and reduce those forces, make them more combat-ready, reduce the bloated officer corps and number of generals, and adapt those forces to modern war. Serdyukov clashed with Baluyevsky over the economics of this reform, forcing the latter to resign.[177] But as part of that process, he said that, "one of the key goals of the reforms is the creation of a combat-ready, mobile, and fully armed army and navy which are prepared to participate in, at a minimum, three regional and local conflicts [presumably at one time]."[178]

Serdyukov's remarks require amplification. But they came at a time when it was clear that Russia could not win such wars easily as the case was in Georgia; the victory was unsatisfying and a pretext for the launching of Serdyukov's reforms. Moreover, given the Russian threat assessment that sees the United States standing behind such wars, the Russian nuclear arsenal as the deterrent that prevents or threatens to prevent foreign intervention in such wars on its periphery, like those Serdyukov says Russia must fight, and its clear doctrinal commitment to the first-use of nuclear weapons if necessary, this statement suggests an enhanced willingness to use those weapons in a warfighting context, precisely because such wars can easily overstep their territorial or strategic limits. This is especially dangerous because today and for several future years, nuclear weapons will take precedence over other forms of weaponry in state spending plans.

Especially at a time of what will surely be protracted economic crisis, such massive spending projects on defense reform and procurement would appear to be singularly unjustified and even in defiance of pressing strategic domestic needs in health science, infrastructure, etc. Nevertheless the regime, clearly still led by Putin despite President Medvedev's visible chafing at the bit, seems intent on restoring still more of the Soviet and Stalinist heritage.[179] This immense expansion of defense spending takes its point of departure not only from the visible economic recovery by 2007, but also from the assessment of current military trends, which the Security Council then described:

> Drastic changes have occurred in the geopolitical and military situation in the world and in the nature of threats against national security, which makes it nec-

essary to revise the specific tasks facing the Russian Armed Forces and related security agencies.[180]

Richard Weitz has summarized the trajectory of defense spending since 2007, which is a very confusing since funds are added in the middle of the year and much spending is hidden from view.

> In 2007 the Russian government approved a $240 billion rearmament program that will run though 2015. In February 2008 Russia's Ministry of Defense announced that it would further increase the military budget by about 20 percent, allocating approximately one trillion rubles (about $40 billion) to military spending in 2008. Following the August 2008 war in Georgia, the Russian government announced it would increase the defense budget yet again in order to replace the warplanes and other equipment lost in the conflict as well as to accelerate the acquisition of new weapons designed since the Soviet Union's dissolution. This year [2008] the Russian military will spend over $40 billion. The figure for 2009 should exceed $50 billion.[181]

Even though defense spending has been steadily rising and was projected before the crisis to rise still faster, the war in Georgia and the visible animosity to America, has led the regime to embark on a return to Stalinist military planning. *Nezavisimaya Gazeta* reported that the Ministry of Defense has already begun working on a 10-year plan for arms procurement and reequipment from 2011-20 that will be sent to the Duma for approval in 2010. This program grows out of the failure of the current arms program from 2006-15 that was budgeted at 5 trillion rubles ($154 billion). Typically that plan proved to be "ineffective and expensive, leading to delays in introducing new armaments."[182] Indeed, "Not a single one of the previous arms programs was fulfilled even at 20 percent of the planned level. Even the existing program, which came about, during the years of oil-sale prosperity, is not being fulfilled."[183]

While this failure reflects upon the continuing failure of the defense industrial sector to respond to market conditions after 1991, it has not only led to ever greater state control of that sector, but also to Stalinist answers. Thus, even in late 2008, when crisis was apparent, Moscow sought to accelerate the 2006-15 plan that has totally failed to date and compress it so that it will be completed by 2011 when the new plan, which certainly entails even more state control and thus guaranteed suboptimal outcomes, is to begin.[184] Indeed, as a result of the crisis, the unending inflation in Russian defense industry and its inability to function in a market economy, the government had to cut the 2009 defense budget by 15 percent and, despite its denials, is now cutting procurement.[185] Thus by July 2009, funding cuts were hampering the acquisition of manpower for the planned new permanent readiness units, construction of the Yuri Dolgoruky class of nuclear-powered ballistic missile submarines (SSBNs), and funding for the development of foreign naval bases.[186]

THE LAST STAGE OF THE DEBATE IN 2009

This debate clearly did not end in 2008 or even when it was originally supposed to end in 2009. Thus, the Security Council was reportedly supposed to accept the national security strategy at its meeting on February 20, 2009.[187] But that meeting did not occur until March 24, suggesting further objections. Yet the leaked portions of the document that were revealed in early 2009 accurately foreshadowed the actual text of the document and will be examined when we discuss the actual strategy document.[188]

Apparently one major reason for the postponement of the appearance of the security strategy was the continuing aggravation of the current economic crisis. It has worsened to the point where the overall economy shrunk by 10.1 percent from January-June 2009.[189] By all accounts, this forced the drafters and the Security Council, not to mention those who would have to approve the document, to assert the importance of economic factors as a part of security. Thus in his address to the Security Council on March 24, 2009, President Medvedev explicitly said that economic security was a part of national security. But beyond that he also insisted that the national security strategy must be considered in the light of the need for serious strategic planning. In this context he again referred to the strategy's purpose of coordinating the state, saying that,

> We have had departmental priorities dominate us for a long time, which does not always facilitate effective attainment of common strategic objectives. Such fragmentation hinders the country in moving forward. . . . The state intends to get rid of fragmentation with a common procedure for preparing documents and with close coordination among the federal center, the regions, and municipalities, as well as civilian society. In fact we are talking about forming a strategic planning vertical under the direction of the head of state. . . . It unquestionably must rest on a precise regulatory base.[190]

Here again, we see the priority placed on achieving coordination through centralization, the eternal mantra of Russian officialdom, as well as the priority attached to perfection of the existing power vertical. So it is hardly surprising that President Medvedev also insisted on the need for strategic planning and tied the new strategy to the documents listed above that also reflected the state's overarching strategies in a host of economic areas, and to a classified "List of Criteria and Indicators of the Level of National Security."[191] However, the economic crisis was not the only factor that led the Council to send the document back for revision, even though by all accounts the fundamental points that were later published were agreed upon. According to several accounts, by March 24, it was clear that a serious change in U.S. policies was underway, and at least some of those who participated in the meeting decided against publishing this document before President Medvedev's first meeting with President Obama in London on April 1 so as not to compromise chances for further development of this welcome turn in foreign policy.[192]

However, there is more to this meeting. At the meeting Patrushev again reiterated the line that the original order for rewriting the national security strategy was in 2004 but had been delayed for "various reasons." Moreover, he again said that the last one was in 1997, a direct slap at Putin, suggesting the tensions inherent in the tandem with President Medvedev.[193] Moreover, the worsening economic situation and the fact that on March 23, the EU, without warning, announced its plan to help Ukraine reform its gas infrastructure, throwing a major monkey wrench into Russian strategy, apparently played a role in sending the document back for revisions.[194] These factors appear to have been the pretexts for a debate that clearly got out of hand and out of President Medvedev's control, necessitating the revision of the document.

After the session, Nikolay Patrushev, Chairman of the Security Council, acknowledged that many new, and at times diametrically opposite proposals were set forth during the discussion, regardless of the fact that there already had been formal agreement on the strategy among all the members of interested departments and the Security Council on the eve of the session. A source in the Administration of President Medvedev told Gazeta that nearly all of the participants had proposed new amendments to the strategy in the closed part of the session. The source made the following statement to the Gazeta correspondent: "The discussion was so animated that, as a result, a decision was made to add new clauses to the strategy. But its basis remains unchanged."[195] When we analyze the actual published text, this conclusion appears to be accurate, for it conforms in many ways to excerpts leaked well before its publication, e.g., in January 2009.[196]

THE SECURITY STRATEGY

The Security Strategy begins by asserting quite falsely that Russia has overcome the economic-political crisis of the last century.[197] This assertion may have seemed correct in 2007-08, but by the time it was published, it became a mocking indicator of the cognitive dissonance of the Russian leadership concerning the real situation in Russia. It then proceeds to say that due to this success, the government is moving to a new state policy in the national security sphere based on earlier documents like the long-term socio-economic development plan until 2020. After defining its basic terms of reference, the security strategy goes on to situate Russia in a context of globalization and interdependence. These processes increase the vulnerability of all members of the international community to new challenges and threats. So very early on, we are told that Russia faces new and increased threats. Moreover, this process coincides with the advent of a qualitatively new geopolitical situation in which new centers of economic growth (Russia among them, but also Brazil, India, and China) and political influence are becoming stronger. This situation is fostering a trend, "Toward searching for the resolution of existing problems and the settlement of crisis situations on a regional basis, without the participation of non-regional forces."[198] In other words, Russia's growing clout is enabling it to exclude (or at least to demand the exclusion) of extra-regional actors from the CIS—or so it maintains.

Thus, early on, three themes of the document are presented: (1) Russia's recovering capability, (2) the increase of new threats to it, and (3) the decline of older centers of power like the United States as Russia rises, a situation that should foster sphere of influence crises and security management trends in the world. This analysis directly ties Russia's alleged economic and political revival to its capacity to exclude all foreigners from the CIS, in fact an attempt by Russia to embrace the unembraceable and overtax its real capabilities. Nonetheless, the strategy then argues that Russia has sufficient potential (note the distinction between potential and reality) to count upon being considered among the leading states in the world economy (and presumably international politics). The strategy then outlines some negative trends. They include the implicit reference to U.S. unilateralism and use of force, contradictions among primary participants in world politics, WMD proliferation and the possibility of proliferation to terrorists, ever more sophisticated forms of illegal cybernetic and biological activity, growing information confrontation (a concept derived from Russian military writing on IW), religious radicalism, ethnic and national hatreds, worsening demographic situations globally, increased drug trafficking, and organized transnational crime.

On this basis, the strategy forecasts that that long-term focus in world politics will "be concentrated on the possession of sources of energy resources, notably in the Middle East, on the Barents Sea shelf and in other areas of the Arctic, in the Caspian Sea Basin, and in Central Asia."[199] Then we come to the issues of proliferation in North Korea and Iran and conflicts in the Middle East, South Asia, and Africa that will have a negative impact on world politics in the (undefined) middle term.[200] Thus, the document here expresses a visible ethnocentrism since energy is Russia's most important instrument of foreign policy and its only competitive economic asset on a grand scale. This prognosis thus displays a very narrow nationalist concept of what world politics will be and harks back to Leninist postulates that made the struggle between imperialism and socialism (to use his terms) in the 1920s the question of questions in world politics. This idea is clearly related to the view, common in elite circles, that Russia, "sees itself as a country that is self-sufficient."[201] Second, the idea that the struggle for resources will be the driving factor in these struggles and that implicitly the West wants to exploit Russia's resources and weaken it evokes Marxist-Leninist perspectives about the start of wars and again follows the approach laid out by Gareyev. Nonetheless this section remains the General Staff's viewpoint; a concurrent article in the journal *Voyennaya Mysl'* (*Military Thought*), the General Staff's house organ, openly argued that not only are the foreseeable wars of the next decade going to grow out of the rivalry for control over energy resources, leading to spheres of influence and rival hostile military blocs, but also that Russia in the future will confront the threat of separatism and aspirations "**to control not only the natural wealth of the territory, but most of all overturn its system of values**, outlooks, and replace them from outside the uniqueness (*Samobytnost'*) and self-identity of the people."[202]

Furthermore, the strategy expressly states that the resolution of emerging problems by military forces is not excluded "under the conditions of the competitive struggle for resources," a trend that would disturb the areas near Russia's borders and those of its allies (presumably the CIS).[203] Furthermore, NATO enlargement, the advance of U.S. military power to Russia's borders, and the attribution of global military powers to NATO without UN sanction are unacceptable to Russia, which demands that it be treated with equality and have Russia's legitimate interests taken into account as a condition for strengthening overall security in the Euro-Atlantic region. Similarly, Moscow seeks equal relations with Washington with a view to resolving outstanding arms control, proliferation, and regional issues.[204]

The strategy then proceeds to outline Russia's national interests, which are developing democracy (i.e., Russia's so called "sovereign democracy," which is anything but a democracy) and the economy's competitiveness. Notably, and this clearly reflects the government's priorities, these interests come before ensuring the Russian Federation's territorial integrity and constitutional order. This order of precedence suggests that neither Russia's territorial integrity nor sovereignty over that territory is at risk, but rather that the economy is a security threat by virtue of its uncompetitive nature and that the governmental leadership grasps its fundamental illegitimacy. Only then does the last major interest of turning the Russian Federation into a world power aimed at maintaining strategic stability and mutually beneficial partnerships in a multipolar world — the real foreign policy goal — come into view.[205]

The next section postulates the goal of preventing global and regional wars and conflicts as well as conducting strategic deterrence to ensure Russia's security. This deterrence goes beyond nuclear deterrence to include the armed forces, the economy, and further development of military-patriotic education of the citizenry, another sign of the intrinsic weakness of the state and the (traditional Russian) sense that the population is not sufficiently attached to it.[206] From here, the strategy then states a long list of threats to military security, which start and end with the United States. The absence of a reference in this list to terrorist threats is noteworthy, possibly a sign that Moscow thinks it won in Chechnya. China too is implicitly omitted from this list, which clearly points to the United States alone as a threat. Indeed, official statements refuse to acknowledge a Chinese threat, a sure sign of deliberate policy guidance because in fact Russian nuclear forces in Asia are configured for deterring China.[207]

What is also notable about these particular threats is that none of them relate to what is commonly called asymmetric or unconventional war. Indeed, the document as a whole is written in such a way as to ignore completely the Asia-Pacific dimension of Russian security policy, hardly a sign of systematic thinking or policy consensus about this region. Instead, it focuses on military threats that are all high-tech, large-scale conflicts reflecting the unreadiness of the military-political leadership for such irregular actions. Moreover, again no mention is made of the North Caucasus, which is ablaze with insurgency. Moscow thus again falls victim here to a strategic myopia and a grossly inflated threat assessment. Specifically,

> The following are threats to military security: the policy of a number of leading foreign countries aimed at achieving overwhelming supremacy in the military sphere, first of all in strategic nuclear forces, through the development of precision-guided information, and other high-tech means of conducting armed combat, strategic weapons with non-nuclear warheads, the formation of a global missile defense system on a unilateral basis, and the militarization of near-earth space—developments capable of resulting in a new spiral of the arms race – as well as the proliferation of nuclear, chemical, and biological technologies and the production of weapons of mass destruction or their components and delivery systems. The negative impact on the state of the military security of the Russian Federation and its allies is aggravated by the withdrawal from international understandings in the weapons limitation and reduction sphere, and also by actions at the destabilization of state and military command and control, missile attack warning, and outer space monitoring systems, the functioning of the strategic nuclear forces, nuclear munitions storage facilities, the atomic energy industry, atomic and chemical industries, and other potentially dangerous facilities.[208]

In this context, it is again worth noting that while the document talks of the need to reform Russia's armed forces and defense industrial sector, the key emphasis resides, as before, on nuclear weapons and the maintenance of deterrence through them.[209]

This neglect of what is commonly called asymmetric war or other synonyms for these phenomena is another sign of the authors' inability to move beyond traditional Russian thinking. As all students of Russian military history know, wars of empire, terrorism, asymmetric, guerrilla wars, etc., have all been integral parts of Russian military history, and today are in effect the main activity on a day-to-day basis of the armed forces in the North Caucasus. So this omission reveals to us a continuing disposition to think of future war only in terms of major conventional, if not nuclear, war, or in other words World War III.[210] As Christopher Bellamy observes, there are many reasons for this omission. First, a military structured as hierarchically as is the Russian military from the top down, finds it difficult to come to terms with the unexpected, elusive character of unconventional kinds of war. Second is the belief that the real threat is the big war and, if you can handle that, you can handle anything. Moreover, the army until recently has been dominated by a mindset that looked not to the local wars after 1945 but to World War II for inspiration in thinking about future conflicts. And last, to the extent that there may be any systematic thinking about such "brush-fire" wars, Bellamy argues that it may be in the archives of the MVD since its Internal Troops, the VVMVD, are the ones fighting it, for the most part.[211]

Thus, official thinking is still caught up in big power and big war scenarios. This is evident from the speeches of President Medvedev and Defense Minister Anatoly Serdyukov to the March 17, 2009, Ministry of Defense Collegium. President Medvedev, for example, said that the first mission is to improve the troops' readiness and their quality, but first of all that of the Strategic Nuclear Forces. The regular troops must also be converted to a state of permanent readiness. Then comes another invocation of the need for "optimizing" their structure and numbers, and only third comes equipping them with the newest arms. No doubt this is both a cause and an effect of the fact that the Russian defense industry has completely failed to meet this challenge since 1991 despite endless reorganizations. He also emphasized the urgency of creating rapid reaction forces for the CSTO, a task that is now underway.[212] Thus, President Medvedev fully subscribes to the priority of major conventional if not nuclear war. But this is not his view alone. In fact, it is Putin's parting bequest on hierarchy of missions for the defense establishment, in his speech of November 20, 2007, to the Armed Forces Leadership conference: preserving nuclear force capability and increasing its combat readiness, optimizing the General Purpose Forces' capability to neutralize threats to Russia's security early in the cycle of their appearance, and only then technical re-equipping of the army, navy and air forces.[213]

Serdyukov's speech was equally revealing concerning the threat assessment. He too emphasized the big war over the smaller phenomena even though, as we shall see, he is aware of the rising incidence of such wars. Nevertheless, the threat assessment corresponds very much with both the preceding discussions we have outlined above and the text of the security strategy. According to Serdyukov,

> The military-political situation has been characterized by the US leadership's striving to achieve global leadership and by an expansion and buildup of mili-

tary presence of the United States and its NATO allies in regions contiguous with Russia. The American side's aspirations were directed toward gaining access to raw-material, energy, and other resources of CIS countries. Processes aimed at crowding Russia [out] from the area of its traditional interests were actively supported. International terrorism, religious extremism, and the illegal arms trade seriously influenced the military-political situation. They have been manifested more and more often in countries bordering on Russia. Georgia's attack on South Ossetia was a direct threat to RF national interests and military security. This attempt to settle the conflict by force was aimed first and foremost at destabilizing the situation in the Caucasus. **On the whole the analysis of the military-political situation permits a conclusion about the growing likelihood of armed conflicts and their potential danger to our state** (bold by author).[214]

Not only did Serdyukov buy the General Staff threat assessment, he intensified it by saying that the likelihood of threats to Russia in the form of wars and military conflicts is increasing. Yet the share of modern armaments in the armed forces only makes up 10 percent of the Russian arsenal, and only 19 percent of defense spending was earmarked for reequipping the army and navy in 2008, in line with that being a third priority behind organizational reform and maintenance of the nuclear forces.[215] Moreover, the ongoing reform of the Russian army that began in 2008 is intended to make that army more capable of fighting the smaller wars that characterize our time, e.g., Israel-Hezbollah, not a large-scale conventional war against NATO which in any case is a chimera, given NATO's well-known debilities. Thus, we have a threat assessment that is at odds with the direction of defense reform (although the latter increasingly looks like it will fail to achieve all its goals due to bureaucratic obstruction and lack of funds) and that gives little or no guidance concerning the threats of today in the North Caucasus, or to China, the rising Asian power.

In this connection, it looks like Russia, in the event of the war that its doctrine seemingly envisages, will only be able to fight it by going nuclear in a first-strike mode, or by threatening to do so. Thus, the process by which the General Staff and military-political elite is allowed to dominate threat assessments and securitize them across foreign policy based on the presupposition of conflict is leading to a dead end and irreconcilable contradictions in Russian defense strategy and policy, and in procurement from the stricken defense industrial sector. The ensuing outcome is one in which Russia pursues a policy based on the expectation of conflict with all its partners except China, even though they are in no way threatening it militarily, builds its military forces and doctrine for conflicts that either are unlikely or that will result in mutual suicide, neglects the conflicts that threaten it right now and in the future, e.g., China and Iran, and by virtue of its political-economic system has brought its defense industry to its knees. The visible signs of a dead end, even collapse of the conventional forces in the navy's case (which is now thinking of buying foreign ships) cannot be obscured any longer.[216] So much for self-sufficiency.

THE SECURITY STRATEGY: DOMESTIC ASPECTS

Turning to domestic security, the strategy lists the threats in the field of state and public security, and they are quite conventional in terms of Russian thinking (the usual kinds of intelligence threats, terrorist activities, extremist actions by nationalist, religious, or other ethnic organizations and structures, and transnational organized crime).[217] Here, along with rather conventional listings of the actions undertaken by the state to prevent those threats, including countering corruption (a vain hope in today's Russia), enhanced interagency coordination, and improvement of their quality, the strategy proclaims that, "the social responsibility of the agencies that provide state and public security is being increased."[218] This last statement underscores the authorities' hidden, but still visible fear of public unrest, a fear magnified by the events in Iran and Xinjiang, and its efforts to cope with that fear by granting ever wider formal powers to the state's police agencies to suppress and preempt dissent.

For example, on July 6, 2009, Russia's Ministry of Communications posted Order Number 65 on its official website. This order obliges the postal services to make available all private mail and data on senders and addressees to the FSB on demand. It also cancels the privacy of electronic correspondence, forcing operators to grant the FSB access to their electronic databases. No such law was ever promulgated by the Soviet government, which conducted such activities anyway. And this order duly contravenes the UN's 1976 International Covenant on Civil and Political Rights based on the Universal Declaration of Human Rights, as well as Article 23 of the Russian constitution that proclaims the full privacy of telephone, postal, and other communications, and states unequivocally that only a court can remove this right. This order parallels the MVD's ongoing efforts to monitor public attitudes to forestall public protests over worsening economic conditions. The MVD is also forming an elite brigade called "avant-garde" that will specialize in maintaining public order during large-scale demonstrations and can be deployed across Russia at short notice. Not only is this a giant step towards re-imposing totalitarian controls, it also betrays the fear, if not panic, of the authorities in the climate stimulated by the unrest in Xinjiang, Iran, and Moldova amid the current economic crisis.[219]

The security strategy then proceeds to advocate the strengthening of the state border, citing, like those assessments listed above, the possibility of escalation of existing conflicts and the incompletion of the legal registration of Russia's state borders with those of adjacent states. This concern naturally flows into a discussion of the inadequacies of border security organizations relative to threats of terrorism, drug running, and organized crime. This requires multifunctional and high-tech cooperation of border forces with neighbors like Kazakhstan, Ukraine, etc. The document then advocates enhancing the ability of the government to respond to emergency situations, upgrading their equipment, and developing technologies for informing and warning the population and taking preventive steps.

The following section on enhancing citizens' quality of life expresses the securitization dynamic at work. It demands greater social and property equality, radical improvement of the demographic situation over the long-term, housing, good jobs, regulation of the financial banking system, and efforts to combat organized crime. It cites the struggle for energy resources and Russia's technological backwardness as increasing the strategic risks of dependence on change from external factors. This section then lists food security, preservation and development of cultural institutions, etc., as arenas of government activity.[220] The document then follows into an extended discussion of the need for economic growth, strongly reiterating the threat that technological backwardness and dependence upon raw materials, mainly energy exports, present to Russia. It cites the symptoms of the current crisis: not only reduced rates of economic growth, inadequate effectiveness of state regulation, trade and payments deficits and reduction in budget revenues, but also shortages of resources, and increase in "dishonest" competition against Russian interests; the document calls, *inter alia*, for multilateral energy cooperation.[221] Following this, the document then proceeds to an extended discussion of science, education, health care, and the overall national economy, all of which should come under increased state regulation and control, and clearly securitizes these areas of national life.[222]

NUCLEAR AND OTHER MILITARY ISSUES

In this section, we see Russia's continuing insistence on its nuclear policy. First, we see that Russia still says that strategic stability with the United States is a condition of Russia's secure development. We must understand that, for Russia, strategic stability has a different meaning than it does here. Russia's arms control posture represents its continuing demand for substantive, if not quantitative, parity, as well as for deterrence with a perceived adversarial United States in order to prevent Washington from breaking free of the Russian embrace and following policies that Russia deems antithetical to its interests.[223] Moreover, that parity is calculated not just globally but in regional balances as well, so that Russia also demands a qualitative or substantive parity with America at various regional levels, most prominently Europe. Russia's demand for restoring parity at both the global and regional levels entails not an unreachable numerical parity, but rather a strategic stability or equilibrium wherein both sides' forces are held hostage by each other in a deterrent relationship and where the United States cannot break free to pursue its global or regional interests unilaterally, or what Moscow *calls* unilaterally. In other words, only if the United States freezes its strategic development can Russia develop stably! Therefore, it should not surprise us that the document goes on to say that Russia insists on stability and predictability in the strategic offensive weapons sphere and attaches special importance to new, "full-format" bilateral understandings on further limitation of strategic offensive weapons. Furthermore, Russia will promote the involvement of other nuclear states to maintain strategic stability (as it defines the term) globally.[224]

Russia then proceeds to justify its military presence in the CIS and in other states on the basis of international law as a means of promoting conflict resolution and maintaining "strategic stability and equal strategic partnership."[225] The conclusion here is that unless Russia can project its power in this way, strategic stability will be eroded. In other words, a neo-imperial policy is the only guarantee of Russia's internal stability. After pledging its determination to enforce existing arms control agreements, both nuclear and conventional, there is no mention of its unilateral and extra-legal suspension of participation in the CFE treaty. The document then reaffirms participation in UN-sponsored peace support operations and also states that Russia will undertake all necessary efforts at the lowest level of expenditure to maintain parity with the United States in strategic offensive weapons and under conditions of the deployment of U.S. missile defenses and implementation of the global strike concept. This, of course, is a reiteration of existing policy.[226] But it reflects Russia's belief that it is confronting nuclear and conventional threats from the United States to which it must reply by nuclear means.

CONCLUDING POINTS OF THE SECURITY STRATEGY

The strategy's concluding section on organizational-legal development fully reaffirms the securitization of domestic policy and the expansion of state supervision called for here. It calls upon the government to draw up a series of all-encompassing strategic plans that comprise the entire socio-economic life of the order. Specifically it says that,

> The Russian Federation Government and the federal executive authorities concerned are to draw up a system of strategic planning documents: the Russian Federation Long-Term socio-Economic Development Blueprint, Russian Federation socioeconomic development programs for the short term, development strategies (programs) for individual sectors of the economy, development strategies (programs) for the federal districts, socioeconomic development strategies and integrated programs for the Russian Federation components, interstate programs that the Russian Federation is involved in implementing, federal (departmental) targeted programs, the state defense order, the blueprints, doctrines, and fundamentals (primary directions) of state policy in the national security sphere and in separate areas of the state's domestic and foreign policy with the participation of the Russian Federation components' state authorities based upon the Russian Federation Constitution and Russian Federation federal laws and other normative legal acts.[227]

This would be a tall order for a state that was supremely efficient (at least in a relative sense). But in a state that is an autocracy with no rule of law, where the government freely flouts the constitution and other laws with impunity and is riven with corruption, this is a recipe for more chaos and failure. In turn, that chaos and failure will only, as has historically been the case, generate more calls for *kontrol* and centralization and the next loop of the unending spiral. Even if here again the state urgently calls for overcoming Russia's technological lag in information science, telecommunications, and communications "that determine the condition of national security," as well as for developing the technologies for managing ecologically dangerous facilities, the military, and national information infrastructure, as well as enhancing information security, this charge has been compromised from the outset due to the nature and scope of ineffective governmental control, which is reiterated throughout the document.[228]

Finally, the strategy concludes with a listing of the primary characteristics of the condition of national security that are designated for assessing the state of national security. These characteristics are the level of unemployment, the ratio of the incomes of the 10 percent of the most-well to do and the 10 percent of the most disadvantaged, the consumer price growth level, the state's foreign and domestic debt as a percentage of gross domestic product (GDP), the level of resource support for healthcare, education, culture, and science as a percentage of GDP, the level of the annual renewal of weapons, military, and specialized equipment, and the level of support in terms of military and engineering–technical cadres.[229] While these indices reflect a welcome appreciation of key economic factors as being important measurements of the state's development, they still reflect the legacy of an excessive militarization of state thinking. Furthermore and unfortunately, if we are to believe what the Russian press is saying, Russia, according to these categories, is already failing to meet the standards laid out for it by the government.

TOWARDS A POLICE STATE

No sooner than the strategy saw the light of day, the critics attacked it. This, of course, is to be expected in politics; nevertheless these analyses and critiques reveal the document's tendencies, direction, and, in some cases, failings. These critiques pertain to both domestic and foreign policy. Several commentators pointed out the fact that while some have called this a "liberal" document due to its stress on economics, in fact it is anything but liberal. Thus, for example, even though President Medvedev directed the authors to stress human rights, the rights included here are limited to "life, security, labor, housing, health and a healthy lifestyle, accessible education, and cultural development."[230] Indeed, in that respect this marks a regression since those are the rights guaranteed by the Soviet constitutions, and we know what those were worth. This document thus regresses from the 2000 national security concept that talked about the rights of the individual, society, and the state. This document does not even mention individual rights as a separate category but only in conjunction with the rights of the society and state. In this context, it should also be noted that Kommersant reported as well that an earlier section calling for and substantiating the need for a "highly professional community of Russian

Federation Special Services [i.e., secret police]," was omitted.[231]

The same omissions apply to property rights. As Tatyana Stanovaya wrote,

> The liberalism in economics is also highly conditional. The preferred economic model actually is strictly coordinated (the policy of import substitution and support for the physical production sector), presupposing the continued national control of resources, the development of innovation, and the modernization of the economy. There is no mention of the protection of private property rights, fair competition, decreased monopolism, and lower administrative barriers, and not one word about free enterprise.[232]

Indeed, as another report observed, "The main food threat is from the seizing of the national grain market by foreign companies and the uncontrolled spread of food products obtained from genetically modified vegetation."[233] The same applies to the takeover by foreign firms of the pharmaceuticals industry, which is not surprising given the quality of healthcare in Russia.[234] As the writer of the article pointing this out noted, there is "No Need To Threaten Us, We Are Frightened of Ourselves."[235] Only a frightened, insecure country with a Third World-like perspective on security could make such a statement, which is indicative of the real state of affairs rather than the unsustainable and deliberately inflated notions of superpower status. This pervasive sense of threat, coupled with the implicit xenophobia of such policy statements and the economic character of the strategy, belies any hope of Russia becoming one of the five top economies by 2020, even if energy prices take off beyond previous highs. Given the nature of the overall economy and its boom or bust character, its reality as a noncompetitive high-cost production platform and the increasing state control of key sectors, such an outcome is unlikely.[236] Even if it occurs in terms of GDP, it will only represent an unbalanced economy and inflated energy sector. Such novel features of the security strategy like its announcement of multiple indices for tracking overall economic development were affected by the government's actual unwillingness to assume responsibility for the true state of affairs. Thus, in the final draft, specific benchmarks for measuring poverty and food costs "were removed to reduce the liability of the government for their performance."[237] As the great Russian pre-revolutionary historian Vasily Kliuchevsky observed, "the state grew fat while the people grew thin."[238] This swelling of the state may be observed from the following report by the newspaper, *Gazeta*, on April 29, 2009. The report stated that not only must Patrushev report annually on the course of the implementation of the strategy, but every ministry and department must also now prepare strategy documents, presumably along the same lines.

> At the operational conference of the Security Council at the end of last week the government was instructed to prepare a full list of such documents within three months. Ahead of the 24 March conference the ministries and departments had already presented a list of 135 different strategies, concepts, and principles in the most diverse spheres — from the banking sector to the agro-industrial complex — which should be developed in the future within the framework of the country's overall strategic planning.[239]

In other domestic policy areas the situation is no better. As Keir Giles has noted in his analysis

> Culture plays a prominent role in the document. The recently-declared struggle with the "falsifiers of history," the program to roll back views of history to the Soviet cult of victory, is referred to with "attempts to re-examine views on Russia's history" noted as a threat. Social cohesion can be improved by fostering the "spiritual unity of the Russian Federation's multi-ethnic people," by such means as resisting orientation to the "spiritual needs of marginal strata," which is "a primary threat to national security in the cultural sphere." Culture is to be directed abroad, too, with "use of Russia's cultural potential in support of multilateral international cooperation" — which the producers of Moscow's Eurovision extravaganza will have found particularly topical.[240]

Giles also calls attention to the fact that no mention is made of how Russia will overcome its demographic threat, perhaps the greatest threat to national or societal security, other than the suggestion that on top of their other responsibilities the national security forces should "create conditions for — stimulating fertility."[241]

This bizarre recommendation, on top of the growing state control throughout the economy, the emphasis on social and state rights at the expense of the individual, and the pervasive sense of threats throughout both the domestic and foreign policy sectors all point not just to a swelling state sector, but also to a police state. This is a police state, and not just in the Latin American sense of the term where the police rule and stifle dissent while running a crony-based economy not unlike Russia's. Rather, given the state's swelling responsibilities for culture, the economy, and the special services, including responsibility for being a kind of Ministry of Love to increase the population, we are talking about the old-fashioned dream of the tsars and of many absolutist German states. This is the so-called "well-ordered police state where supposedly there was a government of laws but where in fact the police not only stifled political rights but also played an educational and paternalistic role throughout many, if not all spheres of social activity."[242] Admittedly in contemporary terms this comes close to a kind of Fascism, but defining that term is laden with difficulties that would take a book to sort out.[243]

Nonetheless, the drift towards a police state in both its earlier and current meanings is clearly apparent from this document and concurrent state policies. There is ample evidence that this danger is growing as is the manifestation of popular unrest due to the current economic crisis. An April 2009 report outlined quite clearly the threat perceived by the authorities, one that wholly belies the faked confidence presented in the security strategy. Specifically it stated that,

> The Russian intelligence community is seriously worried about latent social processes capable of leading to the beginning of civil wars and conflicts on RF territory that can end up in a disruption of territorial integrity and the appearance of a large number of new sovereign powers. Data of an information "leak," the statistics and massive number of antigovernment actions, and official statements and appeals of the opposition attest to this.[244]

This report proceeded to say that these agencies expected massive protests in the Moscow area, industrial areas of the South Urals and Western Siberia, and in the Far East, while ethnic tension among the Muslims of the North Caucasus and Volga-Ural areas is also not excluded. The author also invoked the specter of enraged former army officers and soldiers, who are now being demobilized because of the reforms, are taking to the streets with their weapons. But while this unrest threatens, the government is characteristically resorting to strong-arm methods to meet it. In other words, it is copying past regimes (not least Yeltsin's) in strengthening the Internal Troops of the MVD, and now other paramilitary forces as well.[245]

More soberly, this report, along with other articles, outlines the ways in which the internal armed forces are being strengthened. Special intelligence and commando subunits designed to conduct preventive elimination of opposition leaders are being established in the VVMVD. These forces are also receiving new models of weapons and equipment, armored, artillery, naval, and air defense systems! In 2008, 5.5 billion rubles were allocated for modernization of these forces. Apart from the already permitted "corporate forces" of Gazprom and Transneft that monitor pipeline safety, the MVD is also now discussing an *Olimpstroi* (Olympics construction) army, and even the Fisheries inspectorate is going to create a special armed subunit called *Piranha*.[246]

While the threat assessment may be hysterical, it is hardly beyond the special services to fabricate such assessments to frighten the authorities into giving them more resources. After all, we have seen them and the army do so above. But what is not hysterical is the account of these new paramilitary forces, another sure sign of a Third World system as well as of both an ancient and modern police state. Thus a new special elite police unit called *Avangard* (Avant Garde) is being established in the Moscow region to ensure law and order during mass rallies and relieve the police of some of their burden.[247]

The foreign and defense policy tendencies of the strategy are not any better. For example, although the sections on foreign and defense threats clearly point to Washington they omit the name of the United States. Indeed, it is omitted throughout except to refer to it as a partner or potential partner with Russia, no doubt in deference to the Obama administration's efforts to reset its relations with Moscow and the imminence of the summit with President Obama. Yet, as the usually well-informed analyst Dmitri Trenin points out,

> The opinion that has predominated in our country to this day that the "reset" is above all Washington's apology for the mistakes of the earlier Bush Administration and their rectification certainly does not correspond to the idea of the current team in the White House. For example, in our country the concept of the "reset" is understood as almost the willingness in current conditions to accept he Russian point of view of the situation in the Near Abroad which essentially is wishful thinking.[248]

Thus, Russia still remains trapped in its ethnocentric hall of mirrors, an approach that inevitably breeds disappointment when reality turns out to be different than had been imagined, and which leads to more self-pity and demands for vindication given America's hostility.

Similarly, Lilia Shevtsova observed that in 2008 Lavrov said that the era of Western civilization was over and that Russia was ready to offer its norms and principles, but now President Medvedev says here, and in his address to the G-20 in London, that we have no other choice but that of the West. In other words, foreign policy is subordinated to the ruling elite's quest for power, and there are serious gaps in trying to formulate a clear strategy of foreign policy in this and other cardinal documents.[249] Likewise, Fedor Lukyanov derided the intellectual incoherence of the document and flayed the foreign policy establishment for its institutional weakness, omission of threats from the Far East, surrender to the reigning expediency, and mechanistic fusion of concepts taken from different sources that are either empty or contradictory.[250]

Critics of the strategy's provisions for defense and security were no less caustic. Even though the strategy calls for the development of the military infrastructure, improving the system of the state's military organization, and transition to qualitatively new armed forces, nothing is said as to how this will be achieved or paid for. In fact, given the delusional quality of the document's assessment of Russia's economic position, it already is the case that defense reform is running into serious problems and that the defense industry cannot meet its new requirements.[251] Nor does the document specify how Russia's goals of energy security are to be met without a call for multilateral coordination on energy policies, which is quite unlikely given Russia's energy policies.[252] Finally, defense correspondent Alexander Golts flayed the document even though he thought it was not as bad as it could have been, since it removed the specific name of the United States and NATO in advance of the summit from all of the sections detailing foreign threats.[253] Golts easily discerned the factional in-fighting behind the strategy, and clearly stated that the winner was the FSB since the section on threats from foreign intelligence agencies specified "reconnaissance and other activities of special services and organizations of foreign states," singling out the word "other" as giving the FSB the right to declare any activity they dislike as subversion or the work of foreign intelligence agencies. Furthermore, he claims that the battle over defense reform is ongoing with no winners as yet. All these are signs that the document was written with extremely general definitions of the conceivable threats but gave no answer as to how to meet them.[254]

CONCLUSIONS

Close reading of the national security strategy indicates that Golts was right. Indeed, the Siloviki won most of the debate. The threat assessment directly descends from those advanced by military spokesmen beginning in 2004 and adopted by Putin in his subsequent speeches even if there is a bow to omitting the specific mention of the United States and NATO. Although it cannot be proven, there is reason to suspect that the large increases in defense spending in 2004-09 are at least partly attributable to their success in persuading the government to adopt this threat assessment. Moreover, the government, even though it had to cut procurement by 15 percent in 2009, is now saying that it will not cut defense spending in 2010. Thus the defense sector's victory on the issue of threats to Russia apparently has successfully translated into the acquisition of greater resources. But this victory remains partial, as the defense reform points in a direction away from a conflict with NATO and the United States on the basis of that threat assessment. Therefore, the large-scale military opposition to the reform, either to parts of it or to the whole plan, is consistent with the threat assessment that it persuaded the government to adopt. Meanwhile, Russia is stuck with a military that is maladapted to current threats and riven with rising corruption, and a defense sector that cannot produce what the military either needs or wants.

Thus, we see that the success in persuading the government of a threat assessment is rooted in the predisposition of the political leadership to accept that view of the world, a view that is rooted in the conservative opposition to reforms going back to the start of Yeltsin's, if not Gorbachev's, presidency. For example, Yevgeny Primakov, Yeltsin's foreign intelligence director, then Foreign Minister, and later Prime Minister, observed that, "The unlikely possibility of future world wars is not the same as the advancement of world security. Only the nature and scale of the threat has changed."[255] Only because of civilian political leadership with the predisposition to see the world in this way (i.e., with a presupposition of conflict, and with a growing domestic political need to incite a concept of Russia as a besieged fortress) was the military able to persuade it of the rightness of its threat assessment. However, this same elite, led by Putin, saw Russia's weakness as being, first of all, economic and geoeconomic as opposed to the older view represented by Tyushkevich and others like him. As a result, the government, though responsive to calls for greater defense spending, has steadfastly held to the view that the overall economy must first be repaired.

But this outcome too has its own irony. In prioritizing the economy as the area that must be addressed first, and with it the quality of Russian governance, the Putin administration, and now that of President Medvedev, has been unable to think of a way of doing this that does not revert to the inherently suboptimal Muscovite paradigm of a neo-tsarist, autocratic structure of government based on a patrimonial view of the state, its emancipation from all laws and checks upon its actions, a circumscribed right of property, the imposition of a service state upon the governing elite, and the continuing quest for empire.[256] As the debate leading up to the publication of the national security strategy and the strategy itself show, an ever greater belief that the entire national economy is a proper subject of securitization that must be subjected to ever greater state regulation, control, and centralization came along with the heightened sense of growing threat. Indeed, the strategy itself, as noted above, is a call to the most traditional kind of tsarist centralization and demonstrates that the Russian state in its present form, like a dog chasing its own tail, cannot escape from the charmed circle of its inherent pathologies. So while those who argued for the primacy of economic consideration in Russia's security policy won their point, they did so in a hideously disfigured and transformed way that perverted the meaning of their discourse. They lost more than they won.

The results of these processes are visible to everyone. The economy is not responding to what appears to be positive changes occurring elsewhere. The defense sector cannot meet the expectations and goals set for it by the government. Yet the response is ever greater centralization and development of ever more instruments of repression. Although Moscow regularly complains about U.S. policies not being in the spirit of the Obama administration's "reset," it steadfastly pursues a policy of raising tensions and trying to force its power upon a recalcitrant CIS, whether it is rumors of another war in Georgia, gas threats, and heightened tensions over the Black Sea Base in Sevastopol all directed at Ukraine, forcing another military base on Kyrgyzstan, or a refusal to work to prevent Iranian nuclearization by genuine pressure upon Iran.

Ultimately, the result is a state that demands a greater sphere of untrammeled freedom of action for itself, seeks a status in world politics that it does not have the means to sustain, and sees all its potential interlocutors mainly as enemies.

Lenin's critics attacked him for having introduced "a state of siege in Russian social democracy." He then enlarged and globalized that condition into a permanent factor of Russia's defense and foreign policies. Unfortunately, the current regime wants to retain not just the tsarist system and status, but also Lenin's a priori perception of that state of siege as its watchwords and guides to conduct. As long as this quixotic mixture holds sway, not only can Russia not achieve liberty, security, and genuine prosperity, neither can its neighbors do so. Behind the superficial swagger of the national security strategy, there exists a state condemned to perpetual instability, insecurity, and conflict with its potential partners and neighbors by its political leadership. On that basis, one might write documents like this national security strategy, but in fact, as with this document, all such documents are written on the wind as long as Russia remains trapped within and by its history.

ENDNOTES - CHAPTER 1

1. *Natsional'naya Strategiya Bezopasnosti Rossii, do 2020 Goda*, Moscow, Russia: Security Council of the Russian Federation, May 12, 2009, available from *www.scrf.gov.ru*, in English, it is available from the *Open Source Center Foreign Broadcast Information Service, Central Eurasia* (henceforth *FBIS SOV*), May 15, 2009, in a translation from the Security Council website available from *www.scrf.gov.ru* (henceforth NSS).

2. "Russian Security Council Develops New Concept of National Security, Says Ivanov," *RIA Novosti*, September 29, 2004.

3. Natalia Ratiani, "National Security Strategy Is Being Aligned With Practice," Moscow, Russia: *Izvestiya*, February 3, 2005, *FBIS SOV*.

4. *Agentstvo Voyennykh Novostey Internet Version*, in Russian, December 28, 2007, *FBIS SOV*.

5. *Ibid.*

6. Pavel Felgenhauer, "Medvedev, Military Promote Different Outlooks for Russia," *Jamestown Eurasia Daily Monitor*, January 24, 2008, gives sources for both speeches.

7. *InternetWebDigest.RU*, in Russian, June 19, 2007, *FBIS SOV*.

8. *Ibid.*; Gennady Miranovich, "Interview With General of the Army Makhmut Gareyev," Moscow, Russia: *Krasnaya Zvezda,* in Russian, February 21, 2007, *FBIS SOV*; Stephen Blank, "Military Threats and Threat Assessment in Russia's New Defense Doctrine and Security Concept," Michael H. Crutcher, ed., *The Russian Armed Forces at the Dawn of the Millennium,* Carlisle, PA: Center for Strategic Leadership, U.S. Army War College, 2001, pp. 191-220, also published as, "Military Threats and Threat Assessment in Russia's New Defense Doctrine and Security Concept," *Treadgold Papers*, No. 31, Tacoma: University of Washington Press, 2001.

9. Olga Bozhyeva, "On Guard: False March To the West: Nobody Knows What the Army Should Be Like In the Light Of New Threats," Moscow, Russia: *Moskovskiy Komsomolets*, in Russian, February 15, 2007, *FBIS SOV*.

10. Indeed, this rivalry goes back at least a generation to the 1970s as Dale Herspring has pointed out in *The Soviet High Command: Personalities and Politics 1967-1989*, Princeton, NJ: Princeton University Press, 1990.

11. Dmitri Trenin, "U.S.-Russian Relations Were At a 25-Year Low," *Transatlantic Internationale Politik*, Vol. X, No. 3, Summer, 2009, available from *www.ip-global.org/archiv/volumes/2009/ summer2009/---u-s--russian-relations-were-at-a-25-year-low---.html*.

12. The most recent example is William Browder, "Russian Sharks Are Feeding On their Own Blood," *Financial Times*, July 7, 2009, available from *www.ft.com*.

13. Keir Giles, *Russia's National Security Strategy to 2020*, Rome, Italy: NATO Defense College, 2009, pp. 3-4.

14. *Ibid.*

15. *Interfax*, in Russian, June 13, 2009, *FBIS SOV*; *Interfax*, in English, August 25, 2009, *FBIS SOV*.

16. General S. A. Tyushkevich (Ret.), "Shaping Military Ideology," *Military Thought* No. 4, 2004, p. 162, this is the English language version of the General Staff Journal, *Voynnaya Mysl'*.

17. Pavel Felgenhauer, "Russia's Imperial General Staff," *Perspective*, Vol. XVI, No. 1, October-November, 2005, available from *www.bu.ed./iscip/vol16/felgenhauer*.

18. Tyushkevich, p. 162.

19. *Ibid.*, bold in original.

20. *Ibid.*, p. 163.

21. "Russian TV Considers Potential Military Threats," *BBC Monitoring*, August 29, 2009.

22. Alexander Rzheshevsky, "Far East Military Threats: Old and New," Moscow, Russia: *Parlametnyskaya Gazeta*, in Russian, May 24, 2005, *FBIS SOV*.

23. *Ibid.*

24. *Ibid.*

25. *Ibid.*

26. *Agentstvo Voyennykh Novostey*, Internet Version, In English, February 16, 2007, *FBIS SOV*.

27. General of the Army Yuri Baluyevsky, "The General Staff and Objectives For Military Development," Moscow, Russia: *Krasnaya Zvezda,* in Russian, January 25, 2006, *FBIS SOV.*

28. *Ibid.*

29. *Ibid.*, bold by author.

30. *Ibid.*

31. Marcel De Haas, "Russia's Upcoming Revised Military Doctrine," *Power and Interest Review*, February 26, 2007, available from *www.pinr.com.*

32. *FBIS SOV,* January 25, 2006.

33. Oleg Gorupay, "A Strong Russia," *Krasnaya Zvezda*, in Russian, February 13, 2007, *BBC Monitoring*, February 13, 2007, available from Lexis-Nexis.

34. Rostov na Donu, *"Voyenny Vestnik Yuga Rossii,"* in Russian, November 20, 2006, *FBIS SOV.*

35. *Ibid.*

36. *Ibid.*

37. For a fuller discussion of this point, see Stephen Blank, "Web War I: Is Europe's First Information War a New Kind of War?" *Comparative Strategy*, Vol. XXVII, No. 3, 2008, pp. 227-247; Stephen Blank, "Threats To and From Russia: a Reassessment," *Journal of Slavic Military Studies*, Vol. XXI, No. 3, Summer, 2008, pp. 491-526.

38. *FBIS SOV*, March 31, 2006.

39. *Ibid.*

40. *NTV* in Russian, August 15, 2007, *FBIS SOV.*

41. Gareyev, 2007, p. 4; Baluyevsky, p. 19.

42. Gareyev, p. 4.

43. Igor Kotenko and Alexander Ulanov, "Agent-Based Modeling and Simulation of Network Softbots' Competition," in Enn Tyugu and Takahira Yamaguchi, eds., *Knowledge Based Software Engineering: Proceedings of the Seventh Joint Conference on Knowledge-Based Software Engineering,* Amsterdam: IOS Press, Frontiers in Artificial Intelligence and Applications, Vol. 140, 2006, pp. 243-253.

44. Stephen Blank, "Class War on the Global Scale: The Culture of Leninist Political Conflict," Stephen J. Blank *et al.*, *Conflict, Culture, and History: Regional Dimensions,* Maxwell AFB, AL: Air University Press, 1993, pp. 1-55.

45. Marcel De Haas, "Russia's New Military Doctrine: What Will It Be Like?" Moscow, Russia: *Nezavisimoye Voyennoye Obozreniye,* in Russian, April 13, 2007, *FBIS SOV,* April 13, 2007.

46. Gennadiy Mironovich, "Interview With General of the Army Makhmut Gareyev," *Krasnaya Zvezda,* in Russian, February 21, 2007, *FBIS* SOV; De Haas, "Russia's Upcoming Revised Military Doctrine."

47. *Ibid.*

48. *Ibid.*

49. *Ibid.*; M. A. Gareyev, "The Academy of Military Sciences in 2001-2005: Achievements and Problems," *Military Thought,* March 31, 2006, *FBIS SOV.*

50. Felgenhauer, "Medvedev, Military Promote Different Outlooks for Russia."

51. "Vystuplenie Dmitirya Medvedeva na II Obshcherossiiskom Grazhdanskom Forume," January 22, 2008, available from *www.government.ru*; *Radio Free Europe Radio Liberty Newsline,* January 30, 2008.

52. Matlock and Graham's remarks were delivered at the program to kick off the Century Foundation's release of a series of

papers on the U.S.-Russia relationship, Washington, DC, June 22, 2009, see International Affairs: Working Group on U.S. Policy Toward Russia, available from *www.tcf.org*.

53. *Ministry of Foreign Affairs Internet Version,* "Russian President Addresses Munich Forum, Answers Questions on Iran," February 12, 2007, *FBIS SOV*, the question and answer session from which these remarks are taken are not on the *kremlin.ru* website.

54. "Interview with General Yuri Baluyevsky, First Deputy Defense Minister and Chief of the Russian Federation Armed Forces General Staff," *Rossiyskaya Gazeta*, February 21, 2007, *FBIS SOV*.

55. Luke Harding, "Russia Assesses Option To Co-Host US Missile Defense Shield," June 11, 2009, available from *guardian.co.uk*.

56. Vladimir Putin, "Speech and the Following Discussion at the Munich Conference on Security," *FBIS SOV*, February 12, 2007.

57. De Haas, "Russia's Upcoming Revised Military Doctrine."

58. "Interview with Sergei Rogov by Vadim Solovyev," *Nezavisimaya Gazeta Online*, in Russia, April 2, 2009, *FBIS SOV*.

59. Pavel Felgenhauer, "Russian Security Council Plans to Draft Military Doctrine," *Eurasia Daily Monitor*, March 22, 2007.

60. Elizabeth Wishnick, "The Securitization of Chinese Migration to the Russian Far East: Rhetoric and Reality," *Security and Migration*, Forthcoming; Kristian Atland and Kristin Van Bruusgaard, "When Security Speech Acts Misfire: Russia and the Elektron Incident," *Security Dialogue*, Vol. XL, No. 3, 2009, pp. 335-336.

61. Edwin Bacon and Bettina Renz with Julian Cooper, *Securitizing Russia: The Domestic Politics of Russia*, Manchester, UK: Manchester University Press, 2006, pp. 10-11.

62. Kristian Atland and Torbjorn Pedersen, "The Svalbard Archipelago in Russian Security Policy: Overcoming the Legacy of

Fear—Or Reproducing It?" *European Security*, Vol. XVII, Nos, 2-3, June-September, 2008, pp. 230-231.

63. Gareyev, "The Academy of Military Sciences in 2001-2005: Achievements and Problems."

64. Atland and Van Bruusgaard, p. 350.

65. *Interfax*, in English, November 16, 2006, *FBIS SOV*.

66. Elizabeth Sieca-Kozlowski, "From Controlling Military Information To Controlling Society; "The Political Interests Involved in the Transformation Of the Military Media Under Putin,"*Journal of Small Wars and Insurgencies,* Vol. XX, No. 2, June 2009, pp. 300-318.

67. Dmitry Litovkin, "Guerilla Or Energy?" *Izvestiya Moscow Edition*, in Russian, January 24, 2007, *FBIS SOV*.

68. *Ibid.*

69. Bozhyeva.

70. Felgenhauer, "Medvedev, Military Promote Different Outlooks for Russia."

71. *FBIS SOV*, November 23, 2004.

72. *FBIS SOV*, May 15, 2006.

73. *FBIS SOV*, November 23, 2004.

74. Giles, p. 2.

75. *Interfax-AVN Online*, in English, December 1, 2008, *FBIS SOV*.

76. Giles, pp. 2-3.

77. *Interfax-AVN*, in English, March 24, 2009, *FBIS SOV*.

78. Vladimir Ivanov, "The Secret Strategy of Russia," *Nezavisimaya Gazeta*, in Russian, March 26, 2009, *FBIS SOV*.

79. Giles, p. 3.

80. *Ibid.*

81. "Interview With Sergei Rogov, Director of the USA and Canada Institute," *Nezavisimoye Voyennoye Obozreniye,* in Russian, April 3, 2009. *FBIS SOV.*

82. "Interview With Nikolai Patrushev Secretary of Russian Federation Security Council, by Izvestiya Managing Editor, Elena Ovcharenko," *Izvestiya Online, Moscow Edition,* in Russian, May 13, 2009, *FBIS SOV,* May 14, 2009.

83. George Yaney, *The Systematization of Russian Government: Social Evolution in the Domestic Administration of Imperial Russia, 1711-1905,* Champaign-Urbana: University of Illinois Press, 1973; George Yaney, *The Urge to Mobilize: Agrarian Reform in Russia, 1861-1930,* Champaign-Urbana: University of Illinois Press, 1982.

84. Irina Isakova, *Russian Governance in the Twenty-First Century: Geo-Strategy, Geopolitics and Governance,* London, UK: Frank Cass Publishers, 2004.

85. General Makhmut A. Gareyev, "Concepts: Topic: Russia Must Become a Great Power Again: The Practice of Long-Range Strategic Planning Must Be Introduced," *Voyenno-Promyshlennyi Kuryer,* in Russian, January 16, 2008, *FBIS SOV,* January 19, 2008.

86. *Ibid.*

87. *Ibid.*; Sergei Ivanov, "Russia Must Be Strong," *Wall Street Journal,* January 11, 2006, p. 14.

88. Stephen Blank, *Russia and Arms Control: Are There Opportunities For the Next Administration?* Carlisle, PA: Strategic Studies Institute, U.S. Army War College, March 2009.

89. *Ibid.*

90. *FBIS SOV,* January 19, 2008; See also President Medvedev's "Speech to the Beginning of the Meeting of the Security Council on [the] National Security Strategy of the Russian Fed-

eration Through 2020 and Measures Necessary to Implement It," available from *www.kremlin.ru*, March 24 2009 (henceforth Medvedev Speech).

91. "Putin Interviewed by Journalists from G8 Countries—text," available from *www.kremlin.ru*, June 4, 2007; Federal News Service, *Testimony of Secretary of Defense Robert M. Gates to the Subbcommittee on Defense, Senate Appropriations Committee*, June 9, 2009, available from Lexis-Nexis, June 26, 2009.

92. See Dale Herspring, Chap 2 of this volume.

93. *Ibid.*

94. Felgenhauer, "Russia's Imperial General Staff."

95. "Part Of Russia's New Military Doctrine To Be Classified-General Staff," *Interfax-AVN Online*, in Russian, August 11, 2009, *FBIS SOV*.

96. Interview With Russian Federation Security Council Secretary Nikolai Patrushev," *Izvestiya*, in Russian, October, 14, 2009, *FBIS SOV*; David Novak, "Report: Russia To Allow Pre-Emptive Nukes," Associated Press, October 14, 2009.

97. *Ibid.*

98. Colonel I. A. Shapovalov, Colonel Ya. A. Zhaldybin, and Captain First Rank V. P. Starodubtsev, "Rossiya I Vyzovy XXI VEka," *Voyennaya Mysl'* (*Military Thought*), No. 5, May, 2009, pp. 13-17.

99. *FBIS SOV*, January 19, 2008.

100. *Ibid.*

101. Atland and Pedersen, pp. 230-231.

102. *FBIS SOV*, January 19, 2008.

103. Anatoly Tsyganok, "Who and What Threatens Russia?" *Segodnya.ru* in Russian, January 11, 2009, *FBIS SOV*.

104. *FBIS SOV*, January 19, 2008.

105. Bacon, Renz, and Cooper, pp. 10-11.

106. Atland and Pedersen, p. 237.

107. *Ibid.*, p. 245.

108. Bacon, Renz, and Cooper.

109. *FBIS SOV*, May 15, 2009.

110. Available from *www.kremlin.ru/eng/sdocs/news.shtml*.

111. *Interfax-AVN*, in Russian, August 11, 2009, *FBIS SOV*.

112. Bacon, Renz, and Cooper, pp. 15-16.

113. *Interfax*, January 10, 2006.

114. Stephen Blank, "Putin's Presidency and Russian History," *Russian History*, Vol. XXXVI, No. 1, 2009, pp. 88-116.

115. Bacon, Benz, and Cooper, p. 16.

116. See the discussion in Barry Buzan, Ole Waever, and Jaap de Wilde, *Security: A New Framework for Analysis*, Boulder, CO: Lynne Rienner, Publishers, 1998, and the works cited there for a full examination of this point.

117. Jutta Brunee and Stephen J. Toope, "Canada and the Use of Force," *International Journal*, Vol. LIX, No. 2, Spring, 2004, p. 259.

118. Stephen Blank, "The 18th Brumaire of Vladimir Putin," in Uri Ra'anan, ed., *Flawed Succession: Russia's Power Transfer Crises*, Foreword by Robert Conquest, Lanham, MD: Lexington Books for Rowman and Littlefield, 2006, pp. 133-170.

119. Alexander Golts and Tonya Putnam, "State Militarism and Its Legacies: Why Military Reform Has Failed in Russia," *International Security*, Vol. XXIX, No. 2, Fall 2004, pp. 121-159; Alek-

sandr' Golts, *Armiya Rossii: 11 Poteryannykh Let,* Moscow, Russia: Zakharov, 2004.

120. Stephen Blank, "From Kosovo to Kursk: Russian Defense Policy From Yeltsin to Putin," *Korean Journal of Defense Analysis,* Vol. XII, No. 2, Winter, 2000, pp. 231-273.

121. "Dmitry Medvedev Signed an Executive Order on Russia's National Security Strategy Through to 2020," available from *www.kremlin.ru/eng/text/nes/2009/05/2163230.shtml.*

122. Pavel Felgenhauer, "Russia's Defense Modernization Without a Doctrine," *Eurasia Daily Monitor,* March 26, 2009.

123. Stephen Blank, "Threats To and From Russia: a Reassessment," *Journal of Slavic Military Studies,* Vol. XXI, No. 3, Summer, 2008, pp. 491-526; Stephen Blank, *Towards a New Russia Policy,* Carlisle, PA: Strategic Studies Institute, U.S. Army War College, February 2008; *Radio Free Europe Radio Liberty Newsline,* November 9, 2006; Maria Raquel Freire, "The Many Sides of Deterrence: Threat Perception and Image Building in Russia," paper presented to the Annual Convention of the International Studies Association, New York City, February 2009.

124. *Agentstvo Voyennykh Novostey Internet Version,* in Russian, January 16, 2007, *FBIS SOV.*

125. Oleg Gorupay, "Krepkaya Armiya Rossiya," *Krasnaya Zvezda,* January 23, 2007; Felgenhauer, "Russian Security Council Plans to Draft Military Doctrine."

126. Felgenhauer, "Russian Security Council Plans to Draft Military Doctrine."

127. *Ibid.*

128. Felgenhauer, "Russian Security Council Plans to Draft Military Doctrine"; Stephen Blank, "Web War I: Is Europe's First Information War a New Kind of War?" *Comparative Strategy,* Vol. XXVII, No. 3, 2008, pp. 227-247.

129. Stefan Wagstyl and Edward Luce, "US and Russia Square Up Over Missile Shield," *Financial Times*, July 3, 2009, p. 2.

130. *Radio Free Europe Radio Liberty Newsline*, November 9, 2006; Vladimir Isachenkov, "Spy Chief: West Wants to Split Russia," Associated Press, October 10, 2007.

131. Lynn Berry, "Shake-up In Russia's Security Council," Associated Press, July 18, 2007; "Russia's Security Council Secretary Igor Ivanov Resigns," July 18, 2007, available from *www.Pravda.ru*.

132. "Russia's Angry New Military Doctrine," *Jane's Intelligence Digest*, September 7, 2007, available from *www4.janes.com/subscribe/jid/doc*.

133. Dmitriy Litovkin, "Part of the Military Doctrine Will Be Classified," *Izvestiya*, August 12, 2009, *FBIS SOV*, August 16, 2009.

134. "Russia's Angry New Military Doctrine."

135. *FBIS SOV*, December 28, 2007.

136. *FBIS SOV*, January 19, 2008.

137. Vladimir Lutovinov, "A Strong State-Guarantee of Defending Civilian: A Strategy of National Security Is Increasingly Important," *Voyenno-Promyshlennyi Kuryer*, in Russian, October 1, 2008, *FBIS SOV*.

138. Gareyev, 2007, p. 4; Baluyevsky, p. 19.

139. Gareyev, p. 4.

140. Bacon, Renz, and Cooper, p. 53.

141. *Aktual'nye Zadachi Razvitie Vooruzhennykh Sil' Rossiiskoi Federatsii*, 2003, available from *www.mil.ru* (henceforth Aktual'nye Zadachi).

142. *Ibid*.

143. "Address by Defense Minister Sergei Ivanov, "Russia's Armed Forces and Its Geopolitical Priorities," February 3, 2004, available from *www.polit.ru*, *FBIS SOV*.

144. A. Y. Mansourov, "Russia's 'Cooperative' Challenge to the New Alliance Strategy of the United States of America," *KNDU Review* (Korean National Defense University Review), Vol. X, No. 1, June 2005, p. 146.

145. OSC (U.S. Open Source Center) Analysis: *Russia: Focus of Threat Perception Shifts to Peripheral States,* March 6, 2006, available from *www.opensourcecenter.gov*.

146. "Russia Not Set to Fight NATO-Chief of General Staff," *Interfax AVN News Agency Website,* April 3, 2006.

147. *Krasnaya Zvezda*, in Russian, February 7, 2003, *FBIS SOV*.

148. *Moskovskiy Komsomolets,* in Russian, January 9, 2003, *FBIS SOV*.

149. *FBIS SOV*, December 28, 2007.

150. Stephen Blank, "A New Russian Defense Doctrine?" *UNISCI Discussion Papers* (Madrid, Spain), No. 12, October, 2006; Pavel Felgenhauer, "Russian Security Council Plans to Draft Military Doctrine," *Jamestown Eurasia Daily Monitor*, March 22, 2007.

151. *Ministry of Foreign Affairs Internet Version,* "Russian President Addresses Munich Forum, Answers Questions on Iran," February 12, 2007, *FBIS SOV*. The question and answer session from which these remarks are taken are not on the *kremlin.ru* website.

152. "Interview with General Yuri Baluyevsky, First Deputy Defense Minister and Chief of the Russian Federation Armed Forces General Staff," *Rossiyskaya Gazeta*, February 21, 2007, *FBIS SOV*.

153. Dmitri Trenin, "Russia Redefines Itself and Its Relations With the West," *Washington Quarterly*, Vol. XXX, No. 2, pp. 95-105.

154. Moscow, *Agentstvo Voyennykh Novostey, Internet Version*, in English, February 14, 2007, *FBIS SOV*.

155. "Putin Interviewed by Journalists from G8 Countries—text," June 4, 2007, available from *www.kremlin.ru*.

156. *Internet web Digest*, in Russian, January 31, 2007, *FBIS SOV*; "Interview With Yuri Baluyevsky by Yuri Gavrilov," *Rossiyskaya Gazeta*, in Russian, February 21, 2007, *FBIS SOV*.

157. Viktor Litovkin, "V Yazyke Ultimatov," *Nezavisimaya Gazeta*, June 25, 2007; Viktor Yuzbashev, "Illusory Moratorium," *Nezavisimoye Voyennoye Obozreniye*, in Russian, May 30, 2007, *FBIS SOV*, May 31, 2007; Remarks of Colonel Albert Zaccor to the Conference, "The Role of the Black Sea Region in the Transatlantic Security Agenda," Center for Strategic and International Studies, Washington, DC, June 21, 2007.

158. Martin Walker, "NATO Means Business to Protect Pipelines," *UPI*, October 13, 2005; " US Missile Plans 'a Clear threat' to Moscow: Russian General," AFP, January 22, 2007; "NATO Should Play Greater Energy Security Role, Envoy," June 29, 2007, available from *www.serbianna.com*.

159. Zaccor.

160. "Bush Troop Redeployment Plan: A Threat to Russia," *Current Digest of the Post-Soviet Press*, Vol. LVI, No. 33, September 15, 2004, pp. 1-5.

161. "Russia Says US Democracy Criticisms is Unfair," *Reuters*, June 29, 2007.

162. Dmitri Solovyov, "Russia Says It Must Have Nuclear Parity With U.S.," *Reuters*, December 7, 2007.

163. "Speech and the Following Discussion at the Munich Conference on Security, February 10, 2007"; Open Source Committee, *OSC Analysis*, "Russian Commentators Debate 'Besieged Fortress' Rhetoric," *FBIS SOV*, June 22, 2007.

164. Philip Hanson, "The Turn to Statism in Russian Economic Policy," *The International Spectator*, Vol. XLII, No. 1, March, 2007, pp. 54-55.

165. As Defense Minister, Sergei Ivanov implicitly admitted as much. Sergei Ivanov, "Russia Must Be Strong," *Wall Street Journal*, January 11, 2006, p. 14.

166. Julian Cooper, "The Funding of the Power Agencies of the Russian State," *Power Institutions in Post-Soviet Societies*, No. 6-7, 2007, available from *www.pipss.org*.

167. Ellen Barry, "Russia's Neighbors Resist Wooing and Bullying," *New York Times*, July 4, 2009; Dmitri Trenin, "Russia Reborn," *Foreign Affairs*, Vol. LXXXVIII, No. 6, November-December, 2009, pp. 64-78.

168. Richard Sakwa, "Putin's Foreign Policy: 'Transforming the East'," in Gabriel Gorodetsky, ed., *Russia Between East and West: Russian Foreign Policy on the Threshold of the Twenty-First Century*, London, UK: Frank Cass, 2003, pp. 176-177.

169. Mohammad Ayoob, "From Regional System to Regional Society: Exploring Key Variables in the Construction of Regional Order," *Australian Journal of International Affairs*, Vol. LIII, No. 3, 1999, pp. 247-260; Mohammad Ayoob, "Inequality and Theorizing in International Relations: The Case for Subaltern Realism," *International Studies Review*, Vol. IV, No. 3, 2002, pp. 127-148, and the works cited therein.

170. As quoted in Mikhail Alekseev, *Regionalism of Russia's Foreign Policy in the 1990s: A Case of "Reversed Anarchy,"* Donald W. Treadgold Papers, Tacoma: University of Washington, Henry M. Jackson School of International Studies, No. 37, 2003, p. 12.

171. Amitav Acharya, "Human Security and Asian Regionalism: A Strategy of Localization," in Amtiav Acharya and Evelyn Goh, eds., *Reassessing Security Cooperation in the Asia-Pacific: Competition, Congruence, and Transformation*, Cambridge, MA: MIT Press, 2007, p. 241.

172. Cooper.

173. "Russia's Security Strategy Considers New and Old Challenges," *Deutsche Welle*, June 7, 2009, available from *www.dw-world,de/dw/article/0,4459148,00.html*.

174. Colonel-General Leonid Ivashov (Ret.), "Security—Russia's Chief National Project," *Nezavisimoye Voyennoye Obozreniye*, in Russian, June 12, 2008, *FBIS SOV*; Simon Saradzhyan, "Armed With Nukes and a Vague Plan," *Moscow Times*, July 18, 2008, in *Johnson's Russia List*, July 18, 2008; Mark A. Smith, *Russian Domestic Policy: A Chronology: January-March 2008*, Advanced Research Assessments Group, 2008, available from *www.defac.ac.uk/ARAG*.

175. *Agentstvo Voyennykh Novostey Internet Version*, in Russian, August 1, 2008, *FBIS SOV*; Open Source Committee, *OSC Analysis*, in English, August 1, 2008, *FBIS SOV*.

176. *FBIS SOV*, August 11, 2009.

177. Stephen Blank, *A New Russian Army?* Carlisle, PA: Strategic Studies Institute, U.S. Army War College, forthcoming.

178. Viktor Litovkin, "The Minister of Defense Is Rethinking Strategy," Moscow, Russia: *Nezavisimoye Voyennoye Obozreniye*, in Russian, January 8, 2009, *FBIS SOV*, January 8, 2009.

179. "Medvedev Criticizes Putin's Cabinet On Economy," *Radio Free Europe Radio Liberty*, January 11, 2009; Isabel Gorst, "Medvedev Aims a Swipe At Putin Over Economy," *Financial Times*, January 12, 2009; Medvedev's Assertiveness Troubles Putin," *Financial Times*, December 30, 2008, available from *www.ft.com*.

180. Quoted in Richard Weitz, "Strategic Posture Review: Russia Resurgent," *World Politics Review*, January-February, 2009, p. 58.

181. *Ibid.*, pp. 58-59.

182. Martin Sieff, "Russia Reveals New 10-year Arms Plan to Upgrade Armed Forces," *UPI*, January 20, 2009, available from *www.upi.com*.

183. Dmitry Litovkin, "The Army Will Become a Trillionaire," *Izvestiya*, in Russian, January 20, 2009, *FBIS SOV*.

184. Sieff.

185. Stephen Blank, "The Political Economy of the Russian Defense Sector," in Jan Leijonhielm and Frederik Westerlund, eds., *Russian Power Structures: Present and Future Roles in Russian Politics*, Stockholm: Swedish Defense Research Agency, 2008, pp. 97-128; Stanislav Secrieru, "Illusion of Power: Russia After the South Caucasus Battle," *CEPS Working Document*, No. 311, February, 2009, p. 5, available from *www.ceps.be* (CEPS stands for Center for European Policy Studies); Alexander Chuykov, "Bulava and Dolgoruky Unveiling," *Argumenty I Fakty*, in Russian, June 18, 2009, *FBIS SOV*.

186. Alexander Chuykov, "Bulava and Dolgoruky (Unveiling)," *Argumenty Nedeli Online*, in Russian, June 18, 2009, *FBIS SOV*; Alexander Chuykov, "The Crisis Has Caught Up with the Military Bases," *Agumenty Nedeli Online*, in Russian, June 25, 2009, *FBIS SOV*; Moscow, Russia: *Prime-TASS Online*, in Russian, June 29, 2009, *FBIS SOV*.

187. Roger McDermott, "Russia Flexes Its Military Muscle," January 4, 2009, available from *www.guardian.co.uk*.

188. *Ibid.*

189. Catherine Belton, "Russian Economy Plummets 10.1%," *Financial Times*, July 15, 2009, available from *www.ft.com*.

190. "Beginning of Meeting With the Security Council On National Security Strategy of the Russian Federation Through 2020 and Measures Necessary to Implement It," The Kremlin, Moscow, Russia: March 24, 2009, available from *www.kremlin.ru*; Vladimir Kuzmin, "Authority: the President, Vertical Steps: Dmitry Medvedev Conducted a Security Council Session," *Rossiyskaya Gazeta*, in Russian, March 25, 2009, *FBIS SOV*; Anastasia Novikova and Denis Telmanov, *Gazeta.ru*, in Russian, March 25, 2009, *FBIS SOV*.

191. Anastasia Novikova and Denis Telmanov, *Gazeta.ru*, in Russian, March 25, 2009, *FBIS SOV*.

192. Vladimir Soloviev, "Russia Will Reset Its National Security Strategy," *Kommersant*, March 25, 2009, in *Johnson's Russia List*; *ITAR-TASS*, in English, March 25, 2009, *FBIS SOV*.

193. Felgenhauer, "Russia's Defense Modernization Without a Doctrine."

194. "Beginning of Meeting With the Security Council On National Security Strategy of the Russian Federation Through 2020 and Measures Necessary to Implement It."

195. Novikova and Telmanov, *FBIS SOV*, March 25, 2009.

196. McDermott.

197. *NSS, FBIS SOV*, May 15, 2005.

198. *Ibid.*

199. "Russia Sees Itself as a Country That Is Self-Sufficient," Interview of Russian Defense Minister Sergei Ivanov, *Der Spiegel*, February 9, 2007, *www.mil.ru/eng/12005/12061/12059/18891/index.shtml*.

200. *Ibid.*

201. "Russia Sees Itself as a County That Is Self-Sufficient," Interview of Russian Defense Minister Sergei Ivanov, *Der Spiegel*, February 9, 2007, available from *www.mil.ru/eng/12005/12061/12059/18891/index.shtml*.

202. Colonel I. A. Shapovalov, Colonel, Ya. A. Zhaldybin, Captain First Rank V.P. Starodubtsev, "Rossiya I Vyzovy XXI VEka," *Voyennaya Mysl'*, No. 5, May 2009, pp. 13-14.

203. *NSS, FBIS SOV*, May 15, 2009.

204. *Ibid.*

205. *Ibid.*

206. *Ibid.*

207. Anatoly Tsyganok, "Military Reform Through the Eyes of the General Staff," *polit.ru*, in Russian, August 7, 2009, *FBIS*

SOV, August 14, 2009; Stephen Blank, "Russia's Strategic Dilemmas in Asia," *Pacific Focus*, Vol. XXIII, No. 3, December, 2008, pp. 271-293.

208. *FBIS SOV*, May 15, 2009.

209. *Ibid.*

210. Christopher Bellamy, "Catastrophes to Come: Russian Visions of Future War, 1866 to the Present," Lubica Erickson and Mark Erickson, eds., *Russia: War, Peace, & Diplomacy: Essays in Honour of John Erickson*, London, UK: Weidenfeld & Nicholson, 2004, pp. 24-26.

211. *Ibid.*

212. Text of Speeches by President Dmitry Medvedev and Defense Minister Anatoly Serdyukov at a Defense Ministry Collegium, Samara Volga Inform, in Russian, March 17, 2009, *FBIS SOV*.

213. "Opening Remarks by President V.V. Putin in Defense Ministry," Moscow, Russia, available from *www.kremlin.ru*, November 20, 2007, *FBIS SOV*.

214. *FBIS SOV*, March 17, 2009.

215. *Ibid.*

216. Reuben F. Johnson, "Russian Navy Facing 'Irreversible Collapse'," *Jane's Intelligence Weekly*, July 13, 2009; Reuben F. Johnson, "The Fleet That Had To Die: The Russian Navy's 'Irreversible Collapse'," *The Weekly Standard*, July 15, 2009, available from *www.weekystandard.com/Utilities/printer_preview.asp?IdARticle=16 731&R=1626A1BCE2*.

217. *NSS, FBIS SOV* May 15, 2009.

218. *Ibid.*

219. Stephen Blank, "Iran, Xinjiang, and Democratization in Eurasia: The Impact of Recent Upheavals," Central Asia Caucasus Analyst, August 19, 2009, p. 220.

220. *FBIS SOV*, May 15, 2009.

221. *Ibid.*

222. *Ibid.*

223. Dmitri Solovyov, "Russia Says It Must Have Nuclear Parity With U.S.," *Reuters*, December 7, 2007; *Interfax*, in English, October 1, 2004, *FBIS SOV*.

224. NSS, FBIS *SOV*, May 15, 2009.

225. *Ibid.*

226. *Ibid.*

227. *Ibid.*

228. *Ibid.*

229. *Ibid.*

230. Giles, p. 7; Tatyana Stanovaya, "Security By Means of Economic Development," May 18, 2009, available from *www.politkom.ru*, in Russian, *FBIS SOV*.

231. *Ibid.*

232. *Ibid.*

233. Yuliya Kalinina, "No Need To Threaten Us, We Are Frightened of Ourselves," *Moskovskiy Komsomolets Online*, in Russian, May 14, 2009, *FBIS SOV*.

234. Giles, p. 10.

235. Kalinina, *FBIS SOV*, May 14, 2009.

236. Anastasiya Novikova, Denis Telmanov, and Olga Pavlikova, "The National Security Strategy of the Russian Federation Is Ready," *Gazeta Online*, in Russian, April 29, 2009, *FBIS SOV*.

237. Quoted in Roger McDermott, "Russia's National Security Strategy," *Eurasia Daily Monitor*, May 19, 2009.

238. Giles, p. 10.

239. Novikova, Telmanov, and Pavlikova.

240. Giles, p. 7.

241. *Ibid.*, p. 10.

242. Marc Raeff, *The Well-Ordered Police State: Social and Institutional Change Through Law in the Germanies and Russia, 1600-1800*, New Haven, CT: Yale University Press, 1983.

243. Robert O. Paxton, *The Anatomy of Fascism*, New York: Vintage Books, 2005.

244. "Russia On the Brink of Civil War," *Vlasti*, in Russian, April 19, 2009, *FBIS SOV*.

245. *Ibid.*

246. *Ibid.*

247. *RIA Novosti*, in Russian, May 28, 2009, *FBIS SOV*.

248. Trenin is quoted in Sergei Strokan and Dmitry Sidorov, "In the World: and Now the Rest," *Kommersant Online*, in Russian, July 27, 2009, *FBIS SOV*.

249. "Interview With Lilia Shevtsova of the Carnegie Endowment," *BBC Monitoring*, June 26, 2009 from *Johnson's Russia List*.

250. Fedor Lukyanov, "Security For the Future," *Gazeta.ru Online*, in Russian, May 14, 2009, from *Johnson's Russia List*.

251. Giles, p. 8.

252. McDermott, "Russia's National Security Strategy."

253. Alexander Golts, "The Landscape After the Battle," *Yezhenedevnyi Zhurnal*, in Russian, May 20, 2009, *FBIS SOV*.

254. *Ibid.*; Alexander Golts, "A Strategic Hodgepodge," *The Moscow Times*, May 19, 2009.

255. Primakov quoted in Andrei Davydov, "USA-PRC-Russia: The 'Triangle' 35 Years On," *Far Eastern Affairs*, Vol. XXXVI, No. 1, 2008, p. 25.

256. Stephen Blank, "Putin's Presidency and Russian History," *Russian History*, Vol. XXXVI, No. 1, 2009, pp. 88-116, and the sources cited there.

CHAPTER 2

IS MILITARY REFORM IN RUSSIA FOR "REAL"? YES, BUT...

Dale R. Herspring

There is little doubt that the Dmitry Medvedev administration and its defense secretary, Anatoliy Serdyukov, are very serious about reforming the Russian military. In comparison with other military reforms introduced since the collapse of the Union of Socialist Republics (USSR), this one is for real. Indeed, this writer will argue that the closest comparison of these reforms, in terms of magnitude, is the early communist period when a totally new structure was imposed on the remnants of the Bolshevik Army. Those who followed the tank heavy, mass Soviet and Russian militaries until the mid-2000s will probably be hard pressed to recognize the new structure emerging. It is a far more flexible, smaller, and lethal armed force.

The problem facing the Kremlin, however, is that a "revolution in military affairs" — to steal a phrase from the late Marshal Nikolai Ogarkov — involves much more than structural or personnel changes. Moscow must also produce an efficient, effective, flexible and lethal military if it hopes to compete with other modern militaries around the world. The key question is whether the Kremlin can successfully deal with four major problems confronting it: Russia must overcome its technological inferiority, learn how to delegate authority, find a way to eliminate the ever-present corruption, and find a way to make the military attractive to young Russian men. If it does not deal with these issues, Russia will face the probability of repeating its horrible performance in the 2008 war with Georgia. Only the next time, the consequences could be far worse.

CORRUPTION AND THE WAR IN GEORGIA

Before proceeding, a few words are needed by way of background. In this writer's opinion, the structural and personnel changes currently under way are a combination of two events. The first was Sergei Ivanov's decision to commission an audit of the military budget in 2007. During the audit, he discovered that corruption was even worse than expected. For example, on April 3, 2008, the Audit Chamber announced that more than 164.1 million rubles had been stolen from the ministry through fraud and outright theft. According to another report, the Ministry of Defense (MoD) "accounts for 70 percent of the budgetary resources used for purposes other than those officially designated."[1] Recognizing that the MoD could not continue business as in the past, Russia's then president, Vladimir Putin, decided to shake up the ministry. He did so by appointing Serdyukov, a civilian official from the Tax Service, to become the new defense minister.

The second trigger event was the Kremlin's miserable performance in the war with Georgia. The conflict highlighted the shortcomings, failings, and decrepit condition of both Russia's weapons and personnel. In fact, the lessons learned from the Five Day War were so shocking and had such serious implications that the reinterpretation of the conflict from a Russian military perspective would become the *causes belli* for the radical and sweeping changes in Russian conventional forces.

While it is not possible to include all the complaints by senior officers, it is worth considering some of them. In May 2009, former airborne intelligence chief Colonel Pavel Popovskich highlighted the backward looking, dated condition of combat training within Russia's elite forces when he observed,

> Our army is still being trained based on regulations, which were written in the 1980s! The regulations, manuals, combat training programs, and the volumes of standards have become obsolete. An old friend recently sent the volume of standards that is in force, which we already wrote about in 1984, 25 years ago. . . . If the airborne troops have remained at that prehistoric level, then we can confidently say that the General Staff and the rest of the troops will continue to train for a past war.[2]

The General Staff quickly concluded that "only one-fifth of the troops are in complete readiness."[3] Officers were no better. As one source put it,

> We had to search one person at a time for lieutenant colonels, colonels, and generals throughout the Armed Forces to participate in combat operations. Because [of] the table of organization (paper divisions and regiments) commanders were simply not in a state to solve combat issues.[4]

There were also problems with command and control. The most incredible aspect of the war was that the General Staff, normally in charge of such operations, was absent. The reason was that on October 8, the Main Operations Directorate and the Main Organizational/Mobilization Directorate were in the process of moving from their current headquarters to the old Warsaw Pact headquarters. Many of them learned about the Georgian War from the radio or TV.[5] The situation was made worse by the absence of a commander of the main intelligence directorate, the *Glavnoye Razvedyvatel'noye Upravleniye* (GRU). The old commander, Colonel General Aleksandr Rushin, had been sacked by Serdyukov and had not yet been replaced.[6]

Another source complained that "the command structure, just as on 22 June 1941, waited for an order from the political leadership to make a retaliatory strike and open fire."[7] There was also the problem of a lack of unified command, a point made especially clear by Vitaly Shlykov, who is widely recognized as one of Russia's leading analysts on the Russian military. As he noted,

> And here once again the subject of united commands surfaces. Why was aviation late in appearing? Could the Ground Troops Commander have given orders to the pilots? Of course not. This all had to go through a superior level — approval time was needed. . . . . With the current system of leadership, it could not have been otherwise not only for the Armed Forces but for the country's defense as well.[8]

Shlykov also pointed to the equipment shortages — the Russian armed forces "had neither the GLONASS space system nor satellite-guided projectiles nor precision missiles or laser illuminated projectiles."[9] There was also a lack of "Friend or Foe" identification equipment. The same was true of the much proclaimed Mi28N, *Nochnoy Okhonik*, as well as the Ka50 and Ka-52 helicopters. For the most part, the army operated without the helicopters so critical to infantry operations.[10] The army's performance was also heavily criticized. In August 2008 the independent Russian military newspaper, *Nezavisimoy voyennoye obozreniye* (NVO) pointed out that 60 to 75 percent of the 58th Army's tanks deployed in the theater of operations were in fact old T-62s, T-72Ms, and T-72BMs, none of which would withstand Georgian anti-tank warheads.[11]

There was also criticism of the air force's performance. "The loss of four aircraft in a confrontation with a country that does not even have a single fighter and possesses very feeble ground-based troops of national air defense (PVO)—this gives cause for extremely serious reflection."[12] Continuing along the same vein, the writer commented,

> Never mind about breaching NATO's [the North Atlantic Treaty Organization] air defenses, we are simply incapable of breaching an air defense. We have no UAVs [unmanned aerial vehicles], we are very badly off as regards REB [electronic warfare equipment] and precision weapons, and the gap between us and the West is widening fast.[13]

Another officer summed up the military's view of the operation when he commented, "It turns out that a 21st century army did not go into battle—it was a Soviet army with models from the 1960s and 1980s in the past century. For this reason, rather than a no-contact war, we had classical all-arms battles."[14] Finally, there were even complaints about the clothes worn by the soldiers. "It would seem that the Central Clothing Directorate regularly reports on the order to supply new models of field clothing and gear, however, the soldiers and commanders in this conflict as before look like Ossetian volunteer militiamen, that is, they are dressed as if everyone dresses however they feel like dressing."[15]

The bottom line was that the Russian military needed change. To quote a Russian expert, "we need to work on the state's entire military infrastructure, radically change our weaponry and command systems, and prepare for wars of the 21st Century."[16] The same need was evident for other components of the military. To quote General Vladimir Shamanov, at that time head of the Training Directorate,

> The entire complex of weapons must be moved to qualitatively new parameters. This will require upgrading the system of command and control of subunits and units at the tactical echelon, upgrading means of tactical reconnaissance, and combining the two components with ground artillery and tank subunit fire control systems. That is the world trend of future battle by combined arms subunits, and in building competitive Ground Troops, we too cannot fight further by antiquated methods. [17]

Something also had to be done to reduce corruption, while at the same time streamlining the Russian military so it would be in a position to deal with another Georgia. Russia won in Georgia through sheer mass. What if the better equipped Georgian Army had stood and fought, and not run away from the battle? Change was critical. And while many Russian officers agreed change was needed, few had any idea of just how radical these changes would be. In fact, several of these officers, including then Chief of the General Staff General Yuri Balyuevskii, would soon find themselves out of the military either because they resigned or were forced to leave.

MILITARY REFORM IS FOR "REAL"

The New Minister.

In the beginning, Russian officers did not take Serdyukov seriously. Indeed, in the words of one source, his appointment created "confusion" within the ranks.[18] No one knew what he would focus on or how he would deal with this very conservative and insular organization. He was a civilian with minimal military experience. Given the organization's problems with corruption, many assumed that his primary focus would be on that issue.

In the meantime, Serdyukov was given the nickname *bukhalter,* a derisive term meaning someone whose only job is to shuffle papers. In addition, his decision to bring 20 civilian auditors with him to find the money made him even less welcome. At the very beginning of his term, it indeed seemed that those who thought his primary focus would be on auditing the armed forces appeared to be right. "Defense Minister Anatoliy Serdyukov has begun a financial audit of his department," an article in Izvestiya reported. "As part of this, the first appointees from the Federal Tax Service . . . have appeared on Arbat Square."[19]

Welcome or not, Serdyukov soon made it clear that he meant business beyond simple auditing. For example, during a trip to St. Petersburg in March 2007, he went to the Navy's Nakhimov School unannounced. Instead of entering through the front door, he went in using the back one. In the process, he discovered horrible, inadequate sanitary arrangements, damp college cadets' rooms, water in the basement, fungi on the wall, and crumbling plaster."[20] As a result, chief of the college Rear Admiral Aleksandr Bukin was immediately fired and dismissed from the Naval service.[21]

Then Serdyukov turned his attention to getting rid of excess property, weapons, and bases owned by the armed forces. Conceptually, his primary focus was on how to bring the Russian armed forces into the 21st century. With that in mind, he believed that it was time to introduce radical changes into the military—to move it from a mass mobilization based army to one that was flexible, lethal, and easily transportable to wherever needed. A Russian military expert explained what Serdyukov had in mind when he observed that the old force structure was created to ensure that there would never be a repeat of the disaster of 1941. Russian forces, he explained, were structured so that they would have a powerful forward grouping to deal with mass attack. Now, however, Moscow faced a NATO that did not have enough forces to threaten the country. "At the present, the threat has gone somewhere very far away. Therefore, it has become unnecessary for us to maintain a rather costly, cumbersome mobilization army that is ineffective in performing peacetime missions. Now, we will have peacetime forces — covering forces in a special period, consisting of units fully up to strength and combat-ready," the so-called "permanent readiness units" — units that can be deployed anywhere at any time.[22]

Russian officers, however, faulted Serdyukov for not linking his proposed changes with existing military doctrine. In fact, when the proposal was introduced, it bore little resemblance to existing doctrine. For Russian officers, doctrine is of critical importance. The normal procedure is for the Russian military to await the production of the country's "National Security Doctrine." Once that is published, the General Staff will put together a military doctrine. The latter has been the key document for the armed forces. It provides the generals and admirals with a guide to what weapons to buy as well as what kind of wars to prepare for and under what kind of conditions. However, the best Serdyukov was able to do was promise that the country would have a new military doctrine by the end of 2009.[23]

The executive order that President Medvedev signed on May 13, 2009, replaced the country's 1997 National Security Concept. The new document is a hodgepodge of vague, sometimes confusing statements about every kind of threat the country could face in the future. As a consequence, it does little to provide the military with the kind of guidance it needs. According to this document, Moscow's biggest threat is

> the policy of some foreign states aimed at attaining an overwhelming military superiority, particularly in the area of strategic nuclear weapons, through targeted, informational, and other high-technology means of conducting armed conflict, non-nuclear strategic arms, the development of missile defenses, and the militarization of space.

In other words, Moscow faces just about any kind of threat imaginable, except one of the most likely, asymmetric warfare such as that faced by the United States and its allies in Central Asia today.[24]

Personnel Changes.

Serdyukov was determined to ensure that Russia would make radical changes, especially in the personnel area. After all, what good were the many thousands of officers in what some Russians have called the country's "warehouse army." These officers sat around and kept skeleton units and their equipment in operating condition in case there was a major war one day. After all, the West did not have anything like the 3:1 or 2:1 officer/enlisted ratio. Serdyukov realized it was time for major surgery.

As a consequence, the officer corps was cut from 355,000 (there were 400,000 slots, but only 355,000 were filled when the cutback began) to 150,000.[25] The new army would have approximately 1 million men under arms. The number 150,000 was based on NATO's model of about 1 officer for every 15 soldiers. In the Russian context, the nature of these cutbacks was staggering. For example, the number of generals on active duty was cut from 1,107 to 886 (primarily in logistics), and the roster of colonels fell from 23,663 to 9,114. Majors were cut from 99,550 to 25,000, while the number of captains declined from 90,000 to 40,000. The only officer rank that grew was lieutenants, who increased by 10,000.[26] All parts of the army were hit hard. The medical staff lost 10,000 officer positions and as many as 22 military hospitals were closed.[27] In addition, 80 percent of all lawyers were shown the door.[28] All but 20 officer positions in military media organizations were eliminated, with the exception being those working for the military's main newspaper, *Krasnaya zvezda*.[29] By 2016, Serdyukov declared that the size of the Russian Army would total 1,884,829, including one million servicemen.[30]

One unique aspect of military reform, which preceded Serdyukov, was the decision to cut the duration of conscript service to 1 year. From a military standpoint, a year provides insufficient time to train a soldier. One critic argued that the shortened time of service "will lead to a drastic decrease in the Russian Army's qualification."[31] The problem of decreased conscript service is aggravated by Russian demographic trends combined with poor health conditions among Russian youth. One report noted, for example, that "it can be said that no more than 40-45% of the conscripts will be able to serve in the army, and the number of conscripts aged 18-19 will go down to 35% by 2025."[32] Another change introduced by Serdyukov's reorganization plan was his physical fitness tests. Those who were overweight could and would be released from active service—a bit of a shock to those of us who had become accustomed to equating rank with an officers' girth.[33] In the first part of 2008, 26 percent of all young officers failed the physical fitness test.[34]

Meanwhile, it is also worth noting that there has been a drastic cutback in military educational institutions, because, with the cutback in forces, the military did not need as many facilities. According to then Army General Nikolay Pankov, educational institutions were only 60 to 70 percent full. The logical decision was to combine them. Pankov explained that, "[c]utting redundant establishments of higher education is a painful, but necessary, process. If we do not undertake it today, we shall, in the near future witness the slow but inevitable decline of our military education system."[35] Pankov also maintained that there was widespread duplication in the educational system. In another interview, he stated, "[d]epartmental egoism has led to a situation in which there is widespread duplication of the training of officers in related military specialties in military institutions of higher education of different subordination."[36] To deal with the problem, the number of such institutions was reduced from 65 to three military educational centers, six academies, and one military university (the much smaller General Staff Academy). Needless to say, a large number of faculty (almost exclusively military officers) were also made redundant.

Major changes have also been introduced at the General Staff Academy. Of the 17 chairs the Academy had, only two (the art of war, and national security and defense) remain. In the past there were 100-120 graduates each year. This year, the Academy has only 16 students at the one-star level, while the curriculum has been revised. The first year will focus on

> military disciplines at the operational and strategic levels. During their second year, military topics will account for only 20 percent of the curriculum. This will permit students to take courses in areas such as law and finance, taught by tutors from "high-profile universities."[37]

Serdyukov also took on two of the most powerful military institutions in the Russian Army, the General Staff and the MoD. The Kremlin decided that too many uniformed officers worked in Moscow. Accordingly, officers in the MoD and the General Staff will be reduced by a factor of 2.5 over a 4-year period—from a total of 27,873 officers to 8,500.[38] Serdyukov even took on the GRU, the Main Intelligence Directorate's military's intelligence organization. It was announced in early April 2008 that the GRU would be cut by more than 40 percent.[39] Then, rumors began to circulate that a number of Spetsnatz commando units would also be cut. In response, Major General Valentin Korabelnikov resigned in April 2008. He reportedly could not live with Serdyukov's plan for reforming the GRU as a part of the overall restructuring plan.

Serdyukov's restructuring of the aforementioned units was child's play in comparison with his plans for the major services. Of the 340 units and formations in the Air Force, 160 were disbanded, and the number of air regiments was also reduced. A total of 50,000 positions were cut.[40] This translated into about a 30 percent decrease of Air Force officer positions. As Colonel General Alezandr Zelin, the commander in chief of the

Air Force, put it, "We will have to reform over 80% of Air Force units, of which 10% will be disbanded, 22% will be redeployed and reformed, and 68% will have a change in staff."[41]

The Navy was also hit hard by Serdyukov. To begin with, it was ordered to pack up and move its headquarters from Moscow to St. Petersburg. While that might seem to make sense—after all, St. Petersburg was traditionally its headquarters and is a lot closer to open water than land-locked Moscow—the move was a serious threat to the Navy's ability to function in the intricate and volatile world of intra-military politics. Forcing the Navy to move to St. Petersburg would take the admirals out of the bureaucratic battle for resources in Moscow. As one source put it, "You cannot keep traveling to Moscow on every issue, or it will be necessary to establish a branch of the Main Staff on the Red Army express train."[42] Simple matters like cocktail parties can be very important when it comes to "meeting and dealing" with critical decision makers. Therefore, it is not surprising that the Navy resisted. Sixty-three former senior admirals protested the action, followed by an argument by the admirals that moving the headquarters to St. Petersburg threatened the country's nuclear deterrent because there was no command and control system there for the navy's nuclear missile launching submarines. Admiral Kasatonov stated, "All of the command and control systems of not only the Navy, but of all branches of the armed forces are in Moscow. . . . This is a dangerous and serious experiment, which will cost the state dearly."[43] In April 2009 the transfer process was suspended. In addition to strong resistance on the part of the Navy staff against relocating, a lack of money contributed to the decision. "Kommersant's source in the

Defense Ministry links the reluctance to the lack of the majority of admirals and senior officers of Navy Main Staff to leave Moscow. . . . Of the Main Command's 800 staffers, only 20 came out in favor of the move."[44] The move has since been suspended.

The Ground Troops were also hit hard by major changes. For example, Serdyukov announced that the number of units and formations in the Ground Troops would be reduced by 11 times its current size, "from 1,890 to 172."[45] This structural change was accompanied by a modification of the existing four-tier command relationship to a new three-tier command structure. The old relationship included four levels of command: military district, army, division, and regiment. In an effort to improve flexibility, Serdyukov decided to move to a system that went from: military district to army to brigade. This modification was sharply criticized. As former Defense Minister Pavel Grachev put it,

> I believe that the "district-army-division-regiment" system should be preserved because transition to a brigade system would negatively impact on the state of our country's combat readiness. First, the Russian Federation in terms of area is too big a state, which is surrounded by too many probable adversaries. Second, transition to the American brigade structure would create a number of difficulties organizationally and would require additional amounts of material and funds. [46]

One writer, who came to Serdyukov's defense, argued that the new system is superior to the old one. For example, he noted, that a regiment cannot exist outside of a division and that it is almost impossible for a regiment to conduct independent operations:

It has a weak rear and everything it needs is in the division. That is why it was not regiments, but battalion and regimental task forces that operated in South Ossetia from the makeup of the 19th and 42nd motorized rifle divisions. They were reinforced by assets from the division and adjacent subunits, which immediately made the other units non-combat-effective and their commitment and effective actions no longer could be counted upon.

A brigade is an independent tactical unit. It already has everything necessary, including rear services and means of reinforcement. A "combat" motorized rifle brigade that has taken losses can be withdrawn to the rear and replaced by another, while the means of reinforcement will remain in place, but a division with beaten-up "combat" regiments will have to be removed entirely. . . . [47]

In addition, the Ground Forces will continue to be divided into six military districts and seven operational commands. Remembering the chaos of the Georgian operation, district commanders were given command of all units and formations in their district, with the exception of the Strategic Rocket Forces. This creation of a unified command structure will result in the deployment of about 90 brigades in the various military districts.[48]

The only units exempted from this structural modification are the airborne units. They were left practically untouched for several reasons. First, the airborne units are the best trained and most ready units in the army (except perhaps for the Naval Infantry and Spetsnatz). They are the rapid response units of the Russian military, and one of the most powerful generals in Russia, Vladimir Salamanov (who this author considers to be an officer with a future and a potential Chief of the General Staff) took command of them. His status serves to underline the importance and esteem of this elite group of soldiers. They are the only unit that will not be forced to convert from the regimental system in favor of the brigade. To quote one source, "The Airborne Troops will consist of four divisions and one separate airborne brigade as before."[49]

In comparison, of all the branches affected, none was hit harder than the Rear Services. Moscow undertook an effort to streamline the supply process. To overcome problems with redundancies, logistics between the services are being integrated in a Public Joint-Stock Company. The idea was to disband the roughly 200 service oriented logistical bases in favor of 34 integrated ones. Military units will be supplied by district depots. "For instance, if a missile brigade is in Tver, it will be supplied with food, clothes, fuel, lubricants, and so forth from the nearest depots in the Moscow Military District."[50] In the process of integrating services, 40 percent of all officers, including a number of generals, were eliminated. This amounted to a total of 12,500 lost positions, including 5,600 officers and warrant officers. In addition, 23 to 40 percent of all civilian posts were eliminated.[51] That meant that a little over 300 individuals would remain in the Rear Services' central apparatus.[52] In addition, a number of functions were civilianized. For example, the catering services will use civilian enterprises to provide fuel as well as the provision of bathing and laundry services for the troops.[53]

Another indication of how sweeping Serdyukov's personnel reforms were was found in the Railway Troops, which were also subjected to radical reforms. Although they do not actually conduct combat operations, the Railway Troops were transformed in exactly the same manner as other forces and combat arms. By the end of 2009, the Railway Troops will be divided into four territorial commands and separate railroad brigades.[54] The way the railway troops will be transformed emphasizes the mechanical manner in which Serdyukov's reform agenda has been implemented. With the exception of the airborne units, his reform is a one-size-fits-all approach. The various units are being treated the same, without reference to doctrine, concepts, threats, or even technical requirements or the need to monitor progress.

One of the more shocking changes came in July 2009. In the past, many Russian officers had resisted the idea of chaplains, worrying that Imams could radicalize the increasing proportion of Muslim soldiers in the Russian military. However, Medvedev changed the rules on July 25, 2009, when he pledged to hire chaplains for the military from the major religious groups in Russia.[55] It had become obvious that the disbandment of the political officers in the early 1990s had created a gap. There was no one to take care of the spiritual needs of soldiers, or provide the personal touch needed to deal with the plethora of personal problems they faced. The rule was that if at least 10 percent of the members of a unit belong to a particular religion, then a priest from that religious confession should be attached to the unit. The plan encompassed four major religious groups: Russian Orthodox, Jewish, Muslim, and Buddhist. The chaplains would remain civilians and be paid at the level of a deputy brigade commander.

CHALLENGES

The Military's Response.

It should come as no shock to learn that the senior military reacted very negatively to Serdyukov. This was particularly true of the ranking officers. For example, General Yuri Balyuevskiy, Chief of the General Staff, was firmly opposed to Serdyukov's policies. Balyuevskiy submitted his resignation on three different occasions before it was accepted. Indeed, he had been given permission to stay in for an additional 3 years (he was over 60 and therefore needed special permission), but made a point of quitting before his time in office expired. As far as this author can determine, all officers at the three or four star level in key bureaucratic positions either submitted their retirement papers or were fired. Among the remaining officers, "[i]t is no secret that the absolute majority of the officer corps, which is going to be cut by more than half in the next 3 years, have reacted negatively and in a number of cases with hostility to these reforms."[56]

Not only was Serdyukov cutting the military to the point where officers were losing their jobs *en masse*, he was destroying what many of them considered to be the pride of their lives—the Russian Military! To quote a well-known military expert: "[a]fter all the reductionism, GRU intelligence has actually been destroyed. Management in the General Staff has been destroyed. Vertical troop command and control at all levels has been destroyed."[57] Then, he began selling off military assets in Moscow. The idea was to sell buildings and property no longer needed by the military and to use the resultant money to help pay for the infrastructure improvements needed to attract young men to join the professional military Serdyukov was attempting to create. The same was true of antiquated weapon systems, equipment, and unused bases. In early 2008, for example, he stated that 4,000 tanks would be scrapped.[58] Then he sold excess military real estate on Moscow's elite Rubelvskoye Shosse for 2.606 billion rubles.[59]

The response to Serdyukov's plans to downsize the officer corps was particularly negative, not surprising given that it impacted thousands of officers, many of whom found themselves suddenly in the civilian world. According to one source, "[i]t is symptomatic that a number of publications compare Serdyukov and Boris Yeltsin's first Prime minister the late Egor Gaydar—one 'destroyed' the country's economy, while the other will 'destroy' its Army."[60] There were also repeated requests for detailed information on the reform plan since few knew or understood exactly what Serdyukov had in mind. The regime responded by sending out senior officers to visit the headquarters of various troops to explain what Moscow had in mind.

> Next week, members of the Defense Ministry's board, including deputy ministers, will travel to military districts, the fleet and the central command departments of the Armed Forces' units to inform their personnel of the whole set of the (ministry's) planned reforms.[61]

In the eyes of many, these visits did little to enlighten those most directly impacted by the reform process.[62] In addition, the Medvedev administration made an effort to rationalize the discharge process. For example, those who had less than 10 years of service were provided with retraining and severance pay. Those who had 10-19 years service got an apartment only. Those with more than 20 years, including service in "hot spots" and remote garrisons got an apartment and a pension.[63] The opposition continued to the point that the new Chief of the General Staff, General Nikoklai Makarov, allegedly issued an order on November 11 which barred officers from publicly discussing military reform.[64] The military leadership denied issuing such an order, but few believed it.

> There is no unambiguous confirmation that the directive . . . . doesn't exist, especially since Deputy Head of the Gosduma Committee for Defense Mikhail Babich did not say that he had not seen such a directive. And second, the public has experience with such denials. In the spring of this year, the Ministry of Defense tried to prove Balyuevskiy was not retiring.[65]

Creating a Noncommissioned Officer Corps.

A key element of the current reform plan is to create a noncommissioned officer (NCO) corps similar to those existing in many Western militaries. This is a radical departure from the past, where regular officers have generally played the roles normally assigned to NCOs in Western armies.[66] Creating a NCO corps will not be easy. It goes against one of the most deeply held attributes of the Russian military, the refusal to delegate authority. However, if NCOs are to lead troops as in the West, senior officers must learn how to delegate authority; NCOs are only effective if they are permitted and encouraged to show initiative.

Unfortunately, even if the Kremlin could convince senior officers to delegate authority, Moscow has run into other major problems in developing an NCO cadre. For example, after considerable fanfare, a new program was set up to train NCOs in six military higher education facilities in a new 10-month program. However, this program ran into problems and had to be delayed. "Defense Ministry higher educational institutions, which were to begin training contract NCOs on 16 February, were unable to select a sufficient number of candidates due to the aspirants' low educational level and poor health."[67] The educational problems were so bad that;

> [a]t the military VUZs in Ryazan and Omsk as many as 60 percent of those tested were incapable of solving quadratic equations, while half of them were unable to do calculations involving simple fractions and decimals. Yet this is the eighth or ninth grade standard in high school.[68]

It is not clear at this time whether they will be able to fill these slots in September 2009. This is a very serious problem because there are a total of 250,000 NCO slots to be filled.[69]

Professional Soldiers.

A related personnel issue has been the problematic effort to recruit professional soldiers—the so-called *kontraktniki*. While the program has been under way for a number of years, the decision to move from a primarily mass-based army to one based on permanent readiness units has put increased pressure on the MoD to find and recruit professional soldiers. In addition to the NCOs, the military needs regular soldiers, whose job it will be to fight wars, whether in Chechnya or elsewhere. According to statistics collected by the military, the news is not good: "Only 17% of contract soldiers are firm when it comes to the possibility of a contract extension, 27% reject the possibility, and 7% are ready to be discharged at the first occasion."[70] According to a specialist in the field, this lack of interest shows the ineffectiveness of the recruitment program.[71] The Ground Forces Commander commented rather bluntly:

> I am not happy when a low staffing level is observed in joint formations and military units which have been changed over to a contract manning method, when the training level hardly differs at all from that of joint formations and units which are manned with conscript service members.[72]

To make matters worse, these *kontrakniki* are drawn from the least desirable segment of the population. To quote General Vladimir Shamanov, at the time head of the Main Department for Combat Training and Service of the Russian Armed Forces:

> [T]he Russian Army, plagued by small money allowances, is actually 'picking leftovers' on the labor market of law-enforcement bodies. The so-called 'military guest-workers'—notorious for poor health and unprofessionalism—are signing up for the army and the navy.[73]

Not surprisingly, they are among the most undisciplined group in the military. "According to the Chief Military Prosecutor, the number of infractions by contract service members for the past year rose by 50.5%."[74] They are also unreliable. In 2008 one source stated: "5,000 contract soldiers willfully left the service and 10,000 tore up their contracts."[75]

There is little question about what is needed to make the *kontraktniki* program attractive: money, money, and more money. According to the Federal Service for Government Statistics, in 2008, the average salary in Russia was 17,900 rubles, while contract personnel (*kontraktniki*) were offered the starting salary of 8,000 rubles (somewhat more if the individual is assigned to a combat zone). Overall, MoD statistics show that the average salary for a *kontraktniki* in 2009 was 1.5 times lower than the average salary in the country.[76] Not only are the salaries modest by Russian standards, Moscow has not done nearly enough to build the kind of physical infrastructure that would make the military attractive to young men. Many of them are soon married, and they expect not only decent housing for themselves and their familiess, they look for the kinds of schools, hospitals, recreational facilities, and stores that would make military life attractive. This is a fact recognized by almost all of the country's military and civilian leaders, but moving from a predominantly conscript army to a professional military—which requires a higher degree of education and dedication—is not an easy or inexpensive task, as Western militaries have learned.

Officers.

Based on the discussion above, it should come as no surprise that the Russian officer corps is in a state of chaos. Officers have lost the critical element of career predictability. Often, they do not know if they will be in uniform next year, or even next month. Indeed, there are rumors that senior officers are "selling" letters of recommendation that will permit an officer to remain on active duty.[77] In short, morale among officers is very low.

If morale problems among officer were not enough, problems with crime and corruption appear to have increased dramatically. Note the following:

> If crimes by officers throughout the country in general hold to their normal level, meaning that every fourth criminal is an officer, then, in the 42nd Motorized Rifle Division, which deployed to Chechnya, the situation is much worse, with more than half the crimes in the unit committed by the officer corps. The situation is also bad in the Airborne Troops, the Space Troops, the Air Force, the Volga-Urals Military District, North Caucasus Military District and the Moscow garrison. There almost a third of all crimes reported last year were committed by officers.[78]

Crime is not limited to lower and mid-level officers. The same source noted that "In 2004, only three generals were tried, but in 2008, 20 were." The bottom line is that officer crimes are out of control. "The crime rates are the highest over the past 10 years. Officers are responsible for more than 2,000 crimes, with one-third of these linked to corruption."[79]

The Technological Lag.

Of all the problems facing the Kremlin, the most serious nonpersonnel issue is the technological lag Russia faces vis-a-vis the West. The Soviet military was behind the West in a number of areas, but remained competitive. However, the loss of 10 years—in essence most of the 1990s, when very little was done to modernize Russian weapons systems—resulted in the Russian Army fighting the Georgia conflict with a 1970s/1980s-era military. In spite of considerable efforts by the military industrial complex under Sergei

Ivanov's leadership, with a few exceptions, the Russian military remains far behind the West.

The Navy.

The Navy has probably been in the news more than the other services, but for the incorrect reasons. The Kremlin's inability to develop the long-range ballistic Bulava missile has been a major embarrassment not only for the Navy, but for the MoD as well. The plan to develop the Bulava missile program goes back to 1998. It was intended to become the Navy's primary ballistic missile. It has been repeatedly tested, but has failed in seven out of 11 test launches since 2004.[80] It is still not ready to be deployed. In July 2009, it was tested again but self-destructed 20 seconds after launch from the submerged *Dmitri Dunskoy*. Indeed, far more is involved than just the Navy's acquisition of its latest submarine-launched ballistic missile (SLBM). The Navy refitted the *Dmitri Donskoy* to carry Bulava missiles. Without these missiles, the *Donskoy* is unarmed. The situation is even worse for the Project 995 (Borey) class submarines. The lead boat, the *Yuriy Dolgorukiy*, is ready to go to sea, but it too lacks its SLBMs. There are two more sister boats in production, the *Aleksandr Nevsky*, and the *Vladimir Monomakh*, both of which are designed to carry the Bulava missile. None of these boats, though, will be able to enter combat duty until the Bulava works. There were suggestions that Moscow might try to arm these submarines with an existing SLBM, the Sineva, but Admiral Vladimir Vysotkiy, the commander of the Russian Navy, rejected that option.[81] In mid-July, Moscow's top missile designer, who had been the chief engineer designing the Bulava, resigned after the latest Bulava failure.

The difficulties with the Bulava missile represent only the Navy's latest problems. In the long run, they are perhaps not even the service's most important challenge. A bigger potential problem stems from the fact that the majority of Moscow's ships have been in service for 20 or 30 years and possess technology from the period when they first became operational. One expert commenting on the Pacific Fleet observed that the situation is so bad that "The Americans, Japanese, and Chinese can simply disregard the surface component of the Pacific Fleet."[82] The Russian Navy has received a total of only four new warships in recent years. One of them, a nuclear submarine, was in the shipyard under construction since 1993. Another submarine, the *St. Petersburg*, was begun in 1997; it was "under construction for 10 years, and for 2 years has been unable to complete its sea trials because of —judging from everything—serious technical problems." Another warship, a corvette, was under construction for 7 years.[83] All of this led one well-known Russian analyst to remark,

> The present catastrophe is comparable only with what occurred with the navy during the years of the Civil War and its subsequent destruction. While during the oil and gas boom of the 2000s, the Navy actually received nothing, now during a serious crisis, there are no doubts the Navy will perish in the next few years. This is not an assumption, this is a fact. We are on the edge of a precipice; we are falling into it; and the bottom is in sight.[84]

The situation from a technological standpoint has deteriorated to the point where Vysotskiy suggested he might purchase an amphibious assault ship of the Mistral Class from France.[85] It is unlikely that the few who follow Russian military developments would have anticipated a Russian admiral going abroad to purchase warships.

The Army.

In spite of the report that Moscow is planning to cut the number of tanks of various makes from 23,000 to 2,000,[86] there is little doubt that the tank will remain an important part of the Ground Forces' inventory. The only problem, according to some Russian analysts, is that, technologically, Russian tanks may not be up to the job. For example, at present, the main battle tank is the T-90. According to one Russian source, "[T]he military-technical level factor of the T-90 tanks is 1.5, the M1A2 tanks have 2.2, the BMP-2, 1.0, and the American M2A2 fighting vehicle is 1.87."[87] Looking at the T-90, this analyst argued that

> ... not only does it not have an on-board information management system, but it also lags behind the M1A2 SEP Abrams, the Leopard - 2A6, the Leclerc and the Challenger 2 with respect to firepower and armor protection. In addition, the T-90 is totally defenseless from the upper hemisphere and bottom.

In addition, the writer continues, "foreign precision-guided weapons will not permit the previously mentioned vehicles to accomplish the combat mission since they will kill them already prior to reaching the forward edge of the battle area." Turning to kill probability, the author argues that "the T-90 will destroy the M1A2 with a probability of no more than 0.2, but the M1A2 insures the destruction of the T-90 with a probability of no less than 0.8 for a firing range of two kilometers." The author also maintains that NATO tanks have "superiority not only in the penetration of armor-piercing sabot rounds, but also in firing accuracy at ranges of 2.5-3 kilometers."[88]

According to Russian sources, Western ground superiority is not just about tanks. As one expert put it, "[a] NATO division, equipped with modern control communications, and navigation equipment exceeds a modern Russian division, produced on a 1980 model, by more than three times in combat effectiveness."[89] The problem does not stop here. Moscow has been forced to purchase UAVs from Israel, and it will have to find a foreign replacement for its vintage Global Navigation Satellite System (GLONASS). Indeed, it appears that Moscow's generals are prepared to go abroad to find replacements for a good number of their outdated systems.

The Air Force.

The most important technological system sought by Russian Air Force officers has been acquiring a fifth-generation fighter comparable to the American F-35. It was planned to become airborne in 2000, but it is still not flying. One source maintained that it will take 7 to 10 years to build the aircraft.[90] Not only that, but it is reportedly not a genuine fifth-generation fighter. Rather, "it turned out that this machine can only be regarded as a fifth-generation prototype, since it possess neither the specific on board equipment nor the engine."[91]

Meanwhile, another critic, a retired Air Force colonel, maintained that only 30 to 35 percent of the Air Force's aircraft inventory is in operational condition. He added that this figure includes aircraft whose service life is projected to be "down to 5-10 hours, or even less."[92] The critic went on to blast the situation inside the Air Force; for example, he noted that the Air Force was to get new planes in 2020, and then asked the rhetorical question, "What will they fly until then?" Furthermore, this critic listed a number of other weaknesses and misleading indicators of improved effectiveness. Addressing the reported increase in pilots' flying time, he noted that, besides an increase in available fuel, it also "reflects a reduction in the number of flight personnel."[93] The retired colonel also claimed that Air Force training was abysmal, with no specialized practice ranges or complex battle simulation forms, and with insufficient training for flight leaders. In addition, he argued that intelligence-collecting equipment and radio electronic warfare assets are outdated, and claimed that most ordnance consists of "free-fall bombs, dirigible bombs, and rockets, mostly designed and manufactured in the 1970s or even 1960s."[94]

Defense Production.

While Sergei Ivanov appears to have had a positive impact on the defense industry since he assumed responsibility for its oversight, it remains beset by serious problems. "The Russian military industrial complex is basically equipped with aging Soviet equipment, and in need of fundamental modernization."[95] Most of the complex's staff is either made up of newcomers or consists of scientists and engineers ready for retirement. To take one example, the ammunition production sector faces very difficult problems.

> The safe storage life has expired for the ammunition, which was produced in the USSR (shells, mines, aerial bombs, etc.), and it can be used only for shooting prac-

tice, hardly risking either people's lives or the integrity of the armaments (they can be prematurely exploded). There is virtually no where to produce new ammunition, due to the fact that the ammunition enterprises have become obsolete, and previously qualified personnel have left and are no longer qualified.[96]

The same author claims that to deal with the problem, the defense industry sector would have to receive 5 percent of the gross domestic product (GDP), something that is not likely to occur.[97]

CONCLUSION

There is no doubt that the Kremlin is aware of the depth of the problems facing the armed forces. Faced with the world economic crisis, the Kremlin announced in February 2009 that the MoD's budget would be cut by 15 percent.[98] Even so, these cuts were aimed primarily at capital construction and renovation. The social aspect was to remain unchanged, while the money intended to pay for military reform was "retained in its entirety."[99] In March, it was announced that the MoD's budget would be reduced by only 8 percent.[100] In practical terms, this meant a cut of 115 billion rubles. Of the remaining budget, 36 percent (approximately 520 billion rubles) was devoted to procurement, maintenance, and the development of farms.[101] According to President Medvedev:

> We practically have not amended any parameters of the financing of our armed forces, the army and navy. We have reduced none of the military programs, neither in terms of improving the defense capacity nor social programs that are being implemented in the armed forces, including programs dealing with creating the basics for life. I mean housing.[102]

Given the choice between putting most of the budget into improving or building up weapon systems or into personnel-related costs, the MoD appears to have focused on the latter as a "priority."[103] The MoD appears to believe it will do little good to attempt to overcome its technological lag until it has carried out structural reform and attracted the officers and NCOs it needs to build a modern, flexible, technically sophisticated and lethal army. That is certainly a rational and defensible decision.

The problem with the MoD's choice, however, is that, with the exception of a few weapon systems (the SA-300 comes to mind), the Kremlin may face the prospect of falling further and further behind the West technologically. On the other hand, that may not be as important as it was during the Cold War. The Kremlin knows that it is not about to be attacked by NATO or China. Seen from the Kremlin's perspective, a greater danger is posed by the potential for small conflicts that could arise around its periphery—*a la* Georgia.

Moscow is not about to halt entirely its efforts to produce or purchase modern weapon systems. New and modernized weapon systems and equipment will continue to dribble into the Russian military inventory. With a smaller military, numbers are no longer as important. At least Moscow can rationalize its weapon systems--purchasing, for example, one type of tank. These weapons may not be up to the standards of the West, but they will be sufficient for carrying out military operations that may develop on Moscow's periphery. By 2020, the date most often repeated by Russian military leaders, their services should be equipped with new, more technologically sophisticated weapons and equipment. How comparable they will be to weapons in the West from a technological standpoint remains to be seen.

The Kremlin and the MoD are haunted by the specter of the Georgian conflict. This has forced them to look through the manifest of Russian officers to try to find enough pilots to fly the planes or enough ground leaders with sufficient combat experience or appropriate training. There is little doubt Moscow does not want to repeat the mess that was the invasion of Georgia, and getting the right people in place to help avoid that appears to be its number one goal at present.

So what does this reform mean from a policy standpoint? For the time being, the MoD is likely to focus inward as it attempts to get its military house in order. That does not mean that the Russian armed forces will not answer the call again as they did in the case of Georgia. However, given the enormity of their personnel, equipment, and weapons systems problems, one suspects that Russia's first concern will be with finishing the reform process while it begins to rebuild what is clearly an antiquated and exhausted armed forces.

ENDNOTES - CHAPTER 2

1. "Defense Ministry Will Shed Excess Equipment," RFE/RL Newsline, April 3, 2008, available from *www.rferl.org/content/Article/1144084.html*. See also "Russian Official Says 30 Percent of Military Budget Lost Through Corruption," *Agentstvo Voyennykh Novostey*, July 2, 2008; *also in* World News Connection (hereafter as WNC) (articles available by subscription from *WNC.fedworld.gov/index.html*).

2. "Confusion Reigns in the Russian Troops," May 19, 2009, available from *www.utro.ru, (Russian language website)*; also in WNC, May 19, 2009.

3. "Russian Army Changing its Image," *Gazeta,* November 10, 2008, available from *www.gazeta.ru*, (primarily Russian language); WNC, November 11, 2008.

4. "Officers are Being Retrained as Building Managers," *Moskovskii Komsomolets,* December 23, 2008, available from *www.mk.ru/,* (Russian language); *also in* WNC, December 24, 2008.

5. Sword of the Empire," *Zavtra,* October 5, 2008, available from *www.zavtra.ru/,* (Russian language); also in in WNC, October 6, 2008.

6. *Ibid.*

7. "The Lessons of Basic Training," *Novoye Vremya,* August 9, 2008, available from *www.nv.am/,* (Russian language); in WNC, August 19, 2008.

8. "Disarmed Forces of the Russian Federation; Our Army Continues to Win Only Through its Fighting Spirit," *Moskovskii Komsomolets,* August 23, 2008, available from *www.mk.ru/*; also in WNC, August 23, 2008.

9. *Ibid.*

10. "The Rearming Race: Russian Army Promised New Weapons," *Vremya Novostey,* September 11, 2008, available from *www.vremya.ru/,* (Russian language); also in WNC, September 12, 2008.

11. "The Lessons Learned of the 5-Day War in the Transcaucasus," WNC, August 29, 2008. See also "RF Combat Operations in Georgia Marred by Poor Intelligence, Obsolete Equipment," *FK-Novosti,* August 22, 2008; also in WNC, August 23, 2008.

12. "The Lessons of Martial Success and Failure," *Nezavisimoye Voyennoye Obozreniye,* August 27, 2008, available from *nvo.ng.ru/,* (Russian language); also in WNC, August 28, 2008.

13. *Ibid.*

14. "The Lessons of Basic Training."

15. "War in the Background of the Caucasus Mountain Range: Russia's Army Encountered for the First Time an Enemy, Who has State-of-the-Art Weapons," *Voyenno-Promyshlenny Kuryer,* August 31, 2009; also in WNC, September 12, 2008.

16. Sebastian Smith, "Russia's Georgia Victory: Blitzkrieg or Bluff," *Georgian Daily Independent Voice*, August 21, 2008, available from *georgiandaily.com/index.php?option=com_content&task=view&id=6375&Itemid=132*; also in American Free Press August 21, 2008, and WNC, August 22, 2008.

17. "After Peace Enforcement," *Krasnaya Zvezda*, December 3, 2008; also in WNC, December 4, 2008.

18. "Russia's Generals Don't Believe that the New Defense Minister Can Help the Military," *Versiya*, No. 8, February 26, 2007.

19. "Anatoliy Serdyukov Studying Defense Ministry Finances," *Izvestiya*, March 27, 2007, available from *www.izvestia.ru/*, (Russian language); also in WNC, March 28, 2007.

20. "Serdyukov is an Army Outside of a Parade Formation," *Rossiskaya Gazeta*, May 14, 2007, *http://www.rg.ru/, (Russian language);* also in WNC, May 15, 2007.

21. *Ibid.*

22. " What Kind of Army Will Russia Get," *Argumenty Nedeli Online*, May 22, 2009; also in WNC, May 23, 2009.

23. See "Russia to Have New Military Doctrine by the End of 2009," *ITAR-TASS*, December 15, 2008, available *from www.itar-tass.com/eng/*.

24. The document is available in Russian from *www.serf.gov.ru*. The title of one article in the Russian press probably said it best in its title, "All is Clear with Russia's Security. But Nothing is Understandable," *Moskovskiy Komsomolets Online,* May 15, 2009, available from *www.mk.ru/*; also in WNC, May 16, 2009.

25. "The Army Needs to be Protected from Dilettantes," available from *www.utro.ru,* October 22, 2008; also in WNC July 24, 2008.

26. "No One Needs a War, But Russia is Ready," available from *www.utro.ru*. November 20, 2008; also in WNC, November 21, 2008.

27. "Russia to close 22 Military Hospitals, cut over 10,000 Medical Officer Posts," *Interfax*, May 27, 2009.

28. "Military Reform 2009-2013," *Nezavisimoye Voyennoye Obozreniye*, January 1, 2009; also in WNC, January 2, 2009.

29. "Defense Ministry to Close Officer Jobs in Military Media," *Interfax-AVN online*, December 3, 2008; also in WNC, December 04, 2008.

30. "The Courageous Account: The Experts on Reform," *Vremya Novostey*, January 23, 2008; also in WNC, January 23, 2008. The number in excess of one million servicemen, presumably refers to civilians working for the MoD.

31. "The Soldier Has Become More Educated than the Officers," *Nezavisimaya Gazeta*, January 24, 2008; also in WNC, January 5, 2008.

32. "Number of Army Conscripts to Decline Due to Poor Health," *Agentstvo Voyennyk Novostey*, September 26, 2009.

33. "They Wanted to Do it in the Best Way Possible. But it Turned Out the Other Way Around," *Nezavisimoye voyennoe obozreniye*, April 15, 2008, in WNC, April 16, 2008.

34. "Russian Military Battles Overweight Soldiers," *The Times* (London), April 11, 2008; "Russian Defense Ministry Introduces Stricter Fitness Requirements," *Agentstvo voyennykh novostey*, June 24, 2008, in WNC, June 25, 2008.

35. "Cuts in Russian Military Higher Educational Establishments Will Start in 2009," *Interfax AVN Online*, December 23, 2008.

36. "Interview with General Pankov on Changes in Military Education," *Voyenno Promyshlennyy Kurier*, January 19, 2009; also in WNC, January 20, 2009.

37. "Russian CGS Quizzed about Military Reform," *Interfax-AVN Online*, June 7, 2009; also in WNC, June 8, 2009.

38. "Within the Framework of Reform of the Russian Federation Armed Forces," *Voenno Promyshlennyy Kurier*, October 29, 2008; also in WNC, April 29, 2009.

39. "The Ownerless Nuclear Football," *Nezavisimoye Gazeta*, April 4, 2009; also in WNC, April 5, 2008.

40. "More than 50,000 positions are being cut, Military Reform 2009-2012," *Nezavisimoye Voyennoye Obozreniye*, January 1, 2009; also in WNC, January 2, 2009.

41. "Around 30% of Russian Air Force Officers to be Dismissed During Reform," *Interfax*, February 11, 2009; also in WNC, February 12, 2009.

42. "Multibillion Zigzag: Defense Ministry is Conducting an Operation to Move the Main Naval Staff from Moscow to St. Petersburg," *Nezavisimoye Voyennoye Obozreniye*, January 5, 2009; also in WNC, January 5, 2009.

43. "The Black Sea Fleet is Being Demoted," *Moskovskiy Komosmolets*, February 11, 2009; also in WNC, February 12, 2009.

44. "Admirals Suffer Fear of the Sea, Navy Main Command Cannot be Moved from Moscow to the Baltic," *Kommersant*, April 22, 2009, available from *www.kommersant.ru/*, (Russian language); also in WNC, April 23, 2009.

45. "Reform Under the SECRET Classification: Two Months Have Passed Since Defense Minister Anatoliy Serdyukov Announced the Decision, Which if 'Carried Out' will Radically Change the Military," *Nezavisimoye Voyennoye Obozreniye*, December 21, 2008; also in WNC, December 22, 2008.

46. "We Should Not Be Learning from Those That Want to Conquer Us!," *Nezavisimoye Voyennoye Obozreniye*, March 25, 2009, in WNC, March 26, 2009. See also "The Courageous Accountant: The Experts on Army Reform," *Vremya Novostey*, January 23, 2008; also in WNC, January 30, 2008.

47. See "What Kind of Army Will Russia Get?"

48. "Russian Army to Form About 90 Brigades by End of 2009," *Interfax-AVN Online*, June 18, 2009, in WNC, June 19, 2009. See also Anatoliy Tyganok, "Reform with no Foundation," *Sovetskaya Rossiya*, February 25, 2009, in WNC, February 26, 2009.

49. "Russian Army to Switch from Divisional to Brigade System of Forming Units," *Agentstvo Vvoyennykh Novostey*, September 12, 2008, in WNC, September 12, 2008.

50. "Russian Army's Rear Services Face Personnel Cuts, Switch to Civilian Suppliers," *Rossiyskaya Gazeta*, November 24, 2008, in WNC, November 26, 2008.

51. "The Generals Went to the Officers: Defense Ministry Begins an Advocacy Campaign," *Nexzavisimoye Voyennoye Oborzreniye*, December 20, 2008, in WNC, December 21, 2008; "Almost One Half of Rear Services' Servicemen to Shed Epaulets," *Gazeta Online*, May 18, 2009; also in WNC, May 19, 2009.

52. "Blow to Rear Services," available from *www.Gazeta.ru*, (*www.gazeta.ru/english/*); also in WNC, November 26, 2008.

53. "Rear Services on the Road of Reform," *Krasnaya Zvezda*, November 26, 2008; also in WNC, November 29, 2008.

54. "New Look—Same Content," *Nezavisimaya Gazeta*, May 24, 2009; also in WNC, May 25, 2009.

55. "Medvedev Supports Attachment of Priests to Military Units," *ITAR-TASS*, July 21, 2009; also in WNC, July 22, 2009.

56. "Purge of General Staff Has Begun. Dmitry Medvedev Will Tell Those Who Remain About New Benefits," *Nezavisimaya Gazeta*, November 10, 2008; also in WNC, November 11, 2008.

57. "Virtual Appearance and Actual Essence," *Marketing I Konsalting*, March 28, 2009; also in WNC, March 29, 2009.

58. See "Defense Ministry will Shed Excess Equipment."

59. "Russian Defense Ministry Plans to Sell 20 to 50 Unused Sites," *ITAR-TASS*, May 27, 2008; also in WNC, May 28, 2008.

60. "Serdyukov is Reforming Army from Underground," *Nezavisimoye Voyennoye Obozreniye,* December 10, 2008; also in WNC, December 13, 2008.

61. "Top Defense Ministry Officials to Explain Russian Army Reform to Servicemen," *Interfax AVN Online,* November 21, 2008; also in WNC, November 22, 2008.

62. "Russian Army Reform May Have Negative Consequences—Experts," *Interfax,* December 15, 2008; also in WNC, December 16, 2008.

63. E-mail from Colonel (Ret.) Igor Obraztsov, December 30, 2008, to the author.

64. "MOD Rebutal," *Argumenty Nedeli,* December 1, 2008; also in WNC, December 4, 2008.

65. "Ministry of Defense Unconvincing Refutation," *Nezavisimaya Gazeta,* December 4, 2008; also in WNC, December 9, 2008.

66. See e.g., "New Army Can Be Created Only From Scratch," *Nezavisimoye Voyennoye Obozreniye,* May 23, 2009; also in WNC, May 24, 2009.

67. "Defense Ministry Was Unable to Select Contract NCO Candidates," available from *www.Gazeta.ru,* February 24, 2009; also in WNC, March 14, 2009.

68. "NCO - No Comrade for the Cadet. Training of the Professional Junior Commanders Had Ground to a Halt," *Gazeta,* March 27, 2009; also in WNC, February 28, 2009.

69. "Sergeant or Senior Sergeants," *Voyenno-Promyshenny Kuryer,* May 26, 2009.

70. "NCO - No Comrade for the Cadet. Training of the Professional Junior Commanders Had Ground to a Halt," *Gazeta,* March 27, 2009; also in WNC, February 28, 2009.

71. "Putting a Good Word for the Poor Soldiers," *Nezavisimaya Gazeta,* May 28, 2009; also in WNC, May 29, 2009.

72. "Conscript Soldiers Still the Foundation of the Army," *Nezavisimaya Gazeta*, June 2, 2009; also in WNC, June 3, 2009.

73. "Russian Army in Need of Professionals," *ITAR-TASS*, September 23, 2008; also in WNC September 24, 2008.

74. "Mercenaries Not Required: More than Money Needed to Make Contract Service Attractive," *Nezavisimoye Voyennoye Obozreniye*, June 10, 2009; also in WNC, June 11, 2009.

75. "Around 2,000 Legal Violations Registered at Draft Offices in 2008," *Interfax*, February 25, 2009; also in WNC, February 26, 2009.

76. "Army of the Unemployed," *Novyee Izvestiya*, January 15, 2009; also in WNC, January 16, 2009.

77. "Are Personnel Being Given Efficiency Reports for Cash? Officers Believe it is Possible to Avoid Reduction by Bribery," *Moskovskiy Komsomolets*, December 6, 2008, available from *www.mk.ru/*; also in WNC, December 7, 2008.

78. "Military Honor is Being Disbanded," *Moskovskiy Komsomolets*, July 30, 2009, available from *www.mk.ru/*; also in WNC, August 1, 2009.

79. "Crime Rates in Army Highest Over Past Ten Years—Prosecutor," *ITAR-TASS*, July 9, 2009; also in WNC, July 10, 2009.

80. Nabi Abdullaev, "Designer Quits After the Missile Failure," *The Moscow Times.com*, July 23, 2009, available from *www.cdi.org/russia/Johnson/2009-138-25.cfm*.

81. "Vladimir Vysotksiy Cites Causes of Bulava Problems," *Kommersant*, July 28, 2009; also in WNC, August 1, 2009.

82. "Russian Navy on Foreign Ships," *Nezavisimoye Voyennoye Obozreniye*, July 24, 2009; also in WNC, August 1, 2009.

83. *Ibid.*

84. *Ibid.*

85. "Russian Navy Considers Acquisition of Mistral Class Assault Ship," *ITAR-TASS*, August 4, 2009; also in WNC, August 5, 2009.

86. "The General Staff is Cutting Tanks to the Bone," *Nezavisimaya Gazeta*, July 10, 2009; also in WNC, July 11, 2009.

87. "The Russian Army Doesn't Have any State of the Art Tanks: A Magical Technique Transforms Old Armored Vehicles into New Ones," *Nezavisimoye Voyennoye Obozreniye*, January 4, 2009; also in WNC, January 5, 2009. According to this source, "The military-technical level factor is obtained as a result of multiplying these partial factors. The indicator for the T-90 tank is 0.7 less than for the M1A2 tank, which lulls one into complacency. You think, 0.7 - we will overtake them during modernization. So, false impressions are being created. The military-technical factor is convenient for briefings to the highest leadership, who can really get upset if it hears the truth about armored vehicles' actually poor combat specifications (armor protection, firepower, mobility, and command controllability)."

88. *Ibid.*

89. "Money for Modernization of Production and the Army," *Nezavisimoye Voyennoye Obozreniye*, December 23, 2008; also in WNC, December 24, 2008.

90. "Flight Testing of Fifth-Generation Aircraft for Russian Air Force to Begin this Year," *RIA-Novosti*, August 6, 2009; also in WNC, August 6, 2009.

91. "Defense Military Shelves its Weapons," *Moskovskiy Komsomolets*, June 22, 2009; also in WNC, June 23, 2009.

92. "Air Force is Air Weakness: What Hides Behind the Pictures of Parades," *Sovetskaya Rossiya*, August 7, 2009; also in WNC, August 8, 2009.

93. *Ibid.*

94. Ibid.

95. "Money for Modernization of Production and the Army," *Nezavisimoye Voyennoye Oboreniye*, December 23, 2008; also in WNC, December 24, 2008.

96. "Lopped-off Army," *Vremya Novostey*, March 10, 2009; also in WNC, March 12, 2009.

97. "At the First Stage - 8%: the MoD is Cutting the Budget 8%," *Vedomomsti*, March 10, 2009; also in WNC, March 15, 2009.

98. "Russian Defense Budget to be Cut by 15% in 2009," *Interfax, AVN Online*, February 12, 2009.

99. "Lopped-off Army," *Vremya Novostey*, March 10, 2009; also in WNC, March 12, 2009.

100. "At the First Stage - 8%: the MoD is Cutting the Budget 8%," *Vedomomsti*, March 10, 2009; also in WNC, March 15, 2009.

101. *Ibid*.

102. "Russia Maintains Spending Despite Crisis," *Zvezda Television*, July 14, 2009; also in WNC, July 21, 2009.

103. "Chances and Finances," *Voyenno-Promyshlennyy Kuryer*, May 11, 2009; also in WNC, May 12, 2009.

CHAPTER 3

OPERATIONAL ART AND THE CURIOUS NARRATIVE
ON THE RUSSIAN CONTRIBUTION:
PRESENCE AND ABSENCE OVER THE LAST
2 DECADES

Jacob W. Kipp

INTRODUCTION:
WORKING WITH MARY FITZGERALD ON
SOVIET MILITARY THEORY

During much of the 1980s, I had frequent opportunities to work with Mary Fitzgerald on a range of topics associated with the Revolution in Military Affairs (RMA) and Soviet concepts of future war. We took part in various conferences, gave papers, and wrote articles on Soviet and Russian military strategy and doctrine. We were both regular attendees at David Jones' summer workshop at his home in suburban Halifax, Nova Scotia. We also worked together on several projects for the Office of Net Assessment of the U.S. Department of Defense (DoD). In all these efforts, Mary always focused on the policy implications of Russian developments for U.S. national security strategy, to which she brought her own insights on such topics as the role of space in Soviet military doctrine and the implications of the RMA for Russian military reform. Both of us devoted considerable attention to the development of *voennaia sistemologiia* (military systemology) as a new discipline with military science. The new discipline had radical implications for military art, especially operational art.

This chapter will address the curious narrative of the influence of Soviet operational art on the development of Western concepts of operational art and its subsequent disappearance from the common analytical narrative. It will conclude with a plea for the serious study of military systemology as an alternative reconceptualization of operational art. In particular, military systemology meets the needs of the "informatization" of military art closely tied to the forecasting studies conducted regarding the nature of future war.

OPERATIONAL ART IN THE WEST: FROM BLITZKRIEG AND DEEP OPERATIONS TO CAMPAIGN DESIGN

The origins of operational art are much disputed. Some historians have traced the art to Napoleon's great victories during the Jena Campaign.[1] For David Chandler, the leading student of Napoleonic warfare of his generation, the "heart" of the Napoleonic concept of warfare was "the *Blitzkrieg* attack aimed at the main repository of the enemy, the center of gravity, his army."[2] A series of battles—linked by rapid maneuver and culminating in the defeat of the enemy army in a single final engagement—became the dominant paradigm. In this view, operational art is a legacy of the great captains and the West's "military revolution," with a lineage from Napoleon, through Von Moltke, to the practitioners of *Blitzkrieg* in the 20th century.[3] From this perspective, the evolution of warfare was linear and anchored in the experiences of West European armies. Other historians have disagreed with this line of development. They see fundamental differences in warfare as practiced by the "great captains" and what emerged as modern warfare in the late 19th century. These same authors have looked to the military experience outside of Western Europe that they argue has shaped a more complex evolutionary path in a way that includes more emphasis on crisis and solution than on a direct line of development.

Robert Epstein has attributed elements of operational art to the later campaigns of the Wars of Napoleon, pointing to features in the Franco-Austrian War of 1809 and thereafter. Epstein, the senior historian with the School of Advanced Military Studies of the U.S. Army, laid out such a thesis in his book, *Napoleon's Last Victory and the Emergence of Modern War*. He pointed to the scale of operations, innovations in command and control, and increased firepower of the contesting sides to perceive the emergence of mass war on the model of the American Civil War. The similarities of the opposing French and Austrian forces led their commanders in "distributed maneuvers" across two theaters of war producing broad operational fronts in which battles became both sequential and simultaneous, but ultimately indecisive.[4] The crisis of modern warfare that Epstein noted deepened in the course of the 19th century when mass armies gave way to mass industrial warfare.

This line of thought was developed by Epstein's colleague, James Schneider. While analyzing the development of the Soviet system for mass industrial war, he looked to the origins of modern war and operational art in the American Civil War, a topic studied by the Soviet theorists of operational art in the 1920s.[5] Here the emphasis was upon the impact of industrial production on the making of war.[6] "Vulcan's anvil" laid the foundations for modern total war through the conduct of operational art. The ties of both scholars to the School of Advanced Military Studies are not accidental, for both were part of the effort to introduce the study of the "operational level of war" to the U.S. Army in the 1980s in conjunction with the development of "AirLand Battle."[7]

Both Epstein and Schneider were correct in their examination of the origins of operational art and the connections between the crisis of the command and control of mass armies and the impact of mass industrialization, of fire and maneuver on the conduct of campaigns.[8] This crisis in its evolving stages was quite real and affected the application of military art for the next century. One line of military theory that was developed in Western Europe embraced Helmut Von Moltke's application of successive operations to rapid decision in short decisive warfare. Another line emerged out of the American Civil War and the transformation of that war from one shaped by visions of decisive battle into one of protracted attrition warfare throughout multiple theaters of war. Both these lines of development would finally lead to a crisis of maneuver under the domination of fire power in the stalemate of trench warfare in World War I. This interpretation fits completely with that developed by Soviet military theorists.[9] While both lines of thought embraced elements of operational art and the rejection of what Georgiy Isserson, a Red Army theorist and major contributor to the development of deep operations theory, would call "the strategy of a single point," neither gave birth to "operational art" as an explicit concept.[10] The German General Staff might focus upon operations on an extended line, but its strategic dilemma of war on two fronts pushed its thinking toward *Blitzkrieg* and the rapid annihilation of the opposing army. The American experience, while rich during the Civil War, in the absence of evident strategic threats and the slow professionalization of Army leadership, never became institutionalized through the systematic study of that experience as being the organization of successive operations into protracted campaigns and multiple campaigns into final victory.

THE AMERICAN PRISM ON OPERATIONAL ART

As Bruce Menning has suggested, the American military's interest in operational art was a direct consequence of the Cold War and the associated study of Russian and Soviet military history.[11] Here primary emphasis fell upon the three military concepts articulated in the 1920s: operational art, deep battle, and deep operations.[12] This understanding appears to be self-evident. American commanders, preparing to conduct the defense of Western Europe as part of the North Atlantic Treaty Organization (NATO), confronted in the Soviet and Warsaw Pact forces arrayed across the Iron Curtain, the heirs of the units and formations that had conducted operational maneuver in a series of campaigns leading to the defeat of the Wehrmacht and its allies, which began with the Stalingrad counteroffensive in November 1942, and continued to the Berlin operation in April-May 1945. In the course of those operations, the Red Army destroyed the great bulk of the Wehrmacht's land power.[13]

But the interest in operational art in the 1980s was new and reflected an intense debate over the role of conventional forces in a European general war. Strategic nuclear parity and modernized theater nuclear arsenals called into question the political-military context of war in Europe. Both Soviet and Western military thinkers had returned to the role of conventional forces in the initial period of a Warsaw Pact-NATO conflict and were seeking means to achieve military objectives that would lead to a successful political outcome without escalation into theater nuclear war and a general strategic nuclear exchange.[14] The objective was not enhanced warfighting capabilities to defeat the Warsaw Treaty Organization (WTO) but to extend the credibility of deterrence into the conventional phase of a future conflict in such a fashion as to reduce the risks of nuclear escalation. Distinguished British soldier and intellectual Sir John Hackett made such a conflict the topic of his novel, *The Third World War, August 1985*, which appeared in 1978 and was a thinly veiled call for NATO force modernization.[15]

In the context of these developments, the linage of operational art became an issue of some debate. Some authors saw the interest in operational art as based upon the theoretical innovations of Mikhail Tukhachevsky, the repressed but acknowledged father of deep operations, but also recognized its significant theoretical potential for conventional war under the conditions of nuclear-parity, and emerging concepts for non-linear conventional warfare between NATO and the WTO.[16] Other authors have pointed to the intellectual firmament of the Post-Vietnam era as the catalyst that brought the U.S. Army to embrace the "operational level of war" in 1982 and then "operational art" in 1986.[17] But the American interest was initially centered in one service, the U.S. Army, and within that army in the Training and Doctrine Command (TRADOC), the Combined Arms Command, and the Command and General Staff College.[18] For planning purposes, the U.S. Army accepted the existing Military Decision Making Process (MDMP), which had been developed for training staff officers in operational planning. The movement preceded but was influenced by the push for Jointness that developed as a result of Goldwater-Nicholas Act, which was intended to reduce the services' power and to strengthen the authority of the Secretary of Defense, the Chairman of the Joint Chiefs of Staff, and theater commanders.[19] The Army's interest in operational art came out of a focus on tactical dilemmas that had emerged during the Cold War but never took on a strategic cast. The U.S. Army War College maintained its focus on strategy in its many forms—National Security Strategy, National Defense Strategy, and National Military Strategy—while acknowledging the linkage between theater strategy and campaign planning that was the domain of the combatant commands charged with commanding U.S. military forces in various regions of the globe. Joint Doctrine defined operational art as: "the use of military forces to achieve strategic goals through the design, organization, integration, and conduct of strategies, campaigns, major operations, and battles."[20]

Goldwater-Nicholas refocused the institutional relations of those responsible for the formulation and implementation of strategy and gave Joint Doctrine a prominence it had not enjoyed before. It recast professional military education to take on a more joint flavor and contributed to the founding of a number of institutions that addressed the operational level of war or the operational art with the explicit task of making them masters of the Joint Operational Planning Process (JOPP).[21] Coming at the end of the Cold War and the disappearance of the foe, which had brought about the focus on operational art, this transition left operational art as something of an overripe fruit too long on the vine. In this new security environment and in the absence of threat, it appeared to be a concept without a rationale or intellectual platform. The U.S. Army's Center for Military History undertook the publication of a volume devoted to the history of operational art in the late 1980s, but with the end of the Cold War the volume's publication was delayed until 1994.[22] A second volume by Michael Krause and R. Cody Phillips on historical perspectives on operational art, which had its origins in the same period, did not appear until 2005.[23] In this volume, Operations DESERT SHIELD and DESERT STORM could be portrayed as the maturation of operational art, but ground maneuver represented the short and final stage of a conflict framed by a theater-strategic build-up and a protracted, independent air operation.[24] U.S.-led coalition forces defeated a supposedly Soviet-style army just as the Soviet Army was about to disappear with the collapse of the state that had given it birth.

GOING BEYOND OPERATIONAL ART

Taking a term from Soviet military writings, U.S. military analysts began to speak of an RMA that was radically reshaping warfare by means of automated command and control, precision strike systems, and the integration of "system-of-systems" and "network centric" approaches to future conflicts.[25] Erik Dahl even argued that network-centric warfare had invalidated most of the principles associated with operational art.[26] In the 1990s, the role of the air operation took on even greater importance as a means of conducting precision strikes throughout the depth of the enemy's defenses, making possible maneuver by precision strikes as an independent campaign unto itself. In this context, operational art, which was very much a landpower oriented concept, gave way to "Effects-Based Operations" conducted in accordance with a systems approach and by aviation and cruise missile strikes alone.[27] NATO's Operation ALLIED FORCE against Yugoslavia during the Kosovo campaign became the model for such an operation. Diplomacy and coercive force could be applied without the complications of introducing ground forces into the conflict.[28] The post-Cold War evolution of U.S. security policy towards collective security under NATO through peacekeeping peace enforcement, then towards counterterrorism, and finally toward counterinsurgency seemed to marginalize the place of operational art. These newer concepts, which once again conflated strategy and tactics into one rapid seamless operation, offered the promise of strategic annihilation without the need to engage in operational maneuver or face the prospects of conducting successive operations with pauses to regroup forces.

Critics claimed that NATO's "air operation" violated joint doctrine. In fact, Operation ALLIED FORCE was inconsistent with joint doctrine in both word and spirit. As early as 1991, *Joint Publication 1, Joint Warfare of the U.S. Armed Forces*, and subsequently *Joint Publication 3-0, Doctrine for Joint Operations*, applied the term joint campaign to every campaign, whether fought on land, at sea, or in the air.[29] While attributing the air operation to the political leadership and the influence of contemporary air power theorists, the critics ignored that the decision to go to war had been made under NATO auspices and had required considerable diplomatic bargaining to obtain the Alliance's approval. Therefore the resort to an exlcusive air operation represented a political decision at the highest level of the Alliance. This fact confirmed again that operational art in practice shaped considerably by political and strategic considerations.

Others saw the potential for an asymmetric response to such capabilities where "the distinction between war and peace will be blurred to the vanishing point."[30] Conflict would be nonlinear with no distinction between peace and war or between civilians and military. William Lind and his coauthors in their discussion of Fourth-Generation Warfare envisioned future conflicts where advanced technologies meet the asymmetric threat of terrorism and treat operational art as a historically conditioned construct that had passed its utility with the end of *Blitzkrieg* and irrelevant to the conduct of Fourth Generation Warfare.[31] Operation ENDURING FREEDOM against the Taliban in Afghanistan in this interpretation demonstrated what Special Forces combined with local insurgents and modern air power could achieve.[32] Under the banner of Transformation, then Secretary of Defense Donald Rumsfeld guided his CENTCOM commander's, General Tommy Franks, preparations for such a lightening campaign in Iraq. Fewer ground forces, great reliance upon "shock and awe," and the maximum imposition of effects upon the enemy's military forces to bring about their rapid and decisive defeat and the seizure of Baghdad. Initial studies of the war by leading military historians concentrated on the successful advance to Baghdad, and not its aftermath, and judged the military effort an outstanding success.[33] Later studies were much more critical and saw in the initial planning the seeds of the insurgency that emerged in the aftermath of the initial campaign. Tom Ricks, defense correspondent for the *Washington Post*, simply labeled the war a "fiasco."[34] The reemergence of insurgency in Afghanistan cast Operation ENDURING FREEDOM in a different light as well.

Brigadier General Huba Wass de Czege, U.S. Army (Ret.), has written about the intellectual milieu that gave birth to the School of Advanced Military Studies and to AirLand Battle Doctrine as one dominated by the reconsideration of Clausewitz and Jomini "to transform an abstract strategic idea of ends, ways, and means into appropriate and concrete tactical actions. This feat of conceptual acrobatics is operational art."[35] Wass De Czege, went on to note that "the old industrial age analogy derived conceptual aids are outdated and unhelpful because the standard of conceptual acrobatics demanded by 21st century missions is much higher."[36] He concluded that the doctrinal innovations of the 1990s, which were supposed to transform operational art to meet the demands of post-modern warfare, "undermine[d] critical and creative thinking and promote[d] conceptual rigidity and illogic."[37]

OPERATIONAL DESIGN, NOT OPERATIONAL ART

The protracted insurgencies which emerged in Iraq and Afghanistan did bring renewed interest in operational art, but the discussion became framed by the Global War on Terrorism (GWOT) and the "long war" against Islamic terrorism and insurgencies. In a series of annual war games known as Unified Quest, TRADOC sought to address the complexity of conflict that could evolve from regular warfare into insurgency and noted the need for discourse between the operational commander and his theater-strategic higher headquarters in the face of an adaptive enemy. In contrast to conventional operations which addressed structured technical problems, the emerging situation posed a wide range of complex and unstructured problems that were not amenable to technical solutions. This led to the exploration of systemic operational design (SOD) as developed by Shimon Naveh and his colleagues at the Operational Theory and Research Institute in Tel-Aviv, which made design a necessary precursor to operational planning when confronted by unstructured problems. This new emphasis on design arose out of the very different security problems facing Israel as a result of the Oslo peace process and the continuing threat of Palestinian terrorists. Naveh drew heavily on systems theory, complexity theory, and on post-modernism as found in French philosophy (by authors Gilles Deleuze and Felix Guattari), literary theory, and architecture. Naveh advocated an approach that would "liberate" practitioners from the dichotomy of theory and practice.[38] In his earlier major work on operational art, Naveh had highlighted Soviet operational art for special attention because it combined a systems approach with an emphasis upon shock and disruption in the conduct of deep operations. Naveh noted the Soviet design of combat formations (i.e., the tank army, forward detachment, and shock army) to execute deep operations and use of echelonment in the development of the attack to ensure shock in the execution of a deep operation.[39] The need for liberation from operational art in this context was the result of an adaptive opponent who no longer practiced mass industrial war but had adopted the instruments of insurgency and terrorism to conflict in the 21st century. SOD in this case was evolutionary in its admission of its tie to operational art, but also transcendent as a result of the evolution of military art under new social, political, and strategic circumstances.

As TRADOC Pamphlet 525-5-300 stated, the war game had revealed bias in traditional planning: "In contrast, American and Soviet operational planners traditionally perceived operational art in a much different context. Both typically address [sic] conventional contests between regular armies rather than the complexity of irregular warfare."[40] The result of these efforts was the publication in early 2008 of a new pamphlet, 525-5-500, *Commander's Appreciation and Campaign Design*.[41] The emphasis was upon the application of complexity theory to a systemic approach to the campaign design incorporating "a cognitive model intended for use by commanders charged with designing, planning, and executing military campaigns."[42] Design in this context was supposed to provide a means of dealing with complex or wicked problems which demanded a systems frame to understand the interactions of a self-organizing system and lead to the articulation of a problem frame by which to address key challenges before beginning conventional military planning. In short, design would give depth and character to a commander's guidance.

SYSTEMS THEORY AND SOVIET OPERATIONAL ART: PAST AS PROLOGUE

This very lively and productive debate would seem to have little relationship to the development of operational art in the Soviet Union. But that is not, in fact, the case. Milan Vego, a leading scholar on operational art, has called into question Naveh's interpretation of Soviet operational art, questioning its ties to general systems theory and its emphasis upon shock. Vego points out that the acknowledged "father" of general systems theory, Ludwig von Bertalanffy, an Austrian biologist, did not write about "general systems theory" and its application to open (i.e., biological) systems until decades after 1945; his work on General Systems Theory did not appear until 1968. He argues that the Soviet approach to the conduct of operations was systematic, but not systemic. Vego denies Naveh's claim that Soviet operational art had anything to do with systemic "shock" (*udar*) as that concept was always associated with destruction. "In Soviet military theory and practice disruption was always a means to *facilitate* destruction, not a substitute for it."[43] As this chapter will make clear, the theory of operational art was, in fact, far broader than this characterization. Soviet systems thinking emerged out of a murky confluence of Marxist ideas about the dialectic and organizational theory tied to philosophy and biological sciences.[44]

This seeming contradiction between two eminent scholars over the nature of Soviet operational art has its roots in Soviet political and military history. The development of operational art was a good deal more complex than presented in Western Cold War scholarship. In part, this is the result of the very nature of the Soviet system, where the Communist Party kept a very strict control over the writing of history and spent a good deal of time reshaping the narrative to fit current political and ideological requirements. Declared enemies of the state became nonpersons, and then after decades the Party could rehabilitate that nonperson, often posthumously, and their contribution to the construction of socialism reintegrated as part of a new Party narrative of the past. The struggle with "bourgeois falsifiers" of the history of the Great Patriotic War became a well-funded cottage industry. At the same time, military affairs were treated as an area where the demands of state security limited access even to published documents, not to speak of military archives. Secrecy (*sekretnost'*) extended even into the banal aspects of life—a sausage recipe at a meat processing plant could be a matter of state secrecy, and God protect any naïve foreigner who took a photograph of a man in uniform, a bridge, or a factory. The organs of state security under their various names from the Cheka to the KGB took up the role of protecting state secrets throughout Soviet society. All of this is described in detail by Vladmir Shlapentokh in his book, *A Normal Totalitarian Society*.[45]

To untangle the riddles (*zagadki*) of Russian and Soviet military history which affected Western understanding of the origins and development of operational art (*operativnoe izkusstv*), one must come to grips with the forces that shaped its narrative from late imperial Russian to the end of the Soviet Union.[46] Yuri M. Lotman, the eminent culturalist, has written extensively on the problem of language, semiotics, and history. Addressing intelligence from a semiotic perspective, Lotman reduces it to three functions:

1. the transmission of available information (of texts);

2. the creation of new information (of texts which are not simply deducible according to set algorithms from already existing information, but which are to some degree unpredictable); and,

3. memory (the capacity to preserve and reproduce information as texts).[47]

Lotman addresses the development of semiotics as a discipline and the relationship between semiotics and structuralism. He notes that both have over the last few decades "lived through testing times" in the Union of Soviet Socialist Republics (USSR) and the West. Here he points to a particular difference relevant to our problem. In the Soviet Union, semiotics and structuralism had to confront persecutions and ideological attacks followed by "a conspiracy of silence or embarrassed semi-recognition." In the West, semiotics and structuralism had to withstand the test of fashion in which they became a craze and were taken beyond the limits of science.[48]

In semiotic terms, we have addressed the Western proclivity for making a concept into a fad and the reaction against it in the history of operational art from the 1980s to the present. This chapter will now try to address the opaque world of "persecutions and ideological attacks" that were part of the mystery of operational art in the Soviet Union. Our primary problem will be the semiotic field of memory, or the writing of history. Much will depend on the availability of texts and the narratives created to explain them. It is a bloody tale, which might be expected in military history, but here it involves the attempt to exterminate or transform ideas by eliminating their authors physically and in history.

"Operational art" as a recognized term in discussions of military art emerged out of the caldron of war and revolution that engulfed tsarist Russia and gave birth to Bolshevik Russia. A society torn apart by war came into the hands of a revolutionary party intent on telescoping a world war into the world revolution. This existential gamble by Lenin and Trotsky stood Marxism on its head. That gamble failed when Germany did not become the vanguard of the world revolution. Instead, the Bolsheviks found themselves operating in a society torn asunder by class and ethnic conflict and surrounded by hostile states. War and preparations for war became a prominent feature of the state that emerged during the civil war and foreign intervention and throughout the rest of Soviet history.

To survive, the regime adapted extreme measures until they became an ingrained part of the edifice itself.

Consumed by fears of encirclement and conscious of its own backwardness, the regime offered the world two contradictory images: the agent of human progress for abolition of want and alienation, and the secret police state which used terror to construct a utopia and employed every means available to conceal every contradiction and its own backwardness. Under Lenin, the regime was willing to embrace the use of specialists (*spetsy*) in the economy, professions, and military as necessary.[49] The advocate of the leading role of the party of professional revolutionaries, who read and reinterpreted Clausewitz to serve the cause of world revolution, was willing to embrace *spetsy*, the products of the old regime and members of the "bourgeois intelligentsia" to make War Communism work. The author of the utopian *State and Revolution*, with its withering away of the state, could pragmatically embrace the use of bourgeois specialists to keep the Bolshevik regime in power, even as he distrusted them as class enemies.

Critics of Bolshevism were quick to note the risk that Lenin's "party of professional revolutionaries" would turn into the authoritarian ruling class—reigning over a weak and poorly developed proletariat and a backward peasantry. One answer to this dilemma was the creation of a proletarian culture outside the Party's control. One of the chief theorists of this position was A. A. Bogdanov. A Social Democrat, science-fiction writer, and early Bolshevik, Bogdanov abandoned politics to devote his efforts to the study of philosophy in the forms of empiromonism and tectology (*tektologiia*) or "the universal science of organization." For his studies on the former topic, he became the object of Lenin's attack as an ideological enemy of dialectical materialism.[50] Both topics related to knowledge of knowledge itself, which Bogdanov saw as properly concerned with the examination of forms of knowledge as to their genesis, evolution, and existential importance. A given social milieu conditions a particular worldview or ideology, which might evolve in response to the emergence of a new social milieu or regress and become conservative as the social milieu that engendered it decayed.[51]

Bogdanov refused to join the Bolshevik regime after it seized power, even when his brother-in-law, Anatoly Vasil'evich Lunacharsky, then serving as the newly appointed Commissar of Enlightenment (NARKOMPROS) for Lenin's regime, invited him. Bogdanov and Lunacharsky had worked closely together in an effort to create a proletarian culture among Russian workers. But Bodganov refused the offer on the basis of the social content of War Communism—which he viewed as replacing the social milieu of the factory with that of the barracks—and repeated his warning of the danger of party replacing class and the imposition of authoritarian control in the place of culturally-derived consciousness.[52]

Bogdanov's criticism of the regime at this stage did not preclude him from leading the *Proletkult* movement or from serving as President of the Academy of Social Sciences. His ideas on the science of organization had a following within the Scientific Organization of Labor (*Nachnaia organizatsiia truda*) Movement, which carried scientific management into the Red Army. In his analysis of the situation confronting Bolshevik Russia at the end of the Civil War, Bogdanov adopted a new terminology in referring to the existing class structure and place of the *spetsy* now engaged in managing state economic and military institutions. His term was "Organizer Intelligentsia" (*organizatorskaia intelligentsia*), in which he included state bureaucratic, technical, and social group—a class without class consciousness or organization; "*an sich*" (in itself) but not "*fuer sich*" (for itself). Bogdanov referred to World War I as a "war of exhaustion between competing blocs" of monopoly capitalists, and he warned of the tendency of the emergence of "military-state capitalism" in confrontation with "a besieged communism." In such a contest, the danger was that the organizer intelligentsia could emerge as a class, conscious of its own power and practicing a new militarism in both the military state capitalist system and in the besieged communist system.[53] That fear, as we shall see, was not confined to Bogdanov but infected much of the Soviet elite, including Joseph Stalin.

In the immediate context of civil war, Bogdanov's warnings went unappreciated, and he abandoned *Proletkult*, when his presence led to accusation of anti-Leninist agitation and ideological sabotage. In his last years, he focused his efforts on leading the Institute for Blood Transfusions, laid the foundation for a system of blood banks across the USSR, and died as a consequence of one of his own transfusion experiments in 1928. Bogdanov, under Stalinism, became just Lenin's foil and an ideological caricature. His publications were confined to "special" (i.e., closed) collections. Yet, as one recent author has pointed out: "His mature system, set forth in *Tectology: The Universal Science of Organization,* anticipated many of the ideas of later systems theory and cybernetics, and played an important role in the development of systems thinking in the Soviet Union."[54] Bogdanov's appreciation of the early Soviet regime provides us with a look at the social milieu that gave birth to operational art as a theoretical construct of military art.

There were roughly six periods of Soviet military historiography:

1. the early years of Soviet power from the revolution through the civil war to the New Economic Policy (NEP), when open debate in professional military periodicals was tolerated and even encouraged (1917-28);

2. Stalinism during the consolidation of absolute control from the First Five Year Plan and Collectivization through the Great Terror to the pre-war period (1929-41);

3. the Great Patriotic War and Stalinism triumphant (1941-53);

4. the "thaw" and Nikita Khrushchev's de-Stalinization (1953-64);

5. mature socialism and the cult of Brezhnev to the interregnum (1964-85); and,

6. perestroyka, glasnost, and the end of the Cold War and the final crisis of the Soviet system.

Western studies of the Soviet military thrived during two of these periods: that of Khrushchev's de-Stalinization and that of Mikhail Gorbachev's perestroyka. Following the collapse of the Soviet Union, Boris Yeltsin's Russia became an especially hospitable environment for such historical studies. General Dmitri Volkogonov, former Deputy Chief of the Soviet Army's Main Political Administration and then a Yeltsin confidant and historian of Stalinism, supported greater access to military archives for Russian and foreign scholars.[55] The last decade under Vladimir Putin has seen a return to a more authoritarian and closed environment, though not a totalitarian one. Access for individual historians depends on connections in high places and the regime's attitude toward the topic under consideration.[56]

These circumstances have had a particular impact on the study of the history of Soviet operational art in the West. In the post-war era, Cold War antagonism and the absurd claims associated with the cult of Stalin undermined any credibility for Soviet studies of the war. Stalin, the authoritative voice on all matters, spoke of the "five permanently operating factors" — the stability of the rear, the morale of the army, the quantity and quality of divisions, the armament of the army, and the organizing ability of the command personnel — to explain Soviet victory and cast into the shadows the initial defeats of the Red Army.[57] Moreover, the dominance of the cult of Stalin in any discussion of war in any open source was anchored in banality and devoid of critical enquiry. The mania for secrecy made senior professional discussions in journals like *Voennaia mysl'* (*Military Thought*) and *Morskoi Sbornik* (*Naval Digest*) inaccessible except to a narrow circle of Western scholars and analysts.[58] Raymond L. Garthoff was the first scholar to make significant use of Soviet materials to study the Soviet way of war in the early 1950s, but his approach remained the exception and not the rule.[59] In the absence of a credible interpretation of the war on the Eastern Front, Western scholars gave increasing credibility to German accounts of the war.[60] Captured German archival materials were available in the National Archives and a flow of memoirs and studies from former German generals appeared. Soviet victory in such accounts had three sources: the insanity of Corporal Adolph Hitler, General Winter, and Russia's peasant masses.[61] Writing in the mid-1980s, Colonel David Glantz drew much the same conclusions regarding how "[t]he dominant role of German source materials in shaping American perceptions of the war on the Eastern Front and the negative perception of Soviet source materials have had an indelible impact on the American image of war on the Eastern Front."[62]

The evaluation of Soviet materials on the history of the Red Army and the Great Patriotic War began to change slowly after 1956 and the beginning of Khrushchev's de-Stalinization process. As Khrushchev's "Secret Speech" to the Twentieth Party Congress made clear, Stalin's military leadership was a topic open to criticism. Khrushchev blamed Stalin for the Soviet Union's defeats in the initial period of war, accused him of panic in the face of the initial assault, and noted the impact that Stalin's pre-war purges had on military leadership.[63] Hand-in-hand with de-Stalinization went a "thaw" in the system, which included the rehabilitation of certain purged personalities, including military leaders and theorists, who had become class enemies and wreckers under Stalin.

Attention to operational art as a distinct topic in the Western study of the Soviet military system began with John Erickson. He traveled to the USSR, made use of libraries, talked with veterans and scholars, and got access to newly opened materials whose authors had been repressed under Stalin. In his wide-ranging study of the Soviet High Command, Erickson was the first Western scholar to draw attention to an area of military art between strategy and tactics. Erickson called it "operating art" and defined the term on the basis of the *Great Soviet Encyclopedia* and upon Garthoff's comment regarding General A. A. Svechin's use of the term to link tactics and strategy and that "operating art . . . grew out of an idea developed by the tsarist army." However, Erickson's discussion related specifically to the role of the "operating art" on setting "the essential line of its [tactics'] work."[64] Erickson's definition, however, does not discuss the relationship between strategy and operational art, which was the critical focus of Svechin's treatment of the term. But Svechin was not a figure of primary interest to Erickson, who was addressing Soviet preoccupation with war in the late 1920s. Erickson conflated the operating art into a discussion of only one particular form of operations, the deep operation with mass mechanized forces. Erickson's primary lens for looking at Soviet interwar military affairs was the freshly opened materials relating to Marshal Mikhail Tukhachevsky. Former Guard's officer in the tsarist army, escaped prisoner of war, Bolshevik hero of the Civil War, the father of "deep battle," and the champion of mechanization, tactical aviation, and the airborne forces, Tukhachevsky and the young Red Commanders repressed with him became, in the early 1960s, the alternative explanation for Soviet military successes in the later stages of the Great Patriotic War. Their genius provided the ideas that the Party might use to rebuild in the aftermath of Stalin's disasters. In the two-volume collection of Tukhachevsky's essays published in 1964, Marshal S. Biriuzov wrote of Tukhchevsky: "It can be said without exaggeration that M. N. Tukhachevsky, in accordance with his multifaceted activities, was one of the brightest and most progressive leaders of our army and did much for the development of Soviet military theory and the structure of our Armed Forces."[65]

Tukhachevsky had exactly the right credentials for the anti-Stalinist campaign. He was a Red Commander from the Civil War who had taken seriously the Party's guiding role and the place of ideological orthodoxy in shaping the Red Army. His credentials as a Party member and defender of Bolshevism extended to his role in the suppression of the Kronstadt naval mutiny and the anti-partisan operations he conducted during the Tambov peasant revolt.[66] He was also an avowed enemy of *voenspetsy* (military specialists) as incompetents who could not fight "class warfare" or as wreckers seeking to undermine Soviet power from within.[67] He was also the avowed champion of strategic annihilation as the point of departure for the development of the Soviet military mobilization society and for the actual conduct of warfare. Appointed Chief of Staff of the Red Army by Mikhail Frunze, Tukhachevsky was the model of the young Red commander created by the Civil War. His vision was one of mass industrial war conducted by mechanized forces created by the Stalinist/Bolshevik transformation of Soviet society. His contributions were profound and spoke to the nexus among war plans, mobilization requests, and investment strategy within Soviet economic plans.[68] Here was a victim of Stalin's terror who could posthumously continue his service to the Soviet system.

There was, of course, the ambiguous legacy of his campaign against the Poles in 1920. In that campaign, his objective had been not just the defeat of the Polish Pans but the overthrow of the Versailles system and the ignition of the world revolution in Germany. In the single largest and most ambitious offensive of the Bolshevik regime down to the Great Patriotic War, Tukhachevsky had routed the Poles in Belorussia and pursued them to the banks of the Vistula. At Warsaw, the Polish Army rallied and with Allied assistance smashed into the flank of Tukhachevsky's overextended forces, driving units into East Prussia, and defeating the Red Army. A compromise peace with Poland ensured that Poland would be considered a major threat to the Soviet Union and a further basis for clandestine cooperation between the Reichswehr of Weimar Germany and the Soviet Union. That defeat became one of the most important topics of study for the Red Army in the 1920s, with Tukhachevsky himself contributing to the critique.[69] Who was responsible for the defeat on the Vistula was a topic of keen debate in the Red Army. Tukhachevsky pointed to the role of the First Cavalry Army under Semeon Budenny in the defeat. In August 1920, the Revolutionary Military Council had resubordinated First Cavalry Army from Southwestern Front to the Western Front in support of Tukhavchevsky's advance into Poland, where its shock was supposed to draw Polish forces towards the threat to Lublin. Instead, the First Cavalry Army had ended up in heavy fighting around Lvov and not advancing on Lublin as Tukhachevsky had ordered, and thereby removed the maneuver threat to the Polish defenses along the Vistula. In this case, the issue became part of the debate over the Polish campaign and created some long-term tensions between Tukhachevsky and the three leaders of the First Cavalry Army—Budenny, Klimenty Voroshilov, and Stalin.[70]

Joining Tukhachesky in this narrative of Soviet interwar military development was another Red Commander from the Russian Civil War, leader of the Red Army during the early NEP, and the primary theorist of Soviet military doctrine, Mikhail Frunze. Frunze could claim to be an "old Bolshevik"—i.e., one of those who joined Lenin's Bolshevik Party at its very founding in 1903. During the Civil War, he had led Bolshevik forces in Turkestan and then defeated

Baron Wrangel's forces in the Crimea to effectively end the Civil War. Frunze contributed to the emerging de-Stalinized version of the Soviet military past. Through him, the discussion of Soviet military doctrine could be linked from the era of Lenin down to the present. Preparations for "a long, persistent war to the death" with the encircling capitalist powers could thus have a non-Stalinist voice.[71] Like Tukhachevsky, he could also be treated as a victim of Stalin through his death while undergoing surgery in October 1925.[72] The most important point was to assert the centrality of the revolutionary origins of the Red Army, its class origins and the negation of any ties between the tsarist army, which had fought national wars in the interests of the ruling class as embodied in autocracy and the Red Army of Workers and Peasants.[73] In this fashion, it was quite possible for Western scholarship to depict Soviet military thought as self-generated and even to claim that Frunze was the "Red Clausewitz."[74]

In this narrative, Stalin's purges of the military in the late 1930s were depicted as one of the primary causes of Soviet military incapacity before and during the initial period of war with Nazi Germany. The Winter War with Finland was a disaster. Soviet advances into Poland and Romania had exposed many operational problems, and German successes in Poland and the Battle of France had demonstrated the correctness of Tukhachevsky's vision of a large mechanized formations capable of conducting deep operations. Changes were underway when the Germans unleashed Barbarossa, and the initial Soviet failures could be put directly at Stalin's door.[75]

After the fall of Khrushchev and the consolidation of mature socialism under Leonid Brezhnev, the Party line on the Great Patriotic War became notably less anti-Stalinist and more willing to depict Stalin as the architect of victory. The first indicator of this change came in 1967, when Alexander Nekrich's critical volume on Soviet unpreparedness for Hitler's invasion was subjected to ideological attack as being unpatriotic and anti-Soviet and the book was taken out of circulation.[76] True, Brezhnev did create his own curious "cult" around the fighting at Malaia Zemlia in which he had taken part as a *politruk* (political officer). In the forward to the third edition of Marshal Georgiy Zhukov's memoirs, Marshal A. M. Vasilevsky, Zhukov's close collaborator and wartime Chief of the Soviet General Staff, had pointed out that Marshal Zhukov's views on the role of the Central Committee of the Communist Party of the Soviet Union (CPSU) as "that staff from which came the highest political and military direction of military actions."[77] This turn of events did not undo the criticism of Stalin, but made it much less sharp and radically reduced its explanatory role. This did not affect the presentation of operational art as being expressed in the form of multifront, mechanized operations but that was now conducted under the threat of the probable use of nuclear weapons. Soviet military studies focused upon the role of operational art in "the initial period war," which in its Cold War context meant NATO versus the WTO.[78]

It is in this context that John Erickson made his fundamental contribution to Western understanding of Soviet strategy and operational art in his two-volume history of the war on the Eastern Front, the subtitle of which was *Stalin's War with Germany*. His first volume, *The Road to Stalingrad*, appeared in 1975. The second volume, *The Road to Berlin*, appeared in 1983. Both volumes received extensive praise in professional journals for their scholarship and sweep. In these volumes, Erickson focused on Soviet strategy and operational art. The two volumes were reprinted by Yale University Press 1999 and were described "as the most comprehensive and authoritative study ever written of the Soviet-German war."[79] The only complaint about the volumes was the lack of good operational maps to follow the flow of the campaigns across the Soviet Union and Eastern Europe.

At this time Western analysts and soldiers took on the task of understanding their Soviet opposites as something more than a grey mass of men and equipment and began a deeper study of Soviet military art and operational art. Driving this new look were objective circumstances. Nuclear parity which was achieved by the USSR under Brezhnev demanded a new look at the content of NATO's strategy of "flexible response." At the same time, the initial success of Egyptian arms in crossing the Suez Canal and disrupting the Israeli defense plan in 1973 brought new attention to the role of conventional forces in the initial period of a NATO-WTO war in Europe. Soviet theater-nuclear modernization and the deployment of the SS-20 intermediate range ballistic missile (IRBM) demanded further adaptation of the role of conventional forces in NATO defense. A window for maneuver warfare under the threat of nuclear escalation appeared. Ironically, the first successes in looking at Soviet military sources as a means of reappraising the Soviet military threat came not from land power but among naval specialists.

The study of Soviet sources, which both Garthoff and Erickson had championed, became a broadly accepted approach among Western scholars in the late 1960s and early 1970s. Robert Herrick broke ground for such studies with his analysis of Soviet naval strategy. While not focusing on operational art and far removed from the threat posed by the Red Army in Central Europe, Herrick's study stimulated a major exploitation of Soviet sources by a wide circle of analysts and scholars.[80] These discussions played a positive role in reframing the U.S. Navy's appreciation of Soviet naval power and contributed to the emerging maritime strategy of the 1980s.[81] David Jones of Dalhousie University carried this line of inquiry into Soviet military history and affairs by founding an annual publication "designed to assemble and organize in a standard format all basic relevant information on Soviet military affairs, together with analytical topical discussions, documentation, and bibliography."[82]

In this timeframe, professional military interest in operational art emerged in the U.S. Army and in other NATO armies, and led to deeper consideration of what the Soviet military meant by *operativenoe iskusstvo* (operational art). The context was one of strategic nuclear parity, escalating theater nuclear arsenals, and concern about the conventional offensive of Soviet forces in the aftermath of the initial successes of Egyptian forces against the Israeli defenses along the Suez Canal during the Yom Kippur War of 1973. This process began with the debates surrounding TRADOC's publication of *Field Manual (FM) 100-5, Operations*, in 1976 and continued into the 1980s and the end of the Cold War.[83] Peter Vigor framed the challenge in the classical language of "maneuver war" and *Blitzkrieg*. He took his model of a Soviet theater offensive from the Soviet operations in August 1945 against the Japanese Kwantung Army.[84] Colonel Glantz, who was then only beginning his career as one of the chief Western students of Soviet military history, used the term "operational art" to describe the conduct of theater-strategic operations by the Soviet Armed Forces.[85] In this context, Glantz linked together Svechin's definition of operational art and Tukhachevsky's concept of deep operations in his discussion. What was not yet apparent is how these concepts were linked and from where Svechin had developed his initial concept of operational art. To these two questions would be added still a third: How had Svechin become relevant after so many years of neglect, and how was his "intellectual rehabilitation" related to changes in Soviet defense policy under perestroika and glasnost?[86] David Glantz's contribution to our understanding of the linkage between Soviet strategy and operational art has been profound because he has effectively deconstructed the dominant Soviet narrative of the history of Red Army operations on the Eastern Front by calling attention to the "forgotten operations," which the Soviet narrative treated as "blank pages." His work on the Rzhev operation of November 1943, was an important contribution to this work.[87]

What was reemerging was the necessity for reflection (*razmyshlenie*) upon strategic choices based on an assessment of the probable war confronting the state and the economic means available to prepare for and conduct such a war. This had been the area of competence of the General Staff. But the General Staff was subordinated to the Ministry of Defense. Its opposition to the deployment of limited forces to Afghanistan in 1979 had been ignored. Now events were posing a profound challenge to the dominant concept regarding the desirability and even necessity of seizing the strategic initiative and mounting offensive operations in the initial period of war. In his discussion of Soviet strategic command and control (*upravlenie*) in the post-war period, Andrei Kokoshin calls attention to the ossification of the system of command and control under the leadership of a Ministry of Defense, charged with managing all functions connected with the raising and training of operational formations. In this context, the General Staff lost its function as "the brain of the army." The conflict between the defense manager, Marshal Dmitri Ustinov, and the Chief of the General Staff, Marshal Nikolai Ogarkov, who was positing an RMA that would demand a profound transformation of the Soviet military because of the appearance of new weapon systems based on automated command and control, electronic warfare, and "weapons based on new physical principles," which was reshaping conventional warfare. In the struggle between Ustinov and Ogarkov, the former won because of his membership in the Politburo, and Ogarkov was removed as Chief of the General Staff.[88] Explicit to this reflection was the hegemony of strategy over operational art and recognition of operational art as something more than preparing for the conduct of offensive operations in the initial period of war. At this time, Soviet analysts, including those in the Main Intelligence Directorate (GRU), were engaged in the assessment of the implications of a profound shift in the articulated U.S. strategy. The Reagan administration had begun to speak of an "early victory in a protracted conventional war," which some believed was radically reshaping the U.S. mobilization concept in case of war. The production and availability of precision-strike weapons were raising the possibility of mass fires of such weapons destroying forward-deployed conventional forces to disrupt operations in the initial period of war. The United States was moving away from the mass production of conventional weapon systems, (i.e., tanks) and toward the mass production of precision-strike systems. The implications for the conduct of conventional operational maneuver were profound. The shift called into question the mobilization for mass industrial war, which the Soviet Union had built in the 1930s, perfected during the Great Patriotic War, and sustained throughout the Cold War, even when nuclear weapons had become the core of both nation's strategic postures. As Western military thought returned to the role of conventional forces in the initial period of war, the Soviet Union faced a crisis regarding the very foundation of its conceptualization of operational art.[89]

As part of that debate, General-Major V. V. Larionov and A. A. Kokoshin championed a doctrine of sufficient defense, using the Battle of Kursk to support the possibility of an asymmetric response to the threat of an opponent's offensive operations. At Kursk, the Soviet Stavka had made a conscious choice to stand on the defense to meet and defeat the German summer offensive against the Kursk bulge in order to drain German mechanized forces and to set conditions for a Soviet offensive towards Belgorod-Kharkov, as well as create conditions for the liberation of the Ukraine to the Dnieper River.[90] Kursk was the last major Soviet counteroffensive where Soviet forces first blunted a German offensive and then mounted their own offensive — the other two instances were the Battle of Moscow of December 1941 at the end of the German fall offensive to seize the Soviet capital, and the Stalingrad counteroffensive at the end of the German summer offensive to cut Soviet communications in the south and seize the resources in the Caucasus. In both these cases, the counteroffensive was imposed upon Soviet forces by the success of Wehrmacht offensive operations and arose only when those forces continued their advance after operational culmination. In the Battle of Kursk, the Soviets had adopted an operational plan accepting a premeditated defense based upon the deep echelonment of the defense.[91] The political context of the proposal put forward by Larionov and Kokoshin was one of political-military disengagement between NATO and the WTO under a strategy of demilitarizing the Cold War and robbing the United States of an enemy. Within the Soviet Union, glasnost was making possible the addressing of the "blank pages" of Soviet history in a more systemic fashion.

The full appreciation of this change of intellectual climate is hard to overestimate. It produced opportunities for much deeper studies of Soviet military history, theory, and art. Deeper studies of the Russian imperial army provided greater linkages between its history and that of the Red Army of Workers and Peasants. With regard to operational art, Bruce Menning provided a detailed picture of the evolution of the tsarist army from the aftermath of defeat in the Crimean War to the aftermath of defeat in the Russo-Japanese War, and set the stage for what Russian General Staff officers called the problem of "modern war."[92] At the same time, Glantz began an in-depth study of Soviet operations in the Great Patriotic War at the Combat Studies Institute of the U.S. Army Command and General Staff College, including work on Soviet airborne forces and the Soviet offensive against Japan in August 1945.[93] He continued this work through a series of symposiums on various operations at the U.S. Army War College and later under the sponsorship of the Soviet Army Studies Office.[94] These efforts also led to the founding of the *Journal of Soviet Military Studies*, now the *Journal of Slavic Military Studies*, which he continues to edit. Soviet operational art has been and remains a major theme for its articles. Glantz went on to be one of the most prolific authors on Soviet operations in the Great Patriotic War and provided support and encourage to a younger generation of scholars in the West and in Russia to study such operations.[95] Both Menning and Glantz were among the founders of the Soviet Army Studies Office (SASO), which was created in 1986 on the order of General William Richardson, the Commander of TRADOC. Its mandate was to engage in open-source analysis of the Soviet military on the model of the Soviet Studies Research Center (SSRC) at Camberley, England, which performed the same function for the British Army's Battle Command Doctrine.[96] The Director of SSRC, Christopher Donnelly, published an important study of the Red Army.[97] Both SASO and SSRC collaborated in the exploitation of Russian publications and even in gaining access to Russian military archives during perestroika. As an historian, the author of this chapter was particularly interested in the origins of operational art and began to explore the linkages between tsarist military experience and the development of the concept of operational art.[98] At the same time, the author was also drawn toward the study of military foresight and forecasting in the Soviet Union, a topic he has continued to address down to the present essay.

OPERATIONAL ART, MILITARY SYSTEMOLOGY, AND FUTURE WAR

It is precisely in this area where what General Makhmut Gareyev has called the labor of Sisyphus has been richly conditioned by systems theory and military systemology for almost 3 decades. Systems theory emerged as a major part of Soviet military science in association with the military technical RMA associated with the advent of long-range ballistic missiles and nuclear weapons in the 1950s. General-Major V. K. Kopytko, the former deputy chief of the Chair of Operational Art at the Academy of the General Staff, has treated the entire period from 1954 to 1985, as a single whole dominated by the appearance of nuclear weapons and ballistic missiles. These weapons became the primary means for the destruction of the enemy, but their use was increasingly seen as catastrophic and operationally counterproductive. Colonel-General Adrian Danilevich, who was a senior special assistant to the Chief of the Operations Directorate of the General Staff in the 1970s and early 1980s, speaks of this period in slightly different terms, and refers to 1950-60 as the period of the acquisition of nuclear weapons, which was followed by the era of "nuclear euphoria" from 1960-65.[99] By the late 1950s, under the leadership of Khrushchev, the Soviet Union embarked upon the Military-Technical Revolution in which nuclear weapons and ballistic missiles were seen as the new definition of national power. Since the Soviet Union was undergoing a demographic crisis because of the low birth rate during the war, this revolution was supposed to provide security while the number of ground, air, and naval forces were reduced. The strategic concept for such a military posture was laid out in the three editions of Marshal V. D. Sokolovsky's *Military Strategy* between 1962 and 1968 and focused upon nuclear warfighting as the dominant characteristic of modern war.[100]

The euphoria was followed by what Danilevich called a "descent to earth" after the ouster of Khrushchev and a growing realism on the limited utility of nuclear weapons, which lasted from 1965 to 1975. It was during this period that the General Staff began to consider a first conventional phase to a NATO-WTO war. Originally thought of as a matter of a few hours, by the end of the period it was considered possible that the conventional period could last as long as 6-7 days.[101] Operational art during this period made its reappearance as a relevant part of military art during the initial period of war. However, it was still nuclear-armed missile forces that fundamentally shaped the nature of future war and expanded the effects that could be achieved. The deployment of forces under the conditions of the possible employment of nuclear weapons demanded greater mobility and protective systems against radiation for armor combat systems. The forces developed for this operational environment were designed to conduct operations for which there was no practical experience. Troops could exercise the doctrine and operations research professionals might find ways to simulate the conduct of operations, but the actual impact of nuclear weapons on the conduct of operations simply lacked any empirical test to evaluate theory and correct doctrine. Modeling a NATO-WTO conflict that included the prospective linkage of conventional, theater-nuclear, and strategic forces posed a profoundly difficult problem.

Soviet military specialists, led by Colonel-General Andrian Danilevich, Senior Special Assistant to the Chief of the Operations Directorate of the Soviet General Staff, began to examine the possibility of an extended conventional phase of a NATO-WTO war.[102] This was undertaken in the context of strategic nuclear parity and modernized theater nuclear arsenals, particularly the solid-fuel SS-20 IRBM. In the early 1970s, the General Staff assumed that nuclear first-use by NATO might occur at first at the main defensive line in Germany, and that NATO would always use nuclear weapons to defend the Rhine barrier.[103] When Marshal Nikolai Ogarkov became Chief of the General Staff in 1977, the conventional phase of NATO-WTO conflict was expected to last 5-6 days. By 1979, the General Staff had concluded that the conventional phase of the strategic operation could extend into France. And by 1980-81, the General Staff's expectations were for the entire NATO-WTO war to remain conventional. The logic of this conclusion was based on the assumption that by 1981, nuclear use would be catastrophic and operationally counterproductive.[104] The Soviet General Staff concluded that a theater-strategic offensive based upon a modernized concept of deep operations could be effective in case of a NATO-WTO war. This option did not exclude theater nuclear use, but assumed NATO would initiate such use. The model of the conventional operation was the Manchurian Strategic Offensive, but it assumed a NATO attack and an immediate WTO counteroffensive, which would seek to encircle and annihilate large portions of NATO forces and advance to the Rhine, a crossing of which the General Staff assumed would trigger NATO tactical nuclear use.[105]

From 1979 forward, the General Staff also began to examine the possibility of escalation control after nuclear use and addressed the idea of intrawar termination of nuclear use. To be decisive, the Soviet conventional strategic operation depended upon quantitative advantages in men and material. As Danilevich admitted, "the Soviets did not win the Great Patriotic War because Soviet generalship and fighting skills were superior to those of the Germans. The Soviet Armed Forces simply overwhelmed the Germans with superior numbers of airplanes, men, tanks, and artillery."[106] In a general conventional offensive, Soviet forces might commit 40,000 tanks in multiple echelons and at the end of the war have only 5,000 left.

By the early 1980s, the GRU was aware of qualitative improvements in U.S. theater-nuclear forces (ground launched cruise missiles [GLCMs] and Pershing IIs) and emerging enhanced conventional capabilities associated with better command and control and precision strike, by which the United States was seeking to counter Soviet quantity with qualitatively superior conventional weapons systems. What was reemerging was the necessity for reflection (*razmyshlenie*) upon strategic choices based on an assessment of the probable war confronting the state and the economic means available to prepare for and conduct such a war. Marshal Ogarkov took seriously the role of the General Staff as the brain of the army with an unblinking eye on the future evolution of warfare. He began to call attention to an emerging RMA that was affecting conventional forces through automated command and control, informatization, precision, and weapons based on new physical principles.[107] He championed the professionalization of the military, greater control by the General Staff over weapons development, and force structure changes, including the abolition of National Air Defense Forces (*PVO Strany*).

To counter NATO's emerging theater nuclear and conventional capabilities, Ogarkov embraced a new organizational concept, which Gareyev had proposed: the Operational Maneuver Group as a countermeasure to NATO's emerging capabilities. High maneuverability of specially designed brigades would permit penetration and raiding on an operational scale and would make enemy counterstrikes more difficult.[108]

These trends posed a profound challenge to the dominant concept regarding the desirability and even necessity of seizing the strategic initiative and mounting offensive operations in the initial period of war. In his discussion of Soviet strategic command and control (*upravlenie*) in the postwar period, Andrei Kokoshin has called attention to the ossification of the system of command and control under the leadership of a Ministry of Defense charged with managing all functions connected with the raising and training of operational formations. In this context, the General Staff lost its function as the brain of the army. The conflict between the defense manager Marshal Dmitri Ustinov and the Chief of the General Staff, Marshal Nikolai Ogarkov, who was positing an RMA that would demand a profound transformation of the Soviet military because of the appearance of new weapon systems based on automated command and control, electronic warfare, and weapons based on new physical principles, which was reshaping conventional warfare. In the struggle between Ustinov and Ogarkov, the former won because of his membership in the Politburo, and Ogarkov was removed as Chief of the General Staff.[109] Shortly thereafter, Ustinov died.

Explicit to this reflection was the hegemony of strategy over operational art and recognition of operational art as something more than preparing for the conduct of offensive operations in the initial period of war. At this time, Soviet analysts, including those in the Main Intelligence Directorate of the GRU, were engaged in the assessment of the implications of a profound shift in the articulated U.S. strategy. The Reagan administration had begun to speak of an "early victory in a protracted conventional war,"[110] which some believed was radically reshaping the U.S. mobilization concept in case of war. As noted above, these trends called into question the basis upon which Soviet theory and operations had rested, specifically with regard to the importance of forward deployed masses of forces rather than of masses of precision-strike weapons.

As Western military thought returned to the role of conventional forces in the initial period of war, the Soviet Union faced a crisis to the very foundation of its conceptualization of operational art.[111] The new ideas championed by Larionov and Kokoshin described above reflected a fundamental reconceptualization of the strategic environment in which the Soviet military would henceforth operate. The political context of the proposal put forward by Larionov and Kokoshin was one of political-military disengagement between NATO and the WTO under a strategy of demilitarizing the Cold War and "robbing the U.S. of an enemy."[112] They were seeking to restore the linkages among policy, strategy, and operational art at a particularly difficult moment in national history. As part of that debate, as we have noted, General-Major V. V. Larionov and A. A. Kokoshin championed a doctrine of sufficient defense, using the Battle of Kursk to support the possibility of an asymmetric response to the threat of an opponent's offensive operations. Larionov, Kokoshin, and General Vladimir Lobov reintroduced the military and the Soviet public to Svechin's frame for strategy.[113]

Within the Soviet Union, glasnost was making possible the addressing of the "blank pages" of Soviet history in a more systemic fashion. It became increasingly possible to speak of the costs of Soviet victory in the Great Patriotic War, and to call into question the rationality of offensive warfighting based upon mass industrial war in the context of nuclear parity and the emerging revolution in conventional capabilities. Such criticism undermined the legitimacy of the Soviet Armed Forces, as it called into question the ideology, institutions, and values of the Soviet system, leading to what William Odom called the collapse of the Soviet military and ultimately the Soviet system.[114]

Soviet operational art, which emerged out of the Stalinist system designed to fight and win a total war, collapsed in the face of a qualitative shift in the nature of future war, from an industrial model to one based on information and control. That shift posed a problem for Party control that Leonid Brezhnev was unwilling and unable to address. As Vitaly Shlykov observed, "Stalin created a unique system for the preparation of the economy to mobilize for war. . . ."[115] It was a system that would finally break the Soviet Union, not in war but under the burden of perpetual preparation for war on all fronts and by all means.[116] The Soviet political leadership during the period of stagnation and the post-Brezhnev interregnum had been slow to respond to this systemic challenge. It failed to take timely and vigorous actions. In a society supposedly dominated by long-range, rational, central planning, this revealed glaring flaws in the edifice of "mature socialism." N. N. Moiseev, former head of the Academy of Sciences Computing Center and a leader in Soviet military simulation work, observed that ideological dogmatism, careerism, and bureaucratic inertia precluded a timely and effective response to this pressing challenge. The command system which had worked during the Stalin industrialization, the Great Patriotic War, and even the nuclear and space challenges, would not meet this new challenge.[117] Cybernetics and the challenge of creating an information society posed problems that the Stalinist model, in an even less repressive form, could not answer. Mass was no longer sufficient to win wars or to guide a society and economy.

With the end of the Soviet Union in 1991, the mobilization base for mass industrial war disappeared in Russia. The General Staff has continued to study the evolution of military art and speculate on the nature of future war. Much of that speculation concerns the definitions of the threats to Russia and the capacity of the national economy to adapt to the informatization of warfare.[118] Military systemology has been an integral part of systems studies in the Soviet Union and Russia. The integration of systems theory, cybernetics, and dialectical materialism was the hallmark of discussions about the philosophical bases of systemology.[119] The collapse of the Soviet Union did not lead Russian systemologists to jettison dialectical materialism as a field theory supporting systems theory. This approach permitted the development of systems environmental frames, the treatment of complex, self-organizing systems; and "presents the prospect of the formulation of the idea creation of an applied dialectic as the highest formal logical apparatus of systems theory and the theory of control."[120] On several occasions over the last 2 decades, the author has examined Russian military analysts' attempts to formulate a compelling vision of future war upon which to base force structure and weapons acquisition. In the first such effort, the author concluded that the Communist Party's ideological hegemony would preclude the free-ranging of systems theory and systemology to the study of future war.[121] Following the collapse of the Soviet Union, Russian systems theorists had wide ranging opportunities to apply systems theory to military foresight and forecasting, but they found the political leadership deeply concerned with the political, social, and economic transformation of Russia, and more concerned with cutting defense spending than addressing the problem of future war.[122] Stumbling into a disastrous war in Chechnya did not fundamentally change the Yeltsin administration's appreciation of the necessity of such studies since it assumed that the international system after the Cold War posed no serious threats to Russian national interests. Russia had achieved a strategic partnership with the United States, and was managing its relations with NATO in a fashion that took account of Russian concerns. Russian troops were deployed as part of NATO's implementation force (IFOR)/stabilization force (SFOR) in Bosnia-Herzegovina. This situation changed radically in 1999 when NATO intervened against Yugoslavia over Kosovo conducting an air campaign to compel Serbian President Slobodan Milosevic to surrender the province. The campaign put an end to Moscow's assumptions about a strategic partnership and raised the importance of the issue of future war for the Russian political elite.[123]

With the rise of Valdimir Putin, defense became a priority and defining the nature of the future conflicts for which Russian forces would have to prepare became an immediate and salient issue. NATO's intervention in Yugoslavia in the form of a noncontact air campaign of compellence, which relied upon precision strike systems, seemed to pose a threat to Russia in case of another war in Chechnya. The Russian responses came in June with the symbolic romp of Russian paratroopers from Uglivic to Pristina and the first-major, post-Cold War strategic military exercise, ZAPAD-99, which was based on a scenario in which NATO attacked Belarus from the Baltic States, and in the face of Russia's failed conventional defense, Russia initiated a limited first-strike by nonstrategic nuclear forces to bring about the deescalation of the conflict.[124]

The corpus of literature about the future in the pre-1999 period laid out the major themes which would became more robust and ubiquitous over the next decade. Gareev, who, on his retirement from the Russian Armed Forces, emerged as founder and president of the Russian Academy of Military Sciences, presented one of the first major studies in the mid-1990s. In that work, Gareev argued that nuclear war and general conventional war were unlikely. Therefore, the threat of local conflicts becoming local wars and escalating into regional conflicts could not be excluded. Gareev described forecasting future war to be like "the labor of Sisyphus"—necessary, difficult, and constantly subject to reassessment on the basis of changes in the international environment, the evolution of weapons technology (which he saw as accelerating), and the changing domestic political and socio-economic climate. The post-Cold War utilization of military power would shift to one dominated by the "indirect approach associated with B. H. Liddell Hart" and reflects the strategic choices of hegemonic maritime power.[125]

General-Major Vladimir A. Slipchenko, who on retirement joined Gareev as Vice President of the Academy of Military Sciences, focused on the lessons learned from Operation DESERT STORM and saw that conflict as the harbinger of future war under the impact of the RMA. Such a conflict would be nonlinear, noncontact warfare involving deep strikes with precision-guided missiles as a form of compellence. Slipchenko considered the current environment when only one hegemonic power possesses large arsenals of such weapons to be a temporary condition and believed that the emerging "sixth-generation warfare" would continue for decades and would see such systems become the property of other great powers.

Slipchenko published *Voina budushchego* (War of the Future) in 1999 and would later claim that NATO's war plan confirmed his forecast.[126] Unlike Western discussions of fourth and fifth generation warfare, Slipchenko grounded sixth-generation warfare as emerging from nuclear warfare, which he identified as the fifth generation. Slipchenko also observed that sixth-generation precision strikes could have effects similar to those of nuclear weapons, thereby blurring the distinction between advanced conventional systems and the next generation of nuclear weapons.[127] Slipchenko noted the risks involved in this development, which he believed would undermine deterrence and lead to other states seeking to acquire nuclear weapons when they faced disarmament by the threat of advanced conventional weapons.

Rear Admiral V. S. Pirumov, an expert in radio electronic warfare, had already commented on the impact that advances in precision-strike systems and electronic warfare had on naval combat in the Falklands War.[128] On his retirement from the Navy, he became the driving force in the organization of the Section on Security and Geopolitics of the Russian Academy of Natural Sciences. Pirumov wrote about the use of advanced weapons systems, automated command and control, and electronic warfare during Operation DESERT STORM.[129] Pirumov published widely on the informatization of warfare as a major development that would impact national defense.[130] He became the scientific advisor to the Security Council under President Yeltsin, and in that capacity led a collective effort to establish the foundations of Russian National Security Policy based on a systems approach. This work involved a sharp break with Soviet experience and was based on a review of national security systems in other states. The project set out to define the institutions that formulate national security policy and it articulated a method for evaluating the international environment and Russia's national interests. A product of the era of strategic partnership, it reflected a relatively benign appraisal of the international system and of the external threats confronting Russia.[131]

The author who most directly addressed the evolution of operational art under conditions of the Revolution in Military Affairs was General-Major Viktor Riabchuk, a veteran of the Great Patriotic War and Professor of Operational Art at the former Frunze Combined Arms Academy. Riabchuk sought to apply military systemology to operational art in the epoch of deep precision strikes.[132] Riabchuk emphasized the increased role of knowledge management in command and control, and spoke of making the command and control of combat the cardinal skill of the commander and demanding that he acquire the capacity to manage information to ensure a systemic understanding of the environment, his own forces, and those of the enemy. In this manner, power can be effectively deployed against critical subsystems of the enemy and bring about collapse without having to engage in annihilation.[133] Such an approach in Riabchuk's case does not embrace post-modern discourse but still depends on the creation of robust mathematical models of complex systems and demands that the commander have the necessary skills to appreciate their application and to draw conclusions from them.[134]

Over the last several years, the place of military systemology in Russian military science has become more pronounced. Debates over the nature of future war continue and have an impact on the direction of the development of force structure and weapons acquisition.[135] Sixth-generation warfare is now a broadly accepted concept in describing the emerging prospects for military transformation.[136] Admiral Ivan Kapitanets embraced it in formulating the development of naval science in the 21st century and called for a "sixth generation navy."[137] There is, however, a very active debate over the concept of noncontact war, with critics warning of a certain one-sided emphasis on the impact of precision-strike systems.[138] The scholarly debate over the exact role of military systemology in military science continues to be lively, with broad agreement over its utility. The need for a unified approach to military systemology and infomatization of the armed forces has been noted.[139]

Riabchuk continues to lead the discussion of the application of military systemology to forecasting future conflict, which he describes as intellectual-informational confrontation. He has called for the recognition of military systemology in the articulation of military doctrine, which in Russia's case, as in the Soviet case, still addresses the broadest issues of preparation for and conducting war. In his most recent book, he and his son address the proper role of military doctrine both historically and under contemporary conditions. The authors emphasize the value of a system approach for assessing the international environment, national interests, threats, and the means of national defense. They call for a process of periodic review to take into account changes in these systems. Military doctrine, they argue, is the path to victory. Their emphasis is on modern war as an intellectual-informational conflict that demands of commanders and statesmen an understanding of modeling conflict.[140] According to Riabchuk, the appreciation of military systemology is the foundation for a solution to the problem of forecasting under conditions of intellectual-informational confrontation.[141]

This debate—which is recasting Russian conceptions of operational art and military art on the basis of a systems-infused military science addressing complex, self-organizing systems—should be part of the U.S. debate over system-of-systems analysis, effects-based operations, systemic operational design, and campaign design. The lack of U.S. attention to Russian works in this area reflects the increasingly narrow focus of American military analysis and theory, which, since the end of the Cold War, has become increasingly self-referential. Foreign titles in the field are seldom reviewed and even more rarely published in English. This trends flies in the face of a global interest in foreign military theory. A visit to the People's Liberation Army (PLA) book store in Beijing, China, provides immediate evidence of foreign titles in the field. The Chinese are notable for their translations and publications of Russian studies relating to the RMA, including Slipchenko's work on sixth-generation warfare.[142] In this context, it is quite possible that our abiding tendency towards strategic ethnocentrism, our penchant for ignoring truly fruitful and original thinking about war that comes from other countries may contribute to an explanation of the ongoing U.S. difficulties during the past decade in achieving strategic victory in the wars of our time. As Mary Fitzgerald's work and enduring importance show, not only can we benefit from the study of Russian and other foreign scholars' insights into contemporary warfare, should we ignore those writers, we only do so at our own peril.

ENDNOTES - CHAPTER 3

1. David Chandler, "Napoleon, Operational Art and the Jena Campaign," in Michael D. Krause and R. Cody Phillips, eds., *Historical Perspectives of the Operational Art*, Washington, DC: The U.S. Army Center for Military History, 2005, pp. 27-65. Recent scholarship has traced the origins of operational art even further into the past back to the wars of Frederick the Great, and consider it to have been shaped by a Franco-Prussian dialectic reaching from Frederick the Great to Napoleon's campaign of 1813. See Claus Telp, *The Evolution of Operational Art, 1740-1813: From Frederick the Great to Napoleon*, London, UK: Frank Cass, 2005. Telp emphasizes the shift from limited, protracted war under Frederick to Napoleon's military art, which gradually led to the structuring of campaigns into distributed maneuvers leading to decisive battle. In all these cases, the great commanders are in a situation like that of Monsieur Jordain, the protagonist of Moliere's play, "Le Bourgeois Gentilhomme," in that they were practicing an art they did not name and seem to have been unaware of this category of military art between strategy and tactics. This is precisely the position taken by Gunther Rothenburg in his classic study of the Napoleon's art of war, where he spoke of strategy and tactics and referred to immediate maneuver to contact as "grand tactics." See Gunther E. Rothenburg, *The Art of War in the Age of Napoleon*, Bloomington: Indiana University Press, 1978, pp. 146-156.

2. Chandler, p. 27.

3. On this view, see Clifford J. Rogers, ed., *The Military Revolution Debate: Readings on the Military Transformation of Early Modern Europe*, Boulder, CO: Westview Press, 1995; Geoffrey Parker, *The Military Revolution: Military Innovation and the Rise of the West, 1500-1800*, Cambridge, UK: Cambridge University Press, 1996; and MacGregor Knox and Williamson Murray, eds., *The Dynamics of Military Revolution, 1300-2050*, Cambridge, UK: Cambridge University Press, 2001.

4. Robert M. Epstein, *Napoleon's Last Victory and the Emergence of Modern War*, Lawrence: University Press of Kansas, 1994. There is a curious aspect to the discussions of Napoleon's application of operational art: few references are made to his campaign of 1812 against Russia and the factors that contributed to the destruction of La Grand Armee in the course of that campaign.

5. James J. Schneider, "The Loose Marble—and the Origins of Operational Art," *Parameters*, March 1989, pp. 85-99; and James J. Schneider, "Theoretical Implications of Operational Art," in Clayton R. Newell and Michael D. Krause, eds., *On Operational Art*, Washington, DC: The U. S. Army Center for Military History, 1994, pp. 17-30. The problem with finding the origins of operational art in the American Civil War was well expressed by William McElwee in his study of warfare between the wars of Napoleon and World War I. The American practitioners had been amateurs. They solved many problems of industrial war by trial and experiment, but had not created an institution to preserve those lessons as the Army's dismal performance in going to war with Spain revealed. See William McElwee, *The Art of War from Waterloo to Mons*, Bloomington, IN: Indiana University Press, 1974, pp. 114-116, 147-183.

6. James Schneider, *The Structure of Strategic Revolution: Total War and the Roots of the Soviet Warfare State*, Novato, CA: Presidio Press, 2005.

7. William R. Richardson, "FM 100-5: The AirLand Battle in 1986," *Military Review*, Vol. 66, No. 3, March 1986, pp. 4-11; Huba Wass de Czege, "Lessons from the Past: Making the Army's Doctrine 'Right Enough' Today," *Landpower Essay*, No. 06-2, September 2006. On the origins of AirLand Battle, see John L. Romjue, *From Active Defense to AirLand Battle: The Development of Army Doctrine, 1973–1982*, Fort Monroe, VA: U.S. Army Training and Doctrine Command, 1984, pp. 66–73.

8. The author herewith candidly acknowledges his connections to the works of both scholars. He recommended Professor Epstein's work on Napoleon to the University Press of Kansas and served as dissertation advisor to Professor Schneider for his dissertation, which became the basis of his book. At that time, I was doing my own initial work on the theory and practice of operational art in the Soviet Union.

9. V. G. Kulikov, "operativnoe iskuustvo" ("Operational Art"), in *Sovetskaia voennaia entsiklopediia*, Vol. VI, Moscow, Russia: Voenizdat, 1978, pp. 53-54.

10. G. S. Isserson, *Evoliutsiia operativnogo iskusstva* (*Evolution of Operational Art*), Moscow, Russia: Voenizdat, 1937, pp. 96-97. Isserson spoke of the evolution of strategy from that of a single point, to that of an extended line as practiced by Moltke, to the problem of the emergence of the continuous front and the deepening of the theater of operations that gave rise to the problem of breaking through a prepared defense and finding means to conduct follow-on operations into the depths of the enemy's defenses.

11. Bruce W. Menning, "Operational Art's Origins," *Military Review*, Vol. 77, No. 5, September-October 1997, pp. 32-47. Soviet authors were well aware of the absence of operational art from the vocabularies of Western militaries. In a book of translated essays on the conduct of operations by U.S. and NATO authors, its editor, A. Kh. Monza, stated: "Military theorists in the USA and other imperialist powers, divide military art into strategy and tactics. Questions, which Soviet military science treats as operational art, are looked upon by bourgeois military theorists as part of strategy and part of tactics." See A. Kh. Monza, ed., *O soveremnnykh operatsiiakh* (*On Contemporary Operations*), Moscow, Russia: Voenizdat, 1962, pp. 9-10. On the other hand, recent Western scholarship nods in the direction of the Soviet origins of the term operational art, but then ignores that problem. Claus Telp in his study of operational art in the 18th and early 19th century treats the Soviet origins in a passing reference: "The term 'operational art', coined by Soviet military theorists in the interwar period, has received increased attention in military circles with the debate on the comparative NATO (North Atlantic Treaty Organization) and Warsaw Pact operational capabilities in the 1970s and 1980s." The note following this sentence makes reference to works by three authors, A. S. H. Irwin, Brian Holden Reid, and J. J. G. Mackenzie, two of whom are British senior officers and one a professor at King's College in London. See Telp, *The Evolution of Operational Art, 1740-1813*, p. 1.

12. David Glantz, *Military Operational Art: In Pursuit of Deep Battle*, London, UK: Frank Cass, 1991. Glantz's many contributions to the study of Soviet operational art while he was assigned to the Combat Studies Institute, the U.S. Army War College, and Soviet Army Studies Office laid the foundation for the U.S. Army's understanding of the theory and practice of Soviet operational art.

13. For an excellent account of those operations in a single volume, see David M. Glantz and Jonathan M. House, *When Titans Clashed: How the Red Army Stopped Hitler*, Lawrence, KS: University Press of Kansas, 1995. Glantz had served as an intelligence officer with U.S. Army Europe and so had a professional interest in the details of the opposing forces.

14. Jacob W. Kipp, "Conventional Force Modernization and the Asymmetries of Military Doctrine: Historical Reflections on Air/Land Battle and the Operational Manoeuvre Group," in Carl G. Jacobsen, ed., *The Uncertain Course: New Weapons, Strategies and Mind Sets*, Stockholm International Peace Research Institute, Oxford, UK: Oxford University Press, 1987, pp. 137-166.

15. Sir John Wintrop Hackett, *The Third World War, August 1985*, London, UK: Berkeley, 1978. On the impact of U.S. Army doctrine in the 1970s on the debate about operational art, see William K. Sutey, "The Deterrent Value of U.S. Army Doctrine: The Active Defense and Airland Battle in Soviet Military Thought," Ft. Leavenworth, KS: U.S. Army School of Advanced Military Studies, 1993.

16. Richard E. Simpkin, *Race to the Swift: Thoughts on Twenty-First Century Warfare*, London, UK: Brassey's Defence, 1985. See also Richard E. Simpkin and John Erickson, *Deep Battle: The Brainchild of Marshal Tukhachevskii*, London, UK: Brassey's Defence, 1987. Christopher Bellamy also reviewed the developed of deep operations in his study of future land warfare and concluded in 1990 that the era of large-scale operations conducted by mass armies was over and that such operations would be small scale, involve advanced technology, and be conducted by professional elite forces. See Christopher Bellamy, *The Evolution of Modern Land Warfare*, London, UK: Routledge, 1990, pp. 240-243.

17. John S. Brown, "The Maturation of Operational Art: Operations DESERT SHIELD and DESERT STORM," in Krause and Phillips, eds,. *Historical Perspectives of Operational Art*, p. 439.

18. Romjue, *From Active Defense to AirLand Battle: The Development of Army Doctrine, 1973–1982*.

19. James R. Locher III, *Victory on the Potomac: The Goldwater-Nicholas Act Unifies the Pentagon*, College Station: Texas A&M University Press, 2002, pp. 3-14.

20. U. S. Department of Defense, *Joint Forces Employment: Operational Art*, available from *www.dtic.mil/doctrine/jrm/jfe4a.ppt*.

21. Other services did develop senior schools for operational planners. The Air Force created the School of Advanced Aero-Space Studies (SAASS) at the Air University, Maxwell AFB. SAASS, however, focused on aerospace power and strategic issues. The Marine Corps established the School of Advanced Warfighting at the Marine Corps University in Quantico, VA, and in a smaller effort befitting the Corps' size, focused on complex problem-solving and decisionmaking skills at the "operational-level of war." The Joint Advanced Warfighting School was established at the Joint Forces Staff College by the National Defense University in Norfolk, VA, and was tasked with creating "world-class Joint planners." More recently, the U.S. Navy has also expressed interest in the development of such Joint planners.

22. Clayton R. Newell and Michael D. Krause, eds., *On Operational Art*, Washington, DC: The U. S. Army Center for Military History, 1994. Other volumes on the development of operational art appeared in the mid-1990s. Of note were a Canadian volume of collected essays, B. J. C. McKercher and Michael A. Hennessy, eds., *The Operational Art: Developments in the Theories of War*, West Port, CT: Praeger, 1996; and a major study by the Israeli soldier theorist Shimon Naveh, which defined operational art on the basis of Soviet experience as a concept based upon the assumption that the enemy force was a complex system which could be demolished by applying shock throughout the system in the form of deep operations. See Shimon Naveh, *In Pursuit of Military Excellence: The Evolution of Operational Art*, London, UK: Frank Cass, 1997. Naveh's work coincided with the renewed interest within the Israeli Defense Forces in operational art and the creation of the Operational Theory and Research Institute in 1995 to serve as "cultural *agent provocateur*, cognitive enabler, and conceptual promoter." See Shimon Navveh, *Operational Art and the IDF: A Critical Study of a Command Culture*, Washington, DC: Center for Strategic and Budgetary Assessment, September 30, 2007, pp. 1-2.

23. Krause and Phillips, eds., *Historical Perspectives of the Operational Art*, p. iii. Brigadier General John S. Brown in his Foreword to this volume refers to it as "a continuation" of the Newell and Krause volume.

24. Brown, "The Maturation of Operational Art: Operations DESERT SCHIELD AND DESERT STORM," in Newell and Krause, eds., *On Operational Art*, pp. 454-466.

25. On the initial RMA debate, see Thierry Gongora and Harold von Riekhoff, eds., *Toward a Revolution in Military Affairs?* Westport, CT: Greenwood Press, 2000. For the most articulate argument by senior U.S. military specialist for revolutionary change in the conduct of war, see William A. Owens, *Lifting the Fog of War*, New York: Farrar, Straus and Giroux, 2000.

26. Erik Dahl, "Network Centric Warfare and the Death of Operational Art," *Defence Studies*, Vol. II, No. 1, March 2002, pp. 1-24.

27. Thomas Z. Ruby, "Effects-Based Operations: More Important Than Ever," *Parameters*, Autumn 2008, pp. 26-35. Ruby's article, which appeared in response to General James Mattis' memorandum criticizing Effects-Based Operations, developed the case for Effects-Based Operations along lines to be found in the works of John Warden on the capacity of modern aviation to achieve strategic paralysis. See John Andreas Olsen, *John Warden and the Renaissance of American Air Power*, Dulles, VA: Potomac Books, 2007.

28. Dag Henriksen, *NATO's Gamble: Combining Diplomacy and Air Power in the Kosovo Crisis, 1998-1999*, Annapolis, MD: Naval Institute Press, 2007, pp. 189-191.

29. Peter F. Herrly, "The Plight of Joint Doctrine after Kosovo," *Joint Force Quarterly*, Summer 1999, p. 99.

30. William S. Lind, "The Changing Face of War: Into the Fourth Generation," *Marine Corps Gazette*, October 1989, pp. 22-26.

31. Ibid.

32. Paul Wolfowitz, "Thinking about the Imperatives of Defense Transformation," Address to the Heritage Foundation, April 30, 2004, available from *www.heritage.org/research/nationalsecurity/hl831.cfm*.

33. See Williamson Murray and Robert H. Scales, Jr., *The Iraq War: A Military History*, Cambridge, MA: Belknap Press, 2003; and John Keegan, *The Iraq War*, New York: Alfred A. Knopf, 2004.

34. See Thomas E. Ricks, *FIASCO: The American Military Adventure in Iraq*, New York: Penguin Group, 2006; and Michael R. Gordon and Bernard E. Trainor, *Cobra II: The Inside Story on the Invasion and Occupation of Iraq*, New York: Pantheon Books, 2006.

35. Huba Wass de Czege, "The Logic of Operational Art: How to Design Sound Campaign Strategies, Learn Effectively and Adapt Rapidly and Appropriately," unpublished essay, January 2009.

36. *Ibid.*

37. *Ibid.*

38. For a discussion of Naveh's ideas, see the article/interview by Yotam Feldman: "Dr. Naveh, or how I Learned to Stop Worrying and Walk through Walls," *Haaretz.Com*, November 1, 2007, available from *www.haaretz.com/hasen/spages/917158.html*. The reference to walking through walls refers to the tactic adopted by Israeli troops during Operation DEFENSE SHIELD in the assault on Palestinian forces in Nablus in 2002.

39. Shimon Naveh, *In Pursuit of Military Excellence: The Evolution of Operational Theory*, London, UK: Frank Cass, 1997, pp. 209-238.

40. *TRADOC Pamphlet, 525-5-300, The United States Army Full Spectrum Operations Unified Quest*, Fort Monroe, VA: The U.S. Army Training and Doctrine Command, April 22, 2008, p. 39.

41. *TRADOC Pamphlet, 525-5-500, The United States Army Commander's Appreciation and Campaign Design*, Fort Monroe, VA: The U.S. Army Training and Doctrine Command, January 28, 2008.

42. *Ibid.*, p. i.

43. Milan N. Vego, "A Case against Systemic Operational Design," *Joint Forces Quarterly*, No. 2, 2009, pp. 70-71.

44. I. Susiluoto, *The Origins and Development of Systems Thinking in the Soviet Union: Political and Philosophical Controversies from Bogdanov and Bukharin to Present-Day Re-Evaluations*, Annales Acadamiae Scientarum Fennicae, Dissertationes, Humanarum Litterarum., v. 30, Helsinki, Finland, 1982, pp. 16-17. Susiluoto's remarks on the development of cybernetics and system theory in the 1960s in the USSR had all the appearances of the borrowing of foreign innovation: The emergence of cybernetics and systems theory in the Soviet Union during the 1950s has been interpreted in the West as the passive and belated adoption of foreign science. However, he goes on to make the point that there were Russian precursors which impacted the development of such ideas, which he considers "a qualitative change in the development of thought" and the foundation for the emergence of a systems *Weltanschauung*.

45. Vladimir Shlapentokh, *A Normal Totalitarian Society: How the Soviet Union Functioned and How it Collapsed*, Armoonk, NY: M. E. Sharpe, 2001.

46. The term "zagadki istorii" ("Riddles of History") is taken from a popular Russian television series and books by the author and play write Edvard Radzinsky. See Edvard Radzinsky, *Zagadki zhizni i smerti* (*Riddles of Life and Death*), Moscow, Russia: Vagrius, 2003; Edvard Radzinsky, *Zagadki istorii* (*Riddles of History*), Moscow, Russia: Vagrius, 2003; available from *www.locatetv.com/tv/zagadki-istorii/3361034*.

47. Yuri M. Lotman, *Universe of the Mind: A Semiotic Theory of Culture*, London, UK: I. B. Tauris, 2001, p. 2.

48. *Ibid.*, p. 4.

49. S. A. Fediukin, *Sovetskaia vlast' i burzhuaznye spetsialisty* (*Soviet Power and Bourgeois Specialists*), Moscow, Russia: 'Mysl', 1965, pp. 3-12. As Fediukin points out, the Stalinist position on such specialists was one of incompetents and wreckers who stood in the way of building socialism.

50. V. I. Lenin, *Materialism and Emperio-Criticism: Critical Comments on a Reactionary Philosophy*, Lenin Collected Works, Vol. XIV, Moscow, Russia: Progress Publishers, 1972, pp. 17-362.

51. Avraham Yassour, "The Empiriomonist Critique of Dialectical Materialism: Bogdanov, Plekhanov, Lenin," *Studies in East European Thought*, Vol. 26, No. 1, July 1983, pp. 21-38.

52. Aleksandr Bogdanov, "Logika kazarmy i logika fabriki: Otvet Anatoliiu Lunacharskomu na predlozhenie raboty v pravitel'stve, November 19, 1917," ("The Logic of the Barracks and the Logic of the Factory: Answer to Anatolii Lunacharsky's Porposal to Work in the Government") *Nezavisimaia gazeta*, June 11, 1997. See also A. A. Bogdanov (Malinovskii), "Stat'i, doklady, pis.ma I vospominaniia, 1901-1928 gg," ("Articles, Reports, Letters, and Memories, 1901-1928"), in N. S. Antonova and N. V. Drozdova, eds., *Neizvestnyi Bogdanov* (*The Unknown Bogdanov*), Vol 1, Moscow, Russia: ITS "AIRO"–XX, 1995, pp. 189-190.

53. Aleksandr Bogdanov, "Doklad 'Mirovaia voina i revoliutsiia': zadachi i metod. Aprrl' 1921 g." ("Report: World War and Revolution: Tasks and Methods"), in Antonova and Drozdova, eds., *Neizvestnyi Bogdanov* (*The Unknown Bogdanov*), Vol 1, Moscow, Russia: ITS "AIRO" –XX, 1995, pp. 92-107.

54. Anthony Mansueto, "From Dialectic to Organization: Bogdanov's Contribution to Social Theory," *Studies in East European Thought*, Vol. 46, No. 1, March 1996, p. 37.

55. On the situation in Russian archives in the 1990s, see Patricia Kennedy Grimsted, "Increased Reference Access to Post-1991 Russian Archives," *Slavic Review*, Vol. 56, No. 4, Winter 1997, pp. 718-759; and Patricia Kennedy Grimsted and Vladimir Petrovich Kozlov, *Archives of Russia: A Directory and Bibliographic Guide of Repositories in Moscow and St. Petersburg*, Armonk, NY: M. E. Sharpe, 1997. On Volkogonov's own contribution to archival openness, see Library of Congress, Manuscript Reading Room, "Dmitri Antonovich Volkogonov, A Finding Aid to the Collection in the Library of Congress," Washington, DC: 2008, available from *www.loc.gov/rr/mss/text/volkogon.html*.

56. Rachel Donadio, "The Iron Archives," *The New York Times*, April 22, 2007, available from *www.yale.edu/annals/Reviews/review_texts/Donadio_Iron_Archives_NYT_04.22.07.html*.

57. I. V. Stalin, *O velikoi Otechestvenoi Voine Sovetskogo Soiuza* (*On the Great Patriotic War of the Soviet Union*), Moscow, Russia: Voenizdat, 1949, pp. 41-48.

58. As a young scholar in the 1960s working on my dissertation on tsarist naval reform after the Crimean War, I had spent many hours in the New York Public Library's Slavic Reading Room going through *Morskoi sbornik* from its founding in 1849 to the last tsarist issues in 1917. When I was in Poland working on my dissertation in 1968, I got permission to work in the Central Military Library. Needing to check a reference to something from the journal's first number, I asked for the volume of 1849. I got the one from 1949, which I looked through and was surprised to discover looked very much like the pre-revolutionary journal in layout and major topics. I put the issue aside, not thinking about the mistake, and then the librarian came up to me and asked for the number. She informed me that journal had been closed to "foreigners," i.e., Western class enemies since 1947. Needless to say, I made it a habit to read every issue I could get for the period between 1917 and 1946, which gave a very different perspective on the relationship between the tsarist and Soviet navies and raised the issue of continuity and discontinuity in Russian and Soviet naval and military history.

59. Raymond L. Garthoff, *How Russia Makes War: The Soviet Military Doctrine*, London, UK: G. Allen & Unwin. 1954. In his memoirs, Garthoff relates the origins of this volume to the development of RAND as the flag-ship think tank during the early Cold War. He notes that he made use of German wartime documents and "some Soviet military sources not classified but available only in classified collections" at the Central Intelligence Agency Library and Army Intelligence. See Raymond L. Garthoff, *A Journey through the Cold War: A Memoir of Containment and Coexistence*, Washington, DC: The Brookings Institution Press, 2001, pp. 9-10. Grathoff set the context of his study by quoting from Paul Dickson's study, *Think Tanks*: "RAND was the pioneering American institution in the kind of Cold War scholarship that calls for in-

tensive study of a potential enemy from afar." See Paul Dickson, *Think Tanks*, New York: Ballentine Books, 1971, p. 69. Garthoff's volume was the first of its kind by an American scholar on the Soviet military.

60. On the German reports of war on the Eastern Front and their impact on American military historiography, see Dennis Showalter, "A Dubious Hertiage: The Military Legacy of the Russo-German War," *Air University Review*, March-April 1985, available from *www.airpower.maxwell.af.mil/airchronicles/aureview/1985/mar-apr/showalter.html*. On the impact of such studies on U.S. military doctrine, see Kevin Sutor, "To Stem the Red Tide: The German Report Series and Its Effect on American Defense Doctrine, 1948-1954," *The Journal of Military History*, Vol. 57, No. 4, October-December 1993, pp. 653-688.

61. Michael Cherniavsky, "Corporal Hitler, General Winter, and the Russian Peasant," *The Yale Review*, Vol. LI, No. 4, Summer 1962, pp. 547-558.

62. David Glantz, "American Perspectives on Eastern Front Operations in World War II," A paper delivered at the Soviet-American Colloquium on Problems of World War II in Moscow on October 23-26, 1986, Foreign Military Studies Office, available from *fmso.leavenworth.army.mil/documents/e-front.htm*.

63. Nikita Sergeevich Khrushchev, "Special Report to the Twentieth Party Congress of the Communist Party of the Soviet Union,"February 24-25, 1956, available from *www.uwm.edu/Course/448-343/index12.html*.

64. John Erickson, *The Soviet High Command: A Military-Political History, 1917-1941*, London, UK: Frank Cass, 2001, pp. 313, 717. Erickson's volume first appeared in 1962 and quickly became a classic in the field of Soviet military studies. Svechin used the term art in connection with tactics, operations, and strategy. He specifically stated that "tactical creativity is governed by operational art." However, the focus of his work was strategy, or grand strategy in all its complexity. The concept of discourse among civilian political leaders, economic leaders, and military leaders was at the very heart of preparations for and conduct of war. At the very core of strategy was the concept that it was "theory of

art." Into this art, Svechin put a demand for the serious study of military history and a profound understanding of the relationship between theory and practice. The point in war was for strategic leadership to guide the application of operational art so that the separate operations would lead to the military conditions supporting the political leadership's goals. Svechin supported the concept of a general staff as the embodiment of the "integral military leader." On these issues, see Aleksandr A. Svechin, *Strategy*, Minneapolis, MN: Eastview, 1992, pp. 67-101.

65. M. N. Tukhachevsky, *M. N. Tukhachevskii: Izbrannye proizvedeniia* (*M. N. Tukhachevsky: Selected Works*), Moscow, Russia: Voenizdat, 1964, Vol. I, p. 26. The year following the publication of the two-volume collection of Tukhachevsky's writings, the Soviet General Staff published a single volume collection on problems of Strategy and Operational Art. The volume tied together the legacy of Marxism-Leninism and emphasized and gave prominence to the writings of Mikhail Frunze and Mikhail Tukhachevsky and included works by other commanders who had been purged by Stalin. Marshal M. Zakharov, Chief of the General Staff, provided the introduction to the volume. See A. B. Kadishev, ed., *Voprosy strategii i operativnogo iskusstva v sovetskikh voennykh trudakh* (*Issues of Strategy and Operational Art in Soviet Military Works*), Moscow, Russia: Voenizdat, 1969, pp. 1-24. The volume did establish the close linkage between strategy and operational art and emphasized the leading role of strategy in setting the conditions for the planning of campaigns and the conduct of operations. At one point, the volume did note the contribution of studies of World War I to the development of Soviet military theory but then noted that its advocates did not appreciate the mobilization potential of the Soviet state and in a choice between a strategy of annihilation (*sokrushenie*) vs. attrition (*izmor*), they chose giving up Minsk and Kiev to seizing Byalostok and Brest; they rejected Cannae in favor of Poltava or rapid decision by encirclement against a long war of exhaustion. The names associated with this retrograde theory were tsarist officers serving in the Red Army as military specialists (*voenspetsy*), A. A. Svechin and A. I. Verkhovskii.

66. V. M. Ivanov, *Marshal M. N. Tukhachevskii*, Moscow, Russia: Voenizdat, 1990, pp. 185-199.

67. M. N. Tukhachevskii, "Strategiia natsional'naia i klassovaia" ("National and Class Strategy"), in M. N. Tukhachevskii, *Izbrannye proizvedeniia*, Vol. I, Moscow, Russia: Voenizdat, 1964, pp. 31-50. See also Nikolai Nikoforov, "Zabytye stranitsy istorii: Tukhachevskii i Svechin, Istoki protivostoianiia" ("Forgotten Pages of History: Tukhachevsky and Svechin, Sources of Conflict"), *Krasnaia zvezda*, January 11, 1999.

68. Lennart Samuelson and Vitaly Shlykov, *Plans for Stalin's War Machine: Tukhachevskii and Miltary-Economic Planning, 1925-1941*, New York: St, Martin's Press, 2000, pp. 4-8. This volume provides a deeply researched study of the Soviet warfare state, and Tukhachevsky's contribution to the model of total mobilization of society for war.

69. Jacob W. Kipp, "Two Views of Warsaw: The Russian Civil War and Soviet Operational Art, 1920-1930," in B. J. C. McKercher and Michael A. Hennessy, eds., *The Operational Art: Developments in the Theories of War*, West Port, CT: Praeger, 1996, pp. 51-86. See also Norman Davies, *White Eagle, Red Star: The Polish-Soviet War, 1919-1920*, New York: St. Martin's Press, 1972; and Jozef Pilsudki, *Year 1920*, London, UK, and New York: Pilsudksi Institute of London, and Pilsudksi Institute of America, 1972.

70. A. Ia. Soshnikov *et al.*, *Sovetskaia kavaleriia: Voenno-istoricheskii ocherk* (*Soviet Cavalry: A Military-Historical Essay*), Moscow, Russia: Voenizdat, 1984, pp. 91-92. On the impact of the Warsaw campaign on interwar Soviet military thought on operational art, see Jacob W. Kipp, "Two Views of Warsaw: The Russian Civil War and Soviet Operational Art, 1920-1930," in B. J. C. McKercher and Michael A. Hennessy, eds., *The Operational Art: Developments in the Theories of War*, Westport, CT: Praeger, 1996, pp. 51-86.

71. M. V. Frunze, "Edinaia boennaia doktrina i Krasnaia armiia" ("Unified Military Doctrine"), *Voennaia nauka i revoliutsiia* (*Military Science and Revolution*), No. 2, 1921, p. 39.

72. The Soviet treatment of Frunze as a military theorist is quite interesting. General M. A. Gareev noted the relevance of Frunze's contributions to military theory in his book and specifi-

cally pointed to his contribution to the development of operational art as a commander and as a contributor to the development of the theory of "deep operations." See M. A. Gareev, *M. V. Frunze: Voennyi teoretik* (*M. V. Frunze: Military Theorist*), Moscow, Russia: Voenizdat, 1985, pp. 203-205. Gareev also goes on to comment on the unpreparedness of the Red Army for the conduct of defensive operations in the initial period of war against the Wehrmacht's surprise attack. See Gareev. *M. V. Frunze: Voennyi teoretik*, pp. 229-234.

73. M. N. Tukhachevskii, "Strategiia natsional'naia i klassovaia," ("National and Class Strategy"), in M. N. Tukhachevskii, *Izbrannye proizvedeniia*, pp. 31-50.

74. Walter Darnell Jacobs, *Frunze: The Soviet Clausewitz, 1885–1925*, The Hague, The Netherlands: Martinus Nijhoff, 1969. There were, in fact, better candidates for the title, "Soviet Clausewitz." Lenin himself had read and commented on Clausewitz's *On War*. See Jacob W. Kipp, "Lenin and Clausewitz: The Militarization of Marxism," *Military Affairs*, Vol. XLIX, No. 4, December 1985, pp. 184-191. The other candidate was A. A. Svechin, who oversaw the standard modern translation of *On War* into Russia in 1934, and authored an intellectual biography of Clausewitz, had drawn heavily on Clausewitz in his own classic *Strategy*. Svechin, however, had been an intellectual opponent of Tukhachevsky, who had mounted a campaign against him as a reactionary class enemy. On Svechin and Clausewitz, see Jacob W. Kipp, "General-Major A. A. Svechin and Modern War: Military History and Military Theory," Introductory essay for Kent Lee, ed., A. A. Svechin, *Strategy*, Minneapolis, MN: East View Publications, 1992, p. 51. On Svechin's own writings on Clausewitz, see Carl von Clausewitz, *O voine* (*On War*), Moscow, Russia: Gosvoenizdat, 1934; and A. A. Svechin, *Klausevits* (*Clausewitz*), Moscow, Russia: Zhurnal'no-gazetnoe Ob'edinenie (Journal and Newspaper Association), 1935.

75. This particular narrative ignores the Soviet operational-strategic success against the Kwantung Army during the counteroffensive of August 1939 at Khalkhin Gol. See Alvin Coox, *Nomonhan: Japan against Russia, 1939*, Stanford, CA: Stanford Universiy Press, 1985. On the debates surrounding Barbarossa, see Jacob W. Kipp, "Barbarossa, Soviet Covering Forces and the Initial Period of War: Military History and AirLand Battle," *The Journal of Soviet Military Studies*, Vol. I, No. 2, June 1988, pp. 188-212.

76. A. M. Nekrich, *"June 22, 1941,"* Columbia, SC: University of South Carolina Press, 1968. For a treatment of the attack on Nekrich, see P. G. Grigorenko, "The Concealment of Historical Truth—A public Crime," in P. G. Grigorenko, *The Grigorenko Papers*, Boulder, CO: Westview Press, 1976. Girgorenko's essay circulated in samizdat at the time of the attack on Nekrich.

77. G. K. Zhukov, *Vospominaniia i razmyshleniia (Memoirs and Reflections)*, Moscow, Russia: Izdatel'stvo Agenstva Pechati Novosti, 1983, Vol. I, p. 13.

78. S. P. Ivanov et al., *Nachal;nyi period voiny: Po oputu pervykh kampanii i operatsii vtoroi mirovoi voiny (The Initial Period of War: On the Experience of the First Campaigns and Operations of the Second World War)*, Moscow, Russia: Voenizdat, 1974.

79. John Erickson, *The Road to Stalingrad*, London: Cassell, 2007; John Erickson, *The Road to Berlin: Stalin`s War with Germany*, Volume Two, New Haven, CT: Yale University Press, 1999.

80. The Naval Institute provided the initial forum for these discussions, which were picked up by the Center for Naval Analysis and then were transformed into a collective endeavor under the leadership of Michael MccGwire in the Dalhousie Maritime Forum, which brought together naval officers, analysts, and scholars. On this exploitation of Soviet sources, see Robert Herrick, *Soviet Naval Strategy*, Annapolis, MD: U.S. Naval Institute, 1968; Nicholas George Shadrin, "Development of Soviet Maritime Power," Washington, DC: Georgetown University, 1972, unpublished dissertation; Kenneth Hagan and Jacob Kipp, "U.S. and U.S.S.R. Naval Strategy," *Proceedings*, Vol. C, No. 11, November 1973, pp. 37-42; Michael MccGwire et al., *Soviet Naval Policy: Objectives and Constraints*, New York: Frederick A. Praeger, 1975; Michael MccGwire et al., *Soviet Naval Influence: Domestic and Foreign Influence*, New York: Frederick A. Praeger, 1977.

81. Christopher A. Ford and David A. Rosenberg, "The Naval Intelligence Underpinnings of Reagan's Maritime Strategy," *The Journal of Strategic Studies*, Vol. 28, No. 2, April 2005, pp. 379-409.

82. David R. Jones, ed., *Soviet Armed Forces Review Annual*, Vol. 1, Gulf Breeze, FL: Academic International Press, 1977, p. vii.

83. Richard M. Swain, "Filling the Void: The Operational Art and the U. S. Army," in B. J. C. McKercher and Michael A. Hennessy, eds., *The Operational Art: Developments in the Theories of War*, West Port, CT: Praeger, 1996, pp. 147-172.

84. Peter Vigor, *Soviet Blitzkrieg Theory*, London, UK: Macmillan, 1983.

85. David Glantz, "Soviet Ground Doctrine Since 1845," *Air University Review*, March-April 1983, available from *www.airpower.maxwell.af.mil/airchronicles/aureview/1983/mar-apr/glantz.htm*; and David Glantz, "The Nature of Soviet Operational Art," *Parameters*, Spring 1985, p. 63.

86. A. A. Kokoshin and V. V. Larionov, "Origins of the Intellectual Rehabilitation of A. A. Svechin," *Strategy*, pp. 1-13. See also Viktor Miasnikov, "Kak kovalas' asimmetrichnost'" ("How Asymmetry Was Forged"), *Nezavisimoe voennoe obozrenie* (*Independent Military Review*), October 17, 2008, p. 15.

87. David Glantz, *Zhukov's Greatest Defeat: The Red Army's Epic Disaster in Operation Mars, 1942*, Lawrence, KS: University Press of Kansas, 1999.

88. A. A. Kokoshin, *Strategicheskoe upravlenie: Teoriiam istoricheskii opyt, srvnitel'nyi analiz, zadachi dlia Rossii* (*Strategic Command and Control: Theory, Experience, Comparative Analysis, Tasks for Russia*), Moscow, Russia: ROSSPEN, 2003, pp. 240-246. See also Jacob W. Kipp, "The Labor of Sisyphus: Forecasting the Revolution in Military Affairs during Russia's Time of Troubles," in Thierry Gongora and Harold von Riekhoff, eds., *Toward a Revolution in Military Affairs?* Westport, CT: Greenwood Press, 2000, pp. 87-104.

89. Vitaly Shlykov, "Chto pogubilo Sovetskii Soiuz? Genshtab i ekonomika" ("What Destroyed the Soviet Union? The General Staff and the Economy"), *Voennyi Vestnik* (*Military Messenger*), No. 9, September 2002, pp. 64-93. See also Jacob W. Kipp, "The Changing Soviet Strategic Environment: Soviet Military Doctrine, Conventional Military Forces, and the Scientific-Technical Revolution in Military Affairs," in Carl Jacobsen *et al*, eds., *Strategic Power: USA/USSR*, London, UK: Macmillan, 1990, pp. 435-456.

90. A. Kokoshin and V. Larionov, "Kurskaia bitva v svete sovremennoi obrononitel'noi doktriny" ("The Battle of Kursk in Light of Contemporary Defensive Doctrine"), *Mirovaia ekonomika i mezhdunarodnye otnosheniia (World Economy and International Relations)*, No. 8, August 1987, pp. 32-40. See also Viktor Miasnikov, "Kak kovalas' asimmetrichnost'" ("How Asymmetry was Forged"), *Nezavisimoe voennoe obozrenie*, October 17, 2008, p. 15.

91. V. T. Iminov et al., *Problemy voennogo iskusstva vo vtoroi mirovoi voine i v poslevoennyi period, sic, pp. Strategiia I operativnoe iskusstvo (Problems of Military Art in the Second World War and the Post-War Period)*, Moscow, Russia: Voennaia Ordena Lenina Krasnoznamennaia Ordena Suvorova Akademiia General'nogo Shtaba Vooruzhennykh Sil Rossiiskoi Federatsii, 1995, pp. 193-225.

92. Bruce W. Menning, *Bayonets before Bullets: The Imperial Russian Army, 1861-1914*, Bloomington, IN: Indiana University Press, 1992.

93. David Glantz, "The Soviet Airborne Experience," Ft. Leavenworth, KS: Combat Studies Institute, 1984; and David Glantz, *August Storm: Soviet Strategic Offensive in Manchuria, 1945, Leavenworth Paper No. 7*, Ft. Leavenworth, KS: Combat Studies Institute, 1983; and *August Storm: Soviet Tactical and Operational Combat in Manchuria, 1945, Leavenworth Paper No. 8*, Ft. Leavenworth, KS: Combat Studies Institute, 1983.

94. David Glantz, "1984 Art of War Symposium, From the Don to the Dnepr: Soviet Offensive Operations—December 1942-August 1943, A transcript of Proceedings," Carlisle, PA: Center for Land Warfare, U.S. Army War College, March 26-30, 1984; "1985 Art of War Symposium, From the Dnepr to the Vistula: Soviet Offensive Operations— November 1943-August 1944, A transcript of Proceedings," Carlisle, PA: Center for Land Warfare, U.S. Army War College, April 29-May 3, 1985; "1986 Art of War Symposium, From the Vistula to the Oder: Soviet Offensive Operations— October 1944-March 1945, A transcript of Proceedings," Carlisle, PA: Center for Land Warfare, U.S. Army War College, May 29-23, 1986; and David M. Glantz, ed., *The Initial Period of War on the Eastern Front, 22 June - August 1941: Proceedings of the Fourth Art of War Symposium*, Garmisch, Germany: October, 1987,

Cass Series on Soviet Military Experience, Vol. 2, London, UK: Frank Cass, 1997.

95. This effort began with a general history of the war and continued into both major and minor operations. See David M. Glantz and Jonathan M. House, *When Titans Clashed: How the Red Army Stopped Hitler,* Lawrence, KS: University Press of Kansas, 1995. Among the lesser known operations addressed by Glantz is Operation MARS under the direction of Marshal Zhukov. This set off a major dispute over the nature of the operation, with Russian military commentators labeling it an operation, diversionary. See also David Glantz, *Zhukov's Greatest Defeat: The Red Army's Epic Disaster in Operation Mars, 1942,* Lawrence, KS: University Press of Kansas, 1999; and Alexander Semonovich Orlov, "'Operation Mars': Wage Disaster or Part of the Victory at Stalingrad?" available from *www.armchairgeneral.com/rkkaww2/battles/mars42_Orlov.htm*.

96. On the origins of SASO and its early publications, see Jacob W. Kipp, "FMSO-JRIC and Open Source Intelligence: Speaking Prose in a World of Verse," *Military Intelligence Professorial Bulletin,* January-February 2006, pp. 45-50.

97. C. N. Donnelly, *Red Banner: The Soviet Military System in Peace and War,* Clousdon, Surrey, UK: Jane's Information Group, 1988.

98. Jacob W. Kipp, "Mass and Maneuver and the Origins of Soviet Operational Art" in Karl Reddel, ed., *Transformation in Russian and Soviet Military History: Proceedings of the Twelfth Military History Symposium, USAF Academy, 1986,* Washington, DC: U.S. Air Force Office of Air Force History, 1990, pp. 87-116.

99. John G. Hines, Ellis M. Mishulovich, and John F. Shull, *Soviet Intentions, 1965-1985: Soviet Post-Cold War Testimonial Evidence,* Washington, DC: BDM Federal, 1995, pp. 54-55.

100. V. D. Sokolovsky, ed., *Voennaia strategiia (Military Strategy),* Moscow, Russia: Voenizdat, 1962.

101. Hines, Mishulovich, and Shull, pp. 55-56.

102. Ibid., pp. 19-20.

103. For a look at how the Voroshilov General Staff Academy taught the theater-strategic operation to foreign officers in the mid-1970s, see Ghulam Dastagir Wardak, *The Voroshilov Lectures: Materials from the Soviet General Staff Academy*, Vol. I, Washington, DC: National Defense University Press, 1989, pp. 257-313.

104. Hines, Mishulovich, and Shull, p. 23.

105. Ibid., p. 24. On Western analysis of this option, see P. H. Vigor, *Soviet Blitzkrieg Theory*, Hong Kong: The MacMillan Press, 1985, pp. 183-205.

106. Ibid., p. 25.

107. Jacob W. Kipp, "The Labor of Sisyphus: Forecasting the Revolution in Military Affairs during Russia's Time of Troubles," in Thierry Gongora and Harold von Riekhoff, eds., *Toward a Revolution in Military Affairs?* Westport, CT: Greenwood Press, 2000, pp. 87-104.

108. Hines, Mishulovich, and Shull, pp. 72-73.

109. A. A. Kokoshin, *Strategicheskoe upravlenie: Teoriiam istoricheskii opyt, srvnitel'nyi analiz, zadachi dlia Rossii* (*Strategic Command and Control: Theory, Historical Experience, Analysis, Tasks for Russia*), Moscow, Russia: ROSSPEN, 2003, pp. 240-246.

110. V. V. Larionov *et al.*, *Evoliutsiia voennogo iskusstva: Etapy, tendentsii, printsipy* (*Evolution of Military Art: Stages, Tendencies, Principles*), Moscow, Russia: Voennoe Izdatel'stvo, 1987, pp. 234-245.

111. Vitaly Shlykov, "Chto pogubilo Sovetskii Soiuz? Genshtab i ekonomika" ("What Destroyed the Soviet Union? The General Staff and the Economy"), *Voennyi Vestnik* (*Military Messenger*), No. 9, September 2002, pp. 64-93. See also Jacob W. Kipp, "The Changing Soviet Strategic Environment: Soviet Military Doctrine, Conventional Military Forces, and the Scientific-Technical Revolution in Military Affairs," in Carl Jacobsen *et al*, eds., *Strategic Power: USA/USSR*. London, UK: Macmillan, 1990, pp. 435-456.

112. William E. Odom, *The Collapse of the Soviet Military*, New Haven, CT: Yale University Press, 1998, pp. 388-404.

113. See the essays by Larinov, Kokoshin, and Lobov, A. A. Svechin, ed., *Strategy*, Minneapolis, MD: East View Publications, 1992. See also Andrei Afanasevich Kokoshin, *Soviet Strategic Thought, 1917-1991*, Cambridge: Massachusetts Institute of Technology Press, 1998.

114. William E. Odom, *The Collapse of the Soviet Military*, New Haven, CT: Yale University Press, 1998, pp. 118 ff.

115. Vitaly Shlykov, "Fatal Mistakes of the U. S. and Soviet Intelligence: Part One," *International Affairs*, Vol. XLII, Nos. 5/6, 1996, pp. 158-177.

116. *Ibid.*

117. N. N. Moiseev, *Sotsializm i informatika* (*Socialism and Information Science*), Moscow, Russia: Izdatel'stvo politicheskoy literatury, 1988, pp. 62 ff.

118. Makhmut A. Gareev and Vladimir Slipchenko, *Budushchaia voina* (*Future War*), Moscow, Russia: OGI, 2005.

119. D. M. Gvishiani, "Dialektiko-materialisticheskii fundament sistemnykh issledovanii" ("Dialectical-Materialist Foundation of Systems Research"), in D. M. Gvishiani, ed., *Filosoficheskie aspekty sistemnykh issledovanii: Trudy filosofskogo, metodologicheskogo seminara* (*Philosophical Aspects of Systems Research: Works of the Philosophical-Methodological Seminar*), Moscow, Russia: Vsesoiuznyi nauchno-issledovatel'shii Institu sistemnykh issledovanii, 1980, pp. 3-9.

120. V. A. Kartashev, *Sistema sistem: Ocherki obshchei teorii i metodologii* (*System of Systems: Essays on General Theory and Methodology*), Moscow, Russia: Izdatel'stvo Progress-Akademiia, 1995, p. 398.

121. Jacob W. Kipp, *Foresight and Forecasting: The Russian and Soviet Military Experience*, College Station, Texas: Center for Strategic Technology Stratech Studies, 1988, p. 262.

122. Jacob W. Kipp, "The Nature of Future War: Russian Military Forecasting and the Revolution in Military Affairs, a Case of the Oracle of Delphi or Cassandra?" *The Journal of Soviet Military Studies*, Vol. 9, No. 1, March 1996, pp. 1-45.

123. Jacob W. Kipp, "The Russian Armed Forces, the Draft Military Doctrine, and the Revolution in Military Affairs: The Oracle of Delphi and Cassandra Revisited," in Michael H. Crutcher, ed., *The Russian Armed Forces at the Dawn of the Millennium, 7-9 February 2000*, Carlisle, PA: Center for Strategic Leadership, 2001, pp. 324-334.

124. Jacob W. Kipp, "Russian Non-Strategic Nuclear Weapons," *Military Review*, Vol. 81, No. 3, May-June 2001, pp. 27-38.

125. M. A. Gareev, *If War Comes Tomorrow: The Contours of Future Armed Conflicts*, London, UK: Frank Cass, 1998.

126. Vladimir A. Slipchenko, *Voina budushchego* (*War of the Future*), Moscow, Russia: Moskovskii Obshchestvennyi Nauchnyi Fond, 1999, pp. 35-46.

127. *Ibid.*, pp. 157-207.

128. V. S. Pirumov and R. A. Chervinskii, *Radio-eltronika v voine na more* (*Radio-Electronic Warfare at Sea*), Moscow, Russia: Voenizdat, 1987, p. 77.

129. V. S. Pirumov, "O nekotoryk itogakh i posledstviakh primeneniia sistem i sredstv razvedki, upravleniia i REB v boevykh deistviiakh v zone Persidskogo zaliva" ("On Some Results and Consequences of the Employment of Systems and Means of Reconnaissance, Command and Control, and Electronic Warfare during the Combat Actions of the Zone of the Persian Gulf"), *Geopolitika i bezopasnost'* (*Geopolitics and Security*), No. 2, 1994, pp. 81-84.

130. Vladimir Pirumov, "On the Concept of Russia's National Security," *Russian Executive and Legislative Newsletter*, No. 9, 1995, p. 15.

131. M. I. Abdurskhmanov, V. A. Barishpolets, V. L. Manilov, and V. S. Pirumov, *Osnovy natsional'noi bezopasnosti Rossii* (*Foundations of Russia's National Security*), Moscow, Russia: Izdatel'stvo Druza, 1998.

132. V. D. Riabchuk et al., *Elementy voennoi sistemologii primentel'no k resheniiu problem operativnogo iskusstva i takiki obshchevoiskovykh ob'edinenii, soedinenii i chastei: Voenno-teoreticheskikh trud* (*Elements of Military Systemology Employed in the Solution of Problems of Operational Art and Tactics by Combined-Arms Large Formations, Formations, and Units: Military-Theoretical Work*), Moscow, Russia: Izdatel'stvo Akademii, 1995.

133. V. D. Riabchuk, *Teoriia urpavleniia boem: Nauchnovedcheskii i metodicheskii aspekty* (*Theory of Combat Command and Control: Scientific-Research and Methodical Aspects*), Moscow, Russia: Agenstvo Pechaati Nauka, 2001, pp. 42-54.

134. V. D. Riabchuk, "Elemnty voennoi sistemologii sukhoputnykh voisk" ("Elements of the Military Systemology of Ground Forces"), in V. D. Riabchuk, *Upravlenie, effektivnost', intellekt* (*Command and Control, Effectiveness, Intellect*), Moscow, Russia: Agitiplakat, 2001, pp. 269-278.

135. Makhmut Gareev and Vladirmir Slipchenko, *Future War*, Ft. Leavenworth, KS: Foreign Military Studies Office, 2007.

136. Vladimir Kuzhilin, "Voiny shestvogo pokoleniia" ("Wars of the Sixth Generation"), *Armeiskii sbornik* (*Army Digest*), No. 11, 2002, p. 78.

137. Ivan Kapitanets, "Pozitsiia: Voenno-morskaia nauka i sovremennost'" ("Position: Naval Science Today"), *VPK*, No. 12, December 2004.

138. E. F. Podsobliaev, "Diskussionnaia tribuna: Spornye voprosy teorii bezkontaktnykh voin" ("Discussion Tribune: Controversial Questions of the Theory of No-Contact Wars"), *Voennaia mysl'* (*Military Thought*), No. 2, February 2006, pp. 25-33.

139. Yu. N. Golubev and V. N. Kargin, "Diskussionnaia tribuna: Voennaia sistemologiia and voennaia informatizatsiia:

Edinnstvo konspetual'nykh podkhodov" ("Discussion Tribune: Military Systemology and Military Informatization: Unity of Conceptual Approaches"), *Voennaia mysl'* (Military Thought), No. 6, June 2006, pp. 75-80.

140. V. D. Riabchuk and A. V. Riabchuk, *Voennaia doktrina: Put' k pobede* (*Military Doctrine: The Path to Victory*), Moscow, Russia: Agitplakat MSKH, 2005, pp. 59-92.

141. V.D. Riabchuk, "problemy voennoi nauki i voennogo prognozirovaniia v usloviakh intellektual'no-informatsionnogo protivborstva" ("Problems of Military Science and Military Forecasting under Conditions of intellectual-Informational Conflict"), *Voennaia mysl'* (Military Thought), No. 5, May 2008, pp. 67-76.

142. V. Slipchenko, *PinyDe liu dai zan tsun* (Sixth-Generation Warfare), by Chung Tai Hua, trans., Beijing: Xinhua Press, 2004, The World New Military Revolution Series.

CHAPTER 4

RUSSIAN INFORMATION WARFARE THEORY:
THE CONSEQUENCES OF AUGUST 2008

Timothy L. Thomas*

INTRODUCTION

The August 2008 conflict between Georgia and Russia clarified for Russian leaders the growing influence of information warfare (IW) and exposed several deficiencies in the Russian armed forces in regard to information-based equipment and theory. The conflict also served as the primary motivator for a Russian military reform effort that, in its procurement of new equipment, is sure to include the latest advances in information-technologies. In short, the conflict has wide-ranging implications for future information warfare activities.

Russia's leadership was not taken by surprise over IW's growing importance. For the past several years, Russian political and military figures have written extensively about the impact of the information age on Russian domestic, foreign, and military affairs. In the case of politicians and diplomats, the focus has

---

* The views expressed in this report are those of the author and do not necessarily represent the official policy or position of the Department of the Army, Department of Defense, or the U.S. Government. The Foreign Military Studies Office (FMSO) assesses regional military and security issues through open-source media and direct engagement with foreign military and security specialists to advise army leadership on issues of policy and planning critical to the U.S. Army and the wider military community.

been on writing international strategies and policies designed to shape the information environment to Russia's liking. Considerable time and effort has gone into participation in international forums devoted to information topics, such as the world summits on information societies in Okinawa in 2000, Geneva in 2003, Tunis in 2005, and other such events. Efforts to inject Russian-led information policies into United Nations (UN) discussions have also been persistent. Domestically, politicians have written legislation to confront cybercrime and other internal issues related to the development of an information society. President Dmitriy Medvedev is allegedly an active Internet user who understands the net as an important information weapon, so emphasis on this area should continue. Former President Vladimir Putin was not as enthusiastic in accepting the net as is Medvedev.

Russia's military remained active in a number of information-related areas and also was not taken by surprise in the IW arena. In 2007, Defense Minister Anatoliy Serdyukov promoted Oleg Eskin to the position of seventh deputy defense minister, handling information technology and communications. Under his direction, the military continued to write extensively on IW theory, electronic warfare doctrine and equipment, satellite clusters designed for military purposes, and reconnaissance-strike complexes. In addition, the military continued its focus on two components of IW, its information-technical and information-psychological aspects, as they had done since the concept was first discussed openly. However, advancement in all areas was not performed as quickly as initially anticipated and, when theory was tested in conflict, several weaknesses appeared immediately, most notably problems with communication equipment. The current Russian military reform focus of Anatoliy Serdyukov is designed to correct this and other shortcomings. In November 2008 he replaced Eskin with 39-year-old Dmitriy Chushkin, another sign of his displeasure over the performance of information technologies during the crisis.[1]

This chapter will address two issues associated with these information-related topics in Russia that appeared shortly before and after the August 2008 conflict. Information-related policies of the Russian Federation and their emergence as a key factor in Russia's spiritual and technical development will be discussed, as well as the impact of the recent Georgia-Russian conflict on the future of IW theory, organization, and equipment in Russia. Russian leaders hope that addressing policy and lessons learned now will prevent future failures in information-related areas, especially those of the military.

BACKGROUND ON INFORMATION-RELATED STRATEGIES OF THE RUSSIAN FEDERATION

Russian IW policymakers at the strategic level appear to have adopted a three-pronged approach to information-related developments. This approach, in progress since the late 1990s, has shown steady progress in two prongs, the international and domestic fronts, where the development of policies and doctrines has continued unabated. However, the August 2008 conflict appears to have affected the third prong (military) the most (and provided the greatest controversy).

The first prong of Russia's strategic approach is that politicians and diplomats continue their drive to shape the international information environment, an approach that began more than a decade ago. Russian leaders focused initially on influencing international opinion at the UN through the definition of terms such as information weapons, but they have experienced little progress on this front in influencing international public opinion. However, their efforts continue, and in 2009 several new information-related issues are on the UN agenda. Russia has also focused on shaping international opinion at worldwide conferences on the development of an information society. Armed mentally with the experience of losing an ideology at the end of the Cold War (described by some as "World War III"), Russian strategists understand the important role that information and news play in influencing the minds of its citizens. As a result, Russia should not be expected to back away from continuing this approach either.

The second prong of Russia's strategic approach is that Russian politicians have developed several doctrines and policies to enhance domestic information security, especially the impact of new media on the Russian population. Politicians do not want a replay of the end of the Cold War. These internal policies are aimed at technical issues such as cyber crime and at psychological issues such as the information-psychological stability of society. Leaders have long recognized, from their perspective, an information threat to Russia. In January 2000, for example, Russia's National Security Concept spelled out concern with affairs in the information-technical sphere. It was noted that:

> There is an increased threat to the national security of the Russian Federation in the information sphere. A serious danger arises from the desire of a number of countries to dominate the global information domain space and to expel Russia from the external and inter-

nal information market; and from the development by a number of states of "information warfare" concepts that entail the creation of ways of exerting a dangerous effect on other countries' information systems, of disrupting information and telecommunications systems and data storage systems, and of gaining unauthorized access to them.[2]

In July 2001, Russia published a draft version of a program called "Electronic Russia 2002-2010." Electronic Russia 2002-2010 would enhance domestic information security by creating the institutional and legal environment for the development of an information and communications technology industry that would assist the interaction between the state and society via these technologies. The program was designed to supplement other federally targeted programs (to include but not limited to: Strategy for Russia's Social and Economic Development Until 2010; Development of Electronic Commerce in Russian 2002-2006; the Development of a Unified Educational Information Medium in the Russian Federation 2001-2005; and the Creation and Development of a Special-Purpose Information and Telecommunications System in the Interests of Governmental Bodies 2001-2007).[3]

Russian Professor Aleksandr Selivanov added to this discussion of information security with an article on internal and external IW threats to Russia. He stated that Russia had lost much on the information front in the past 25-30 years. No other weapons have emerged to replace the ideological ones that buttressed the people's souls. For that reason alone, IW remains important. Russia must clarify the direction of information attacks, methods of conducting information operations, and methods of countering them. Without this knowledge, it cannot proceed with confidence in the realm of information security. He notes that the principal method of carrying out information operations is "to form a stratum of people with transformed values in society who actually become carriers of a different culture and of the tasks and goals of other states on the territory of one's own country."[4] Seizure of territory by means of IW, he adds, "presumes 'nontraditional occupation' as the possibility of controlling territory and making use of its resources without the victor's physical presence on the territory of the vanquished."[5]

The third prong of Russia's strategic approach is that Russia's military continues its attempts to modernize its military force and develop the proper military strategy for the 21st century. The recent conflict with Georgia has helped this process pick up speed as the fighting indicated that Russia needs to make significant improvement in command and control and in developing information-based equipment if it hopes to remain competitive in the event of future war. The military's recent focus on reform seems dedicated to making these adjustments happen. In addition to improving tactics and equipment, the Russian military is determined to enhance the psychological stability of its servicemen. *Red Star* (*Krasnaya Zvezda*, the organ of the Ministry of Defense) has printed a number of recent articles dedicated to IW's impact on soldiers' psychological stability. One of these articles noted that only 11 percent of servicemen are currently satisfied with information services the military provides.[6] The government wants to ensure that soldiers get objective information from the new information environment that has surrounded and penetrated the country.[7]

Selivanov wrote that Russia is now obligated to speak about the need for information subunits in the armed forces to shape patriotism and a fighting spirit, to counteract enemy information-ideological operations, and to conduct information-ideological operations against an actual or potential enemy.[8] Thus the reform effort is designed to make improvements in both the technical and psychological components of IW.

These three avenues of approach to information security in Russia are influenced by foreign and domestic events. A look at just seven Russian headlines from 2007-present indicates some of the rationale and concern behind Russia's urgency in handling information security issues:

- "Information technical company head speculates that economic crisis will fuel information security needs;"[9]
- "Growing dependence on computer systems may threaten Russia's security;"[10]
- "National security implications of information warfare analyzed;"[11]
- "Internal, external threats to Russia from information warfare detailed;"[12]
- "Russian General Staff expects cyber war in 2-3 years;"[13]
- "Almost 300,000 hacker attacks on president's website repelled in 2008;"[14]
- "Caucasus conflict prompts Russia to resume development of robotic weapons."[15]

THREE RUSSIAN POLICIES DESIGNED FOR DOMESTIC STABILITY

Russian efforts on the international stage to influence and shape the international environment will not be addressed here as the work on this aspect is too extensive for this analysis. Rather, the focus will remain on Russian internal information-related policies and on military capabilities. This section will discuss three internal policies, to be followed by the section on military issues related to the Georgian-Russian conflict of August 2008. The first policy issue addressed, Russia's 2000 Information Security Doctrine, will be examined in more detail than the other two policies, the 2008 "Strategy of Information Society Development in Russia" and the 2009 "National Security Strategy."

Russia published a very specific and important information-related document in September 2000, the Information Security Doctrine of the Russian Federation. Signed by President Vladimir Putin, Russia's Information Security Doctrine presents the purposes, objectives, principles, and basic directions of Russia's information security. It defines information security as "the state of protection of its national interests in the information sphere defined by the totality of balanced interests of the individual, society, and the state." The doctrine declares that the "implementation of the guarantees of the constitutional rights and liberties of man and citizen concerning activity in the information sphere is the most important objective of the state in the field of information security."[16] Some of the main points of the doctrine are:

- First, the document discusses the national interests of the Russian Federation in the information sphere, including the protection of information resources from unsanctioned access.
- Second, the document examines the types of threats to Russia's information security. These include constitutional rights that protect one's spiritual life, information support for state policy, the development of the information industry, and the security of information.

- Third, the document identifies external and internal sources of threats to Russia's information security.
- Fourth, it outlines the state of information security in the Russian Federation and objectives supporting it, discussing tension between the need for the free exchange of information and the need for restrictions on dissemination of some information.
- Fifth, general methods of information security in the Russian Federation—legal, organizational-technical, and economic—are outlined.
- Sixth, the document discusses several features of information security: economics, domestic policy, foreign policy, science and technology, spiritual life, information and telecommunication systems, defense, law enforcement, and emergency situations.
- Seventh, the goals of international cooperation in the field of information security are discussed, such as a ban on information weapons and the coordination of law enforcement activities.
- Eighth, the doctrine describes the provisions of state policy regarding information security: guidelines for federal institutions of state power, and balancing the interests of the individual, society, and the state in the information sphere.
- Finally, organizational elements of Russia's information security system are described; these include the President, Federation Council of the Federal Assembly, the State Duma of the Federal Assembly, the government of the Russian Federation, the Security Council, and other federal executive authorities, presidential com-

missions, judiciary institutions, public associations, and citizens.[17]

When the information security doctrine was first announced in 2000, it was supported by a series of official proclamations. Official spokesmen reinforced this message. First Deputy of the Security Council Vladislav Sherstyuk, who helped draft the doctrine, claimed that the doctrine would not be used to restrict independent media or control television channels, but asserted that the state must supervise all media, state or private.[18] Anatoly Streltsov, another doctrine author, noted that the components of the doctrine provide for the constitutional rights and freedoms of citizens to obtain and use information, while providing for Russia's spiritual renewal, the development of moral values, patriotic and humanistic traditions, and cultural and scientific potential. Most important, according to Streltsov, was that currently Russia's information security does not fully comply with the needs of society and the state, lacking sufficient legal, organizational, and technical backing.[19]

Information Security in the Sphere of Defense.

Details of the Information Security Doctrine's section on defense are described next. Information security in the defense sphere involves: (1) the information infrastructure of the central elements of military command and control, and the elements of military command and control of the branches of the armed forces and the scientific research institutions of the Ministry of Defense; (2) the information resources of enterprises of the defense complex and research institutions; (3) the software and hardware of automatic systems of command and control of the forces and weapons, arms, and military equipment furnished with computerization facilities; and (4) information resources, communication systems, and the information infrastructure of other forces and military components and elements.[20]

External threats to the Defense Ministry (MoD) include the intelligence activities of foreign states; information and technical pressure (electronic warfare, computer network penetration, etc.) by probable enemies; sabotage and subversive activities of the security services of foreign states, including information and psychological pressure; and activities of foreign political, economic, or military entities directed against the interests of the Russian Federation in the defense sphere. Internal threats included the violation of established procedure for collecting, processing, storing, and transmitting information within the MoD; premeditated actions and individual mistakes with special information and telecommunications systems, or unreliability in their operation; information and propaganda activities that undermine the prestige of the armed forces; unresolved questions of protecting intellectual property of enterprises; and unresolved questions regarding social protection of servicemen and their families.[21]

Ways to improve the system of information security for the armed forces included the refinement of the modes and methods of strategic and operational concealment, reconnaissance, and electronic warfare; and the methods and means of active countermeasures against the information, propaganda, and psychological operations of a probable enemy.[22] The terms information-technical and information-psychological are not used in the information security doctrine, perhaps because military people did not write it. However, its sections on the spiritual and cultural sphere, and the scientific research sphere, do cover the gist of the military's concerns in information-psychological and information-technical realms.

2008/09 POLICIES

Russia has addressed concerns from these year 2000 documents in a number of other documents. In February 2008, Russian President Vladimir Putin approved the "Strategy of Information Society Development in Russia." The strategy has both information-technical and information-psychological overtones. Among the information-technical tasks are: developing modern information and communication infrastructures; developing the Russian Federation's economy using these infrastructures; and developing science, technology, and engineering, as well as training qualified personnel in the field of information and communication technologies. Among the information-psychological tasks are upgrading the quality of education, health services, and social protection of the population; improving the constitutional rights of citizens acting in the information sphere; and preserving the culture, moral, and patriotic principles associated with the public consciousness.[23]

The strategy also discussed how the government of Russia would solve these tasks. The government will formulate basic actions for the development of an information society and create conditions for the implementation of these actions; will define reference values for the development of an information society in Russia; will develop the legislation and updates for law-enforcement's use of information and communication technologies; will create conditions for the intensive development of science, education, and culture (and science-driven information and communication technologies); will enable the improvement of the quality and efficiency of public services for business and citizens; will create conditions for equal access for citizens to information; and will use the capabilities of information and communication technologies for strengthening the defense capacity of the country and the security of the state.[24]

In May 2009, Russia's National Security Strategy was published. It further addressed the concerns expressed in the 2000 National Security Concept. The unclassified version of the strategy, in superficial terms, mentions the global information confrontation; information as a strategic deterrent; information as a means of conducting armed combat; the availability of information technologies (especially telecommunications); the formation of an information and military infrastructure; the importance of information science and information resources; the role of information networks and systems in situation centers; and information and information-analytical support necessary for implementing the strategy.

THE GEORGIAN-RUSSIAN CONFLICT: IW AND MILITARY REFORM

The August 2008 conflict with Georgia occurred midway between Russia's 2008 strategy for an information society and the 2009 national security strategy. The conflict likely influenced the 2009 national security strategy. Information-related aspects of the August 2008 conflict were discussed often in the press of both countries. Russian cyber attacks, Georgians stated, neutralized Georgia's use of the Internet and its ability to talk internally with its citizens. Georgian attacks on Russia were less successful but still merited consideration in the Russian press for their ability to shut down some services. With regard to military equipment dependent on information-based technologies, the Russian military did not do well. Equipment with information technologies were deemed a critical shortcoming that must be fixed. Lieutenant General Vladimir Shamanov, at the time chief of the Main Combat Training and Troop Service Directorate of Russia, stated that troops needed equipment with up-to-date geolocation and telecommunications instruments (to include ensuring uninterrupted telecommunications) integrated into the fire command chain, a top-notch friend-or-foe system, and the ability to improve the resolution power of reconnaissance assets.[25] Command and control equipment often failed and relegated commanders in some instances to using the cell phones of journalists. Precision-guided weaponry did not perform well. The military's poor performance in Georgia served as a catalyst for change and military reform efforts, headed by Defense Minister Anatoliy Serdyukov.

Several prominent Russian authors discussed the good and bad features of Russia's information warfare response months after the conflict ended. Most prominent among them are the Dean of the Russian Foreign Ministry's Academy for Future Diplomats, Igor Panarin; the head of the Institute for Political and Military Analysis Center of Military Forecasting, Colonel Anatoliy Tsyganok; the Deputy Chief of the Russian Armed Forces General Staff, General Anatoliy Nogovitsyn; and Russia's First Deputy of the General Staff, General Aleksandr Burutin.

RUSSIA LOST THE INFORMATION WAR: THREE OPINIONS

Panarin addressed shortcomings with what he termed information-related reform. He offered an interesting plan to correct Russia's information warfare deficiencies. Panarin is a long-time IW specialist and thus understands quite well the ins and outs of the problem. Overall, he was not impressed with Russia's use of IW, noting that in regard to the Georgian conflict "the Caucasus demonstrated our utter inability to champion our goals and interests in the world information arena."[26] Two public groups of Russian experts, Panarin added, had looked at the IW problem in a September round table of the Russian Federation Public Chamber (titled "Information Aggression against Russia: Methods for Countering It"); and an October international conference sponsored by the party "A Just Russia" (titled "Information Warfare in the Modern World"). Panarin concluded that "the geopolitical and geoeconomic role of Russia in the world will be determined to a large extent by whether or not it can create an effective system for information warfare."[27]

Panarin writes that to win the information war, Russia needs a specialized management system and analytic structures that counter information aggression against Russia. The components of such a system are:

    1. Council for Public Diplomacy: includes members of the state structure, media, business, political parties, nongovernmental organizations (NGOs), and so on headed by Prime Minister Putin.

    2. Advisor to the President of Russia for Information and Propaganda Activities: Coordinates activities

of the information analysis units of the President's administration, the Security Council, and several other ministries.

3. State Foreign Affairs Media Holding Company (All-Russia State Television and Radio Broadcasting Company): The government should subordinate this company to the Ministry of Foreign Affairs, where the American experience can be copied.

4. State Internet Holding Company: Create a domestic media holding company for the publishing of books, video films, video games, and the like for dissemination on the Internet.

5. Information Crisis Action Center: Enable the authorities to present commentaries on unfolding events in a timely, real-time manner to the world information arena. "Homework assignments" must be readied in advance.

6. Information Countermeasure System: Create a system of resources to counter information warfare operations by Russia's geopolitical enemies.

7. NGOs: network of Russian organizations operating on Commonwealth of Independent States (CIS), European Union (EU), and U.S. territories.

8. System for Training Personnel for Conducting Information Warfare: Define which institutions will train individuals in this topic. Most likely candidates at the highest level are the Diplomatic Academy of the Ministry of Foreign Affairs and the Russian Civil Service Academy; and at the middle level, Moscow State University, the Higher Economic School, and the Moscow State Institute of International Relations.[28]

Panarin adds that these activities must be unified within the framework of an organizational and analytic system composed of eight parts (diagnostic, analysis and forecasting, organization and management, methodological, consultative, prevention, control, and cooperation); and that information Special Forces must be developed to "prepare for effective operations under conditions of a possible crisis."[29] In summary, Panarin advocated creating his system, strengthening financing for the plan, creating a state/private system for managing activities, creating a state/private system for formulating a positive image of Russia overseas, and expanding the information resources of the Russian speaking populations across the globe.[30]

While Panarin's plan was the most complete, it was not the only one offered for consideration. With regard to other plans like Panarin's, an unattributed report published in *Novyi Region* that was eerily similar to Panarin's stated that "Russia lost the information war in August 2008."[31] This unnamed author recommended improving the information structures available to Russia. Special organization-managerial and research entities for counteracting information aggression should be formed by presidential decision. Information troops should be created composed of state and military news media, people responsive to the needs and interests of Russia in response to a crisis. Information troops would do the strategic analysis of control networks, counterintelligence work, operational concealment measures, information security issues, and security for one's own men and equipment. To insure the proper information impact it is necessary to construct an anti-crisis center, a national media holding company, work with public relations entities, and train specialists in applied journalism as well as military press, radio, and TV journalists. To construct information countermeasures, it is necessary to develop a center for the determination of critically important information entities of the enemy, including how to eliminate them physically, and how to conduct electronic warfare, psychological warfare, systemic counterpropaganda, and net operations to include hacker training. The personnel of information troops would be diplomats, experts, journalists, writers, publicists, translators, operators, communications personnel, web designers, hackers, and others.[32]

In March 2009, analyst Anatoliy Tsyganok also wrote that, at the preliminary stage of the conflict, Georgians won the information war. In Tsyganok's opinion, every agency was unprepared to conduct IW against Georgia. This included the Security Council, the Ministry of Foreign Affairs, and the press center of the Ministry of Defense. The two main goals of IW are to disable an enemy's command and control systems, and to impose on enemy citizens moral norms and cultural traditions that are foreign to them. Tsyganok also recommended creating information troops, as did the two previous authors. They would conduct strategic analysis, information influence, and information countermeasures. His discussion of these categories is identical to the paragraph above, suggesting that it was he and not Panarin who provided the interview to *Novyi Region*.[33]

Tsyganok added three other important facts that he did not cover in his *Novyi Region* interview. They are that IW is a reality of geopolitics that Russia's political elite does not understand; that the Israeli Army is the technological model that Defense Minister Serdyukov's reform should follow; and that a military Global Navigation Satellite System (GLONASS) is badly needed, a system that did not work well against Georgia. Thirty-six GLONASS satellites are needed. Then precision weaponry will work.[34]

RUSSIAN IW DID WELL AGAINST GEORGIA: TWO OPINIONS

There were other opinions that positively assessed Russia's information warfare effort in Georgia. The deputy chief of the Russian Armed Forces General Staff, General Anatoliy Nogovitsyn, is representative of someone who was not at all negative about Russia's information warfare performance during the conflict. He said that "Russian journalists stood united with the Russian army as never before, displaying heroism in covering the events in South Ossetia," and that journalists helped "finding the words and evidence to rebut torrents of lies and rejection, and helped the West to view our operations with understanding."[35]

Colonel P. Koayesov also found more positive than negative in Russia's IW effort against Georgia. He noted that, from a Georgian perspective, the effort began long before hostilities, with the key information warfare themes being Georgia's historic right to South Ossetia, Georgia's legal right to South Ossetia, and Georgia's psychological information pressure on world opinion. Once conflict began, between August 7-8, Georgia organized a denial of service attack against South Ossetian websites carrying information about the progress of the fighting. On August 9, Russian news agencies were attacked, making it difficult to access RIA Novosti in particular.[36] Concurrently, the Georgian leadership organized psychological information pressure on their population from with the country and from abroad. Support from abroad was particularly strong from the Anglo-Saxon media, such as the Cable News Network (CNN), the British Broadcasting Corporation (BBC), Reuters, Bloomberg, and others. Georgian President Mikhail Saakashvili, for example, conducted all of his public statements against a backdrop of the EU flag.[37]

Koayesov defined IW in the following way in January 2009, some 5 months after the conflict ended:

> Information warfare consists in making an integrated impact on the opposing side's system of state and military command and control and its military-political leadership—an impact that would lead even in peacetime to the adoption of decisions favorable to the party initiating the information impact and in the course of conflict would totally paralyze the functioning of the enemy's command and control infrastructure.[38]

IW's two components, from a Russian military perspective, have remained consistent through the years. These two components are information-technical and information-psychological. Koayesov defined the former as "blocking the operation of the enemy's state and military command and control systems" and the latter as "exerting psychological information pressure on its leaders, Armed Forces personnel, and the population."[39] The pillars of U.S. information doctrine, on the other hand, have undergone significant change since the 1990s.

Koayesov describes the damage caused by Russian hackers against Georgia as "significantly more serious." Virtually all of Georgia's national ministries and government departments (along with some news agencies) came under attack. Georgia was forced to find other servers to host its web material. Internet online surveys were an important IW field for Russia, since Russia's actions were viewed as peacekeeping by a majority of voters in a CNN survey, which "obviously CNN terminated very promptly."[40] Blog entries were also more pro-Russian than Georgian. Koayesov summed up his research the following way:

> On the whole it can be noted that whereas the Georgian side built its strategy for waging information warfare at the official level, attempting to convince people through mass exposure in popular, primarily Anglo-Saxon publications, the South Ossetian side gambled on involving as many of its Internet supporters as possible in information warfare...the utilization of "mass information armies" conducting a direct dialogue with people on the Internet is more effective than a "mediated" dialogue between states' leaders and the world's peoples.[41]

FURTHER IW CONSEQUENCES OF THE CONFLICT

Besides plans and positives/negatives, there were rather significant consequences of the conflict that appeared months later after the conflict's lessons had been digested. These consequences and second thoughts by major IW players in Russia are important to consider. One early consequence was the October 2008 announcement of a new military intelligence system. The Strela research and production company reportedly developed a new Internet-based military intelligence system. This system will provide a collective view of the battlefield. Strela also announced the production of a new radar known as Aistyonok and a modified version of the Fara-1 radar. The new Fara-PV radar, with night-vision devices, can open fire on group targets in the total absence of optical visibility.[42]

Another of these consequences appeared in the form of a few statements from Russia's first deputy of the General Staff, General Aleksandr Burutin. He said in an interview on January 29, 2009, that it is "essential to switch from an analysis of the challenges and threats in the sphere of information security to a response and to their preemption."[43] In the sense of preemption, Burutin sounds more like the Chinese. More importantly, Burutin stated that a mechanism should be developed that would require states to "incur liability for what is happening in their information space."[44]

The importance of Burutin's last statement was developed further in the U.S. journal *Parameters*. Authors Stephen Korns and Joshua Kastenberg discussed the issue of cyber neutrality from the perspective of the Georgian-Russian conflict. They asked what a neutral nation can do to remain a cyber neutral when another nation at war (Georgia) uses the servers of a neutral (U.S.) country in order to converse with its own nation after its servers have been neutralized or debilitated by another nation (Russia) with whom it is at war?[45] During the Georgia-Russian conflict, a Georgian website was relocated on a private U.S. information technology (IT) company site, and the company provided a cyber conduit through which Georgia's leadership could talk with its population, apparently without the knowledge or approval of the U.S. Government. Luckily, Korns and Kastenberg note, the Georgian authority sought cyber sanctuary on a U.S. ".com" site and not a ".gov" or ".mil" site. Korns and Kastenberg recommended that the U.S. Government should take steps to determine if it will allow future cyber belligerents to make use of Internet assets in the United States, and, if so, what protocol is appropriate to control the situation.[46] Thus they recommend discussion about the issue of cyber neutrality much as Burutin recommends developing a mechanism for incurring liability. Both nations should talk this through.

A year earlier, in January 2008, Burutin was featured in an article by an unnamed journalist that discussed some conceptual solutions for the conduct of information operations. These solutions were in response to what was described as "other nations developing information weapons and announcing their preparations for the conduct of information warfare." It was announced at the Infoforum at which Burutin spoke that "the goals of war are now achieved not through force but through technological and information supremacy."[47] There is no need to cross borders anymore, according to Burutin, because information weapons can do that for you. An information weapon also combines a low level of expenditure and high effectiveness of employment. The article later stated that "an information weapon's primary destructive factor is the manipulation of the consciousness," and referred the reader to a website run by Sergey Kara-Murza.[48] Kara-Murza is well-known in Russia for his description of western attempts to control Russian public opinion. The article ends noting that information space is now a new theater of military operations.[49]

A month after Burutin's 2009 article, General Nogovitsyn stated that the General Staff will develop a strategy for the state's information defense. This is because IW is a reality, and Russia must be ready to respond to this threat. IW's main tasks will be to destroy the key military, industrial, and administrative sites and systems of an enemy, and to inflict psychological and information damage on the military and political leadership as well as the troops and population through the use of modern information technologies and tools.[50] Nogovitsyn's recommendation was immediately challenged by the Federal Security Service (FSB) of Russia, that stated that the military must be aware that the FSB had already created information-protection mechanisms that are constantly being updated. The FSB spokesman added that "such issues are not under the purview of any one department and should be resolved within the framework of the country's Security Council."[51]

Nogovitsyn defined IW as:

> Conflict among states in the information space with the objective of inflicting damage on information systems, processes, and resources and on critically important structures, undermining the political and social systems, and massively brainwashing troops and the population with the objective of destabilizing enemy society and the state as a whole.[52]

With regard to the latter information-psychological effect, Nogovitsyn added that the human mind is the objective of this aspect of warfare against which different information technologies can be directed. In the information-technical sphere, the focus is on information technology systems of reconnaissance, electronic warfare, command and control, and control of precision-guided munitions.[53]

Also in February 2009, Russia's Chief of the General Staff, General of the Army Nikolay Makarov, stated that a priority for Russia's military is the development of its command and control systems. Problems exist with both components of systems and their tactical specifications in his opinion. A consequence of the conflict was noted in an April 2009 report which stated that Russia had abandoned some 300 outdated military projects following the outcome of the armed conflict in South Ossetia. Vladimir Popovkin, Russian deputy of defense in charge of armaments, added that a project to develop robotic military hardware was reopened and efforts were underway to create a single database that any officer, from a battalion commander to the defense minister, can use.[54]

A MILITARY EXPLANATION OF RUSSIA'S INFORMATION SECURITY NEEDS

In February 2009, deputy chief of the Russian Federation's General Staff, Colonel-General Anatoliy Nogovitsyn, dedicated a lengthy article in *Red Star* to Russia's information security. Only on select occasions has such a high-ranking individual discussed this concept in such detail. The article's in-depth analysis makes it appear to be an update to the military aspect of the 2000 Information Security Doctrine of Russia, although this point is not addressed directly.

Nogovitsyn defined information security as the degree of protection of Russia's national interests in the information sphere, to include the interests of the individual, society, and the state to ensure the formation, use, and development of the information environment. Russian national interests in the information sphere include ensuring Russia's spiritual renewal and preserving moral values and traditions of patriotism; information support to Russia's state policy in the form of reliable communications and accurate public information on significant events; the development of modern information technologies in both domestic and international markets; and protecting the state's information sphere from unsanctioned access.[55]

He listed external information threats to Russia as foreign political, economic, intelligence, and information structures directed against Russia's interest in the information sphere; infringements on Russia's interest in the world's information space to drive it from the information market; the development of information warfare concepts by a number of states; competition to possess information technologies and resources; and the activities of international terrorist organizations. Internal information threats to Russia include the condition of its domestic information industry; the rising influence of organized crime on the lawful interests of citizens, society, and the state in the information sphere; and the insufficient coordination among federal bodies to form a unified state policy that can assure Russia's information security.[56]

Some of the consequences of information security threats to the Russian Federation are described by Nogovitsyn as follows:
- Obstacles can be placed in the path of equal cooperation with other countries.
- Important decisionmaking can be hampered (information manipulations of political decisionmaking present a special danger).
- Russian authority in the international arena can be undermined.
- An atmosphere of tension and political instability in society can be created.
- The balance of interests of the individual, society, and the state can be disturbed.
- State authorities can be discredited.
- Social, ethnic, and religious conflicts can be provoked.
- Strikes and mass disorder can be triggered.
- The functioning of bodies of state authority and the functioning of military command and control can be disrupted.[57]

Nogovitsyn states that the mission of information warfare is to destroy the foundations of national self-awareness and the way of life of the opposing side's state. The philosophical and methodological foundations of cognitive activity must be eroded. Victory in modern war, he argues, much like the Chinese believe, occurs with one "preemptively winning information superiority and only later superiority in the sphere where military operations are going on."[58] This ensures victory in modern war. Primary missions of North Atlantic Treaty Organization (NATO) countries, if they attempt to fight information wars in the coming 2-3 years, Nogovitsyn postulates, include disorganizing the "functioning of key enemy military, industrial, and administrative facilities and systems as well as the information-psychological effect on his military-political leadership, troops, and population" using modern information technologies and assets.[59]

Special features of information warfare closed out Nogovitsyn's article. These features distinguish it from other forms of military operations. They are:
- Developing and employing information weapons is cheap.
- Controlling perception is taking an increased role.
- Increasing complexity of damage prevention and assessment.
- Increasing vulnerability of the state's territory.
- Increasing need for a developed information protection strategy.[60]

In another interview, Nogovitsyn was asked about military reform and the transformation's priorities. He stated that social issues (pay, housing, etc.) were the first and second priorities. The third priority was high-quality training for specialists of sophisticated weaponry and equipment—high-technology equipment. Thus, the information-psychological and information-technical areas received priority placement in the reform effort. In fourth place was the ways and means of employing troops for emerging situations (and not for position warfare or large scale operations), and in fifth place was the development of advanced models of armaments.[61]

INFORMATION-PSYCHOLOGICAL STABILITY OF THE FORCE: RECOMMENDATIONS AFTER AUGUST 2008

Russia's military leadership seems intent, in the course of its military reform effort, to prepare the way for an infusion of new digital patriotic educational materials into the armed forces. A three stage plan is proposed. From 2009-12, the expectation is that a television digital format will be introduced into the garrisons as well as the creation of Internet sites of military print media. Between 2013-17, Internet access will be available for 85 percent of servicemen. Between 2018-20 all barracks will have satellite and cable TV, and there will be 20 newspapers per 100 servicemen.[62]

CONCLUSIONS

Russia is working hard at shaping the international environment to its liking. Its efforts at international conferences and at the UN are indicative of this effort. Russian officials have offered proposals on the development of principles for information and communication technologies, discussed the formalization of terms such as information warfare and information weapons, and have developed government groups of experts to discuss information related topics (the last meeting for this group was in 2009). Russia is also interested in developing an international conference site that will mimic the economic conferences at Davos, probably Garmisch, Germany, as the site for these meetings. For the past few years, Russians have been meeting there to discuss information-related issues in April.

Domestically, Russian policymakers worry about what types of IW activities other nations are running against their citizens. To thwart the further loss of patriotic and other cultural values, Russian leaders have developed a host of policies to ensure that protection is offered to Russia's spiritual values. The war with Georgia forced a host of information security issues to the fore. Communication problems surfaced early as did the performance of precision-guided weaponry. Both issues affected the command and control of Russian troops. These problems served as the primary motivators behind Serdyukov's military reform process.

A short confrontation on the Internet between Russian and Georgian hackers resulted in a wide-ranging discussion about the power of the Internet to influence public opinion during a conflict. Russia's leaders seem keen on harnessing this power. Recently, the Kremlin opened what is known as a "school of bloggers," an indication that President Medvedev's interest in social media is taking on new avenues of approach.[63] Evgeney Morozov, who founded the site, noted that

> extensive "googling" for "Kremlin's school of bloggers" reveals at least one interesting project—Polit-TV.ru—a series of ideological YouTube videos, all

branded with a funny Kremlin-shaped logo, which aim to rally up support for the Kremlin's recent public campaigns.[64]

Russia is addressing its military information warfare problems with more focus than at any time in the recent past. This focus includes the proposed development of several new organizations aimed at better control over the information-technical and information-psychological aspects of information warfare. And for once, these reform efforts appear to have the backing of the political leadership. Overall, one should expect that in the next 10 years significant improvement will be noted in all three prongs of Russia's approach to IW—external, internal, and military. The West would be wise to keep a close eye on how Russia proceeds since there is much to learn from its experiences.

ENDNOTES - CHAPTER 4

1. Yuriy Gavrilov, "General Replaced by a Bureaucrat," *Rossiyskaya Gazeta*, November 25, 2008, as downloaded and translated by the Open Source Center (OSC), document number CEP20081125358012.

2. *Nezavisimoye Voennoye Obozreniye*, Internet version, January 14, 2000, as translated and downloaded from the Foreign Broadcast Information Service (FBIS) website on January 16, 2000.

3. "Federal Targeted Program 'Electronic Russia 2002-2010,'" Russian Government Press Release Number 869, Section Four, Internet *Government.gov.ru*, July 5, 2001, as downloaded and translated by the OSC, document number CEP20010723000238.

4. Aleksandr Selivanov, "How Our Land Can Become Foreign Land: On the Architecture of the 'Information War' Against Russia," *Voyenno-Promyshlennyy Kuryer*, March 21, 2007, as downloaded and translated by the OSC, document number CEP20070321436006.

5. *Ibid.*

6. Nikolay Poroskov, "The 'Brains' Will Take by Storm," *Vremya Novostey*, April 7, 2009, as downloaded and translated by the OSC, document number CEP20090408358001.

7. Anatoliy Bashlakov, "Efficient, Objective, and Accessible," *Krasnaya Zvezda*, March 18, 2009, as downloaded and translated by the OSC, document number CEP20090325548001.

8. Selivanov.

9. *Information Security Doctrine*, Russian Federation Security Council, Internet version, September 13, 2000, as downloaded and translated by the OSC, document number CEP20000913000294.

10. *Ibid.*

11. "Russia calls for International Information Security System," *Interfax*, October 12, 2000.

12. Mikhail Shevtsov, *ITAR-TASS*, 1327 GMT, September 12, 2000, translation downloaded from FBIS.

13. *Information Security Doctrine.*

14. *Ibid.*

15. *Ibid.*

16. *Ibid.*

17. *Ibid.*

18. "Russia calls for International Information Security System," *Interfax*, October 12, 2000.

19. Mikhail Shevtsov, *ITAR-TASS*, 1327 GMT, September 12, 2000, translation downloaded from FBIS.

20. *Information Security Doctrine.*

21. *Ibid.*

22. *Ibid.*

23. *The Strategy of Information Society Development in Russia*, February 7, 2008, Moscow, Russia: pamphlet with both the Russian and English texts, p. 2 of the English text.

24. *Ibid.*, pp. 2-3 of the English text.

25. *ITAR-TASS*, 1301 GMT, September 23, 2008, as downloaded and translated by the OSC, document number CEP20080923950226.

26. Igor Panarin, "The Information Warfare System: the Mechanism for Foreign Propaganda Requires Renewal," *Voyenno-Promyshlennyy Kuryer*, October 15, 2008, as downloaded and translated by the OSC, document CEP20081016548020.

27. *Ibid.*

28. *Ibid.*

29. *Ibid.*

30. *Ibid.*

31. "Russia is Underestimating Information Resources and Losing Out to the West," *Novyy Region*, October 29, 2008, as downloaded and translated by the OSC, document number CEP20081031358001.

32. *Ibid.*

33. Interview with Anatoliy Tsyganok, "Ministry of Defense Planning Informatino Warfare," *Svobodnaya Pressa*, March 17, 2009, as downloaded and translated by the OSC, document number CEP20090318358009.

34. *Ibid.*

35. *ITAR-TASS*, 1503 GMT, February 19, 2009, as translated by the OSC, document number CEP20090219950324.

36. Available from *www.rian.ru*.

37. P. Koayesov, "Theater of Warfare on Distorting Airwaves. Georgia Versus South Ossetia and Abkhazia in the Field of Media Abuse. Fighting by Their Own Rules," *Voyennyy Vestnik Yuga Rossii*, January18, 2009, as downloaded and translated by the OSC, document number CEP20090121358009.

38. *Ibid.*

39. *Ibid.*

40. *Ibid.*

41. *Ibid.*

42. Interfax-AVN online, 0845 GMT October 24, 2008, as downloaded and translated by the OSC, document number CEP20081024950109.

43. "An International Mechanism Requiring States to Incur Liability for 'Information Warfare' is Essential," *Tsentr Parlamentskikh Kommunikatsiy*, January 30, 2009, as downloaded and translated by the OSC, document number CEP20090202358007.

44. *Ibid.*

45. Stephen Korns and Joshua Kastenberg, "Georgia's Cyber Left Hook," *Parameters*, Winter 2008-09, pp. 60-73.

46. *Ibid.*, p. 73.

47. Internet *NEWSru.com*, Janauary 31, 2008, as downloaded and translated by the OSC, document number CEP20080201358004.

48. Available from *www.kara-murza.ru/manipul.htm*.

49. *Ibid.* In 2007, Vadim Fedorov defined an information weapon as "a set of software and hardware means designed to control the information resources of the target and to interfere with the operation of its information systems." See Vadim Fedorov, "Information Wars," *Orlovskaya Pravda*, October 9, 2007, as downloaded and translated by the OSC, document number CEP20071105358002.

50. Dmitriy Usov, "Russia is Preparing for the Wars of the Future: Deputy Chief of the General Staff Anatoliy Nogovitsyn States that an Information Defense Strategy will be Created for the Country," *Vzglyad*, February 25, 2009, as downloaded and translated by the OSC, document number CEP20090227358005.

51. Dmitriy Litovkin, "The General Staff is Preparing for a Cyber War," *Izvestiya*, February 27, 2009, as downloaded and translated by the OSC, document number CEP20090302358005.

52. Anatoliy Nogovitsyn, "Information Security is the Focus of Attention," *Krasnaya Zvezda*, February 27, 2009, as downloaded and translated by the OSC, document number CEP20090303548001.

53. *Ibid.*

54. Interfax, 0754 GMT, April 10, 2009, as downloaded and translated by the OSC, document number CEP20090410964069.

55. Nogovitsyn.

56. *Ibid.*

57. *Ibid.*

58. *Ibid.*

59. *Ibid.*

60. *Ibid.*

61. Aleksandr Tikhonov, "Position Warfare has Outlived its Time," *Krasnaya Zvezda*, April 8, 2009, as downloaded and translated by the OSC, document number CEP20090413548001.

62. Poroskov.

63. Nathan Hodges, "Kremlin Launches 'School of Bloggers,'" *Wired*, available from *www.wired.com/dangerroom/2009/05/kremlin-launches-school-of-bloggers/*.

64. Evgeny Morozov, "What do They Teach at the Kremlin School of Bloggers," *Foreign Policy*, available from *neteffect.foreignpolicy.com/posts/2009/05/26/what_do_they_teach_at_kremlins_school_of_bloggers*.

CHAPTER 5

RUSSIAN STRATEGIC NUCLEAR FORCES AND ARMS CONTROL: DÉJÀ VU ALL OVER AGAIN

Daniel Goure

INTRODUCTION

Arms control is back. Renewal of arms control was one of the issues on which then-candidate President Barack Obama ran. Immediately after taking office, his administration began the process of revitalizing the dialogue with Russia on a range of issues, but none more important than changing the dynamic with respect to nuclear weapons. In a joint statement on April 1, 2009, Obama and Russian President Dimitri Medvedev agreed to begin formal bilateral negotiations to create a new, comprehensive, legally binding agreement to replace the 1991 Strategic Arms Reduction Treaty (START). The Joint Understanding the two governments adopted at their July presidential summit in Moscow commits the United States and Russia to reduce their strategic warheads to between 1,500-1,675, and their strategic delivery vehicles to between 500-1,100. Under the expiring START and the 2002 Moscow Treaty (also known as the Strategic Offensive Reductions Treaty [SORT]), the maximum allowable level of warheads is 2,200, and the maximum allowable level of launch vehicles is 1,600. Both parties made commitments to try to conclude this agreement before START expired in December 2009.

Publicly, the Russian government welcomed the Obama administration's interest in improved relations. In some instances, Russian leaders went even farther, seeming to signal the potential for a radically new strategic relationship between the two countries. The new Russian government even echoed some of the foreign policy themes of its American counterpart. For example, in one of their recent international meetings, President Medvedev joined President Obama in committing "to achieve a nuclear-free world while recognizing that this long-term goal will require a new emphasis on arms control and conflict-resolution measures and their full implementation by all concerned nations."[1]

Many politicians and security experts in the West see the present moment as a chance to pursue the complete elimination of nuclear weapons. They recognize that this will be a difficult and possibly prolonged task. In addition, it is generally agreed in the West that getting to zero will require radical changes in the rules that govern the international system, threat perceptions, and the mechanisms for providing the security of nations. Some groups have gone so far as to argue that attaining the "zero option" will require changes to the basic definition of national sovereignty and state-based security. Daryl Kimball, head of the Arms Control Association, provides an example of this view:

> Principles of peaceful coexistence must be created and observed among major and rising powers, involving notions of equality and reciprocity. The elements of a new nuclear approach must be the dropping of absolute security concepts and practices—*true security is mutual*, not absolute. Absolute security agendas among major powers is a dangerous concept in the 21st century; security through inequality does not work, and the nuclear doctrines of the P-5 [the five perma-

nent members of the U.N. Security Council] must reflect this reality.[2]

Consistent with this end, some groups have gone so far as to conduct an Orwellian rewriting of history. For example, a recent Council on Foreign Relations report noted that, although Russia still poses an existential threat to the United States, "... since the end of the Cold War, Russia has neither shown nor threatened such intent against the United States."[3] This statement implies that the continuing existence of nuclear weapons is somehow irrelevant, even antithetical, to the political relationship between Russia and the United States.

Some experts have suggested that interest in reducing the nuclear threat—particularly that resulting from nuclear proliferation or possible terrorist acquisition of nuclear materials and weapons—is of such a high priority that the United States must accommodate Russia in the bilateral strategic relationship in order to gain Moscow's support on the more important strategic issues. For example, a Russian "sphere of influence" in Eastern Europe, the Baltic states, the Caucuses and Central Asia might be accepted in return for Moscow's assisting Western policies on nonproliferation and the Middle East. This would be akin to welcoming the fox into the henhouse in order to keep out the lesser varmints.

A variant on this theme is to seek to denigrate the importance of possessing nuclear weapons by attacking the strategy that underpins the requirement for them. Like early Christian theologians, these advocates of going to zero nuclear weapons are seeking to rewrite the scripture of nuclear doctrine to ensure that no logical or moral case can be made for their retention. In a recent briefing on 21st century deterrence challenges, Lewis Dunn declared that "deterrence thinking in both countries makes it more difficult to move toward cooperative U.S.-Russia political-strategic relationship."[4] Of course, both sides are somehow equally guilty of this sin. In keeping with this chapter's theme of déjà vu again, I must remind the reader of President Ronald Reagan's famous dictum regarding arms races: to wit, that nations do not fear one another because they arm, but rather arm because they fear one another.

Notwithstanding the enthusiasm with which President Obama's election and his administration's initial arms control actions have been met by many in the arms control community, it might be worthwhile to consider how the other side in the arms control dance might be thinking. It is one thing for U.S. officials and experts to dream of a nuclear free world. It is quite another to assume that their opposite numbers share this vision. Furthermore, even if there is a consensus on the end state, it is not clear that the two sides share a sense of how to get there.

Is it possible that Russia and America might actually adopt the American vision of a nuclear-free world? More modestly, what is the likelihood that the United States will be able to find ways to reduce Russia's clear reliance on nuclear weapons for both military security and political leverage?

RUSSIA'S INTERNATIONAL IDENTITY AND ITS NUCLEAR STRATEGY

It is important to recognize that Russian nuclear weapons have two basic purposes: one military and the other political/psychological. The primary military purpose of Russia's nuclear arsenal is to deter a wide range of threats to Russia's security. The most obvious of these threats is an attack with nuclear weapons on Russia. Since the United States alone possesses sufficient strategic nuclear forces to destroy Russia, deterring that threat is the first consideration in Russian nuclear strategy.

However, Russian national security officials see nuclear weapons as serving other important deterrence functions. During the Cold War, Soviet nuclear doctrine rejected the idea of using nuclear weapons in response to conventional aggression. The Soviet government often sought from the United States a "no first use" pledge. Now, however, circumstances are different. Russian military weakness has made it attractive to emphasize the broader roles of nuclear weapons in deterring other types of threats to Russian security. The new Russian Security Concept promulgated in 2000 declared that nuclear weapons can be used "in the case of the need to repulse an armed aggression, if all other methods of resolving the crisis situation are exhausted or have been ineffective."[5] This formulation looks remarkably similar to the statements of the North Atlantic Treaty Organization (NATO) during the Cold War indicating that the alliance might use nuclear weapons in the event of a Soviet conventional attack on Western Europe.

Russian leaders and defense experts consistently rejected the contention of the Bush administration that the absence of great power rivalry between the United States and Russia meant that it was not necessary for the two governments to enter into new strategic arms agreements. From Moscow's perspective, this policy argument was politically unacceptable since it meant that Russia's interests could be disregarded when it came to subjects such as NATO expansion, the deployment of limited missile defenses in Eastern Europe, or U.S. military operations in Central Asia. It also correctly implied that Russia's conventional military position and economic power were so limited that it could not pose a threat to the United States or its interests.

Today, Russia is in greater need of maintaining the mutual hostage relationship created by strategic deterrence than perhaps at any time since the end of World War II. Moscow understands that it too is bound by that relationship, but considering its relative weakness vis-à-vis the United States this is acceptable, particularly in light of Russia's retention of a large arsenal of theater nuclear weapons and its promulgation of a doctrine of nuclear first use.

Some Russian officials and experts have gone even further in defining potential uses for the country's nuclear forces. Russian nuclear doctrine asserts that nuclear weapons, both strategic and theater, have a role to play in deescalating conventional conflicts. Certain Russian nuclear experts also consider them useful—and even legitimate—means for redressing the balance of forces on the conventional battlefield if the other side strikes certain high value targets. According to one senior analyst:

> Russia may decide to selectively initiate the use of nuclear weapons to "deescalate an aggression" or to "demonstrate resolve," as well as to respond to a conventional attack on its nuclear forces, command, control, communications, and intelligence (C3I) forces (including satellites), atomic power plants, and other nuclear targets.[6]

Russian nuclear exercises reflect, if anything, greater attention to the possible early use of nuclear weapons than during the Soviet Union's Cold War exercises. The *Stabilnost'* 2008 (Stability 2008) set of exercises included scenarios which actually simulated the use of nuclear weapons to achieve a number of missions. Most of these scenarios involved some hypothetical NATO aggression against Russia.

In a larger sense, nuclear weapons are viewed as an all-purpose instrument with which to address most of Russia's military security challenges of the 21st century.[7] Russian political and military leaders and defense analysts, echoing arguments made by their predecessors in the 1980s, have repeatedly argued that the threat of conventional precision-strike weapons could be countered by the employment of theater nuclear weapons.[8] Some Western nuclear analysts share this view. The final report of the Commission on the Strategic Posture of the United States noted that, "[i]ronically, our edge in conventional capabilities has induced the Russians, now feeling their conventional deficiencies, to increase their reliance on both tactical and strategic nuclear weapons."[9]

The second, perhaps more important, role of nuclear weapons for Moscow is essentially political. This role derives from the commonly held belief within the Russian government and among the Russian elite that the fall of the Soviet Union was a political (and one could argue psychological) disaster for Russia. The Russian government and many Russian strategic observers make the argument that the conditions which existed after the collapse of the Soviet Union were fundamentally unstable. They argue that the end of the Cold War was not the result of a change in the nature of the international system but the collapse of one of the two poles that bounded and balanced that system. According to one analyst:

> The elimination (of the Cold War environment) took place not due to dispersion of both poles, but because of the collapse of one of them. Since 1991 — the year of the Soviet collapse — and until the early 2000s, the asymmetry between the two former poles continued to increase. It has happened not only due to Russia's decreasing influence, but also as a result of relative strengthening of political, economic, and military positions of the United States and the Western Alliance as a whole.[10]

A number of Russian publications and commentaries of late have argued that START itself was one of those factors leading to a diminution of Russian security. Those making this case argue that the treaty was forced on a weakened Russia by an American government seeking to enshrine its strategic superiority over Russia.[11]

In addition, the end of the Cold War did not result in a significant decrease in Russia's sense of vulnerability. Russian foreign policy and military leaders continued to view the United States and NATO with suspicion. For example, they believe that NATO's eastward expansion was fundamentally directed against Russia. In addition, the new world disorder that emerged after the Cold War appeared to be creating new instabilities and threats along Russia's borders.[12] According to another source, the Russian General Staff sees nuclear weapons as the appropriate response to what they see as a Russia facing a multitude of grave threats:

> The Russian military is not going to abandon its reliance on nuclear weapons to ensure national security. This is unsurprising under the circumstances, when military threats continue unabated and the Russian general purpose forces are significantly less powerful than the armed forces of the countries competing with Russia on the world stage, not to mention a military-political block such as NATO.[13]

There are certainly some observers in the West who share this viewpoint. One prominent American arms control advocate writes:

> Since the end of the Cold War, Russia has increased the emphasis on nuclear weapons in its security strategy as a hedge against the eastward expansion of NATO, the 200 remaining U.S. tactical warheads stored in six NATO countries and China's small nuclear arsenal. This has led Russia to hold on to its sizable arsenal of tactical nuclear warheads, which independent experts estimate to be as high as 8,000.[14]

Regrettably, the development of these threat scenarios has taken on what at times seems an almost frenetic quality. Former Russian President Vladimir Putin has spent most of the past decade emphasizing the proliferation of security threats to Russia, principally as a result of actions by the United States. According to one well-respected analyst of the Russian political and military scene:

> In his speeches since 2006, Putin repeatedly charged that NATO enlargement, missile defenses, the incitement of terrorism, growing American military emplacement in Central and Eastern Europe, refusal to submit to the United Nations (UN) on questions of using force, calls for democracy in Russia, militarization of space, use of conventional missiles in intercon-

tinental ballistic missiles (ICBMs), development of the Reliable Replacement Warhead (RRW), the use of low-yield nuclear weapons or of conventional missiles atop nuclear launchers for missions hitherto described as nuclear, other new weapons, and the militarization of space all present threats to Russia. These reputedly aim at coercing and marginalizing Russia by means of threats against its vital interests and are allegedly drawing closer to Russia's borders.[15]

No doubt this includes a number of U.S. foreign and security policy initiatives ranging from Washington's withdrawal from the Anti-Ballistic Missile (ABM) Treaty to its refusal to enter into new strategic arms control agreements. But it has been the effort to continue NATO's expansion eastward to include Ukraine and Georgia (a policy reaffirmed by the Obama administration) that has been most difficult for Moscow to accept. As one analyst noted, NATO expansion confirms the almost apocalyptic Russian threat perceptions and justifies its often overly aggressive responses to local incidents:

> Although the victory of Dmitri Medvedev in Russia's presidential elections might change the parameters of Russo-American rivalry for the better, it is unlikely to do so soon. The foundations of today's difficult relationship were put in place in the mid-1990s. Subsequent developments have reinforced these foundations and, in the eyes of Russia's leadership, confirmed their essential validity.[16]

In a 2007 statement during a G-8 Summit, then President Putin asserted that U.S.-Russian relations were returning to the mutually antagonistic stance that marked the Cold War. He went even further, declaring that Russia would take new measures to increase the nuclear threat to the U.S./NATO:

> Of course, we will return to those times. And it is clear that if part of the United States' nuclear capability is situated in Europe and that our military experts consider that they represent a potential threat then we will have to take appropriate retaliatory steps. What steps? Of course we must have new targets in Europe. And determining precisely which means will be used to destroy the installations that our experts believe represent a potential threat for the Russian Federation is a matter of technology. Ballistic or cruise missiles or a completely new system. I repeat that it is a matter of technology.[17]

Some observers argue that the reason Putin's government has sought to focus so intently on projecting an image of a world that poses increasing danger to Russia has little to do with the actual validity of these assertions and much more to do with Russian domestic politics. According to this line of argument, in essence the current Russian leadership's hold on power depends on its ability to demonstrate that they are restoring Russia to its rightful position in the world. One might call this superpower status "on the cheap." According to most indices of national power, Russia today is not even a major player, much less an aspiring superpower. One Russian observer explained the connection between the effort to create a climate of fear and Russia's domestic politics in the following manner:

> Maintaining Russia's superpower ambitions and the domination of the former Soviet space are now crucial to the reproduction of the political system and the self-perpetuation of power. In short, Russia's foreign

> policy has become an important tool for achieving the Kremlin's domestic objectives. And a key foreign policy objective is to create the image of a hostile international environment and demonstrate a strong reaction to which it can legitimize the hyper-centralization of Kremlin power, top-down governance, and its crackdown on political pluralism.[18]

The collapse of Russia's economy following the end of the Cold War, the parlous status of Russian conventional forces, and the sense of proliferating threats, provides a logical argument for increased reliance on nuclear weapons. It is no wonder that under these conditions, Russian political and military leaders were concerned about their country's weakness in relation to potential threats, and that they would view nuclear weapons as being the one capability that guaranteed Russia's ability to deter aggression. Indeed, for many years it appeared as if strategic nuclear weapons were the only factor that contributed to Russia having any relevance in the evolving international system. As one author notes:

> The paradox was that by the early 2000s, Russia, indeed, became an economic dwarf. At the same time, it was able to capitalize on the huge Soviet nuclear legacy. Deployment represents the cheapest phase of the lifetime of intercontinental ballistic missiles (ICBMs), the cornerstone of Russia's strategic nuclear deterrent. Their lifetime is also long, and can be prolonged by relatively inexpensive technical measures. This is why, despite the fact that the air and naval components of the Russian strategic triad experienced a decrease in their alert status due to economic constraints, the land-based forces still remained capable and combat ready.[19]

If anything, secular, demographic, and socioeconomic trends argue that Russia's sense of vulnerability, and its determination to retain its presumed position as America's strategic equal, will only cause it to cling ever harder to the concept of strategic deterrence — and with it the retention of nuclear weapons.

If central deterrence of an attack on the homeland was all that concerned Russia, then achieving a stable nuclear balance might not be a particularly difficult challenge, even if it would undermine the Obama administration's dream of complete and total denuclearization. The real problem is that Russia sees the need for a robust and usable capability to conduct theater-level nuclear strikes. As one analyst pointed out, Russian nuclear strategy requires an ability to hold Europe at risk regardless of the central strategic relationship with the United States.[20]

One way to achieve a unilateral capability is by relying on nonstrategic or tactical nuclear weapons. Here Moscow has a distinct advantage over Washington. The United States deploys forward in Europe at most a few hundred air-delivered nuclear weapons. U.S. aircraft carriers, submarines, and some surface combatants are capable of carrying more nuclear weapons (gravity bombs and cruise missiles), but currently do not. In contrast, Russia is estimated to have several thousand of these nonstrategic nuclear weapons, many of which are deployed forward.[21]

The Russian argument is that NATO expansion eastward plus the clear conventional superiority of the Western alliance over Russia's non-nuclear forces requires a countervailing capability in the form of an expansive Russian arsenal of theater nuclear weapons. This view ignores the political situation in NATO and the inability of the alliance to achieve an effective military response to a relatively small-scale challenge such as Afghanistan. Since the military potential of the West seems to outweigh Russia's, Russian strategists insist they need nuclear weapons to achieve stability. One longtime analyst of Russian strategic thought describes the situation: "In other words, believing a priori that Europe is the site of a presumptive enemy action against it, Russia demands as a condition of its security that the rest of Europe be insecure."[22]

The threat environment fabricated by the Russian government may serve its obvious domestic political needs. The situation, however, creates an important dilemma for Russia internationally: How can Moscow agree to the elimination of its nuclear weapons when they alone are the essential bulwark against those threats? Additionally, what would be the basis for Russia's claim for high international status if Moscow were not to retain one of the world's largest arsenals of nuclear weapons?

Many U.S. observers mistakenly believe that Russia's political and security interests are largely parallel to those of the United States. They assume that the threats the West sees from so-called rogue states and terrorist groups acquiring weapons of mass destruction are those that also concern Russia. This is not the case. The principal danger to Russian security, or more correctly to the security of its leadership's hold on power, is in the absence of nuclear weapons. In this way, Russian leaders are in the same position as Iraq's Saddam Hussein, who needed to pretend to have a program to develop weapons of mass destruction for both security and political purposes. The current Russian leadership needs the aura provided by nuclear weapons for two purposes: as a response to the exaggerated threat perceptions they have put forward, and as a means of holding onto power both internationally and domestically.

One Western political scientist with extensive experience in Moscow made the connection between Moscow's retention of nuclear weapons and Russian political and psychological needs explicit:

> For the post-Soviet Russian elite, nuclear weapons play a major politicopsychological role as one of only two remaining attributes of their country's great power and global status (the other being a permanent seat on the UN Security Council). Over the past 15 years, Russian leaders have been repeatedly "reminding" others, in particular the United States, that Russia is still a nuclear power on par with the U.S. In reality, by doing so they have been reassuring themselves that *not everything is lost* and that Russia will make a comeback as a major world player. Nuclear weapons are a symbol of Russia's strategic independence from the United States and NATO, and their still formidable capabilities alone assure for Russia a special relationship with America.[23]

Before we dismiss the Russian perspective as paranoid, one should remember the recent comments by U.S. Vice President Joseph Biden. During a trip to Eastern Europe and Georgia, located on Russia's borders, the Vice-President was quoted as saying that Russia's weakness would most likely make Moscow more accommodating in planned negotiations on strategic issues.

The above discussion is not intended to suggest that there is no room for progress with Russia on some arms control issues. Rather, it is intended to make two points. First, the idea that nuclear weapons can be rendered irrelevant or even eliminated entirely starkly contravenes Russian views of the role those devices play in their country's security policy and domestic politics. Second, the effort to assuage Moscow's sense of injury over the loss of Russia's position of eminence since the end of the Cold War is both dangerous, since it will feed an exaggerated feeling of entitlement, and ultimately futile.

RUSSIAN INTEREST IN STRATEGIC ARMS CONTROL

As demonstrated by the rapidity with which Moscow responded to the Obama initiatives on a new strategic arms treaty, pursuing arms control agreements with Russia is not impossible. The questions that remain are what kinds of agreements are desirable from a U.S. perspective, and what kinds of agreements are possible from the perspective of the Russian government? The related issue is what price the United States might be asked to pay for an agreement that in theory is in both countries' national interest. An example would be any follow-up nuclear arms agreements that permit Russia to maintain an advantage vis-à-vis the United States and NATO in theater nuclear weapons.

Russia's ostensible interests in strategic arms control, most notably in a follow-on agreement to START that captures the progress made in the Moscow Treaty, are fairly obvious and not unreasonable. Russian strategists wish to see the two sides reduce their inventories of strategic weapons for reasons that will be discussed below. Moscow would like to structure new agreements so as to avoid the costs of investing in a significant number of new strategic and theater nuclear systems. Russia also desires increased predictability and transparency regarding U.S. strategic decisionmaking. Finally, a new agreement would reestablish the primacy of the U.S.-Russian relationship in Washington's eyes, something that Moscow has been trying unsuccessfully to achieve for most of the past decade.[24] This last point is clearly reflected in the following comment by a Russian analyst:

> It was obvious that the United States, for whatever reasons, ignored the Russian direct references to the importance of the strategic stability issue. The U.S. Administration just welcomed the part of Putin's statement about "no threat to the national security of the Russian Federation" and paid no attention to what Russia understood under such a threat. To my view, if we could speak of an American mistake, it was not the decision to withdraw from the ABM Treaty, but to completely ignore the principles which must create the basis for strategic relations with Russia after the Cold War; as well as the inability of the United States to present something instead of the "strategic stability" principle for the discussions and probable acceptance by the two states. And it was not enough to put forward standard ideas of "mutual interests and cooperation." The main problem and the task were to prove that the "strategic stability" principle must go, together with the Cold War and U.S.-Soviet confrontation. Since it has not been done, "strategic stability" continued to play a role of a "mine," which sooner or later could deeply worsen or even undermine U.S.-Russian strategic relations.[25]

In truth, the current Russian drive for a new strategic arms limitation agreement is motivated largely by the progressive obsolescence of Russia's strategic arsenal. Numerous Western sources have pointed out that the majority of Russia's strategic delivery vehicles are rapidly reaching the end of their life spans and will soon have to be scrapped. This condition applies to both the land and sea-based legs of the Russian nuclear triad.[26] As a result, Russia is predestined to a further decline in its strategic force posture to well under 1,000 strategic nuclear delivery vehicles and, at best, only slightly more than 1,000 warheads.

Russia has been deploying, albeit slowly, the Topol-M SS-27 ICBM, which is asserted to have capabilities to counter U.S. strategic defenses. The effort to develop a follow-on submarine-launched ballistic missile (SLBM), the Bulava, has run into technical difficulties, reflected in its repeated test failures. There are reports that the program may be cancelled. At the same time, there is no evidence of a program to design a new missile carrying submarine, something Russia will need to begin developing soon if it is to avoid the problem of having its fleet of "boomers" dwindle to a mere handful. The only leg of the Russian triad that appears sustainable in the medium-term is the bomber fleet, based largely on the venerable TU-95 *Bear*. Like the U.S. B-52, it appears that the *Bear* could be maintained as an operational aircraft until several times the average age of its crew members.

Given these conditions, the reductions in the number of strategic delivery vehicles and warheads Russia requires from a new START agreement have basically been predetermined. Critics of the current proposals point to the fact that influential Russians insist that the outlines of the new agreement do nothing to reduce Russia's strategic nuclear arsenal to levels below those to which aging alone would have required it to go:

> Russian Gen. Nikolay Solovtsov, commander of the Strategic Missile Troops, was recently quoted by Moscow Interfax-AVN Online as saying that "not a single Russian launcher" with "remaining service life" will be withdrawn under a new agreement. Noted Russian journalist Pavel Felgengauer observed in *Novaya*

Gazeta that Russian leaders "have demanded of the Americans unilateral concessions on all points, offering practically nothing in exchange."[27]

What Moscow also desires, and what is in this instance a wish shared by the new U.S. administration, is to import the very intensive verification protocols established in earlier START agreements. This will help both sides achieve some, albeit limited, additional visibility into the strategic nuclear activities of the other side. For Russia, there is almost equal value in a set of full verification arrangements as there are in the reduced numbers themselves.

What are the verification provisions intended to ensure? One of the key issues that will need to be resolved in a new START agreement is that of counting rules. Under the Bush administration, the United States sought to count only operational deployed nuclear weapons. This approach would reflect only the actual number of warheads deployed. It would also allow for former nuclear systems, such as the four ballistic missile submarines converted to carrying conventionally armed cruise missiles, to not count against the START ceilings. This would encourage the conversion of strategic nuclear delivery systems into conventional-only systems, something the United States has been doing. It would also encourage reducing the number of warheads on a delivery vehicle or spreading the total number of allowable warheads across more delivery vehicles, depending on the specific ceilings established for each category.

The Russian government rejects this concept and would like to see the counting rules from earlier agreements imported into the new START agreement.[28] Russian sources assert that it would be wrong to ignore the potential of some U.S. systems to be rapidly uploaded with additional nuclear warheads (or in the case of the converted ballistic missile submarines, with SLBMs). More significantly, given the state of the Russian strategic delivery force, this would allow Russia to maintain a fleet, albeit reduced in numbers, of highly multiple independently targetable reentry vehicle systems (MIRVs), a condition which meets their cost objectives but could be highly destabilizing.[29]

Similarly, the Russian preferred approach would essentially deny the United States the ability to develop so-called prompt global strike capabilities, such as ICBMs or SLBMs armed with conventional rather than nuclear warheads. Most Russian sources see such weapons, with their extreme precision, as a means of circumventing strategic arms control as well as potentially an attempt to develop a new strategic weapon for use against Russia that would slide under any theoretical nuclear use threshold. Russia may also seek to limit other U.S. conventional capabilities with alleged strategic effects, possibly including long-range unmanned aerial systems.[30]

On a related subject, dealerting (that is, reducing the rapidity with which strategic systems can be launched), Russian arms control negotiators have been at best only modestly interested. In the past, Russia has claimed that it had dealerted its missiles by changes in software coding. Repeated studies have made it clear that those de-alerting measures, which are low cost and provide for realerting in a reasonable time period, are almost impossible to verify. Those that are readily verifiable are either extremely expensive or are the equivalent to the dismantlement of the launcher. There does not appear to be an easy solution to this dilemma.

The subject of limits on theater nuclear forces is one that should be addressed even now. It must be addressed if the United States intends to pursue arms reductions below those outlined in the July 2009 Obama-Medvedev memorandem on a post-START agreement. This is a serious problem, as described by former Pentagon official Dr. Keith Payne:

> Russia has some 4,000 tactical nuclear weapons and many thousands more in reserve; U.S. officials have said that Russia has an astounding 10 to 1 numerical advantage. These weapons are of greatest concern with regard to the potential for nuclear war, and they should be our focus for arms reduction. The Perry-Schlesinger commission report identified Russian tactical nuclear weapons as an "urgent" problem.[31]

It seems unlikely that Russia would easily relinquish one of the few areas of military advantage it now possesses. One old-time Cold Warrior, Andrei Kokoshin, now head of the International Security Problems Institute at the Russian Academy of Sciences, recently again made the case for Russia's retention of its superiority in tactical nuclear weapons in light of the threats Russia allegedly must confront:

> Our national security is different (from that of the United States). Tactical nuclear weapons are advantageous for us and necessary for the provision of national security. . . . What matters here is not so much the number of nuclear warheads and their carriers to be stipulated in a would-be treaty. The most important thing is that this treaty must secure for Russia a guaranteed capability of inflicting unacceptable damage in a retaliatory nuclear strike against any country that carries out a nuclear attack on it.[32]

Another issue of interest to many is that of missile defenses, particularly the proposed deployment of a limited U.S. missile defense system in Poland and the Czech Republic. The Russian government and leading Russian strategic experts have been highly critical of the U.S. proposal to deploy such a system. A number of officials have gone so far as to warn that Moscow will take offensive countermeasures, some of which would increase the threat to Europe, in the event that the deployments go forward. On the day President Obama was elected, President Medvedev warned that unless the plan to locate the U.S. missile defenses in Europe was halted, Russia would deploy additional short-range ballistic and cruise missiles that could target the U.S. facilities in Eastern Europe.[33]

Missile defenses, particularly those in Europe, appear to strike at the very heart of the Russian strategic conception and Moscow's requirement to be able to hold Europe at risk regardless of the balance of forces between Russia and the United States. One analyst sought to answer the question why a ballistic missile defense architecture of only 10 interceptors oriented towards the threat from Iran would so antagonize the Russian government:

> Close examination of Russian policy reveals that these defenses entrench the United States in Eastern Europe's military defense and foreclose Russia's hope of intimidating Central and Eastern Europe or of reestablishing its hegemony there and possibly even in the Commonwealth of Independent States (CIS). If missile defenses exist in Europe, Russian missile threats are greatly diminished, if not negated. Because empire and the creation of a fearsome domestic enemy justify and are the inextricable corollaries of internal autocracy, the end of empire allegedly entails Russia's

irrevocable decline as a great power and—the crucial point—generates tremendous pressure for domestic reform.[34]

However, there is an interesting strain of thought in both the United States and Russia regarding a cooperative approach to defending Europe and Russia from third-party missiles. Sources in both countries have proposed a variety of approaches towards achieving cooperative missile defenses, including the use of Russian radars to complement or support the European defense system, or an agreement to suspend actual deployments of defensive missiles pending Iran's testing of a medium-range ballistic missile.[35] Russian Foreign Minister Sergei Lavrov has alternatively warned of Russian countermeasures to a non-Russian missile defense system in Europe and proposed cooperative alternatives. As an example of the latter, he has suggested the need for a common definition of the threat and of an appropriate system to be developed prior to actual deployment:

> The first problem is that we differ in our assessment of the threat of missile proliferation which is the target of the global system of anti-missile defense .... We have agreed that experts will focus on working out a common understanding of the present threat. And the second problem is that for the joint work of Russian and American experts to become more effective, it is necessary to "freeze" the new plan for the deployment of the new installations in Europe.[36]

CONCLUSIONS

The Obama administration and the Medvedev-Putin government approach the issue of strategic arms control from diametrically opposed positions. For the new U.S. administration, the threats of concern are those posed by the nuclear weapons themselves in the event of crises, their potential for being proliferated or falling into the hands of terrorists, and the difficulties of establishing a positive relationship between Moscow and Washington that might result from retaining a secure U.S. nuclear deterrent. This attitude reflects the views held by many U.S. strategists that the issue preventing an improved political relationship between the two countries is the maintenance of a security strategy based on deterrence.

But even were this not the case, the U.S. approach to nuclear arms control is based on a fundamental flaw. As described by Lewis Dunn, it presumes that "in effect, vis-à-vis each other, U.S. and Russian nuclear forces would be moved 'into the backroom' of the political relationship."[37] As this chapter argues, that is precisely the outcome that Moscow seeks to avoid.

For the Russian leadership, the problem is the inherently adversarial nature of relations between these two nations, the potential cataclysmic consequences of which Russians argue can only be held in check by a mutual hostage relationship. For Moscow, nuclear forces are not anachronisms of the Cold War because the essential feature of that era, the enduring rivalry between the main antagonists, continues. Possibly the best description of the Russian view of the connection between politics and nuclear weapons was recently provided by Dr. Stephen J. Blank:

> Thus the fundamental basis of the rivalry with Washington is political and stems from the nature of the Russian political system, which cannot survive in its present structure without that presupposition of conflict and enemies and a revisionist demand for equality with the United States so that it is tied down by

> Russian concerns and interests. From Russia's standpoint, the only way it can have security vis-à-vis the United States, given that presupposition of conflict, is if America is shackled to a continuation of the mutual hostage relationship, based on mutual deterrence that characterized the Cold War, so that it cannot act unilaterally. In this fashion, Russia gains a measure of restraint or even of control over U.S. policy. Thanks to such a mutual hostage relationship, Russian leaders see all other states who wish to attack them, or even to exploit internal crises like Chechnya, as being deterred. Therefore nuclear weapons remain a critical component in ensuring strategic stability and, as less openly stated, in giving Russia room to act freely in world affairs.[38]

While it is certainly possible for the United States and Russia to conclude a new START agreement, and even to make progress on other nuclear issues, it is highly unlikely that the current Russian leadership is willing to go down the path towards complete denuclearization. Nor is it likely that Moscow will be willing to see nuclear weapons relegated to the backroom.

This situation creates a potential dilemma for the Obama administration. It can seek to gain Russian agreement to further nuclear arms reductions beyond the planned post-START levels by reassuring Russia regarding its strategic position. The United States can do this by limiting both the development of advanced conventional weapons and the refitting and modernization of its future nuclear forces. In so doing, Washington inevitably increases the value of Russia's residual nuclear arsenal, making it even harder for Moscow to relinquish those weapons and any perceived advantage that might accrue from superiority in selected aspects of its strategic or theater nuclear posture.

ENDNOTES - CHAPTER 5

1. Daryl G. Kimball, "Taking the Bang out of Nuclear Weapons," *Moscow Times*, April 13, 2009, available from *www.ploughshares.org/news-analysis/blog/taking-bang-out-nuclear-weapons*.

2. *Realizing Nuclear Disarmament*, Report of the UN Issues Conference 2009, Muscatine, IA: The Stanley Foundation, April 2009, p. 11, available from *www.stanleyfoundation.org/publications/report/issues09.pdf*.

3. William J. Perry and Brent Scowcroft, Chairs, *U.S. Nuclear Weapons Policy*, Independent Task Force Report No. 62, New York, Council on Foreign Relations Press, April 2009, p. xii.

4. Lewis Dunn, *21st Century Deterrence Challenges – Exploring Key Issues, Rethinking Traditional Approaches*, May 20, 2009 (hereinafter *21st Century Deterrence*).

5. "Russia's National Security Concept," Washington, DC: The Arms Control Association, January 2000, *www.armscontrol.org/act/2000_01-02/docjf00*.

6. Alexei Arbatov, *Reducing the Role of Nuclear Weapons*, paper presented to the Conference on Achieving the Vision of a World Free of Nuclear Weapons, Oslo, Norway, February 26-27, 2008, pp. 5-6, (hereinafter *Reducing the Role of Nuclear Weapons*).

7. Stephen J. Blank, *Russia and Arms Control: Are There Opportunities for the Obama Administration?* Carlisle, PA: Strategic Studies Institute, U.S. Army War College, March 2009, p. xi, (hereinafter *Russia and Arms Control*).

8. Stephen J. Blank, "Undeterred: The Return of Nuclear War," *Georgetown Journal of International Affairs*, Vol. I, No. 2, Summer/Fall 2000, pp. 55-63.

9. *Congressional Commission on the Strategic Posture of the United States*, Washington, DC: U.S. Institute of Peace, May 6, 2009, available from *www.usip.org/strategic-posture-commission/view-the-report*.

10. Alexander Pikayev, "Arms Control and U.S.-Russian Relations," in Stephen J. Blank, ed., *Prospects for U.S.-Russian Security Cooperation*, Carlisle, PA: Strategic Studies Institute, U.S. Army War College, March 2009, pp. 121-122, (hereinafter *Prospects*).

11. Victor Esin, "Possible Attributes of a New Russian-American Treaty on Strategic Offensive Weapons: The View from Russia," New York: The Carnegie Council for Ethics in International Relations, July 21, 2009, available from *www.cceia.org/resources/articles_papers_reports/0024.html*.

12. Alexei Arbatov, "Terms of Engagement: Weapons of Mass Proliferation and U.S.-Russian Relations," in Blank, *Prospects*, pp. 143-144.

13. Esin.

14. Kimball.

15. Stephen J. Blank, "Threats to and from Russia," *The Journal of Slavic Military Studies*, Volume 21, Issue 3, July 2008, pp. 491-526, abstract available from *www.informaworld.com/smpp/content~content=a901872669~db=all~jumptype=rss*.

16. James Scheer, "Russian and American Strategic Rivalry in Ukraine and Georgia," in Blank, *Prospects*, p. 285, available from *www.isn.ethz.ch/isn/layout/set/print/content/view/full/100?id=97317&lng=en&ord588=grp1&ots591=0C54E3B3-1E9C-BE1E-2C24-A6A8C7060233*.

17. Vladimir Putin, cited in Blank, *Russia and Arms Control*, p. 176.

18. Lilia Shevtsova, "The End of Putin's Era: Domestic Drivers of Foreign Policy," *U.S.-Russian Relations: Is Conflict Inevitable?* Washington, DC: Hudson Institute, June 26, 2007, p. 50, available from *www.hudson.org/files/publications/Russia-version%202.pdf*, (presented as part of Hudson Institute Summer Symposium).

19. Pikayev, p. 124.

20. Blank, *Russia and Arms Control*.

21. Perry and Scowcroft, p. 35 and footnote 32.

22. Blank, *Russia and Arms Control*, p. 9.

23. Dimitri Trenin, *Russia's Nuclear Policy in the 21st Century Environment*, Proliferation Papers, Paris, France: Institut Francais des Relations Internationales (IFRI) Security Studies Department, Autumn 2005, p. 1, available from *www.carnegie.ru/en/pubs/media/73180.htm*.

24. Linton Brooks, "Arms Control and U.S.-Russian relations," in Blank, *Prospects*, pp. 107-108, available from *se2.isn.ch/serviceengine/Files/RESSpecNet/97336/ichaptersection_singledocument/C6424A5A-E95A-41CB-ABA9-DBB716F779F1/en/Ch_3.pdf*, (Brooks chapter revised August 10, 2008).

25. Alexander Savalyev, cited in Blank, *Prospects*, p. 29.

26. Keith Payne, "Arms Control Amnesia," *The Wall Street Journal*, July 9, 2009, p. A11; Perry and Scowcroft, pp. 32-33.

27. Payne.

28. Pavel Podvig, "Formulating the Next U.S.-Russian Arms Control Agreement," *The Bulletin Online*, December 18, 2009, available from *www.thebulletin.org/web-edition/columnists/pavel-podvig/formulating-the-next-us-russian-arms-control-agreement*.

29. Payne.

30. Podvig.

31. Payne.

32. Andrei Kokoshin, "Expert Cautions Russia Against Eliminating Tactical Nukes," *Interfax*, August 14, 2009, available from *gsn.nti.org/gsn/nw_20090814_6996.php*.

33. Stephen J. Blank, "Russia Challenges the Bush Administration," Op-Ed, The U.S. Army's Strategic Studies Institute

Newsletter, December 08, 2008, available from *www.strategicstudiesinstitute.army.mil/pubs/display.cfm?pubID=900*.

34. *Ibid.*

35. Steve Pifer, "A New Approach to Missile Defense in Europe," Washington, DC: The Brooking Institution, July 2, 2008, available from *www.brookings.edu/opinions/2008/0702_missile_defense_pifer.aspx*; Arbatov, *Reducing the Role of Nuclear Weapons*, pp.165-166.

36. Sergei Lavrov, cited in Blank, *Prospects*, p. 40.

37. Dunn.

38. Blank, *Russia and Arms Control*, pp. x-xi.

CHAPTER 6

THE CHALLENGE OF UNDERSTANDING THE RUSSIAN NAVY

Mikhail Tsypkin*

PUTIN'S NAVY

The Russian naval tradition is torn between the desire of Russian politicians to project the image of a great naval power and the reality of Russia as a great land power. In the course of the 20th century, Russia and the Soviet Union tried three times to build a true blue water navy — before World War I, in the late 1930s before World War II, and during the second half of the Cold War (from the 1960s until the late 1980s). In each case, these plans had to be abandoned because a blue water navy turned out to be not crucial for the nation's survival. In both world wars, the Russian Navy — with the exception of its ballistic missile submarine fleet, a part of the strategic triad — was useful on the flanks of the great land battles of the Eastern Front, but did not play an independent role. In the first decade after the Soviet collapse, the real — as opposed to the declaratory — missions of the armed forces were to maintain Russia's sovereignty, to preserve its status as a nuclear superpower, to deal with the brushfire wars in

---

* Mikhail Tsypkin is associate professor of national security affairs at the Naval Postgraduate School. The author would like to express his gratitude to Captain Christopher Bott, U.S. Navy (ret.), for providing a valuable critique of the draft. The views expressed in this paper are the author's, and do not represent the view of the Dept. of the Navy or any other agency of the U.S. Government.

the post-Soviet space and in the North Caucasus and, in a political crisis, to defend the current occupant of the Kremlin from challengers. None of these missions required a blue water navy; accordingly, the Russian Navy, despite regular outbursts of soaring rhetoric from Russian politicians, was allowed to stagnate and deteriorate.

The arrival of Vladimir Putin to the Kremlin, in 2000, appeared to open a new and more ambitious era for the Russian Navy (*Voyenno-morskoi flot* [VMF]). Since then, the Navy has been showered with political attention, received several new ships, sent its ships on global cruises for the first time since the collapse of the Union of Soviet Socialist Republics (USSR), heard promises to build several aircraft carriers, saw combat in the Black Sea, and has sent its attack submarines, for the first time in more than a decade, to the shores of the United States. At the same time, the Russian Navy suffered disasters, including the catastrophic sinking of the *Kursk* nuclear attack submarine, was ordered to remove its main staff from the Russian capital of Moscow to the relative backwater of St. Petersburg, has been downgraded in the plans of military reform, and has fallen behind on the plans to modernize the seaborne leg of the nuclear triad. What does this contradictory record tell us about the future of VMF?

Under Putin, the Russian Navy received a lot of political attention. Within days of assuming the office of the president (on April 3, 2000), Putin signed a detailed document entitled the *Foundations of the Russian Federation's Naval Policy until the Year 2010*. A year later (on July 21, 2001), he approved another major document, the *Maritime Doctrine of the Russian Federation until the Year 2020*.[1] In 2007, the Russian government adopted the *Strategy for the Development of the Shipbuilding In-*

dustry until the Year 2020 and Beyond.[2] The interagency Maritime College (Council) has produced voluminous documentation regarding future plans for the Russian Navy. Russian Navy officers have filled the pages of the *Naval Digest*, their professional journal, with detailed and passionate arguments about the future of the Russian Navy.

In the Soviet era, such abundance of official pronouncements would have been sufficient for a reasonably confident forecast of naval developments. The Soviets had a well-established (however wrongheaded) worldview and goals in international politics; their policy debates were for the most part conducted in secrecy (and thus did not confuse Western analysts) and resulted in settlements that would then be revealed to the world; they also had a mechanism for mobilizing resources that could turn, however imperfectly, intentions into capabilities. Russia, in contrast, is still seeking its position in the world, fluctuating between loud hostility to the West and demands to be accepted as its partner. Russia's policy process is opaque and informal: the highest authority, especially in matters of national security, is theoretically vested in the president. The current incumbent (Dmitri Medvedev) however, appears to play second fiddle to the strongman prime minister (Vladimir Putin), who skillfully balances interests of powerful financial-industrial clans closely connected to the machinery of the Russian state. This political system produces endless intrigue and policy debates, often without an obvious resolution and execution. Finally, Russia's economy is much smaller than the Soviet one, and it no longer has the mobilization mechanisms, such as all-encompassing economic planning and disregard for the consumers' well-being, that allowed the USSR to compete in the military field with more advanced and wealthy countries. Profit seeking has become perhaps the strongest motive in the activities of Russian elites.

Another difficulty in forecasting Russian naval developments stems from the fact that the current naval force is a product of the Soviet era. Recently we have witnessed an increased level of activity by the Russian Navy. One should not, however, make projections on the basis of what we see today. One has strong reasons to doubt that Russian industry will be able to replace the retiring ships. Former Navy commander-in-chief retired Admiral Vladimir Kuroedov recently observed that the Russian shipbuilding industry has been unable to build new ships in a timely fashion, while research, development, and design of new ships capable of deploying far from Russia's shores have been chronically underfinanced.[3]

Russia's unsettled vision of its place in the world had a direct impact on its naval policy. Putin has promoted the image of Russia as a "great power," erasing the "humiliations" of the 1990s. The Kremlin's vision is rooted in the Soviet past: being a great power means being taken as an equal by the United States. This vision is irrational, given the economic and demographic realities, but it is driven by a veritable hostile obsession with the United States among the Russian elites and public. Russian politicians discovered in the 1990s that the Russian public, while reluctant to have their children drafted for military service, associate patriotism with military power. The Russian Navy represents a particularly tempting subject for public relations games. Big ships look even more impressive than marching infantrymen and rolling tanks. Construction of a capital ship can be rightfully presented as a national achievement. The Russian naval tradition is rhetorically linked to one of the few relatively positive figures in Russian history, Peter the Great. The Navy can provide visible proof of Russia's resurgence and growing international activism by its presence in various areas of the world and through port calls. The Russian Navy also includes the platforms of the sea-based leg of the Russian nuclear triad, which is extolled by Russian leaders and media as the key to national defense and to keeping the status of a great power. In the realm of naval policy, being a great power requires having aircraft carriers to match the United States.

VIRTUAL AIRCRAFT CARRIERS

The subject of aircraft carriers surfaced in a very tentative fashion in the *Foundations of Naval Policy* (March 2000). At that time, however, Putin was very concerned about finding ways to fill Russia's treasury by using its natural resources. In response to this imperative, the then Navy commander-in-chief Admiral Vladimir Kuroedov (1997-2005) appealed to Putin's obvious interest in the economic dimension of Russia's maritime policies, especially in the exploration and extraction of Russia's natural resources from the seabed, as reflected in the *Maritime Doctrine of the Russian Federation* (approved in 2001). Both the *Foundations . . . of Naval Policy* and the *Maritime Doctrine* put emphasis on the defense of Russia's sovereignty over mineral and biological resources of the ocean. As far as the Navy's priorities, these documents stress the traditional importance of ballistic missile submarines (SSBNs), as the sea-based leg of Russia's nuclear triad. According to some reports, in 2004, the Ministry of Defense prepared a plan of naval development until the years 2040-50, which put emphasis on defense of Russia's territorial and contiguous waters, projecting naval power for about 500 kilometers (km) from the shore—an antithesis of a blue water navy equipped with aircraft carriers.[4] The issue of a blue water navy complete with aircraft carriers was not to be raised prominently until 2005, by which time the Russian financial situation began to improve drastically, and relations with the United States, which had seemed to have picked up after September 11, 2001 (9/11), began to deteriorate again as a result of Ukraine's "Orange Revolution" of 2004.

On March 25, 2005, the Kuznetsov Naval Academy in St. Petersburg hosted a conference on the "History, Prospects of Development and Combat Employment of Aircraft Carriers in The Russian Navy." Speakers included industry executives and prominent retired admirals, who were all in favor of equipping the Russian Navy with carriers. Carrier enthusiasts argued that Russia needed these ships in order to repulse attacks with cruise missiles—presumably, by the U.S. Navy—against Russia's heartland from the Arctic and Pacific oceans. The likely cost of this undertaking met resistance from the influential Finance Minister Aleksei Kudrin.[5] On August 25, 2005, Putin, while on board the heavy missile cruiser *Peter the Great*, stated that it was time to start long-term planning (beyond 2020) for new weapon systems, reiterated his view that the Navy was critically important for extracting resources from the seabed, and said that the Navy's financing had been increased to 30 percent of the defense budget.[6] Still, there was no apparent rush to build carriers. In early 2006, Minister of Defense Sergei Ivanov said that it was a bit too early to discuss building aircraft carriers, although he recognized that the Russian

Navy would need them. Further, he explained that until 2015, the armaments program treated the Navy as being equally important to the strategic nuclear forces; 25 percent of the weapons acquisition budget in the course of this program would go to the Navy. (Of course, Ivanov neglected to mention the overlap between the budgets of the Strategic Nuclear Forces and the Navy because of the need to build new nuclear submarines carrying SSBNs and submarine-launched ballistic missiles [SLBMs].) The new Navy commander-in-chief Admiral Vladimir Masorin said at the time that the construction of aircraft carriers would not begin before 2015, and until then the shipbuilding program would focus on smaller ships that could escort carriers.[7]

Masorin stated that the Russian Navy, given the budget constraints, could not afford any of the fashionable doctrines that their American counterparts implemented. Instead, the Russian Navy would devise an asymmetrical strategy to deter use of force. The strategy should enable the Russian Navy to prevent a potential adversary from dominating the theater of naval operations and guarantee unacceptable damage to the adversary. In the next 10 years (until 2015), he said, the main task would be to maintain the existing ships in the state of readiness, and prepare ideas and plans for a new generation of navy ships and an adequate support and logistics system for them.[8] Even conceptual work on the design of aircraft carriers was reportedly not included in the 2006-15 armaments plan.[9]

As oil prices climbed throughout 2007 and the first half of 2008, and relations with the West deteriorated even further, the rhetoric about aircraft carriers escalated. In May 2007, a meeting of top Navy brass and leaders of the shipbuilding industry considered the issue of aircraft carriers. A spokesman for the Navy said that the participants believed that Russia needed carriers and that "building a ship of this class would increase the status of Russia as a maritime power. . . ."[10] Admiral Masorin commented in June 2007, that the new Russian carriers would be relatively small (50,000 tons), nuclear powered, and would have about 30 aircraft (fixed wing and helicopters). The beginning of their construction had been originally planned for 2016-17, but may be undertaken earlier, added the admiral.[11] A year later, his successor, Admiral Vladimir Vysotsky, announced that beginning in 2012-13 Russia would start building "five or six" aircraft carriers for its Northern and Pacific fleets.[12] On October 11, 2008, President Dmitri Medvedev visited the Admiral Kuznetsov carrier and confirmed that Russia indeed would build aircraft carriers, the first one to be completed by 2013-15.[13] In November 2008, the media reported that the shipbuilding company Sevmash in Arkhangelsk was selected to build the new carriers and its general manager was already discussing with journalists the upgrades that his shipyard would require to accommodate the construction of carriers.[14] But a sudden rhetorical turnaround was executed in June 2009, when Deputy Minister of Defense for Armaments Vladimir Popovkin stated that the plans to begin building aircraft carriers in 2012 would be postponed indefinitely.[15]

There is likely no single explanation for the sudden blooming and withering of the enthusiasm for carriers. The most apparent reason—the rise and fall of the Russian economy is obvious. The rapid growth of the Russian economy during Vladimir Putin's second term as president (2004-08) produced euphoria among the Russian elite. It is possible that the Russian policymakers, schooled in finance, but not in management of manufacturing industries, failed to appreciate the enormous complexity of building aircraft carriers. They may have seen sufficient financing as the only major condition for such an undertaking. It is likely that the shipbuilding industry encouraged this kind of thinking out of an obvious self-interest, without pointing out to the political leaders that the problems of Russian industry's—an outdated capital plant and a depleted, rapidly aging work force—could not be solved in the short and even medium term simply by an infusion of money.[16] As the realities of the economic crisis set in and forced a sober survey of Russia's economy among the policymakers, the improbability of the aircraft carrier project became obvious to the Kremlin.

It appears that the Russian high command did not have real—rather than rhetorical—plans for building aircraft carriers. In various official pronouncements, the number of carriers fluctuated from "a couple" to five "or" six. This "or" suggests that no plan had ever been approved. Moreover, Admiral Vysotsky, when explaining the Navy's future to journalists of the military daily, *Krasnaya Zvezda*, in February 2009, named the Navy's priorities as; building SSBNs, attack submarines, multipurpose surface ships, strike and reconnaissance systems, command and control, and navigation systems.[17] Carriers were not mentioned. This is a very traditional emphasis (except for SSBNs, which are a part of Russia's strategic nuclear forces) on ships that can defend Russia's contiguous waters.

At his June 5, 2009, press conference the Chief of General Staff Army General Nikolai Makarov warned that rearming the Navy would take a longer time than the other services because of the huge cost: a capital ship, he said, would cost as much as a fully armed division of the ground forces.[18] Several days later, Deputy Minister of Defense Popovkin observed that the Russian high command still had to decide, "[why] do we need these carrier groups? What are our strategic interests in the [distant] regions, what do we have to defend far away [from home]."[19] If the Russian leaders need proof that building carriers would be extremely difficult, the saga of overhauling and upgrading the former *Admiral Gorshkov* for the Indian Navy has definitely provided one. On July 1, 2009, Medvedev visited the Sevmash shipyard, and warned the shipbuilders that they could no longer drag out the *Gorshkov* project, which had commenced in 2004 with the initial completion date of 2008; after huge cost overruns the completion date has been postponed until 2012-13.[20] All of the above suggests that the discussion of aircraft carriers had no concrete plans behind it.

The discussion of carriers, however, reflected certain realities of Russian politics and economy. One was likely a carryover from Putin's successful PR campaign of 2007-08: portraying Russia as a great power was one of its central elements. Another factor behind the aircraft carrier hullabaloo may have been purely commercial. One of the main trends of Putin's industrial policy has been formation of state-controlled giant industrial holdings (which include privately owned enterprises in which the government owns shares) headed by government officials close to Putin. On March 21, 2007, the Russian government created the United Shipbuilding Corporation (USC), to put under the same roof the research and development (R&D) and shipyards involved in design and production of naval ships and weapon systems.[21] The first chairman of the board of the USC was the head of the administration (chief of staff) of the Cabinet of Ministers Sergei Naryshkin, appointed in September 2007.[22] In May 2008, soon after Putin had moved to the post of prime minister, the USC top job went to one of the most powerful figures in Russian business and politics, Deputy Prime Minister Igor Sechin.[23] Sechin reportedly played the central role in the imprisonment of then Russia's wealthiest man, Mikhail Khorodkovsky, and has been accused of profiting immensely from the destruction of Khodorkovsky's oil company YUKOS.[24] One of the most important holdings of the USC is the shareholder-owned Sevmash Shipyard in Arkhangelsk. These shareholders could have profited from stories persistently leaked to the media that Sevmash had already been selected to become the prime contractor to build new aircraft carriers.[25]

THE "NEW LOOK" AND THE RUSSIAN NAVY

The real priorities for the Russian Navy should be viewed in the light of the latest military reform, to which the Russians call "the new look" of the armed forces, probably because all the previous military reforms undertaken since 1991 changed virtually nothing. The decision to seek the new look for the Russian military followed the Russo-Georgian war of August 2008, which demonstrated that the Russian armed forces suffered from numerous serious deficiencies. The essence of the new look is a transformation of the hollow Soviet-type military, which would need to mobilize millions of conscripts to fight, into a much smaller force ready to fight on a short notice. Its structure is also to change, with divisions replaced by brigades, and operational commands (partially modeled on American combatant commands) established in conjunction with existing military districts. This is a step away from preparations to fight an all out war against the North Atlantic Treaty Organization (NATO) towards plans to be ready for regional conflicts along Russia's periphery. This realistic approach recognizes that a large-scale conflict with NATO (or, for that matter, China), is highly unlikely, especially in view of Russia's nuclear arsenal.

Russian experts have had relatively little specific to say about the impact of the new look on the Navy. According to Admiral Vysotskiy, the Navy's missions under the new look have not changed. They include the paramount one of strategic deterrence, plus various missions to defend Russia's interests in the contiguous seas, as well as participation in international United Nations (UN)-sanctioned forces. The priorities in procurement, according to Vysotsky, include SSBNs, multipurpose attack submarines, multipurpose surface ships, as well as reconnaissance; target acquisition; command, control, and communications (C3); and navigation systems.[26] This suggests that the future Russian Navy is supposed to operate with confidence in adjacent seas and embark on selected missions further away from home, such as distant port calls and participation in international efforts against piracy, smuggling, etc.

A practical demonstration of what awaits the Navy under the new look has been provided by the recent decision to operationally subordinate the Black Sea Fleet and the Caspian Flotilla to the commander of the North Caucasus military district/operational-strategic command, a Ground Forces officer. This decision was reportedly prompted by the inability of the amphibious assault ships of the Black Sea Fleet to provide support in a timely fashion to the Russian ground forces fighting Georgian troops along the Inguri River and the Kodori Gorge.[27] The Northern and Baltic fleets will be similarly subordinated to the commander of the Leningrad military district/operational-strategic command, while the Pacific Fleet will be subordinated to the commander of the Far Eastern military district/operational-strategic command.[28]

This approach is a nightmare for the proponents of a Russian blue water navy. The tension between them and the authors of the military reform was expressed in an unprecedentedly shrill article in the August 2009 issue of the *Naval Digest* authored by the retired Navy commander-in-chief Admiral Kuroedov and two other Navy officers. Tellingly entitled, "We Should Continue to Fight for the Russian Navy," the article blames the decline of the Russian Navy squarely on the domination of the military by the Ground Forces: "The main cause of this situation is the navy's complete dependence upon the army's decisionmaking mechanism which has resulted in a low level of financing for the navy." Further, the authors claim that the during the Putin era the Navy received only 12 to 14 percent of the overall military budget, a figure much lower than the 30 percent cited in the past by Putin and Sergei Ivanov. Kuroedov et al., accuse the "hidebound" resistance of failing to recognize the Navy's independence "in any sphere of its current existence," which has resulted in a "tragedy" for the Russian Navy.[29]

It appears that the minister of defense Anatoliy Serdyukov wants to make it very difficult for the Navy to lobby for its interests in Moscow. He ordered the main staff of the Navy to move from Moscow to St. Petersburg, a decision met with a howl of protests.

High-ranking Navy retirees made open protests and active duty naval officers made organized leaks. A move of a government agency from Moscow to St. Petersburg gets the agency in question away from the center of power and makes it less relevant. This is what has happened to the Constitutional Court, a body whose importance in Russia is quite minimal. Moving the main staff from Moscow to St. Petersburg would mean rebuilding the C3 system, reserve wartime command facilities for the Navy, etc. There is no military utility whatsoever in the move—but it certainly puts the Navy brass further away from Putin, Medvedev, and their staffs. It also frees up valuable real estate in the center of Moscow, which the Ministry of Defense can sell, and creates new business in St. Petersburg, the home of both Putin and Serdyukov.

As mentioned earlier, the most significant missions of the Russian Navy are strategic deterrence and projecting power in the contiguous seas. The all-important strategic deterrence mission has suffered a series of significant setbacks. Currently, the Navy is responsible for 172 SLBMs and 612 nuclear warheads (based on 13 SSBNs) out of the total 634 strategic delivery platforms and 2,825 nuclear warheads of the Strategic Nuclear Forces (SNF).[30] If a new arms control treaty between Russia and the United States is signed, the total number of delivery vehicles and warheads of each side will go down to 500−1,100 and 1,500-1,675, respectively, the Russian Navy's share of delivery vehicles may go up to nearly one-half, and the warheads to about one-third of the total. The future of the sea-based leg of the nuclear triad is uncertain because of continuing failures of the Bulava R-30 SLBM. At issue is not just the solid-propellant missile itself, but also the Borey-class SSBN specially built to carry it. If the

Bulava has to be replaced by the existing liquid-propellant Sineva SS-N-23 SLBM, the Borey design will have to be changed to accommodate a large missile. This would be very costly, and will make resources available to the general-purpose naval forces even more scarce. The cost of the sea-based leg of the strategic triad probably explains the huge discrepancy between the Navy's budget figures cited by Kuroedov (12-14 percent of the overall military budget) and the 25-30 percent cited by Putin and Sergei Ivanov.

Resource allocation for the Navy is a difficult process because of the conflicting priorities when it comes to Russia's four fleets and one flotilla. The geography makes such decisions nearly a zero-sum game, since one Russian fleet cannot easily reinforce another in an emergency, and an emergency can easily arise, since three fleets (Northern, Black Sea, and Pacific) and the Caspian flotilla operate in areas with potential for border and other conflicts. The main competition for resources is likely to arise between the Northern and the Black Sea fleets. The Russians have said much about the importance of the Arctic and the Northern Fleets. The Arctic is the home of the majority of Russian SSBNs. The Northern Fleet is the least geographically constrained of all the Russian fleets, providing a relatively easy access to the Atlantic Ocean. The economic potential of the Arctic is deemed to be very considerable: the ice melting may lead to new possibilities for extraction of oil and gas, as well as for opening of regular navigation from Europe to the Far East along the northern edge of Russia. The Northern Sea Route (as the Russian call it) can favorably change Russia's strategic situation by improving the tenuous transportation link of European Russia with the Far East, as well as strengthening Russia's position as the transportation link between Europe, Asia, and North America.

There is potential for conflict over Russia's claims regarding the seabed in the Arctic and the demarcation of the sea border with Norway. Reading the comments made by Russian naval experts, one may conclude that the militarization of the Arctic is inevitable.[31] This is hardly surprising given the self-interest of the Navy, the antagonistic views of the West that have become politically correct in Russia since the late 1990s, and the fact that the Arctic is a hiding place of the Russian strategic deterrent, the SSBNs based in the Kola peninsula.[32] At the same time, as Katarzyna Zyśk observes, the Russian Arctic policy so far has been quite pragmatic.[33] While the Russians created enormous publicity around the stunt of putting the Russian flag on the bottom of the Arctic Ocean, they have not followed through on their rhetoric by unilaterally claiming a large sector of the Arctic. Russia is strategically isolated in the Arctic region and NATO naval forces have easy access there. While the Russians have shown a willingness to demonstrate that their Navy is "back," avoiding direct confrontations with NATO has, so far, been as much the heritage of the Soviet era as the dream of a blue water navy.

One of the highest priorities of Russia's foreign policy under Putin has been creating an exclusive sphere of influence in the post-Soviet states.[34] The Black Sea region has seen the sharpest conflict resulting from Moscow's attempts to implement this policy priority. The prime example was the Russo-Georgian war of 2008, in which the Black Sea fleet saw action. The tensions between Russia and Georgia have been intertwined with the tensions between Russia and Ukraine (Russia has been incensed by Ukraine's support for Georgia), and with the fate of the Black Sea fleet that may lose its base in Sevastopol after 2017. The Russians would like to keep NATO naval forces out of the Black Sea; Admiral Vysotskiy stated that "the non-Black Sea nations have no business in the Black Sea." He emphasized naval cooperation with Turkey (which controls access to the Black Sea) and which goes hand-in-hand with the Kremlin's wooing of Ankara on various energy projects.[35] Unlike in the Arctic, the Russians have more hope of keeping the NATO navies (primarily the U.S. Navy) out, thanks in part to various provisions of the Montreux Convention.

Russia's decision in August 2008 to recognize Abkhazia and South Ossetia guaranteed continuing tension in the Black Sea area for years, if not for decades. The temptation to use force in the Black Sea is much greater for Russia than in the Arctic, since during the Russo-Georgian war NATO demonstrated that it would not defend countries that are not its members, and also because NATO naval deployments to the Black Sea are limited, because of the Montreux Convention preventing aircraft carriers of the Western nations from entering the Black Sea. Recent interceptions of Abkhazia-bound ships by Georgia, and Abkhazian threats to destroy the Georgian ships taking part in such operations raise the specter of a naval conflict involving Russia. The possibility of a conflict with Ukraine over the fate of Sevastopol and the Crimea cannot be completely discounted. In view of this, it is logical that the Kremlin has recently stressed the importance of building up the military infrastructure and buying new ships for the Black Sea fleet.[36] The neighboring Caspian Sea is important for Russia's energy interests and for its influence both in Central Asia and the Caucasus. Thus, the southern flank may very well siphon off resources from the Northern Fleet.

An important recent development indicates the growing interest in littoral operations to support Russia's goals vis-à-vis other post-Soviet nations. While attending a EURONAVAL-2008 exhibition in Paris in October 2008, Admiral Vysotsky expressed open interest in purchasing a Mistral-Class Force Projection and Command Ship, built by the French THALES Corp.[37] Secret negotiations with the French company began at about the same time.[38] On June 24, 2009, Admiral Vysotsky said that Russia might start buying ships abroad.[39] Soon the media began to cite rumors of Russia negotiating a purchase of an aircraft carrier with a French company.[40] In late August 2008, Chief of the General Staff General Makarov confirmed that Russia had indeed entered negotiations with the French company to buy a Mistral-class ship, and hoped to have a contract by the end of 2009.[41]

The Mistral-class are "all-electric ships with an overall length of 199 meters and a displacement of 21,300 tons."

> The . . . concept combines a landing helicopter dock, a floating hospital, an amphibious assault ship, troop transport and a command vessel in a single platform. . . . They have a crew of 160, plus 450 troops, endurance of 45 days, and maximum range of 11,000nm at 15 knots. . . . It can carry up to 16 heavy helicopters and one-third of a mechanized regiment, plus two . . . hovercraft or four . . . landing craft. A high-performance communications suite makes the Mistral ideal as a command vessel. The 750-sq.m hospital features two operating theatres and offers 69 beds. If additional hospital/medevac space is required, the hangar can be converted into a modular field hospital.[42]

Thus, a Mistral-class ship is a potent asset for operations in the post-Soviet region, enabling Russia to carry out amphibious landings and serving as an instrument of psychological pressure: this ship is large, and with its ability to project power on land, any small country would feel threatened if such a Russian ship carrying naval infantry, tanks, and helicopters appears in its vicinity during a crisis in relations with Russia. Moreover, it could do something the Russian politicians craved in vain during the Kosovo war: send a visible signal of Russia's strong displeasure with NATO, and demonstrate its ability and willingness to help its friends.

The biggest question concerning the future of the Russian Navy is the condition of the Russian shipbuilding and manufacturing industry in general. According to a Russian expert, the Navy has received only four new ships since 2000. It can count on buying, in the foreseeable future, one nuclear attack submarine (the *Severodvinsk,* a Yasen' class, project 855), three diesel submarines (the Lada class, project 677), and three corvettes (the Steregushchiy class, project 20380). (This forecast excludes SSBNs.) It has taken nearly 10 years to get the *St. Petersburg*, the first of the Lada class submarines, to the stage of testing. It took 7 years to get the first ship of the Steregushchiy class into service.[43] Such a slow rate, even at the time of increasing defense budgets, suggests serious problems in the shipbuilding industry. Judging from the plans to import a Mistral class ship, the Russian naval command has apparently become quite skeptical about the ability of the Russian defense industry to provide them with all the ships it needs.

The condition of the Russian shipbuilding industry, both civilian and naval, leaves much to be desired and is outside the scope of this chapter. Still, some facts need to be mentioned. The Maritime Council concluded recently that "the shipbuilding industry currently cannot effectively fulfill all the strategic tasks set by the government. . ."[44] Russian shipbuilding exists mostly thanks to Navy orders—more than 70 percent of its contracts are with the Ministry of Defense.[45] This has not made the industry as a whole competitive, because the habit of working for the Navy has made it unable to control costs.[46] The formation of the USC so far has not changed the situation for naval shipbuilding. One of the more recent positive results of the Russian shipbuilding industry, the diesel-electric icebreaker *St. Petersburg*, was built at the Baltiysky Zavod in St. Petersburg by the United Industrial Corporation, and not by the USC.[47]

Without attempting a detailed discussion of the subject, I would like to note that the Russian defense industry as a whole is stuck in transition from a command economy to a market economy. Until this transition is complete, the defense industry will not be a reliable provider of new weapons for the Russian military. The Russian manufacturing industry in general, including the defense industry, suffers from many problems. According to Sergei Chemezov, the general director of the state corporation Rostekhnologii, noted that about 70 percent of the main equipment for Russian machine building (including shipbuilding) is 20 years old, or even older. Only 5 percent of machine tools are 5 years or younger. "The defense industry suffers badly because Russia has fallen behind in computer technology," observed Chemezov.[48] The current economic crisis has hit the defense industry hard: in January 2009 about one-third of defense industry companies were in danger of bankruptcy.[49]

After years of talk about building unmanned aerial vehicles (UAVs), Russia had to begin importing them from Israel. Now it is about to import Mistral class ships from France, thus spelling an end to Russia's dream of being an autarkic, totally self-sufficient military power. The Russian defense industry is not dead by any means, but Russia is no longer an autarkic defense industrial power. Its ability to arm itself will depend on cooperation with other nations and imports. This would obviously have a major impact on such complex weapon systems as modern surface and subsurface navy ships, and on Russia's ability to conduct a foreign policy independent of the influence of the major industrial powers.

CONCLUSION

The ultimate challenge of understanding the Russian Navy lies not in the capabilities of the Russian shipyards or in plans drawn by the Main Naval Staff and redrawn by the General Staff. Measuring strength and weakness in conventional terms is a less reliable forecasting instrument that in the recent past. The rapidly and unpredictably changing international scene can provide unexpected leverage to the weaker actors and paralyze the stronger ones. While the Russian Navy is not likely to project its power in a meaningful way over the world ocean in the foreseeable future, it will be able to serve as an instrument for gaining influence vis-à-vis Russia's smaller and weaker neighbors and for defending the maritime approaches to Russia proper. Therefore we cannot rule out the possibility of further naval or combined operations employing the Navy as one arm of the operating forces on Russia's peripheries. Russia's neighbors are smaller states that depend to a considerable degree on the ability of the United States and other NATO members to project power around the periphery of Eurasia to ensure their stability and security. A physical and psychological exhaustion of the Western alliance may allow even a second-rate naval force to fish in the troubled waters around Russia.

ENDNOTES - CHAPTER 6

1. *Osnovy politiki Rossiyskoy Federatsii v oblasti voyenno-morskoy deyatel'nosty nf period do 2010 goda,* available from *www.morskayakollegiya.ru/printer.php?menu=57&schema=1&id=26; Morskaya doktrina Rossiyskoy Federatsii do 2020 goda,* available from *www.kremlin.ru/text/docs/2001/07/58035.shtml.*

2. *Strategiya razvitiya sudostroitel'noy promyshlennosti na period do 2020 goda i na dal'neyshuyu perspektivu,* available from *www.garant.ru/prime/20071204/92194.htm.*

3. V. Kuroedov, L. Sidorenko, and M. Moskovenko, "Za flot Rossii nuzhno prodolzhat' borot'sia," *Morskoi' sbornik,* No. 8, August 2009, p. 17.

4. Viktor Myasnikov, "Smena morskoi doktriny dorogogo stoit," *Nezavisimoye voyennoye obozrenie* (further—NVO), February 10, 2006.

5. Vladimir Gundarov, "Raspravim kryl'ya nad okeanom?" *Krasnaya zvezda,* April 6, 2005.

6. *Beseda s zhurnalistami po zavershenii morskogo pokhoda,* August 17, 2005, available from *kremlin.ru/text/appears/2005/08/92586.shtml.*

7. Dmitriy Litovkin, "Pochemu Rossii ne nuzhny avianostsy, *Izvestiya,* June 8, 2006, available from *www.izvestia.ru/armia2/article3093648/index.html.*

8. "Razvitiye flota—zadacha gosudarstvennaya," *Krasnaya zvezda* (further—KZ), July 29, 2006, available from *redstar.ru/2006/07/29_07/1_03.html*.

9. Vladimir Zaborskiy, "Bez avianostsev flot schitayetsya ushcherbnym," NVO, July 28, 2007.

10. Andrei Gavrilenko, "Flotu byt' avianosnym," KZ, June 7, 2007.

11. Vladimir Gundarov and Viktor Yuzbashev, "Milliardy dlya 'dlinnoy ruki; v okeane," NVO, June 29, 2007.

12. "Glavkom VMF rasskazal, ka yego vedomstvo usilit yadernyy potentsial Rossii," *Newsru.com*, April 4, 2008, available from *newsru.com/russia/04apr2008/glavkom_print.html*.

13. *Beseda s lichnym sostavom tyazhelogo avianesushchego kreisera "Admiral flota Sovetskogo Soyuza N. G. Kuznetsov,"* October 11, 2008, available from *www.kremlin.ru/text/appears/2008/10/207617.shtml*.

14. "Kuz'kina mat'-2," *Prime-Tass*, November 14, 2008, available from *www.prime-tass.ru/news/show.asp?id=2941&ct=articles*.

15. Denis Tel'manov, "Avianosnym gruppam ne nashli primeneniya," *GZT.RU*, June 18, 2009, available from *www.gzt.ru/print/243906.html*.

16. For details on the situation in the manufacturing sector, see the interview with the director of Rostekhnologii state-owned corporation Sergei Chemezov, in Vladimir Soloviev, "Mashinostroiteli priobreli lobbistov," NVO, May 18, 2007.

17. Admiral Vladimir Vysotskiy, "Izmeneniya flot nazreli davno," KZ, February 11, 2009.

18. "Polnyy tekst vystuplenia General Makarova," *Kommersant Vlast'*, July 13, 2009, available from *www.kommersant.ru/doc.aspx?DocsID=1201042&print=true*.

19. Tel'manov, "Avianosnym gruppam ne nashli primeneniya."

20. Dmitri Medvedev, *Vstupitel'noye slovo na sovheshchanii "O razvitii podvodnykh sil Voyenno-Morskogo Flota Rossii,"* available from *kremlin.ru/text/appears/2009/07/218889.shtml*; "Medvedev prokatilsya na katere v Severodvinske," *newsru.com*, July 2, 2009, available from *www.newsru.com/russia/02jul2009/medvsever.html*.

21. Nikolay Poroskov, "Rossii neobkhodimo yedinoye proektno-konstruktorskoye byuro dlya grazhdanskogo sudostroyeniya," *Vremya novostey*, April 21, 2009.

22. Available from *www.newsru.com/finance/15jun2007/osk.html*.

23. Available from *www.newsru.com/finance/13may2008/sechin.html*.

24. "Khodorkovskiy obvinil Sechina i obyavil sukuyu golodovku," *newsru.com*, January 30, 2008, available from *www.newsru.com/russia/30jan2008/hodor.html*.

25. "'Sevmash' gotovitsya k proizvodstvu avianostsev," *Izvestiya*, March 19, 2009; available from *www.navy.ru/nowadays/concept/reforms/carrierstobe.htm*.

26. Admiral Vladimir Vysotskiy, "Izmeneniya oblika flot nazreli davno," KZ, February 11, 2009, available from *www.redstar.ru/2009/02/11_02/4_03.html*.

27. Viktor Litovkin, "So strategicheskim razmakhom," NVO, September 11, 2009.

28. Viktor Litovkin, "Reforma armii sdelala zakhod v proshloe," *Nezavisimaya gazeta*, September 29, 2009, available from *www.ng.ru/printed/231581*.

29. Kuroedov, "Za flot Rossii nuzhno prodolzhat' borot'sia," pp. 17, 19.

30. Pavel Podvig, *Strategic Fleet*, available from *russianforces.org/navy/*.

31. See, for instance, Rear Admiral A. Yakovlev, "Kto vladeet Arktikoi', tot upravliaet mirom," *Morskoi' sbornik*, No. 9, September 2008, pp. 28-37; A. Smolovskii', "Poslednie voenno-politicheskie sobytiia v Arktike, *Morskoi' sbornik*, No. 12, December 2008, pp. 18-21.

32. See Kristian Atland, "The Introduction, Adoption and Implementation of Russia's 'Northern Strategic Bastion' Concept, 1992-1999," *Journal of Slavic Military Studies*, Vol. 20, Issue 4, October 2007, p. 521.

33. Katarzyna Zyśk, "Russia and the High North: Security and Defence Perspectives," in Sven G. Holtsmark and Brooke A. Smith-Windsor, eds., *Security Prospects in the High North: Geostrategic Thaw or Freeze?* NDC Forum Paper No. 7, Rome, Italy: NATO Defense College, May 2009, p. 106.

34. Arkadiy Moshes, "Bez dorogi," *Yezhednevnyy zhurnal*, June 23, 2009, available from *ej.ru/?a=note&id=92069*.

35. *Sotrudnichestvo rossiyskogo flot s VMS Ukrainy perspektivno – Vysotskiy*, RIA Novosti, July 26, 2009, *available from www.rian.ru/defense_safety/20090726/178699463.html*.

36. Nikolai Poroskov, "*Otrublennaya armiya*," *Vremya novostei*, March 5, 2009, available from *www.vremya.ru/print/224358.html*; *Predsedatel' pravitel'stva Rossiyskoy Federatsii V. V. Putin provel v Sochi soveshchanie po gosoboronzakazu*, August 7, 2009, available from *www.government.ru/content/governmentactivity/mainnews/archive/2009/08/07/6720240.htm*; *Nachalo rabochey vstrechi s Zamestitelem Predsedatelya Pravietl'stva Sergeem Ivanovym*, available from *kremlin.ru/text/appears/2009/07/220134.shtml*.

37. Sergei Ptichkin, "Glavkom pritsenilsya k avianostsu," *Rossiyskaya gazeta*, October 30, 2008, available from *www.rg.ru/2008/10/30/oruzhie.html*.

38. Yuriy Gavrilov, "Frantsuz pod Andreyevskim flagom," *Rossiyskaya gazeta*, August 31, 2009, available from *www.rg.ru/2009/08/31/korabl.html*.

39. Khramchikhin, "VMF RF na zarybezhnykh korablyah;" Ilya Kramnik, "Zagranitsa nam pomozhet," *RIA Novosti*, June 26, 2009, available from *www.rian.ru/analytics/20090626/175492980-print.html*.

40. Kramnik, "Zagranitsa nam pomozhet."

41. Aleksei Nikol'skiy, "Frantsuzskoye sudno Pugacheva," *Vedomosti*, August 27, 2009, available from *www.vedomosti.ru/newspaper/print.shtml?2009/08/27/211666*.

42. Available from *www.globalsecurity.org/military/world/europe/mistral.htm*.

43. Aleksandr Khramchikhin, "VMF RF na zarubezhnykh korablyah," NVO, July 3, 2009; *Oruzhiye Rosii, www.arms-expo.ru/site.xp/049050054053124049051054049.html*, available from available from *www.arms-expo.ru/site.xp/049050054057124049052055056.html*; *Rossiyskiy podvodnyy flot*, available from *submarine.id.ru/sub.php?885*.

44. *Morskaya Kollegiya*, "Obyedinennaya sudostroitel'naya korporatsiya i razvitie rossiyskoy sudostroitel'noy oblasti," available from *www.morskayakollegiya.ru/printer.php?menu=269&schema=1&id=202*.

45. Vyacheslav Rumantsev, "Ozhivut li rossiyskiye verfi?" Rossiyaskaya Federatsiya segodnya, 2009, No. 4, available from *www.russia-today.ru/2009/no_04/04_SF_01.htm*.

46. *Predsedatel' pravitel'stva Rossiyskoy Federatsii V. V. Putin provel soveshchanie po voprosam razvitiya sudostroitel'noy otrasli v Dal'nevostochnom regione*, May 11, 2009, available from *www.government.ru/content/rfgovernment/rfgovernmentchairman/chronicle/archive/2009/05/11/5379145.htm*.

47. Fox Business, *OPK Shipyards Deliver the New Icebreaker "St. Petersburg,"* July 16, 2009, available from *www.foxbusiness.com/story/markets/industries/industrials/opk-shipyards-deliver-new-icebreaker-st-petersburg/*.

48. Vadim Solovyev, "Mashinostroiteli priobreli lobbistov," NVO, May 18, 2007.

49. Oksana Novozhenina and Aleksei Topalov, "Rossiyskiye tekhnologii zayma," *gazeta.ru*, February 25, 2009, *gazeta.ru/*

CHAPTER 7

RUSSIAN MILITARY CHALLENGES TOWARD CENTRAL-EAST EUROPE

Joshua B. Spero

Russia's military strategy toward Central and Eastern Europe (i.e., the lands between Germany and Russia) poses security challenges not only for Europe, but also for Russia's overall national security strategy. Regional security challenges to Europe arise from Russian military threats against Ukraine and Georgia along Russia's western periphery. Indeed, regional security tensions between Russia and Ukraine, and between Russia and Georgia, over the past several years, have also led to tensions between the United States and Europe.[1] Meanwhile, a resurgent Russian military could also threaten longer-term cooperation not only between Russia and Europe, but also between Central and Eastern Europe and Western Europe. Military pressure and even confrontation in this context are signifiers of broader Russo-European geopolitical tensions after September 11, 2001 (9/11) that even stretch into Central Asia and the Caucasus.[2] Thus, Russian military challenges toward Central-East Europe cannot be separated from the geopolitical battles over an economic agenda that are occurring on Russia's western periphery in Eastern Europe and Eurasia (to include Central Asia and the Caucasus).[3]

As Russian military challenges center mainly on Russia's western periphery, its strategy might appear limited to Eastern Europe and Eurasia, rather than to Central-East Europe. The Russian threat of military intervention in Ukraine over the past several years, and the actual Russo-Georgian war in 2008 have driven Western European political considerations and Europe's necessary economic ties with Russia.[4] Indeed, economic and political concerns have fostered more tensions within Europe—between Eastern and Central Europe on the one hand, and Western Europe on the other—than Russian military challenges have. As a result, Ukraine and Georgia have become "geopolitical pivots"[5] in Russian military planning for larger Russian national security strategy toward Europe overall.[6] Given the pivotal Russian energy pipelines that traverse Central-East Europe into West Europe and the expanded European Union (EU) and North Atlantic Treaty Organization (NATO) membership of those same Central-East European countries during the past decade, regional tensions will likely remain high. Therefore, Russo-European security dilemmas center on the following key areas: first, Russo-European energy security challenges; second, tensions over EU integration and eastern outreach; and, third, impact of NATO on East-European and Eurasian security, particularly Afghanistan as post-9/11 military operations there escalate.

RUSSO-EUROPEAN ENERGY SECURITY CHALLENGES

Given the dominant role of energy in contemporary politics and military conflicts in Southwest Asia and the Middle East, Russian and European leaders focus increasingly on the European energy routes through independent Ukraine and Georgia. Regional East European and Eurasian energy security in Ukraine and Georgia may reveal more about Russo-European ties than military confrontation in Central-East Europe.

For West European security calculations, Ukraine and Georgia are more important as political and economic factors than they are as military factors, particularly in terms of West European energy priorities. The Russo-Georgian War in August 2008 and the continual Russo-Ukrainian energy pipeline shutdowns, including the tacit threat of military force most recently in January 2009, have enabled Russia to reassert itself. To a certain extent, West European leaders see territorial war in Georgia and continual gas pipeline confrontation in Ukraine connected to the issue of vital pipeline routes across Europe. These developing regional energy security dilemmas and divisions over Russian military planning and threat perceptions cause tension and increase divisiveness between West and Central-East European leaders. At times, Central-East European leaders have tried to use the United States to leverage West European leaders about resurgent Russia, creating more division among European leaders.[7] Consequently, Russian military objectives appear to have advanced through political and economically focused pipeline rows. Geostrategically, Central-East Europe's integration into the EU and NATO limits Russia's military impact in Europe, particularly without the former Central-East European Warsaw Pact force structure.[8] Yet, it is the vital energy pipelines and supplies from Russia through Eastern Europe and Eurasia that allow Russia's military to reassert itself in Europe. Thus, Russia's energy influences Central-East European challenges for European security more than traditional Russian military planning toward Europe, especially as energy increasingly concerns the EU and NATO.[9]

Such disputes caused great consternation in European capitals and constantly affected Russo-European relations negatively for the past several years, the period from 2008-09 proving especially controversial in Europe. As the first decade of the 21st century ended, German leaders formulated their international security concerns particularly toward Russia in terms of energy priorities and disputes.[10] The economic impact of Russian energy supplies on Europe weighs so much politically in Europe that long-term Russian national security strategy now clearly integrates pipeline politics.[11] For geopolitical pivots such as Ukraine and Georgia, the Russian military sees them as critical to its military resurgence, as well as countering European security expansion.[12] Furthermore, Ukraine and Georgia remain pivotal not only to Russia's southwestern pipeline development, but also to its military strategy for the Nord Stream pipeline expansion. Significantly, the Nord Stream pipeline bypasses some emerging non-Russian southeast European pipelines. Such Russian geostrategic decisions appear to reduce Central-East Europe's security impact by attempting to lessen Russia's pipeline usage through Central-Eastern Europe.[13]

Central-East European leaders remain caught in Russo-European multipipeline developments heading into the second decade of the 21st century's. Central-East European security depends primarily on EU economic integration. Subsequently, Central-East European leaders remain apprehensive about Russian military intentions on their eastern periphery and the impact of the emerging Russo-European Nord Stream pipeline bypassing Central-East Europe. However, additional pipelines intended to bypass Russia into Europe create new Russo-European security dilemmas. The Middle East-Eurasian-Southeast European Nabucco Pipeline is intended to bypass Russia. Coupled with other non-Russian pipelines the following are all envisioned to bypass Russia: the Baku-Tbilisi-Ceyhan Pipeline; the Interconnection Turkey-Greece-Italy-ITGI Pipeline; the Trans-Adriatic Pipeline; the Trans-Caspian Pipeline; and the White Stream Pipeline. These planned, partially built, or functioning pipelines have already increased Russo-European tensions.[14] Some, but not all, pipelines involve Central or Eastern Europe causing even larger European security dilemmas—a number involve Russia as well.

Such geo-economic security dilemmas could also detrimentally affect U.S.-European ties since huge pipeline financing issues seriously affect U.S.-Russian ties. Residual Russian military threats to European pipeline supplies continually hamper the larger international security concerns for both Russo-European and U.S.-Russian ties.[15] The key becomes if European leaders believe Russian military strategy reflects a realistic capability to dominate its western periphery by using energy sources to further military objectives. Prospective non-Russian Eastern European and Eurasian pipelines face tremendous difficulties in fulfilling European energy needs. Security concerns between and among Balkan, Caucasus, and Central Asian countries threaten to slow and even prevent completion of these pipelines.[16] As a result, Central-East European leaders, believing they're already integral to European security, grow more concerned about the geopolitical status between Europe and Eurasia as energy disputes worsen.[17] Such security dilemmas will likely determine the direction of Russo-European relations, particularly with both growing EU Eastern integration and outreach, and declining U.S. European security influence.

EU INTEGRATION AND EASTERN OUTREACH

Some of the roots for Russo-European energy dilemmas stem from the rapid European security integration during the 1990s.[18] From the end of the Cold War to the end of the 20th century, Poland and Germany established critical bilateral linkages that now give Poland an alignment model that it can pursue with Ukraine, a relationship very important to Europe and Eurasia.[19] Russo-Polish tension predominantly centers on independent Ukraine, thus preventing Russia from becoming neo-imperialistic and on Europe continuing to solidify regional democratization.[20] As Zbigniew Brzezinski exclaims, the Polish-Ukrainian "critical core of Europe's security" emanates from linkages of the Franco-German-Polish relationship." This, he contends, draws on the "special geopolitical interest of Germany and Poland in Ukraine's independence." Brzezinski further argues that these linkages underscore the seriousness with which Russia's post-Cold War military strategy envisages European integration without its former western periphery in its sphere of influence. Hence, Brzezinksi asserts that if Ukrainian independence prevails over traditional Russian neoimperialism, given Poland's new found Central-East European regional role, Ukraine "will gradually be drawn into the special Franco-German-Polish relationship."[21]

Many assessments of Polish-Ukrainian ties, then, praise Poland's efforts in the mid-to-late 1990s to reinforce Ukraine's sovereign foreign policy, particularly by pulling Ukraine Westward in its approaches to Europe's international institutions. Ukrainian independence in 1990, and increasing consolidation over its sovereign foreign policy by the end of that decade enabled Ukraine to seek closer European ties.[22] Therefore, Polish-Ukrainian regional security renders an important cooperative political, economic, and military bridging model for Ukraine's European linkages.[23] When bolstered by other European and U.S. support without provoking Russia, Polish-Ukrainian bridging could contribute cooperatively, but how long can Ukraine define its external alignment separately from Russia?

Poland's cooperative bridging with Ukraine during the 1990s, to uphold Ukrainian sovereignty, centered on reorienting Ukraine Westward and establishing a politico-economic bridge to Russia. Warsaw refused to balance Moscow and Kyiv militarily in order to re-integrate politically and economically into Europe. Warsaw argued that Kyiv's sovereignty remained more important for European security than some economic losses.[24] By not aligning with Ukraine or Russia, and by pulling Kyiv and Moscow Westward, Warsaw sought to reduce the security dilemma of one state gaining advantage over the other. Warsaw and Kyiv tried to build economic, political, and military linkages between and among European states, and with Russia to integrate the former Soviet states into Europe—or to build longer-term ties to European institutions without full membership.[25] Despite such policies, Ukraine continues to remain dependent on Russia for energy, even though Russia continually uses that leverage to pressure Ukraine. By extension, Russia's efforts to influence Ukraine by leveraging energy affects Europe politically, economically, and even militarily.[26] From Russia's perspective, such continuing power plays may signify attempts to reintegrate Ukraine into the Russian orbit, potentially with U.S. and European acquiescence.[27] Europeanized Poland may then fail to maintain its open markets and flexible borders with Ukraine, especially with Poland's entry into the EU and NATO during the past decade.[28] At best, Poland's role between the great powers could increase regional stability, allow greater coalition building, and prevent neo-imperial Russia. At worst, Poland's bridging could succumb to EU energy demands and Russia's geo-economic coercion, with tacit European and U.S. approval of the emergence of the several pipelines described above. Some of these pipelines could be built around Poland and Ukraine, and could bring about Ukraine's loss of sovereignty by isolating it from European energy flows and forcing it into greater dependence upon Russia.[29]

For these reasons, energy security policy figures much more prominently in the EU's Eastern outreach, particularly in the aftermath of the January 2009 Russian-Ukrainian disputes, and the subsequent European energy supply cut-off. From 2008-09, EU energy assistance to non-Russian, non-EU states bordering Russia's western periphery increasingly inflamed Russo-European ties over the issue of energy security. EU outreach initiatives consist of financing of and politico-economic support for Southern and Southeast European pipelines to avoid Russia and to delink Europe from Russian pipelines.[30] Instead of corroboration with Russia, EU eastern outreach raises EU-Russian tensions and provokes disagreement at recent EU-Russian Summits.[31] Therefore, the EU enlargement, to include several Central-East Europe states in the 21st century, aimed at integrating Europe actually heightened Russo-European tensions as the EU tried to extend security to former Soviet Republics.[32] Russian military anxiety intensifies as the EU increasingly sees its role throughout Europe, and globally, to support not only politico-economic policies, but also security policies with growing military implications. For the Russian military, the EU's cultivation of its newly forming "Eastern Partnerships" may result in an anti-Russian and greater geo-strategic rivalry than does NATO's impact on Eurasian security. Russian energy resources will continue to fuel European security developments as the attendant geopolitical struggle for oil and gas may give Russia increased influence in Europe.[33]

NATO'S IMPACT ON EAST EUROPEAN AND EURASIAN SECURITY

The EU's moves eastward contribute to the Russian military's unease about Central-East European security, particularly given its constant concerns regarding NATO. Even after the demise of the Union of Soviet Socialist Republic (USSR) nearly 20 years ago, NATO enlargement has not altered Russian military objectives.[34] As the Russian military persists in trying to exploit Central-East European security dilemmas along Russia's western border, Russia sees greater Euro-Atlantic threats moving farther east. NATO's Central-East European enlargement not only includes countries bordering Ukraine and moving closer to the Caucasus (Georgia), but also encroaching upon the three Baltic countries that encircle Russia's Kaliningrad enclave. As a result, Russia's counter-NATO strategy still involves large-scale military exercises directed against former Soviet Republics along its western border.[35] Yet, East European and Eurasian energy security developments also influence Russian military planning for exercises directed more toward Central-East Europe. Consequently, the U.S. military force structure decline in Europe, and its post-9/11 focus on the Middle East and Southwest Asia enable Russia's military to reassert itself in Europe. Hence, Russian military strategy not only focuses on energy security along its western periphery in order to disrupt NATO planning, but it also remains part of the larger Russian national security strategy to exploit new Central-East European security dilemmas.[36]

To exploit NATO, Russia believes it can influence the NATO discussion concerning membership for Ukraine and Georgia as the Alliance grapples with bigger geo-strategic security challenges. On one hand, the Russian military witnesses Central-East European leaders simultaneously aligning with the West and encouraging former Soviet republics to move westward politically. On the other hand, the Russian military sees that many NATO allies, particularly in Western Europe, remain hesitant about voting on any new members for the foreseeable future.[37] Meanwhile, during 2008-09 the U.S. and Central-East Europeans mainly supported potential paths for Ukraine and Georgia NATO membership. At the same time, although NATO allies voiced serious concern over Russian military tensions with Ukraine and the Russo-Georgian War, NATO found itself facing larger security dilemmas. These security dilemmas center on NATO's mission in Afghanistan, which not only move its focus away from Europe, but it also detrimentally affect its consensus.[38] Thus, the consistent threat of Russian military intervention in East Europe or Eurasia, especially regarding energy supplies, significantly impedes a NATO consensus on further enlargement.[39]

To sow even more dissension among NATO members, Russia continually proposes alternative security structures to NATO. Historically, however, Russian proposed alternatives to NATO have failed over the decades. The downfall of the Warsaw Treaty Organization (WTO) and the failed attempt to transform the Organization for Security and Cooperation in Europe (OSCE) into an anti-NATO structure foiled Russian military objectives.[40] Like his predecessors, Russian President Dmitriy Medvedev keeps proposing alternative security structures to NATO and even the EU. His most recent effort concentrates on "the future treaty (that) should include basic principles for the development of arms control, confidence-building measures, restraint and reasonable sufficiency in military development." Furthermore President Medvedev asserts that "certain political forces are still dominated by the logic of mechanistic expansion of military-political alliances." He contends that "alternatively, European security needs better direction with better values," such as "compliance with international law, non-use of force, respect for sovereignty, and adherence of peaceful methods of conflict resolution."[41] Muted European reactions to President Medvedev's proposal thus far exemplify how Russian European security initiatives still fail to replace current structures.[42]

Even though Russian efforts to provide Europe with national security alternatives other than NATO may not have materialized, Russia keeps challenging NATO with its Eurasian based Collective Security Treaty Organization (CSTO). The nearly decade-old CSTO attempt to buttress Russian military strategy consists of Central Asian nations, along with Belarus and Armenia.[43] Yet, recent CSTO developments demonstrate that even its Central Asian members and Belarus do not always succumb to Moscow's authority. To illustrate, Belarus; President Lukashenko, as rotating CSTO Head, actually failed to attend the summer 2009 CSTO Summit, undercutting Russian attempts to make the CSTO a significant security organization.[44] Ultimately, the CSTO may become a mostly Russian-Central Asian focused organization, with CSTO military exercises occurring more often in Central Asia.[45] Though the CSTO may have little impact on European security, its strategic implications in Southwest Asia may be more telling for NATO's increasingly complicated Afghanistan operations.

The irony remains that in the NATO-Russia Council (NRC) Russian military strategy to counter NATO objectives holds greater sway than proposed European alternative security structures do.[46] In the late 1990s, the initiation of the NATO-Russia Council emerged from NATO's enlargement decision and NATO's process to appease Russia. Paradoxically, Russian endeavors to counter NATO rely on more effectively working with NATO in the NATO-Russian Council. Debates within the NATO-Russian Council might provide Russia with its greatest leverage.[47] The most important decisionmaking body in NATO is the North Atlantic Council (NAC), which is the only body in the Alliance that obtains its authority explicitly from the North Atlantic Treaty. Even though the Council is comprised of only NATO members, non-NATO states, such as Russia and Russia's western neighboring states, can still have a significant impact on Alliance decisions by raising their concerns in the NATO-Russia Council.[48] Before the Russo-Georgian War temporarily worsened NATO-Russia ties, Russia threatened NATO concerning NATO Membership Action Plans (MAP) for Ukraine and Georgia. Russian speeches at NATO Headquarters threatened military intervention in Ukraine and Georgia if MAP invitations emerged, and the threats have continued consistently after the April 2008 NATO Summit. These threats caused serious reaction in European capitals[49] and also set the stage for more antagonistic politico-military maneuvering to disrupt NATO consensus, particularly in the aftermath of the Russo-Georgian War in August 2008.

The geopolitical effect of the Russo-Georgian War on NATO-Russia relations became clearer as a result of NATO's temporary suspension of the NRC and some NATO decisions favoring Russian military strategy. The December 2008 NAC session, and the April 2009 NATO 60th Anniversary Summit, demonstrated how the Russian military slowed Alliance inroads made by recent members and aspirant partners. In both NATO leadership gatherings, the Alliance distanced itself on enlargement by the inclusion of Ukraine and Georgia, and retreated on missile defense in Poland and the Czech Republic. Divisiveness among allies grew over Russian military threats on NATO's eastern periphery, especially the post-war breakaway Georgian regions in Abkhazia and South Ossetia. The reduced prominence of the efforts toward enlargement and MAP membership for Ukraine and Georgia in NAC statements, and other Summit declarations underscored the allies' divergence.[50] Indeed, the U.S. missile defense system initiative for Poland and the Czech Republic prior to the April 2008 NATO Summit initially gained Alliance support. However, by the Summit's end, NATO veered away from a U.S.-Central European-NATO effort and in fact, began to focus on a U.S.-NATO-Russian one.[51] By the April 2009 NATO Summit, Russian military objectives appeared to have been affirmed by the April 2009 Summit's declaration on this new approach to missile defense cooperation.[52]

Russian anti-missile defense arguments influenced important West European leaders, such as Germany's, to diverge from Central-East European and U.S. counterparts.[53] Dissension in NATO also emerged as NATO nations downplayed Iranian threats to Europe, while Russia rejected U.S. anti-ballistic missile defense proposals based on Russian territory.[54] By the fall of 2009, the deal to trade-off U.S. missile defense systems in Poland and the Czech Republic by suspending sales of Russian S-300 Surface-to-Air Missile systems to Iran emerged in American-Russian negotiations.[55] Time will tell how both enlargement and missile defense will influence NATO's outreach to Central-East Europe and whether Russian military pressure plays a role in spurring Alliance divisiveness.

As part of NATO's reaction to Russian military concerns, within a year of the Russo-Georgian War, the Alliance tried to reinforce its Partnership For Peace (PFP) outreach efforts to PFP Partners, Georgia and Ukraine, angering Russia.[56] In July 2009, NATO and non-NATO PFP nations conducted military exercises on Georgian territory, including Ukrainian military units. Ostensibly, the NATO exercises were for crisis management training, to show how NATO handles crisis response procedures for counterterrorism missions. Even though counterterrorism missions form the basis for NATO-Russia Council discussions, NATO conducted this exercise near the South Ossetian-Georgian border. The exercise occurred not far from where the 2008 Russo-Georgian War erupted. Consequently, Russia saw the exercise as a provocation.[57] Moreover, the Russian military believed that NATO regrouping toward Georgia and Ukraine masked NATO's true intentions in the Black Sea region.[58] Whether NATO truly revives its enlargement debates for Georgia and Ukraine remains unknown, because key NATO allies such as Germany and France remain apprehensive and cautious. They desire closer ties and compromise with Russia.[59] Therefore, Russia appears to hold greater sway with these NATO members, creating dissent more often than a sense of security that Moscow might engender through any proposed alternative European security structures.

The reinvigorated NATO-Russia Council, however, did lead to mutually beneficial dialogue about Afghanistan.[60] If Russia provides military support for NATO's Afghanistan operations that include Central-East European and Eurasian military organizations, then the essential objectives for NATO's International Security Assistance Force (ISAF) can be achieved. Russia's military priorities in Afghanistan center on continual support for nonmilitary and military supply transit agreements with ISAF. Such agreements utilize Russian territory and airspace. Equally important, ISAF benefits with Russia acting as an intermediary to its Central and South Asian neighbors bordering Iran, Afghanistan, and Pakistan. Russian land-transit arrangements with NATO provide crucial supply and resupply lines to reinforce NATO and non-NATO ISAF forces.[61] Future air transport agreements may also emerge to demonstrate cooperative security measures that help promote NATO-Russia ties, and by extension, exhibit Russia's influence in and around Afghanistan.[62]

Yet, what needs to remain part of any consideration for Russian military strategy toward NATO also arises from Russia's politico-military maneuvering regarding its Afghanistan supply and resupply networks. If Russia exerts itself in the NATO-Russia Council to try to counter NATO initiatives on Central-

East Europe, Russia could conceivably upset ISAF's operational abilities with politico-military trade-offs.[63] Such potential disruption portends more NATO alliance divisiveness over how U.S. and European allies want to approach Russia and subsequent debates to determine if closer military ties with Moscow trump politico-military disputes.[64] Since the Russo-Georgian War in 2008, and the Russo-Ukranian pipeline confrontation of 2009, Alliance decisions have been more accommodating toward Russia, thereby enabling Russia to have greater influence on the shaping of Central-East European security.[65]

CONCLUSION

This analysis demonstrated how the Russian military has attempted to reassert itself in Central-East Europe, and how those attempts are reinforced by key political and economic factors in national security strategy. The analysis showed how the challenges for Russian military strategy lie not only in NATO's eastern enlargement of the former Soviet states on Russia's western periphery, but also in greater EU eastern outreach toward those states. That may explain why Russian influence in the NATO-Russia Council concentrates on increasing Allied divergence, while raising the geopolitical stakes in Afghanistan. Simultaneously, threats by the Russian military to protect Russo-European pipelines underscore how energy security becomes integral to Russian military strategy. If Russia can weaken NATO while countering the EU's attempts to advance militarily, then Russia's military strategy may succeed in derailing Central-East Europe's security efforts.

However, Russian military strategy toward Central-East Europe generates the basis for confrontation in Russo-EU relations. Potential EU development eastward alarms Russia. Furthermore, Central-East European leaders consistently call for Europe's commitment to them via NATO; the EU's drive for pipeline politics and economic maneuverability may yet yield a higher stakes energy security competition. This geopolitical competition may then put Russian military strategy at a crossroads. The geostrategic maneuvering between and among Russia, Central-East Europe, and Western Europe, with the declining U.S. role in Europe, could signal NATO's possible decline.[66] Finally, this may achieve what the Russian military has long determined to be one of its priorities—the weakening of NATO's political and military influence, if not its collapse.[67] Yet, NATO's collapse hinges on its Afghanistan operations, a failure in Southwestern Asia could destabilize the region, cast greater uncertainty throughout Eurasia, and end up harming Russian national security. Thus the paradoxes attendant upon Russian military strategy towards Western and Eastern Europe remain unresolved.

ENDNOTES - CHAPTER 7

1. Andranik Migranyan, "At Last, We can Sum up the Results of the Moscow Summit," *Rossiyskaya Gazeta*, July 27, 2009 available from Johnson's Russia List, #2009-143, *www.cdi.org/russia/johnson*; Eugene Rumer and Angela Stent, "Russia and the West," *Survival*, Vol. 51, No. 2, April-May 2009, pp. 91-104; Sean Kay, "Enhancing Cooperation among the Atlantic Allies," *Global Strategic Assessment 2009: America's Security Role in a Changing World*, Washington, DC: Institute for National Strategic Studies, 2009; Andrew A. Michta, "NATO Enlargement post-1989: Successful Adaptation or Decline?" *Contemporary European History*, Vol. 18, No. 3, 2009, pp. 363-376.

2. "Russia's Neighbors Ask For Protection against the Kremlin," *Nezavisimaia Gazeta*, October 10, 2009, *RIA Novosti*, available from *en.rian.ru/papers/20091210/157189619.html*; A "Security dilemma" defines how states perceive themselves and how they initiate actions toward or respond to the actions of other states that frequently lessen security. See, especially, John H. Herz, *Political Realism and Political Idealism: A Study in Theories and Realities*, Chicago, IL: University of Chicago Press, 1959, p. 4; Robert Jervis, *Perception and Misperception in International Politics*, Princeton, NJ: Princeton University Press, 1976, p. 66; Charles L. Glaser, "The Security Dilemma Revisited", *World Politics*, Vol. 50, No. 1, October 1997, pp. 191, 197; Charles L. Glaser and John C. Matthews, III, "Correspondence: Current Gains and Future Outcomes," *International Security*, Vol. 21, No. 4, Spring 1997, pp.192-197.

3. Edward Lucas, *The New Cold War: Putin's Russia and the Threat to the West*, Houndmills, UK: Palgrave Macmillan, 2008; Stephen J. Blank, *Challenges and Opportunities for the Obama Administration in Central Asia*, Carlisle, PA: Strategic Studies Institute, U.S. Army War College, 2009.

4. "Russia Can No Longer Rely on Energy Charter to Protect its Interests," *Vremaia Novostei*, October 19, 2009, *RIA Novosti*, available from *en.rian.ru/papers/20091019/156520082.html*.

5. Halford J. Mackinder, "The Geographical Pivot of History," *Geographical Journal*, Vol. 23, 1904, pp. 421-444; and Halford J. Mackinder, *Democratic Ideals and Reality*, Westport: Greenwood, 1962. Many prominent works build on Mackinder, assessing small and middle power politics and their regional impact, depicting geopolitical "pivots" globally on every continent in terms of great power state security challenges.

6. "Strategy for the Russian Federation's National Security toward 2020," *Russian Federation President's Office*, May 12, 2009, available from *www.scrf.gov.ru/documents/99.html*.

7. "An Open Letter to the Obama Administration from Central and Eastern Europe," *Gazeta Wyborcza*, July 15, 2009, available from *wyborcza.pl/1,75477,6825987,An_Open_Letter_to_the_Obama_Administration_from_Central.html*.

8. Lincoln Mitchell, "Georgia's Story: Competing Narratives since the War," *Survival*, Vol. 51, No. 4, August-September 2009, pp. 87-100; Vladimir Ryzhkov, "Kremlin Burning Bridges with Every Neighbor," *Moscow Times*, August 4, 2009, available from Johnson's Russia List, #2009-145, *www.cdi.org/russia/johnson*; Anatoly Medetsky, "EU Offers Russia's Neighbors Perks for Energy," *Moscow Times*, May 7, 2009, available from Johnson's Russia List, #2009-85, *www.cdi.org/russia/johnson*; Oleg Nikiforov, "To NATO Via NABUCCO—Nabucco vs. South Stream Pipelines: An Update—Georgia, Azerbaijan, and Other Post-Soviet Countries are Promised A Chance At NATO Membership," *Nezavisimaya Gazeta*, July 28, 2009, available from Johnson's Russia List, #2009-141, *www.cdi.org/russia/johnson*; Clifford Gaddy and Andrew Kuchins, "Putin's Plan," *The Washington Quarterly*, Spring 2008, pp.117-129; Andrew Kuchins and Richard Weitz, With a Reaction by Dmitri Trenin, "Russia's Place in an Unsettled Order—Calculations in the Kremlin," Muscatine, IO: The Stanley Foundation, Working Paper, November 2008.

9. "Energy Security, A New NATO Issue?" Video interview with Thierry Legendre, Policy Advisor in the office of the NATO Secretary General, *North Atlantic Treaty Organization*, January 16, 2008, available from *www.nato.int/cps/en/natolive/opinions_1750.htm*; "Energy Policy for a Competitive Europe," *European Commission: Energy*, August 18, 2009, available from *ec.europa.eu/energy/index_en.htm*; Paul Gallis, *NATO and Energy Security*, Washington, DC: Congressional Research Service, 2006; "NATO Pipeline System," *North Atlantic Treaty Organization*, November 9, 2009, available from *www.nato.int/cps/en/natolive/topics_56600.htm*.

10. Christopher S. Chivvis and Thomas Rid, "The Roots of Germany's Russia Policy," *Survival*, Vol. 51, No. 2, April-May 2009, pp. 105-122; "Meetings with Representatives of various Communities: Speech at 9th Russian-German Public Forum, the Petersburg Dialogue," Munich, Germany; *President of Russia*, July 16, 2009, available from *www.kremlin.ru/eng/speeches/2009/07/16/1106_type82914type84779_219753.shtml*.

11. "Energy in Europe: He Who Pays for the Pipelines Calls the Tune," *The Economist*, July 18, 2009, pp. 47-48; "Russia Prods Europe to Finance Ukrainian Gas Purchases, Warns of New Gas Crisis," *U.S. Open Source Center Report*, July 9, 2009, available

from Johnson's Russia List, #2009-130, *www.cdi.org/russia/johnson*; Svante E. Cornell, Roger N. McDermott, William O'Malley, Vladimir Socor, and S. Frederick Starr, *Regional Security in the South Caucasus: The Role of NATO*, Washington, DC: Johns Hopkins University, 2004; Stephen J. Blank, *Energy and Security in Transcaucasia*, Carlisle, PA: Strategic Studies Institute, U.S. Army War College, 1994.

12. "Large Russian Military Exercise in Baltic Sea Area Involves Tens of Thousands of Troops: Protection of Nord Stream Gas Pipeline Also Being Rehearsed," *Helsingin Sanomat*, International Ed., August 20, 2009, available from *www.hs.fi/english/article/Large+Russian+military+exercise+in+Baltic+Sea+area+involves+tens+of+thousands+of+troops/1135248663305*.

13. "Nord Stream and EU Energy Commissioner Reaffirm Importance of New Gas Supply Routes," *Nord Stream Press Release*, July 16, 2009, available from *www.nord-stream.com/en/press0/press-releases/press-release/article/nord-stream-and-eu-energy-commissioner-reaffirm-importance-of-new-gas-supply-routes.html?tx_ttnews[backPid]=24&cHash= 7d5c017400*; Mark MacKinnon, *The New Cold War: Revolutions, Rigged Elections and Pipeline Politics in the Former Soviet Union*, New York: Carroll & Graf Publishers, 2007.

14. Yulia Nazarova, "Nabucco without Gas: An Update on Nabucco as Five Participants in Nabucco Signed an Agreement in Ankara, Turkey," *RBC Daily*, July 14, 2009, available from Johnson's Russia List, #2009-132, *www.cdi.org/russia/johnson*; Roland Oliphant, "Eradicating the Effect, But Not the Cause Modernizing Ukraine's Pipeline System without Russia's Involvement Could Prove to Be Dangerous," *Russia Profile*, August 3, 2009, available from Johnson's Russia List, #2009-145, *www.cdi.org/russia/johnson*; Svante E. Cornell, Mamuka Tsereteli, and Vladimir Socor, "Geostrategic Implications of the Baku-Tbilisi-Ceyhan Pipeline," in S. Frederick Starr and Svante E. Cornell, eds., *The Baku-Tbilisi-Ceyhan Pipeline: Oil Window to the West*, Washington, DC: Johns Hopkins University, 2005.

15. "An Open Letter to the Obama Administration from Central and Eastern Europe"; Robert Bridge, "The Ukrainian-Russian Brotherhood: Forged in Blood, Broken by Gas," *www.russiatoday.*

com, June 4, 2009, available from Johnson's Russia List, #2009-104, *www.cdi.org/russia/johnson*; "Eastern Europe as a U.S. problem," *RIA Novosti*, July 21, 2009, available from Johnson's Russia List, #2009-137, *www.cdi.org/russia/johnson*.

16. Nazarova, "Nabucco without Gas"; Tatyana Mitrova, "The Magical Paper Pipeline," *Moscow Times*, August 5, 2009, available from Johnson's Russia List, #2009-146, *www.cdi.org/russia/johnson*.

17. K. C. Smith, *Russian Energy Politics in the Baltics, Poland and Ukraine*, Washington, DC: Center for Strategic and International Studies, 2004.

18. See Zbigniew Brzezinski, *The Grand Failure: The Birth and Death of Communism in the Twentieth Century*, New York: Collier, 1989; Jeffrey Simon, ed., *European Security Policy after the Revolutions of 1989*, Washington, DC: National Defense University Press, 1991; Andrew Michta, *East Central Europe after the Warsaw Pact: Security Dilemmas in the 1990s*, New York: Greenwood, 1992; Richard Weitz, "Pursuing Military Security in Eastern Europe," in Robert O. Keohane, Joseph S. Nye, and Stanley Hoffman, eds., *After the Cold War: International Institutions and State Strategies in Europe, 1989-1991*, Cambridge, MA: Harvard University Press, 1993, pp. 342-380; Jacob Kipp, ed., *Central European Security Concerns: Bridge, Buffer or Barrier*, London, UK: Frank Cass, 1993; Ilya Prizel and Andrew A. Michta, eds., *Polish Foreign Policy Reconsidered: Challenges of Independence*, London, UK: Macmillan, 1995; Jeffrey Simon, *NATO Enlargement & Central Europe: A Study in Civil-Military Relations*, Washington, DC: National Defense University Press, 1996; Ilya Prizel, *National Identity and Foreign Policy: Nationalism and Leadership in Poland, Russia, and Ukraine*, Cambridge, UK: Cambridge University Press, 1998; Mark Kramer, "Neorealism, Nuclear Proliferation, and East-Central European Strategies," in Ethan B. Kapstein and Michael Mastanduno, eds., *Unipolar Politics: Realism and State Strategies after the Cold War*, New York: Columbia University Press, 1999, pp. 437-438, 462; and S, Victor Papacosma, Sean Kay, and Mark R. Rubin, eds., *NATO After Fifty Years*, Wilmington, DE: Scholarly Resources, 2001.

19. See Joshua B. Spero, "Great Power Security Dilemmas for Pivotal Middle Power Bridging," *Contemporary Security Policy*, Vol. 30. No. 1, April 2009, pp. 147-171; and Joshua B. Spero, *Bridg-*

ing the European Divide: Middle Power Politics and Regional Security Dilemmas, Lanham, MD: Rowman and Littlefield, 2004.

20. Ilya Prizel, *National Identity and Foreign Policy: Nationalism and Leadership in Poland, Russia, and Ukraine*, Cambridge, UK: Cambridge University Press, 1998, pp. 137-145, 388-396; Zbigniew Brzezinski, "Ukraine's Critical Role in the Post-Soviet Space," in Lubomyr A. Hajda, ed., *Ukraine in the World: Studies in the International and Security Structure of a Newly Independent State*, Cambridge, MA: Harvard University Press, 1998, pp. 3-8; Stephen R. Burant, "Ukraine and East Central Europe," in Hajda, pp. 45-78; and F. Stephen Larrabee, "Ukraine's Place in European and Regional Security," in Hajda, pp. 257-263. See also Samuel P. Huntington, *The Third Wave: Democratization in the Late Twentieth Century*, Norman: University of Oklahoma Press, 1991; Bruce Russett, *Grasping the Democratic Peace*, Princeton, NJ: Princeton University Press, 1993; and Fareed Zakaria, *The Future of Freedom: Illiberal Democracy at Home and Abroad*, New York: Norton, 2003.

21. Zbigniew Brzezinski, *The Grand Chessboard: American Primacy and Its Geostrategic Imperatives*, New York: Basic, 1997, pp. 40-41, 84-86.

22. Taras Kuzio, *Ukrainian Security Policy*, Westport, CT: Praeger/Greenwood, 1995; "Treaty on Friendship, Cooperation, and Partnership between Ukraine and the Russian Federation," in Hajda, pp. 319-329.

23. Fraser Cameron, "Relations between the European Union and Ukraine," in James Clem and Nancy Popson, eds., *Ukraine and Its Western Neighbors*, Washington, DC: Woodrow International Center for Scholars, 2000, pp. 93-106; Kataryna Wolczuk and Roman Wolczuk, *Poland and Ukraine: A Strategic Partnership in a Changing Europe?* London, UK: Royal Institute of International Affairs, 2002.

24. Roman Kuzniar, ed., *Poland's Security Policy, 1989-2000*, Warsaw, Poland: Scholar Publishing House, 2001; Eric A. Miller, *To Balance Or Not to Balance: Alignment Theory and the Commonwealth of Independent States*, Surrey, UK: Ashgate Publishing, 2006.

25. Margarita Mercedes Balmaceda, *On the Edge: Ukrainian-Central European-Russian Security Triangle*, Budapest, Hungary:

Central European University Press, 2000; Roman Wolczuk, *Ukraine's Foreign and Security Policy, 1991-2000*, London, UK: Routledge, 2003.

26. Janusz Bugajski, *Cold Peace: Russia's New Imperialism*, Westport, CT: Greenwood Publishing Group, 2004.

27. Robert Legvold and Celeste A. Wallander, *Swords and Sustenance: The Economics of Security in Belarus and Ukraine*, Cambridge, MA: MIT Press, 2004; Margarita Mercedes Balmaceda, *Energy Dependency, Politics and Corruption in the Former Soviet Union: Russia's Power, Oligarchs' Profits and Ukraine's Missing Energy Policy,1995-2006*, London, UK: Routledge, 2008.

28. "Gazprom stalls over contract on additional gas supplies to Poland," *Gazeta*, July 9, 2009, *RIA Novosti*, available from *en.rian.ru/papers/20090907/156051666.html*; Joshua B. Spero, "The Polish-Ukrainian Interstate Model for Cooperation and Integration: Regional Relations in a Theoretical Context," in Jennifer D. P. Moroney, Taras Kuzio, and Mikhail Molchanov, eds., *Ukrainian Foreign and Security Policy: Theoretical and Comparative Perspectives*, Westport, CT: Praeger, 2002, pp. 155-178.

29. Moroney, Kuzio, and Molchanov.

30. Anatoly Medetsky, "EU Offers Russia's Neighbors Perks for Energy," *Moscow Times*, May 7, 2009, available from Johnson's Russia List, #2009-85, *www.cdi.org/russia/johnson*.

31. Andrew Monaghan, "Russia-EU Relations: An Emerging Energy Security Dilemma," *Pro et Contra*, Vol. 10, Issue 2-3, Summer 2006; "Former Soviet republics hindering improved Russia-EU relations," *Izvestiia*, December 24, 2009, *RIA Novosti*, available from *en.rian.ru/papers/20091224/157344274.html*.

32. Dmitriy Medvedev: Statement following Russia-EU Summit in Khabarovsk, *Kremlin.ru*, May 22, 2009, available from Johnson's Russia List, #2009-96, *www.cdi.org/russia/johnson*; "EU-Russia summit fails to mend rifts," AFP, May 22, 2009, available from Johnson's Russia List, #2009-96, *www.cdi.org/russia/johnson*.

33. Mikhail Zygar, "CDS, Commonwealth of Dependent States, The European Union is about to Establish Eastern Partnership, an Analog to the CIS," *Kommersant*, May 7, 2009, available from Johnson's Russia List, #2009-85, *www.cdi.org/russia/johnson*.

34. Stephen J. Blank and Jacob W. Kipp, eds., *The Soviet Military and the Future*, Westport, CT: Greenwood Press, 1992; Anatol Lieven and Dmitriĭ Trenin, eds., *Ambivalent Neighbors: The EU, NATO and the Price of Membership*, Washington, DC: Carnegie Endowment, 2003.

35. For some of the more recent Russian military exercises and their impact, see "Russia dismisses NATO concerns over military drills with Belarus," November 18, 2009, *RIA Novosti*, available from *en.rian.ru/mlitary_news/20091118/156893946.html*; "Medvedev says Russia-Belarus war games strengthen ties," *RIA Novosti*, August 29, 2009, available from *en.rian.ru/russia/20090929/156293664.html*; "Russia holds large-scale Ladoga-2009 military drills," *RIA Novosti*, August 18, 2009, available from *en.rian.ru/mlitary_news/20090818/155844811.html*; Ilya Kramnik, "Russia demonstrates military machismo in West 2009 war games," *RIA Novosti Opinion & Analysis*, August 9, 2009, available from *en.rian.ru/analysis/20090908/156063504.html*; "Russia sends missile frigate on long-range patrol mission," *RIA Novosti*, September 24, 2008, available from *en.rian.ru/russia/20080924/117072009.html*.

36. "Russia to Have New Military Doctrine by the End of 2009," *ITAR-TASS*, December 15, 2008; "Military Reform 2009-2013," *Nezavisimoye voyennoye obozreniye*, January 1, 2009, *World News Connection*, January 2, 2009; "The Foreign Policy Concept of the Russian Federation," *President of Russia*, July 12, 2008, available from *www.kremlin.ru/eng/text/docs/2008/07/204750.shtml*; Dale Herspring, *The Kremlin and the High Command: Presidential Impact on the Russian Military from Gorbachev to Putin*, Lawrence, KS: University of Kansas Press, 2006; Janusz Bugajski, *Expanding Eurasia: Russia's European Ambitions*, Washington, DC: Center for Strategic and International Studies, November 2008; Stephen J. Blank, *Towards a New Russia Policy*, Carlisle, PA: Strategic Studies Institute, U.S. Army War College, 2008.

37. Adrian Karatnycky and Alexander J. Motyl, "The Key to Kiev," *Foreign Affairs*, Vol. 88. No. 3, May/June 2009, pp. 106-

120; Charles King, "The Five-Day War," *Foreign Affairs*, Vol. 87, No. 6, November/December 2008, pp. 2-11; *www.russiatoday.com*, "ROAR: Biden explains the rules of "reset" to Ukraine & Georgia," July 22, 2009, available from Johnson's Russia List, #2009-137, *www.cdi.org/russia/johnson*.

38. Among many assessments, see analyses from Zbigniew Brzezinski, "An Agenda for NATO," *Foreign Affairs*, Vol. 88, No. 5, September/October 2009, pp. 2-20; Karl-Heinz Kamp, "Toward a New Strategy for NATO," *Survival*, Vol. 51, No. 4, August-September 2009, pp. 21-27; Sean Kay, "Beyond European Security: Europe, the United States, and NATO," in Ronald Tiersky and Erik Jones, eds., *Europe Today: A Twenty-first Century Introduction*, 3rd Ed., Lanham, MD: Rowman and Littlefield, 2007; Andrew A. Michta, *The Limits of Alliance: The United States, NATO and the EU in North and Central Europe*, Lanham, MD: Rowman and Littlefield, 2006.

39. "Antiaircraft Defence at Exercise Ladoga-2009," *The Russian Federation Ministry of Defence: News Details*, August 21, 2009, available from *www.mil.ru/eng/1866/12078/details/index.shtml?id=65914*; "Russia to deploy 2 armies in Belarus for Zapad military drills," *RIA Novosti Military News*, May 6, 2009, available from *en.rian.ru/mlitary_news/20090605/155178281.html*; Sergei Balashov, "An Exercise in Leverage: By Suggesting that Russia Could Forego the Nord Stream Project Vladimir Putin was Merely Flexing Political Muscle," *Russia Profile: Russia Beyond the Headlines*, November 26, 2008, available from *rbth.ru/articles/2008/11/26/261108_leverage.html*.

40. Rumer and Stent, "Russia and the West," pp. 96-98; Ekaterina Kuznetsova, "Russia No Match for NATO," *Moscow Times*, July 9, 2009, available from Johnson's Russia List, #2009-129, *www.cdi.org/russia/johnson*.

41. "Speech at Helsinki University and Answers to Questions from Audience," *Russian President's Website*, April 20, 2009, available from *www.kremlin.ru/eng/text/speeches/2009/04/20/1919_type82912type82914type84779_215323.shtml*; "Russia Views New European Security Treaty As 'Helsinki Plus'," *ITAR-TASS*, April 20, 2009, available from Johnson's Russia List, #2009-74, *www.cdi.org/russia/johnson*.

42. "NATO chief rejects Russia's idea of European security treaty," *Nezavisimaya Gazeta*, December 18, 2009, available from *en.rian.ru/papers/20091218/157289431.html*; "Russia's Europe security pact draft offers mutual military assistance," *RIA Novosti*, November 29, 2009, available from *en.rian.ru/russia/20091129/157030069.html*; "NATO, Russia discuss Medvedev plan for new European security treaty," *RIA Novosti*, July 12, 2009, available from *en.rian.ru/valdai_foreign_media/20091207/157138145.html*; Vladimir Ryzhkov, "Does a new treaty on European security have a future?" March 10, 2009, available from *en.rian.ru/valdai_op/20091003/156332362.html*; "Lithuanian, Belarusian, Ukrainian FMs to discuss cooperation in Kiev," *RIA Novosti*, November 22, 2009, available from *en.rian.ru/world/20091122/156935428.html*; Ilya Kramnik, "Poland, Lithuania and Ukraine to set up 'joint army'," *RIA Novosti Opinion & Analysis*, November 18, 2009, available from *en.rian.ru/analysis/20091118/156890112.html*.

43. "Russia wants CSTO to be as strong as NATO," *RIA Novosti*, May 29, 2009, available from Johnson's Russia List, #2009-100, *www.cdi.org/russia/johnson*; Irina Ionela Pop, "Russia, EU, NATO, and the Strengthening of the CSTO in Central Asia," *Caucasian Review of International Affairs*, Vol. 3, No. 3, Summer 2009, available from *cria-online.org/8_4.html*.

44. Mikhail Rostovsky, "Collective Irresponsibility Treaty: Informal Summit of the CIS Collective Security Treaty Organization is a Demonstration of Russia's Failure," *Moskovsky Komsomolets*, August 3, 2009, available from Johnson's Russia List, #2009-144, *www.cdi.org/russia/johnson*; Ryzhkov, "Kremlin Burning Bridges With Every Neighbor."

45. "Dmitriy Medvedev observed the final active phase of Cooperation 2009 special complex rapid reaction force exercises," *The Russian Federation Ministry of Defence: News Details*, October 19, 2009, available from *www.mil.ru/eng/1866/12078/details/index.shtml?id=68080*.

46. "Georgia officially withdraws from CIS," *RIA Novosti*, August 18, 2009, available from *en.rian.ru/exsoviet/20090818/155839605.html*; "Moscow swaps carrot for stick in CIS policy," *Vremaia Novostei*, June 10, 2009, available from *en.rian.ru/papers/20091006/156370029.html*; Stephen Sestanovich, "What

Has Moscow Done? Rebuilding U.S.-Russian Relations," *Foreign Affairs*, Vol. 87, No. 6, November/December 2008, pp. 25-28.

47. "Fact sheet of NRC practical cooperation," *North Atlantic Treaty Organization: Official Documents*, August 22, 2009, available from *www.nato-russia-council.info/htm/EN/news_41.shtml*.

48. "Chairman's statement Meeting of the NATO-Russia Council in Defence Minister's session in Brussels," *North Atlantic Treaty Organization: Official Documents*, June 13, 2008, available from *www.nato-russia-council.info/htm/EN/documents13jun08.shtml*.

49. "Text of Putin's Speech at NATO Summit," *Unian*, April 18, 2008, available from *www.unian.net/eng/news/news-247251.html*; "Moscow to Prevent Ukraine, Georgia's NATO Admission—Lavrov," *RIA Novosti*, April 8, 2008, available from *en.rian.ru/russia/ 20080408/104105506.html*.

50. NATO Final Communiqué, "Meeting of the North Atlantic Council at the Level of Foreign Ministers Held at NATO Headquarters, Brussels," December 3, 2008, available from *www.nato.int/docu/pr/2008/po8-153e.html*; Steven Pifer, "Averting Crisis in Ukraine," Council Special Report No. 41, *Council on Foreign Relations Center for Preventive Action*, January 2009, pp. 24-28, 44-47; "Medvedev Says Russia-Ukraine Relations at their Lowest Level," *RIA Novosti*, December 24, 2008, *enrian.ru/russia/20081224/119160157.html*; Rumer and Stent, "Russia and the West," pp. 98-99.

51. "NATO chief expects joint missile defense with Russia by 2020," *RIA Novosti*, December 17, 2009, available from *en.rian.ru/world/20091217/157273894.html*.

52. Strasbourg /Kehl NATO Summit Declaration: Issued by the Heads of State and Government participating in the meeting of the North Atlantic Council in Strasbourg /Kehl—Section 54. *North Atlantic Treaty Organization*, April 4, 2009, available from *www.nato.int/cps/en/natolive/news_52837.htm*; "Russia hails military cooperation with NATO," *RIA Novosti*, April 12, 2009, available from *en.rian.ru/russia/20091204/157102656.html*.

53. Rumer and Stent, "Russia and the West," pp. 98-100.

54. "Iran does not have Technology to Build Missile Threatening U.S., Europe—Russian Diplomat," *Moscow Interfax-AVN*, March 27, 2009, available from Johnson's Russia List, #2009-61, *www.cdi.org/russia/johnson*; "Russia rejects US plans for ABM facilities on its territory," *Vesti TV*, June 11, 2009, available from Johnson's Russia List, #2009-110, *www.cdi.org/russia/johnson*.

55. "U.S., Russia trade European missile defense system for S-300 SAMs," *RBC Daily*, September 24, 2009, *RIA Novosti*, available from *en.rian.ru/papers/20090924/156242202.html*; "U.S. uses NATO as a tool to integrate Russia into its project for a new world order—expert," *Kommersant*, December 16, 2009, available from *en.rian.ru/papers/20091216/157260660.html*; Mark Fitzpatrick, "A Prudent Decision on Missile Defence," *Survival*, Vol. 51, No. 6, December 2009-January 2010, pp. 5-12; Oliver Thränert, "NATO, Missle Defence and Extended Deterrence," *Survival*, Vol. 51, No. 6, December 2009-January 2010, pp. 63-76.

56. "NATO chief says no compromise with Russia over Georgia," *RIA Novosti*, December 17, 2009, available from *en.rian.ru/russia/20091217/157268722.html*. NATO's PFP process defines a practical cooperative security framework between NATO and individual non-NATO PFP states, former Warsaw Pact, Soviet Republic, and neutral states. Military or nonmilitary contributions include NATO operations in Bosnia, Albania, Kosovo, and Macedonia. See *Report to Congress on Implementation of the Partnership for Peace Initiative*, Washington, DC: Department of State, 1998, pp. 18-19; *United States Security Strategy for Europe and NATO*, Washington, DC: Department of Defense, 1995, pp. 10-12; and Joshua B. Spero, "Paths to Peace for NATO's Partnerships in Eurasia," in S. Victor Papacosma, James Sperling, and Sean Kay, eds., *Limiting Institutions: The Challenge of Eurasian Security*, Manchester, UK: Manchester University Press, 2003, pp. 166-184.

57. David Nowak, "NATO, partners wrap up Georgia military training," *AP*, May 31, 2009, available from Johnson's Russia List, #2009-101, *www.cdi.org/russia/johnson*; "NATO Turns into 'Blind Rhino' by Refusing to Recognize New Political Realities," *ITAR-TASS*, April 30, 2009, available from Johnson's Russia List, #2009-81, *www.cdi.org/russia/johnson*; Chivvis and Rid, "The Roots of Germany's Russia Policy," pp. 116-117.

58. "NATO offering carrot to ex-Soviet states—analyst," *RIA Novosti*, November 17, 2009, available from *en.rian.ru/russia/20091117/156878177.html*; "Russian patrol boats arrive in Abkhazia to guard border," *RIA Novosti*, December 12, 2009, available from *en.rian.ru/russia/20091212/157208271.html*; "Georgia wants to retrieve 2008 defeat," *Vedomosti*, December 15, 2009, available from *en.rian.ru/papers/20091215/157244170.html*.

59. "Russian envoy says NATO has given up eastward expansion," *RIA Novosti*, October 11, 2009, available from *en.rian.ru/russia/20091110/156785077.html*; "Russian-German aspects of development of military cooperation discussed in Moscow," *The Russian Federation Ministry of Defence: News Details*, November 2, 2009, available from *www.mil.ru/eng/1866/12078/details/index.shtml?id=68558*; "Mistral Warship Offer Symbolizes New Franco-Russian Strategic Partnership," *RIA Novosti*, March 12, 2009, available from *en.rian.ru/valdai_foreign_media/20091203/157079733.html*; "Lack of threat from Russia stumps NATO—analyst," *RIA Novosti*, March 9, 2009, available from *en.rian.ru/russia/20090903/156012964.html*.

60. "Allies agree to resume formal meetings of the NATO-Russia Council," North Atlantic Treaty Organization Website, March 5, 2009, available from *www.nato.int/cps/en/natolive/news_51343.htm*; "Informal NATO-Russia Foreign Ministers Meetings," North Atlantic Treaty Organization Website, Press Release, 2009, 082, Corfu, June 27, 2009, available from *www.nato.int/cps/en/natolive/news_55512.htm?mode=pressrelease*.

61. "Fact sheet of NRC practical cooperation," August 22, 2009; "Press conference by NATO Secretary General, Jaap de Hoop Scheffer after NATO Defence Ministers' working lunch and meeting of NATO-Russia Council at the level of Defence Ministers," *North Atlantic Treaty Organization: Official Documents*, June 13, 2009, available from *www.nato.int/docu/speech/2008/s080613e.html*.

62. "Moscow can increase Obama's chance of success in Afghanistan—analyst," *Nezavisimaya Gazeta*, December 17, 2009, available from *en.rian.ru/papers/20091217/157274919.html*; Rumer and Stent, "Russia and the West," pp. 100-101.

63. "PM Putin hopes for fewer disagreements between Russia and NATO," *RIA Novosti*, December 16, 2009, available from *en.rian.ru/world/20091216/157261263.html*; "NATO wants free oil and gas, Kalashnikovs from Russia," *Nezavisimaya Gazeta*, December 15, 2009, available from *en.rian.ru/papers/20091215/157244170.html*.

64. "NATO seeks more Russian help in Afghanistan," *RIA Novosti*, December 16, 2009, available from *en.rian.ru/russia/20091216/157258159.html*; "Summit Declaration on Afghanistan: Issued by the Heads of State and Government participating in the meeting of the North Atlantic Council in Strasbourg/Kehl on April 4, 2009," *North Atlantic Treaty Organization: Official Documents*, April 4, 2009, available from *www.nato.int/cps/en/natolive/news_52836.htm*; "Weekly press briefing by NATO Spokesman, James Appathurai," *North Atlantic Treaty Organization: Official Documents*, January 28, 2009, available from *www.nato.int/cps/en/SID-A20623A1-B062DB7F/natolive/opinions_50117.htm?selectedLocale=en*.

65. "The West doing Russia's dirty work for the first time," *Kommersant*, October 19, 2009, *RIA Novosti*, available from *en.rian.ru/papers/20091019/156520082.html*; "Russia-NATO relations enter new stage—Medvedev," *RIA Novosti*, December 16, 2009, available from *en.rian.ru/russia/20091216/157256721.html*.

66. "Is NATO an Alliance for the 21st Century?" S. Victor Papacosma, ed., *NATO's Current and Future Challenges, Occasional Papers VI*, Kent, OH: Kent State University, 2008.

67. Andrew A. Michta, "Central Europe and NATO: Still Married, but in Need of Counseling," Report No. 29, Washington, DC: Center for European Policy Analysis, December 2009.

CHAPTER 8

RUSSIAN-CHINESE SECURITY RELATIONS:
CONSTANT AND CHANGING

Richard Weitz

When the new U.S. Director of National Intelligence, Dennis Blair, issued the latest U.S. National Intelligence Strategy in September 2009, the first since 2005, its unclassified version characterized both Russia and China as potential threats, as well as possible partners, to U.S. national security interests. The strategy document described Russia as collaborating with the United States in combating nuclear terrorism, but added that Moscow "may continue to seek avenues for reasserting power and influence in ways that complicate U.S. interests." It also noted several worrisome developments regarding the People's Republic of China (PRC), including its "increasingly natural resource-focused diplomacy" and its rapidly modernizing military.[1] When asked about the strategy document by reporters, Blair confirmed that, "China is very aggressive in the cyber-world, so too is Russia and others."[2]

The governments of Russia and China continue to cooperate on some international security issues while disagreeing on others. These contrasting results have been evident in how the two countries are dealing with the case of Iran's nuclear program and proposals to transform the traditionally bilateral strategic arms control frameworks developed by Moscow and Washington during the Cold War into broader instruments encompassing a wider group of important military powers, including China. More generally, although Russian-Chinese relations are arguably better than at anytime in their history, persistent tensions in certain areas will prevent the two countries from soon becoming close military allies.

NUCLEAR PROLIFERATION AND ARMS CONTROL

In recent months, Western governments have struggled to organize a united front to prevent Iran's feared acquisition of nuclear weapons. Meanwhile, Moscow and Beijing have once again collaborated to resist imposing punitive measures on Iran that would coerce it into adhering to United Nations (UN) Security Council resolutions that demand Tehran to halt its uranium enrichment activities and provide the International Atomic Energy Agency (IAEA) with the information it needs to determine whether past Iranian nuclear research had military purposes. For several years, Russian and Chinese diplomats have also collaborated to weaken sanctions sought by the United States and its allies on North Korea, Burma, Zimbabwe, and other governments engaged in proliferation, human rights, and other activities of international concern.

In the case of Iran, years of Russian and Chinese lobbying have forced Western governments to concede Iran's right to pursue nuclear activities for peaceful purposes such as civilian energy production. Since 2002, the support offered by Moscow and Beijing may have contributed to Tehran's stubbornness during its negotiations with Western governments—led by Britain, France, and Germany. The three countries negotiating on behalf of the European Union (EU), supported at times by the Bush administration and now more explicitly by the Obama administration, have essentially sought a deal whereby Iran would agree to limit its uranium enrichment activities on a voluntary basis and allow IAEA representatives unfettered access to its nuclear facilities. In return, the EU-3 would help develop Iran's civilian nuclear program, provide additional economic and technical assistance, and relax international sanctions imposed on Tehran in response to its suspicious nuclear activities.

Neither Russian nor Chinese leaders want Iran to obtain nuclear weapons. Concerns about Iran's perceived unpredictability and fears about Tehran's long-term ambitions to compete with Moscow for dominance over Eurasia have led Russian leaders to resist Iran's possible acquisition of nuclear weapons. The main Russian worry, however, is that the United States, Israel, and some European governments might employ force to stop an overt Iranian atomic bomb program. A major conflict in the Persian Gulf could lead to a spike in world prices for Russian oil and gas, generating windfall profits for Moscow, but Russian territory lies uncomfortably close to the site of any military operation. Another war could also encourage Islamist extremism or lead to unpredictable regime change in Iran. Russians might also fear that a group within Iran might transfer nuclear explosive devices to a terrorist group, which could use them to try to coerce Russia to change its policies in Chechnya, or they could even employ a nuclear device against a Russian target to retaliate for Russian policies toward Muslims. Chinese policymakers worry more directly how a military conflict involving Iran might adversely affect their energy supplies and other economic interests in the region.

Yet, Moscow and Beijing have been considerably less critical of Iran's nuclear activities than Western governments. During the last few years, Russian officials have been especially stubborn in downplaying Iran's ability to develop nuclear weapons or long-range missiles. Until recently, NATO governments cited an emerging Iranian threat to justify deploying ballistic missile defense (BMD) systems in Poland and the Czech Republic, a strategy strongly opposed by Moscow. Russian objections to the U.S. BMD plans for Eastern Europe had threatened to disrupt the Russian-American negotiations over replacing the expiring START I agreement with another bilateral nuclear arms reduction treaty. Although the two governments have reached consensus on the general limitations on offensive nuclear forces in their follow-on treaty, they remain divided over how to address the issue of missile defenses. Whereas the United States wants to exclude BMD issues from the next treaty, Russian negotiators seek to make further nuclear reductions contingent upon Washington's acceptance of formal limitations on U.S. missile defense programs.

Overall, Russia and China have only modest economic interests in Iran, but certain influential groups in both countries have more extensive stakes, resulting in the two governments pursuing policies more supportive of Iran than is arguably wise for the pursuit of their general national interests. In Russia, groups associated with the defense and nuclear energy sectors see Iran as a lucrative export market for their goods. For the last 2 decades, Russia has been Tehran's main foreign nuclear partner, with the rest of the international community largely eschewing contact with Iran due to its refusal to heed international calls, including UN Security Council (UNSC) resolutions, to constrain its sensitive nuclear activities. Russia also sold Iran billions of dollars worth of conventional weapons, though the planned sale of the advanced S-300 air defense system is apparently on hold.³ In addition, there have been recurring rumors that Russian scientists and private sector entrepreneurs have been assisting Iran's nuclear, missile, and other military-related activities, perhaps without the approval or even knowledge of the Russian government. Supposedly, Israeli Prime Minister Benjamin Netanyahu completed a secret visit to Russia during the summer of 2009 to deliver a list of suspect individuals to the Russian government.⁴

Iran's ties with China encompass both the defense sector and civilian commerce, especially energy. Iran has become one of the PRC's most significant oil suppliers, while Chinese companies provide Iran with important industrial technologies, specialty metals, and other products. Any discussion of Chinese-Iranian relations must start with the fact that Iran has become one of the PRC's most significant sources of foreign energy, supplying Chinese consumers with as much as 15 percent of its imported oil. Beijing has benefited from the reluctance of Western companies to invest in Iran due to the numerous unilateral and multilateral sanctions imposed on its government for its nuclear activities, past support for terrorism, and controversial regional polices towards Israel, Lebanon, and other countries. If anything, Beijing's dependence on Iranian oil should increase in the coming years as China's energy consumption continues to rise.⁵ The governments of China and Iran have signed several multibillion dollar energy framework agreements, though these remain only partly implemented. Chinese and Iranian companies began to finalize specific contracts earlier this year. In January 2009, China National Petroleum Corporation (CNPC) and the National Iranian Oil Company (NIOC) signed a $1.76 billion contract to jointly develop Iran's North Azadegan field, which will produce an estimated 75,000 barrels of oil a day by 2013.[6] Chinese firms have helped modernize Iran's energy industry and other economic infrastructure as well as sold Iranians diverse commercial products.[7] Bilateral trade between the two countries is several times greater than between Iran and Russia. In addition, Chinese companies, such as the PRC defense conglomerate NORINCO, have sold Iran important industrial and military technologies, especially suitable for ballistic missiles. During the 1980-88 Iran-Iraq War, China provided Iran with tanks and other weapons, including special tactical anti-ship missiles.[8] Iranian officials have threatened to use these missiles against American and other ships in the Persian Gulf.[9] The Iraq War that began in 2003 has driven Beijing and Tehran closer, with China eager to secure Middle Eastern oil supplies and Iran seeking to bolster ties with friendly governments to counterbalance an increase in American military threats to Tehran.[10] Iran also receives compensation for these energy ties in the form of Chinese diplomatic support at the UN.

Chinese policymakers presumably appreciate, and Russian observers openly acknowledge, that their countries benefit in several ways from the long-standing confrontation between Iran and the West, providing it does not escalate into war or lead to Tehran's acquisition of nuclear weapons.[11] The friction between Iran and Western countries leaves Russia and China as Iran's major economic partners and, at least in the case of Moscow, placed them in the enviable position of mediator between Iran and the West, with both parties seeking to secure Moscow's support against the other. Russia further benefits from how Iranian-Western tensions exclude Iran from contributing its territory or oil and natural gas to Western-sponsored trans-Caspian energy pipelines that would reduce European dependence on Russian supplies. Tehran's alienation from the West also helps to inflate world energy prices by keeping Iranian oil and especially natural gas sales off international markets. Conversely, a relaxation of Iranian-Western tensions could bring about a further fall in world energy prices, both in the short run due to the decline in global tensions and in the longer run as Western firms resume making large-scale investments in Iranian energy projects. While China would pay less for imported oil, Chinese exporters would suffer economically if Iranian businesses seek to replenish their inventories with Western goods and technologies, diverting purchases away from Chinese (and Russian) firms in the process. Even if Russian and Chinese companies retained their presence in Iran, they would probably need to offer better commercial terms to their Iranian partners if the latter has the option of pursuing deals with Western companies.

Chinese and Russian officials have called on Iran to cease enriching uranium and conduct its nuclear activities in a more transparent manner. Iranian government representatives insist they need to possess indigenous means of making nuclear fuel, but the same technology used to enriched uranium to the level needed to power a commercial nuclear reactor can also be employed to manufacture the more heavily concentrated weapons-grade fissile material needed to power a nuclear explosion. Economic motives can easily be adduced to explain Moscow's opposition to Iran's acquisition of an indigenous enrichment capacity. Until now, Tehran has had to purchase large quantities of Russian uranium fuel to run Iran's Russian-built nuclear reactor at Bushehr. Russian exporters hope to sell Iran the additional fuel needed to run the other nuclear reactors the Iranian government plans to build in the coming years. If Iran can make its own fuel, Russia would lose these markets. China's growing nuclear industry would presumably also like to service the Iranian uranium fuel market without having to worry about domestic Iranian competitors, who would presumably enjoy home field advantage in any direct competition.

The September 17, 2009, announcement by U.S. President Barack Obama that the United States will abandon Bush administration plans to deploy 10 long-range missile interceptors in Poland and an advanced battle management radar in the Czech Republic was welcomed in Moscow, where the intended deployments had aroused sharp Russian opposition. Obama and other U.S. leaders insisted that concerns about Russia did not affect their decision. Instead, they cited new intelligence information indicating that the nature of the Iranian missile threat had evolved in ways not anticipated by the U.S. intelligence community in 2007, when a National Intelligence Estimate (NIE) provided the assessment used by the Bush administration in reaching its East European BMD deployment decision. The Obama administration later confirmed that the U.S. intelligence community had produced a new NIE in May 2009, which reportedly concluded that Iran would take 3 to 5 years longer than anticipated in the 2007 NIE, which set the date as 2015, to construct an intercontinental ballistic missile (ICBM). In contrast, U.S. intelligence has concluded that Iranian scientists and engineers have achieved much more rapid progress in developing shorter-range missiles capable of delivering payloads against targets in Europe and the Middle East, including U.S. forces based there.¹² In a press conference explaining the decision, Secretary of Defense Robert Gates cited the U.S. military's own very rapid progress in developing missile defense technologies, especially regarding the currently available Standard Missile-3 (SM-3) interceptors carried aboard the U.S. Navy's Aegis-equipped destroyers. Gates also pointed to dramatic improvements in airborne, space-based, and ground-based missile sensors, making the single large radar previously planned for the Czech Republic unnecessary.¹³ The Defense Secretary argued that these changes in threat perception and U.S. missile defense capabilities justified Washington's decision to rapidly establish a shorter-range missile shield, based on existing BMD technologies, much closer to Iran. Following creation of this initial shield, scheduled to occur around 2011, the United States would deploy more advanced missile defenses in Europe in phases corresponding to advances in Iran's missile capabilities.

Although denying that concerns about Russia affected their BMD decisionmaking, the Obama administration clearly hoped that indefinitely suspending the Polish and Czech deployments would facilitate negotiation of a new Russian-American strategic arms control agreement before START I expires in December 2009. In practice, the U.S. decision to focus on developing shorter-range BMD might have greater impact on the strategic arms control agreement that Washington intends to negotiate with Russia *after* the immediate START replacement accord. Many members of the Obama administration desire substantially greater reductions in the existing nuclear arsenals of Russia and United States, but Russian strategists have argued that their country must retain sufficient offensive nuclear forces to overcome U.S. strategic missile defenses. A more pressing U.S. objective, however, was to secure greater Russian assistance in constraining Iran's nuclear and missile development programs. Obama sent a letter to Medvedev in February 2009 that reportedly underscored that progress in limiting Iran's nuclear and ballistic missile development efforts would reduce the need for U.S. and NATO missile defenses.[14] Although both governments have rejected the idea of a formal quid pro quo, with Washington abandoning the BMD deployments in return for Moscow's coercing Iran into restraining its nuclear and missile programs, American officials now expected that the Kremlin will show greater flexibility in applying additional sanctions on Iran.

Following Obama's announcement, Medvedev said his government "appreciate[d] the responsible attitude of the President of the United States towards implementing our agreements."[15] The Russian President explained that the U.S. decision created "favorable conditions" for the joint Russian-American threat assessment regarding ballistic missile proliferation that their governments agreed to undertake at their London and Moscow summits earlier this year.[16] He later confirmed that he had cancelled contingency plans to deploy short-range Iskander ballistic missiles in the Russian enclave of Kaliningrad.[17] Although Medvedev said that Russian officials would now "be more attentive to" U.S. security concerns, he insisted that Moscow would not engage in "primitive compromises or exchanges."[18] Russia's envoy to NATO, Dmitry Rogozin, warned Russians against becoming "overwhelmed with some kind of childish euphoria" following Obama's announcement.[19] Prime Minister Vladimir Putin, Russia's most influential policymaker, described the U.S. decision as simply the first step in removing the obstacles to better relations between the two countries. In his first public comments on Obama's announcement, Putin said that, "I very much hope that this right and brave decision will be followed up by the full cancellation of all restrictions on cooperation with Russia and high technology transfer to Russia as well as a boost to expand the WTO [World Trade Organization] to embrace Russia, Belarus and Kazakhstan."[20] Putin's comments at least imply that, when it comes to pressing the fabled "reset button," some influential Russians expect that most of the resetting would occur in Washington.

It is true that Medvedev has not excluded imposing additional sanctions on Iran. On September 25, 2009, when Tehran confirmed to Western intelligence that it had been constructing a secret uranium enrichment facility at Qum, Medvedev stated that, "the information that Iran, over the course of several years, has been constructing an enrichment plant near Qum without the IAEA's knowledge is a cause of serious concern." He insisted that, "The construction of a new uranium enrichment plant contradicts the UNSC's repeated demands for Iran to cease its enrichment activities." Medvedev joined the other five governments negotiating with Iran (this so-called "P-6" consists of all UNSC members as well as Germany, one of Iran's main economic partners) in demanding that the Iranian government allow the IAEA to inspect the new facility as soon as possible. Medvedev further called on Tehran to demonstrate, at its October 1, 2009, meeting in Geneva with the P-6, that it genuinely wants a negotiated solution to the problem created by the uncertain nature of its nuclear program: "This will be possible if it [Iran] comes to the meeting in Geneva prepared to focus on the nuclear issue, take practical steps toward rebuilding trust toward its nuclear program and ensuring its transparency, and demonstrate its readiness to cooperate fully with the IAEA."[21] Previously, including during the week after Obama announced the revised U.S. BMD deployment plans, Russian officials dealing with the Iran case said they would only support additional sanctions if the IAEA provided convincing proof that the Iranian government was seeking a nuclear weapon.[22] Medvedev now cited the revelations about Qum to place the burden of proof on Tehran "to present convincing evidence of its intent to develop nuclear energy strictly for peaceful purposes."[23]

At two news conferences the following day after the G-20 summit in Pittsburgh, Medvedev said that he still preferred to rely on incentives to entice Iran to make its peaceful nuclear energy program more transparent, but if these positive inducements failed to secure the desired favorable response, then "other mechanisms come into force."[24] At a meeting with students and faculty at the University of Pittsburgh, where he told one questioner that Iran had dominated his talks with President Obama, Medvedev explained that, "if all possibilities for influencing the situation have been exhausted, using sanctions according to international law would be possible. On the whole, this is a fairly standard approach. Without speaking about their effectiveness," which Medvedev regularly questions, "sometimes it is necessary to do it."[25]

But Medvedev made similar statements even before the Obama administration announced it would suspend its missile defense deployments in Poland and the Czech Republic, so it remains unclear whether the Russian government has adopted an entirely new position in favor of a stricter approach toward Iran.

For example, Medvedev told the Valdai discussion group of Russia experts in Moscow that, "Sanctions are not very effective on the whole, but sometimes you have to embark on sanctions."[26] Medvedev and other Russian officials can also cite Iran's flexibility at Geneva as a reason for postponing any new sanctions. In addition, Prime Minister Putin, who is thought to exercise great influence regarding Russian policy in this area, has yet to indicate any lessening of his opposition toward additional sanctions. Finally, suspicions persist in Washington that Russian leaders may be calculating that they can gain credit with the Obama administration by publicly appearing to adopt a harsher line toward Iran—which will help the administration deal with critics accusing it of abandoning the missile defense systems intended for Poland and the Czech Republic without receiving any major Russian concessions in return—while anticipating that the PRC will use its veto to block the imposition of new economic sanctions on Tehran, which would sustain Russia's profitable business relations with Iran. Whereas Medvedev hinted several times that he might apply sanctions against Iran for its nuclear activities, the Chinese government more actively opposed the notion of sanctioning Iran further. Even after the dramatic revelations about Qum, a decision by the White House to share U.S. intelligence information about Iran's nuclear program with Beijing (and Moscow),[27] and personal lobbying by President Obama during his meetings with President Hu in New York and Pittsburgh, the Chinese government simply stated that it was following the situation.[28]

Russia and China have acted largely in parallel in the case of Iran, but a small and potentially widening gap has opened between the two governments regarding the global arms control agenda. In his September 2009 speech at the opening of the UN General Assembly, Medvedev returned to an important issue that Russian leaders have appropriately stressed in recent years—the need to transform the primarily bilateral strategic arms control relationship that Moscow and Washington have inherited from the Cold War into one that places greater emphasis on multilateral frameworks. For example, although Medvedev noted that Russia and the United States were making progress in negotiating a replacement for the START Treaty that expired in December 2009, he urged other nuclear weapons states to join the offensive strategic nuclear weapons reduction process, which thus far has been almost exclusively a Russian-American affair. Medvedev also recommended making the 1987 Intermediate-Range Nuclear Forces (INF) Treaty universal. For several years, Russian leaders have complained how this bilateral agreement prevents only Russia and the United States from developing, manufacturing, or deploying ground-launched ballistic and cruise missiles having ranges of 500 to 5,500 kilometers (km). In the case of these arms control and security measures, President Medvedev, like President Obama earlier in the day, stressed in his General Assembly speech that the remaining nuclear weapons states need not wait for Russia and the United States to lead the way.

China is a rising international power and the only acknowledged nuclear weapons state in East Asia. Therefore securing China's involvement is an essential prerequisite to achieving substantial reductions in nuclear weapons. Although the United States and Russia still have much larger nuclear arsenals than China, these two countries will find it difficult to reduce their nuclear holdings below approximately 1,000 warheads unless the PRC commits to limiting its own nuclear arsenal. Otherwise, Washington and Moscow would fear that Beijing could exploit Russian-American reductions to strengthen its own nuclear forces in an effort to become an equivalent nuclear power. Yet, Chinese officials have indicated that they have no intention of joining the strategic arms reduction talks for offensive nuclear systems of intercontinental range until Moscow and Washington reduce their own arsenals to levels approximating that of China. The country's January 2009 defense white paper commented: "The two countries possessing the largest nuclear arsenals bear special and primary responsibility for nuclear disarmament. They should earnestly comply with the relevant agreements already concluded, and further drastically reduce their nuclear arsenals in a verifiable and irreversible manner, so as to create the necessary conditions for the participation of other nuclear-weapon states in the process of nuclear disarmament."[29] Despite concerns that China is positioning itself to "race to parity" following major reductions in Russian and U.S. offensive nuclear forces, in other instances when Moscow and Beijing have proven unable to agree on a common position regarding third-party issues, their governments have tended to ignore or downplay their differences.

A QUESTION OF METRICS

A comprehensive assessment of Russian-Chinese security relations is opportune given that 2009 marks the 60th anniversary of the establishment of the diplomatic relations between Moscow and the PRC. In June 2009, Chinese President Hu visited Russia partly in celebration of the occasion. Citing the high-level exchanges, mutually supportive statements, and other manifestations of Russian-Chinese cooperation in what both governments refer to as their developing strategic partnership, President Medvedev told the China Central TV in an interview on the day of Hu's arrival that he believed that Russian-Chinese relations had reached their highest level in history.[30] In his speech marking the 60th anniversary of the establishment of relations between Moscow and China, Medvedev rhapsodically observed that, "Having analyzed our relations since 1992, I have come to the conclusion that such relations are best described as exemplary."[31] He continued:

> This unique sort of good-neighborliness and friendship between two great powers has made a significant contribution to the formation of a new world order, the strengthening of multipolarity, and the development of respect for those states intent on national development, in compliance with international law. I believe that our experience in reaching agreement on the most difficult issues should be extensively disseminated and recognized as a gift to all humankind. [32]

Hu was a bit more philosophical when he offered his own assessment. The past 60 years, he related, had led him to conclude that healthy Chinese-Russian relations required the two parties to embrace the four principles of "mutual trust," "mutual respect," "mutual understanding," and the search for "common ground," which involves "leaving our differences aside and resolving them through friendly consultations."[33] Yet, he too saw the Chinese-Russian partnership as serving the global good:

> For many years, Chinese and Russian diplomatic efforts have worked tirelessly to ensure peace and stability in the world. In recent years, by extending collaboration and coordinating positions on ways to resolve international and regional issues, we have made persistent efforts to create a multipolar world and to democratize international relations. Sino-Russian relations are indeed an important factor in the positive interaction between the major players in world politics and for the preservation of peace and stability in the world.[34]

Although Medvedev's assessment that Sino-Russian ties have never been better is probably correct, this metric does not present an especially high hurdle. The modern Chinese-Russian relationship has most often been characterized by bloody wars, imperial conquests, and mutual denunciations. It has only been during the last 20 years, when Russian power has been decapitated by its lost Soviet empire and China has found itself a rising economic — but still relatively weak, albeit steadily strengthening — military power that the two countries have managed to reach a harmonious *modus vivendi*. According to various metrics, China now has the world's second or third largest economy, while Russia lags in approximately eighth place and, due to its slower growth rates, is falling further behind. But Russia still has a much more powerful nuclear arsenal.

During the 1990s, Chinese and Russian leaders focused on ensuring their domestic political stability following the political turmoil that accompanied the demise of Chinese and Soviet communism. Russian officials had to manage, simultaneously, the transition from single-party rule to a multi-party state, the conversion of a command economy to one based on largely market principles, and the loss of a global empire. In comparison, Chinese leaders had an easier transition, though they still had to surmount mass protests in 1989 seeking their overthrow and, subsequently, several years of political ostracism by Western governments dismayed by the brutal repression at Tiananmen and elsewhere.

Although both countries have experienced a geopolitical resurgence during the past decade, Chinese and Russian security concerns emanate from different areas with the exceptions of Central Asia and North Korea. Most Russian analysts, typically based in Moscow, perceive their main security challenges to the west and south as well as from the United States. They discount the emergence of a genuine military threat to Russia from China for at least the next decade. With their blessing, the Russian defense industry has sold the Chinese military billions of dollars worth of weapons, though these systems have typically been optimal for fighting a maritime war in the Pacific rather than a land war in the Russian Far East. Chinese policymakers, considering U.S. military forces in the Pacific as well as potentially threatening developments in Taiwan, Japan, India, and North Korea, eagerly bought these weapons.

Many of these harmonious interests persist, but the global economic crisis and other developments have introduced new challenges into the Russia-China relationship. Chinese and Russian officials still decline to criticize each other's foreign and domestic policies. They also have issued many joint statements calling for a multipolar world in which no one country (e.g., the United States) would dominate. Moscow and Beijing uphold traditional interpretations of national sovereignty that exempt a government's internal policies from foreign criticism. They oppose the promotion of American democracy, U.S. missile defense programs, and Washington's alleged plans to militarize outer space. The two countries strive to uphold the authority of the UN, where the Chinese and Russian delegations frequently collaborate to dilute proposed resolutions that would impose sanctions on Burma, Iran, Zimbabwe, and other governments that they consider to be friendly. Since 2005, Russia and China have begun holding major joint military exercises, with the next one scheduled for later this year (2010). In July 2008, they finally demarcated the last pieces of their 4,300-km (2,700 mile) frontier, the longest land border in the world, ending a decades-long dispute. During 2009, their leaders have blamed American economic mismanagement for precipitating a global recession that now threatens their countries' socioeconomic stability.

Nevertheless, Chinese officials evince much greater reluctance than their Russian counterparts to challenge the paramount role of the American dollar or, more broadly, the U.S. role in world politics. Although the inauguration of Obama has not triggered the boost in popular approval of the United States seen in many other countries, Russian and Chinese leaders appear eager to work with the new American administration where possible. The most noteworthy development in their bilateral defense relationship has been the sharp decline in Russian arms sales to China in recent years. The ongoing improvements in China's indigenous defense industry have decreased Beijing's interest in purchasing Soviet-era weapons from Moscow. The Chinese are now demanding that Russia sell the People's Liberation Army (PLA) its most advanced weapons. The Russian government has thus far declined to do so for fear that the Chinese might copy their technology and use it to design superior weapons that Chinese firms can then sell to potential Russian customers at lower prices. Russian officials are similarly reluctant to transfer their best nuclear energy technologies and other intellectual products that could allow lower-cost Chinese manufacturers to displace Russian exports from third-party markets.

The rest of their bilateral energy relationship remains equally problematic. The two governments repeatedly announce grandiose oil and natural gas deals that fail to materialize. Russian energy firms try to induce European and Asian customers to bid against one another. Although this approach enhances Russian bargaining leverage, it reinforces Chinese doubts about Russia's reliability as a long-term energy partner. Russian energy suppliers accepted the recent loans for energy deals only under duress due to the global recession; if oil and gas prices rebound, they might seek to renegotiate the terms of their new deals with China. The two governments remain suspicious about each other's activities in Central Asia, where their state-controlled firms compete for oil and gas. Chinese officials have steadfastly refused to endorse Moscow's decision to recognize Abkhazia and South Ossetia as independent states, which Russia pried from Georgia during the August 2008 war. On the 1 year anniversary of the conflict, the Chinese Foreign Ministry simply repeated Beijing's aspiration that the parties would resolve their conflict "through dialogue and consultation."[35] At the societal level, ties between ordinary Chinese and Russians remain minimal despite several years of sustained efforts by both governments to promote humanitarian exchanges and the study of the other country's language. The Chinese criticize the failure of the Russian government to ensure the safety and respect the rights of Chinese nationals working in Russia. Russians in turn complain about Chinese pollution spilling into Russian territory and worry that large-scale Chinese immigration into the Russian Far East will result in large swaths of eastern Russia becoming de facto parts of China. These differences are not so great as to outweigh their shared interests in maintaining good bilateral relations, but they have reassured other nations that a Chinese-Russian military alliance or even less formal Moscow-Beijing block is unlikely.

ENERGY AND ECONOMICS

In recent months, the focus of the Russian-Chinese relationship has been on energy and economic co-operation. Presidents Medvedev and Hu met at the June 15-16, 2009, Shanghai Cooperation Organization summit in Yekaterinburg, the first ever heads-of-state meeting of the BRIC (Brazil, Russia, India, and China) countries held later in the day on June 16, and then several times from June 16-18 when Hu made a state visit to Russia. While in Moscow, Hu made sure to confer with Prime Minister Putin, still considered Russia's preeminent politician. He also spoke with Russian commercial and society leaders. At the Russia-China Trade and Economic Forum in Moscow, which took place during Hu's visit, some 600 Chinese and Russian business people signed over 40 contracts worth some $3 billion.[36]

In the midst of the global economic slowdown, the focus of media attention was on whether the two nations would make a concerted effort to displace the American dollar as the world's dominant reserve currency. Since he became Russian President in May 2009, Medvedev has been pushing to enhance Russia's role in global financial decisions. A key element of this campaign has been to elevate the status of the Russian ruble, ideally by making it a major world currency and by diminishing the role of the dollar. According to one estimate, the dollar accounts for two-thirds of the world's aggregate foreign currency reserves.[37] Most international trade is also valued in dollars.[38] Medvedev and other foreign leaders have complained that the dollar's unique status gives the United States unwarranted privileges and subjects other countries to the negative consequences of U.S. economic policies. A recent complaint, for example, has been that the large U.S. budget deficits are lowering the value of the dollar holdings of foreign countries.

Despite Moscow's hopes, Chinese officials have been much more reluctant about challenging the dollar's preeminent global position. China holds an estimated $2 trillion in dollar reserves, almost five times Russia's estimated total of slightly over $400 billion.[39] Chinese government representatives have therefore been very cautious about making statements that might depreciate the value of the PRC's holdings, which are the world's largest. China's restraining influence became apparent when the BRIC summit issued a communiqué that, while endorsing a "more diversified" global currency system, did not explicitly attack the dollar or call for new reserve currencies.[40] In their bilateral talks with the Russians, the most the Chinese would consent to was "using national currencies in mutual payments."[41] Medvedev said that, "We agreed to take additional steps in this direction, which may include adjusting our current agreements or giving corresponding instructions to the heads of relevant agencies, such as the finance ministers and the heads of our central banks."[42] A significant indicator of the importance of this agreement is whether the Chinese will consent to purchasing oil in rubles, which Russian officials have defined as a strategic goal. Deputy Prime Minister Igor Sechin, who oversees the government's energy policies and is also Rosneft's chairman, said selling energy in rubles was a "strategic" issue for Russia.[43]

After many years of frustrated deals and false starts, Russia and China now seem on the verge of establishing their long-expected energy partnership. Although Chinese energy demand is soaring and Russia's oil and gas deposits lie much closer than the more distant energy sources of Africa and the Persian Gulf, Russian-Chinese collaboration in this area has always been very limited. Differences over pricing and a failure to develop adequate pipelines as well as other infrastructure have severely constrained Chinese purchases of Russian energy.[44] While the monetary value of Russia's energy exports to China has increased exponentially in recent years, this surge was due to the rising world prices of oil and gas. The actual volume of Russian deliveries has stagnated at relatively low levels.[45]

During 2009, however, the two countries made major progress. The most important development occurred in April, when the Russian and Chinese governments finalized their $25 billion loan-for-oil deal. They had accepted this arrangement in principle in a memorandum of understanding negotiated in October 2008, but it required another half a year of haggling to overcome differences over the rate of the loan and other details. Under its terms, the Development Bank of China will lend Russia's state-run energy companies the money they need to build and operate a 67-km branch line, extending from the Skovordino refinery on the East Siberia Pacific Ocean (ESPO) oil pipeline currently under construction to the Russian-Chinese border town of Xing'an in Heilongjiang province's Mohe county. The China National Petroleum Corp. is constructing a 1,000-km pipeline from Mohe to the refineries located in the Chinese city of Daqing. Russia's Transneft corporation has already begun building the branch pipeline, while Russia's Rosneft energy conglomerate has pledged to pump 300 million metric tons of oil through it during the course of a 20-year period. Roseneft's oil supplies will serve as collateral for a $15 billion loan, whereas the pipeline and related infrastructure will guarantee the $10 billion loan to Transneft.[46] Following the construction of the new pipeline, Russia will have the annual capacity to transport 26 million tons of crude oil to China via pipeline and 11 million tons by rail.[47] The Russian State Duma ratified the bilateral agreement with China in September 2009.[48]

Market conditions rather than a major transformation in Russia-China relations probably account for the recent deal. The Russian government and its state-run energy firms have suffered from declining world demand and prices for Russian oil and gas, sharp reductions in the share value of Russia's heavily indebted energy firms on global stock markets, and surging unemployment and other manifestations of economic retraction in the Russian economy. In addition, Chinese negotiators have achieved some success in securing oil and gas agreements with neighboring Central Asian governments, circumventing Moscow's dominant position in the energy sectors of Kazakhstan and Turkmenistan by, at times, outbidding Russian energy representatives. Beijing has also provided large loans to Moldova, Central Asian countries, and other former Soviet republics suffering during the global recession. Whereas Moscow sees energy as a major, if not the major, tool in advancing Russian foreign policy interests, China can more deftly use its massive financial and other economic resources as instruments of influence, including in the former Soviet territories ruled by Moscow. Against this backdrop, Russian negotiators made concessions they had long resisted concerning PRC demands regarding the price for oil deliveries to China and the terms for the Chinese loans. They also expressed greater openness than they have previously to Chinese direct investment in eastern Russia and Central Asia.[49]

Hu and Medvedev favorably mentioned the oil-for-loans exchange several times during their June 2009 meetings. In a joint press conference with Hu in Moscow, the Russian President assessed the value of the entire deal at around $100 billion. He added that the two governments were considering using the same model to additional energy sectors: "Today, we spoke about using this experience in other forms of energy cooperation, such as gas or coal mining. I think that we may get good results by applying this experience elsewhere."[50] In particular, Russian officials are encouraging consideration of a similar relationship to accelerate plans to sell Russian natural gas to China. The Russian energy giant Gazprom and the Chinese National Petroleum Corporation (CNPC) have been negotiating possible deals since 2004, when they formed a strategic partnership.[51]

During Putin's March 2006 trip to Beijing, Gazprom and the CNPC signed a memorandum of understanding about constructing a 6,700-km Altai pipeline to deliver Russian natural gas to China. At the June 2009 St. Petersburg International Economic Forum, Deputy Prime Minister Sechin told a questioner that Russia was prepared to provide the Chinese as much natural gas as they require: "Whatever amounts they ask for, we have the gas."[52] During Hu's state visit, however, Gazprom announced that it could not deliver natural gas to China in 2011 as planned under the Altai pipeline project because Russian and Chinese negotiators could not agree on a price. Gazprom was supposed to begin building the pipeline, which could deliver over 30 billion cubic meters of natural gas annually to China, in 2008. "As soon as there is a price, we will start the construction, but this is a complicated issue," a senior executive Gazprom observed.[53] At his joint news conference with Medvedev, Hu underlined the importance of accelerating the natural gas discussions. If the two governments follow the precedent set by the oil deal, then China might lend Gazprom the money it needs to construct the Altai pipeline in return for guaranteed gas shipments. These energy-for-loans swaps also circumvent the problem of the low level of reciprocal Chinese and Russian foreign direct investment in each other's enterprises, Russian Foreign Minister Sergey Lavrov characterized this mutual investment as "insignificant" in a late March interview with a Chinese newspaper.[54]

When commenting on Chinese-Russian economic ties, Medvedev took care to cite the 2008 figure of $55 billion in two-way trade. Bilateral trade has fallen from the record level of the previous year, due to the global economic slowdown and especially the collapse in world prices for Russian oil, gas, and other raw material exports.[55] Russia's trade envoy to China said that two-way trade had decreased to $7.3 billion during the first quarter of 2009, a 42 percent drop-off.[56] Ironically, the decrease in the value of Russian exports to other countries has been even greater, resulting in China's overtaking Germany to become Russia's leading trading partner during the first 4 months of 2009.[57]

Even so, Chinese-Russian trade remains seriously imbalanced. Whereas before 2007, Russia racked up steady surpluses thanks to large deliveries of energy, arms, and high-technology goods. During the last 2 years, the terms of trade have been shifting markedly in China's favor due to a decrease in Chinese purchase of weapons systems and other high-technology items and growing Russian purchases of cheap Chinese cars, electronics, and other consumer goods. At present, Russian exports to China consist overwhelmingly of commodities, especially natural resources like oil and timber, while China sells mostly consumer goods such as household appliances, machinery, and other higher-value products to Russia. As a result of the recent collapse in world prices for Russia's natural resources and decreasing Chinese purchases of Russian high-technology goods, Russia experienced a $13.5 billion trade deficit with China last year.[58] Medvedev said that he and Hu "talked at length about changing the structure of commodity turnover, opportunities for increasing the share of machinery and technical products, [and] the share of high-tech products in our commodity turnover structure."[59] The two men signed a memorandum of understanding to promote mutual trade in high-tech products, but similar efforts to rebalance their commerce have had little effect in the past. Chinese firms importing advanced technologies still look most often to Western countries rather than Russia.

MILITARY SALES AND EXERCISES

One of the reasons for Russia's deteriorating terms of trade with China has been the sharp decline in Chinese purchases of Russian arms in recent years. After the United States and European governments imposed an arms embargo on China following the 1989 Tiananmen Square incident, China became one of Russia's most reliable purchasers of imported arms. In any given year, Beijing bought between one-fourth and one-half of Russia's weapons exports. During most of the past 2 decades, Russian military exports to China constituted the most important dimension of the two countries' security relationship. Russian firms derived substantial revenue from the sales, which helped sustain Russia's military-industrial complex during the lean 1990s. For its part, China managed to acquire advanced conventional weapons that its developing defense industry could not yet manufacture. China was able to purchase certain weapons systems from Brazil and Israel as well, but their portfolio of exportable arms is limited. In addition, the United States pressured Russia to curtail its sales of advanced systems to China.

Recent years have seen a major change in the Russian-Chinese arms relationship. The volume of Russian weapons sales to the Chinese military has experienced a precipitous decline. The major reason for this transformation has been that the PRC's defense industry has become capable of manufacturing much more sophisticated armaments. Moscow now confronts the choice of either accepting a greatly diminished share of the Chinese arms market or agreeing to sell even more advanced weapons to Beijing. In addition to threatening existing force balances in East Asia, such transfers could further strengthen the PRC's ability to compete for sales on third-party markets.

Thus far, surging Russian arms sales to other countries have allowed Russian policymakers to accept the decreasing Chinese military purchases rather than risk the transfer of new technologies. For example, Russian officials decided against selling Su-33 multirole fighter planes for use on China's future aircraft carriers after Beijing sought to purchase only two planes for a trial. Russian policymakers feared that Chinese experts simply wanted to study the warplanes to reverse engineer or otherwise copy them.[60] Even so, the threat to Russian arms exports presented by the global recession may cause more Russians to seek short-term profits by allowing the sale to the PRC of even their most advanced systems.

Whatever the problems with their bilateral arms relationship, the Russian and Chinese militaries have developed a more professional and balanced relationship with each other. During the Cold War, the Soviet and Chinese armed forces faced each other across the world's longest border as enemies. They even engaged in a small-scale shooting war in the late 1960s over contested islands lying along a shared river. During the 1990s, the two defense establishments largely ignored each other since their attention was focused elsewhere. Now the relationship is evolving further, becoming better institutionalized and integrated. As befits two large and powerful neighbors, the senior military leaders of Russia and China now meet frequently in various formats. The two defense communities also conduct a number of exchanges and engagements. The best known are the major biennial military exercises that they have been holding since 2005, but smaller-scale encounters are constantly occurring. In April 28, 2009, Russian Defense Minister Anatoly Serdyukov and his Chinese counterpart, Liang Guanglie, announced in Moscow that the two countries would conduct 25 joint maneuvers in 2009 alone as well as boost other defense cooperation.[61] In September, the Chinese and Russian warships engaged in counterpiracy missions in the Gulf of Aden arranged to conduct Joint Exercise Blue Peace Shield 2009. They practiced communication links, coordinated resupply efforts, and joint live-firing and helicopter operations.[62] They then rehearsed searching, locating, and detaining a pirate ship.[63]

Another major exercise, Peace Mission 2009, took place from July 22-27, 2009. It began with a single day of political-military consultations among senior Russian and Chinese defense personnel in Khabarovsk.[64] The operational phases of the exercise took place in northeast China, at the Taonan training base in China's Shenyang Military Area Command. Both parties spent 3 days jointly planning and organizing for a hypothetical combined anti-terrorist campaign. The most important exercise segment was a live-fire drill at the base, which occupied 90 minutes on the last day.[65] About 1,300 military personnel for each country participated in some phase of the exercise. The Russian air force contributed about 20 military aircraft to the maneuvers in China, including Su-25 and Su-27 combat jets, Su-24 bombers, Mi-8 helicopters, and Il-76 transport planes.[66] The air force considered but declined to deploy strategic bombers.[67] The Chinese military sent about an equal number of combat aircraft, one of which crashed a few days before the exercise began. The Russian ground forces included BMP-1 and BTR-70 armored vehicles as well as T-80 tanks.[68] A Russian airborne assault unit practiced parachuting from Il-76s.⁶⁹ The Chinese armed forces contributed artillery, air defense, army aviation, and special forces contingents, as well as logistical support to both sides.⁷⁰ Peace Mission 2009 differed from the previous two exercises in the series in certain respects. The operational phase of the drills occurred only on Chinese territory. The single day of discussions at Khabarovsk gave the appearance of an attempt to involve Russian territory in some direct capacity. Fewer troops participated than in previous years, though some of the weaponry employed was more sophisticated.⁷¹

BORDER SECURITY ISSUES

Unlike during the Cold War, Russia and China no longer fear engaging in a shooting war. The two countries have largely accepted their common border. Russia's first president, Boris Yeltsin, made border management a priority for his administration, for understandable reasons that he cited in July 1995: "China is a very important state for us. It is a neighbor, with which we share the longest border in the world and with which we are destined to live and work side by side forever."⁷² Lavrov reiterated such sentiments in March 2009, when in an interview with a Chinese newspaper he cited the Chinese proverb that, "A close neighbor is better than a distant relative." Lavrov added that, "Russia and China objectively have the closest relations, owing particularly to geographical proximity and long historical ties."⁷³

In July 2008, Lavrov and Chinese Foreign Minister Yang Jiechi signed a treaty in Beijing that formally ended their 4 decades' old border dispute. The accord finally demarcated the last pieces of their 4,300 km (2,700 mile) frontier, the longest land border in the world. The deal ended a disagreement that in 1969 led to a brief shooting war between the two countries over some contested islands along the Amur River. According to the Chinese media, the Russian government made the most concessions, yielding half of Heixiazi (Bolshoi Ussuriysky in Russian) island and all of Yinlong (Tarabarov) island.[74] As a result, the Russian government withdrew its official presence from 174 square km (67 square miles) of territory that had been the site of bloody clashes in 1969.[75] One reason why this last segment of the frontier along northeast China proved the most challenging to resolve was that the Heixiazi/Bolshoi Ussuriysky Island involves inhabited lands. Since the small Russian community on the island did not want to relocate or become part of China, the two governments drew the boundary in such a way that the populated areas fell within the new Russian half of the island.[76] Since then, the Joint Russian-Chinese Border Commission has redirected its work from demarcating the boundary to confirming that the existing border corresponds to the agreed frontier.

That Russia conceded more than China can be interpreted in two ways. On the one hand, Russian policymakers might have considered themselves to be in a weak position vis-à-vis the PRC, on multiple levels. In terms of demographics, trends are clearly moving in China's direction. The ethnic population of the Russian Far East continues to decrease due to many Russians' migration westward and the failure of efforts to get more Russians to move eastward. At the same time, the ethnic Chinese population across the border in northeast China is growing. Russian border control officers would find it much easier to prevent mass illegal ethnic Chinese immigration into Russian territory if they enjoyed the active collaboration of PRC authorities. Another consideration influencing Russian policy was probably a desire to strengthen Sino-Russian ties at a time when Russian-Western relations remain problematic. In addition, the Russian government might have felt sufficiently confident in its reviving military power to yield control of most of the disputed regions to China. Despite Beijing's ongoing military buildup, Russia's armed forces still enjoy considerable advantages, in both the nuclear and conventional realm—though at present both countries' forces are concentrated in other theaters and would find it logistically difficult to rapidly reinforce their border region. Given these considerations, Russian policymakers may well have decided that sacrificing most of the remaining territory in dispute constituted a well-considered gambit that would yield Moscow much greater net benefits in terms of Chinese goodwill and concrete economic advantages. Lavrov observed that, "Both sides have kept in mind the long-term benefit, building a friendly neighborhood, and peace and development. So neither party is just discussing the issue of territory—but also further refining the border in more detail."[77] In fact, the two delegations spent most of the talks discussing how to improve bilateral economic cooperation.[78] According to Lavrov, the PRC government also met another Russian concern by agreeing to cooperate further with Russia on regulating labor migration, including by jointly establishing insurmountable barriers for illegal migrants."[79]

Despite their border agreements, tensions surrounding the Russian-Chinese border periodically reappear, such as when the Chinese government first learned that two Russian coast guard ships had sunk a freighter owned by the Hong Kong-based J-Rui

Lucky Shipping Company on February 15, 2009. The vessel, *New Star*, was registered with Sierra Leone, Africa, and using that country's flag of convenience.[80] Ten of the 16 crew members were Chinese citizens, while six were from Indonesia, including the captain. Of the eight who died when the ship sank 80 km (50 miles) off the Russian port of Nakhodka, seven were Chinese nationals.[81] Although the Russian authorities initially sought to depict the affair as a simple disaster at sea, the Russian Federal Security Service (FSB) later confirmed, after video clips of the incident began appearing in the Russian media, that the Russian coast guard had shot at the ship to prevent its unauthorized departure from Nakhodka.[82]

A company representative said the *New Star* had arrived at Nakhodka in late January 2009 with a cargo of rice. The intended buyer complained that the rice had gone bad, rejected the consignment, and demanded compensation for the cancelled transaction.[83] After repeatedly being denied permission to leave port, the Chinese ship decided to depart anyway. Following the sinking, the owners demanded compensation from Russian authorities for violating international law and the crew's human rights.[84] Russian officials state that they had impounded the *New Star* to investigate allegations that the vessel had been involved in smuggling. They blamed the ship's captain for causing the deaths by leaving port on January 12 without permission and ignoring repeated Russian orders to halt. The Russians claimed they had tried to communicate with the captain by radio, had employed light signals, and then fired hundreds of warning shots. They then tried to disable the vessel by aiming bullets at the stern with a 30-mm automatic cannon. Although the captain eventually reversed course to return to port, the damaged freighter soon sank in the rough seas. The stormy weather also hampered the Russian rescue efforts, which managed to save the passengers aboard only one of the two lifeboats.[85]

Revelations about the incident produced sharp protests in the Chinese media, which ran stories recounting how Czarist Russia had seized the land around Nakhodka from a weak China during the 19th century and citing examples of how contemporary Russians mistreat Chinese nationals.[86] On February 19, China's Vice Foreign Minister Li Hui summoned Russia's ambassador to express Beijing's "shock and deep concern over this incident."[87] The Chinese Foreign Ministry also attacked what Beijing termed Russia's inadequate efforts to rescue the crew and Moscow's refusal to conduct a joint investigation or brief the Chinese authorities about the results of their own inquiry (which later absolved the Russian border guards of any responsibility for the sinking) until it had been completed. Zhang Xiyun, director-general of the ministry's Department of European-Central Asian Affairs, characterized the Russian attitude as "hard to understand and unacceptable."[88] But as is typical with such incidents, both governments subsequently decided to play down the affair. Media coverage of the incident ended, while stories about the 60th anniversary of ties between Beijing and Moscow and positive coverage of Russia became predominant.[89]

IMMIGRATION ISSUES

Even though few Russians worry about a potential military clash with the PRC over border issues, many of them expect that existing trends, left unaltered, will result in China's de facto peaceful annexation of large parts of eastern Russia. These unwelcome indicators include the declining ethnic Russian population in the Russian Far East, Chinese interest in increasing its access to the region's energy and other natural resources, the growing disparity in the aggregate size of the Chinese and Russian national economies due to China's higher growth rate, and suspected large-scale illegal Chinese immigration into the Russian Far East. Many Russians fear that the presence of large numbers of Chinese workers in Russia, at least in areas neighboring the PRC such as the Russian Far East, will compromise Moscow's control over the regions. If many Chinese move in to eastern Russia, and if they retain their family ties and allegiance with their homeland, the Russian Far East could become annexed de facto by China. Although the Russian Federation is the largest country in the world in terms of territory (9.6 million square km versus China's 3.7 million), the PRC has almost 10 times as many people as Russia (1,305 million versus 143 million according to 2005 figures).[90]

The Russian communities located near China are especially uneasy about the PRC's enormous population, their economic dependence on Chinese trade and investment, and distant Moscow's seeming inability to curtail the population drain from the Russian Far East or bring about the region's economic rehabilitation. Even Russians outside the region are uneasy about future trends. During a July 2000 visit to the Russian Far East, Putin remarked that, "If we don't take concerted action, the future local population will speak Japanese, Chinese, or Korean."[91] In December 2005, Russian Interior Minister Rashid Nurgaliev reaffirmed that illegal immigration presented a threat to the security of the Russian Far East.[92]

Such remarks reflect Russian awareness of the stark demographic and economic contrasts along the Russian-Chinese frontier. According to the 2002 Census, the entire Russian Far Eastern Federal District had a population of 6.7 million inside a territory of 6.2 million square kms (over one-third of the total area of the Russian Federation).[93] These figures equate to an average population density of slightly more than one person per square km, making the Russian Far East one of the most sparsely populated areas in the world. The region's population has been rapidly declining since the dissolution of the Soviet Union, falling by over 500,000 inhabitants since 1992, or approximately 20 percent. During the Soviet period, the federal government provided extensive subsidies (for travel, housing, and other services and amenities, including higher salaries compared to what workers earned in other Soviet regions) to induce people to reside and work in eastern Russia despite its harsh climate. The Russian Federation could not afford to continue these money transfers, contributing to the mass exodus from the region as well as a sense of alienation from the rest of Russia among those who remain. Some forecasts estimate that only 4.5 million Russians will live in the region by 2015.[94] In contrast, over a hundred million Chinese live in the border provinces of Heilongjiang, Jilin, and Liaoning. The disparity in population densities on either side of the border is already greater than that existing between any other two countries.[95]

Given the large number of people located so close to one another, some Chinese laborers invariably look for jobs in Russia, where they often can find employment more easily and earn higher wages than if they stayed at home. Estimates are that, at any one time, as many as one million Chinese citizens may reside somewhere in Russia. Chinese workers are common in many rural areas throughout the Russian Far East. In addition, Chinese merchants and small businessmen are visibly concentrated in urban ghettos in large cities such as Irkutsk, Khabarovsk, and Vladivostok. They often find a niche in the underdeveloped retail and service sectors of the Russian Far East.[96] Chinese citizens typically perform labor in eastern Russia — especially in agriculture, forestry, construction, and small retailing — that many Russians either shun or are unwilling to relocate from other regions of the country to perform. Some 20,000-30,000 Chinese nationals, ranging from a few business entrepreneurs and diplomats to merchants and laborers, also live in Moscow.[97] Very few of these Chinese legally immigrate to Russia. Most Chinese nationals either enter on term-limited visas, which they then overstay, or simply cross over illegally. Nonetheless, Russian fears about the number of Chinese nationals seeking to reside in Russia for a lengthy period were clearly exaggerated as were fears that if Russia opened its borders to limited Chinese immigration that the influx of workers would lead to a Chinese ethnic onslaught were clearly exaggerated.

Thus far, most Chinese traders and laborers see Russia as a place to work and make money — not as a permanent home. Many Chinese entering Russia — as well as the large number of Russians visiting China — seek to buy goods and then, by evading tariffs and customs duties, resell the items at profit in their home market. Organized crime groups, sometimes with branches in both countries, often facilitate this exchange by forging travel documents, assisting with smuggling operations, or providing other support.[98] Some analysts even foresee a decline in the number of Chinese nationals seeking work in the Russian Far East.[99]

Despite the limited number of Chinese actually seeking to stay in Russia permanently or at least for a long time, the Russian government has sought to address this problem before it becomes more serious. Russian officials also want to appear responsive to popular concerns about illicit Chinese immigration regardless of the actual number of unauthorized residents. The Russian authorities have tried to deal with the demographics issue through a combination of tailored policies to promote the economic development of the Russian Far East, which aim to make the region more attractive for Russian workers and their families, as well as with more general solutions aimed at reversing Russia's overall demographic decline.

At its December 2006 session, the Russian Security Council created a State Commission for the Development of the Far East, under the chairmanship of then Prime Minister Mikhail Fradkov, and with several other ministers as members.[100] Putin's presidential envoy to the region, Kamil Iskhakov, said the commission could function as a de facto federal government ministry for the Russian Far East.[101] When he visited Vladivostok on January 27, 2007, Putin indicated that the government might spend an additional 100 billion rubles ($3.8 billion) to construct a resort and associated infrastructure on the nearby Russky Island, which would host the 2012 Asian Pacific Economic Cooperation (APEC) summit.[102] The following month, Fradkov said that the envisaged spending program would help stimulate economic growth throughout the Russian Far East in such sectors as energy, transport, and shipbuilding.[103] During his visit to the September 2007 APEC summit in Sydney, Konstantin Kosachyov, head of the Russian parliament's international affairs committee, said that the Russian government wanted to entice the country's Asian neighbors into supplying financial and technical assistance to develop the Russian Far East because "the development of Russia as a whole is impossible" without it.[104] Nevertheless, in December 2007, Prime Minister Viktor Zubkov acknowledged that the government's plans for developing the Russian Far East, seen as essential for minimizing the demographic imbalance between district and neighboring Chinese provinces, remained underfunded and behind schedule.[105] The region's main port of Vladivostok was rocked by mass protests early in 2009 after the Russian government, seeking to protect the domestic automobile industry, increased customs duties on used Japanese cars. Entrepreneurs had been importing these vehicles into the Russian Far East and then reselling them elsewhere in Russia at a considerable mark-up.

Solving the demographic problems of the Russian Far East will also require action to reverse the overall decline in the ethnic Russian population of the Russian Federation. Putin called Russia's demographic challenge the country's most critical national security threat in his May 2006 annual address to the Russian Federal Assembly.[106] From 1992 to early 2005, the population of the Russian Federation fell from 148.3 million to 143.5 million. This decline would have been even steeper were it not for the 6 million immigrants during this period. Many of these individuals were ethnic Russians who found themselves inside the other newly independent Soviet republics after the Union of Soviet Socialist Republic's (USSR) unexpected dissolution. The Russian Statistics Service estimates that without further immigration, Russia's working age population could decline by 18-19 million during the 2005-25 period, equivalent to almost 30 percent of the current 67 million economically active Russian citizens. In October 2007, the Russian government adopted new initiatives to increase birth rates, decrease mortality, improve public health care, and make national immigration policies more effective. Even if the government succeeded in raising the country's low birth rate, however, the entry of the new young workers into the national labor force would not occur until after 2025.[107]

In order to address popular concern, the authorities have taken several steps to curb the commercial activities of illegal immigrants. In October 2006, Putin directed the government to establish quotas for foreign workers and to allow them to work in Russia for only 90 days during any 6-month period.[108] Starting on April 1, 2007, moreover, the government forbade foreigners from selling goods directly to Russian citizens in retail marketplaces in Russia. Non-Russian citizens legally working in Russia must restrict their retail activities to support functions such as cleaning, loading, and managing these operations.[109] To enhance enforcement, the government increased the fines imposed on businesses employing illegal immigrants.[110] Although these measures are primarily directed toward immigrants from Central Asia, they also affect those from China, with potentially negative effects on the Russian economy. In June 2009, for instance, the Putin administration closed the massive Cherkizovsky market, where thousands of foreign merchants, many from Central Asia and China, sold fake designer clothing and other goods smuggled into Russia. The decision to close the bazaar seems to have resulted from a dispute between its owner and Putin, but the effect was to force many Chinese merchants out of business and induce the Chinese government to send a delegation to Moscow to discuss the issue.[111] Its head, Deputy Commerce Minister Gao Hucheng, released a statement calling for Russian restraint: "In light of the development of the Sino-Russian strategic partnership, China urges the Russian side to take a historical perspective, legally resolve the situation and protect Chinese merchants' legal rights."[112] Chinese officials subsequently worked with their Russian counterparts to address the "gray customs" problem by which Chinese traders used their Russian connections to evade Russian customs and sell goods inside Russia without its government's approval.[113]

These restrictions on foreign business activities have led many Chinese traders to return home, which in turn has weakened Russia's integration into the ethnic Chinese commercial networks that support economic activities in much of East Asia.[114] Yet, one reason the authorities have cracked down on non-Russian commercial activities is to lessen ethnic tensions by appearing to meet the concern of Russian nationalist groups. A series of violent attacks against non-Slavic foreigners in Russia have occurred in recent years, including assaults at the Cherkizovsky bazaar. Ethnic Chinese have occasionally been killed by members of these racial gangs. In January 2007, Putin denounced xenophobia as well as ethnic and religious intolerance as threats to Russians' human rights and the country's security.[115]

The Chinese authorities, while pressing the Russian government to protect the safety and rights of Chinese nationals living in Russia, have sought to assist Russian officials to manage the immigration problem. Article 20 of their 2001 bilateral Russia-China friendship treaty commits both governments to "conduct cooperation to crack down on illegal immigration, including the crack down on illegal transportation of natural persons via its territory."[116] Furthermore, during President Hu's visit to Moscow in 2006, the two governments agreed to draft a joint plan to develop Russia's eastern and China's northeastern regions. The cooperative regional investment agreement signed by Russia's Vnesheconombank, the regional government of Krasnoyarsk Territory, and China's State Bank for Development envisages joint Sino-Russian efforts to promote construction, transportation, agriculture, public utilities, the service sector, and the development of natural resources.[117] Thus far, the main result of these initiatives has been to encourage Chinese investment into eastern Russia.[118] As of May 2009, Medvedev was still calling for coordinated development plans by China and Russia for their border regions.[119] It was only at their September 23, 2009, meeting in New York, on the sidelines of the opening of the UN General Assembly session, that Presidents Medvedev and Hu actually approved the joint program.[120] If the Russian Far East continues to remain largely unaffected by Russia's general economic revival, or if the share of Chinese ownership of the infrastructure and natural resources in the Russian Far East continues to rise, then Russian fears about becoming a natural-resource appendage of the PRC will return, adversely affecting the long-term prospects for enduring Russian-Chinese security ties.

STATEMENTS AND ACTIONS

In April 2009, Lavrov argued that two core principles defined the "Russia-China strategic partnership":

Firstly, Russia and China have a common vision of the contemporary world and of its development trends; a

> common vision of ways to tackle global and regional problems based on international law, a more central role for the UN, and multilateral diplomacy. Secondly, Russia and China, in the framework of the approaches I have set out, always support each other on concrete issues that directly affect the national interests of Russia and China.[121]

In public, officials of both countries enunciate a shared vision of how they want world politics to run. Their joint statements call for a multipolar international system in which the UN and international law dominate decisionmaking on all important questions, including the possible use of force. In a break from their earlier communist-based world view, they stress the value of traditional interpretations of national sovereignty rather than the promotion of universal democratic values or other ideologies. They also regularly endorse each other's policies and refrain from criticizing one another. Yet, their actual policies frequently diverge, with Moscow and Beijing focusing on different priorities. Besides joint declarations and common actions in the UN, they rarely act in concert on concrete issues.

As a general rule, Russian and Chinese officials avoid criticizing each other's domestic policies. Russian representatives have not challenged the Chinese government's repression of civil liberties, including in Tibet or Xinjiang, and have not supported American-backed efforts to criticize China's internal policies. They also have not refrained from selling military technologies that the Chinese military and police could use to repress domestic opposition. Chinese officials have reciprocated by not joining Western criticisms of Putin's authoritarian tendencies or Russian policies in Chechnya. The lengthy joint statement both governments issued in June 2009 to mark their

60th anniversary contained an interesting extension in the section in which the two governments pledged mutual support for their sovereignty and territorial integrity. In the past, China had backed Russia's control over Chechnya while Moscow endorsed Beijing's position regarding Taiwan. On this occasion, the Russian government affirmed that Tibet as well as Taiwan "are inalienable parts of the Chinese territory," while the Chinese side supported "Russia's efforts in maintaining peace and stability in the region of Caucasus," which might be read as including Georgia in the South Caucasus as well as Chechnya and the other troubled Russian provinces in the North Caucasus.[122] The following month, after the Muslim minority region of Xinjiang experienced widespread ethnic riots, the Russian Foreign Ministry backed the Chinese crackdown in the region. "We would like to reaffirm that the Russian side regards Xinjiang as an integral part of China, and what is happening there as an exclusively internal matter of the PRC," Ministry Spokesperson Andrei Nesterenko told reporters at a July 9 briefing. "We hope that the actions being undertaken within the law by the Chinese authorities to maintain public order in Xinjiang will soon help to normalize the situation in that area."[123]

Both the Russian and the Chinese governments have expressed concern about the efforts by the United States and its allies to strengthen their BMD capabilities. In December 2008, for instance, Russian Defense Minister Anatoliy Serdyukov said that he had discussed the missile defense issue when he met with Chinese Defense Minister Liang Guanglie in Beijing. According to Serdyukov, the two governments shared a concern "that the USA's global missile defense system could potentially upset the strategic balance among the leading nuclear powers."[124] Their apparent fear is that these strategic defense systems, in combination with the strong American offensive nuclear capabilities, might enable the United States to obtain global nuclear predominance, as claimed in a widely cited *Foreign Affairs* article.[125] Yet, while Russian attention has been focused on the U.S. BMD systems planned for Poland and the Czech Republic, Chinese policymakers have been most worried about the expanding U.S.-Japanese BMD research and development program. A particular Chinese concern is that the system might eventually cover Taiwan, which could embolden Taiwanese separatist aspirations if it appeared to negate the capacity of China's growing fleet of medium range missiles to bombard the island.[126] Despite the professed concern of both Russia and China about U.S. missile defense plans, the two governments have restricted their cooperative measures to counter it to the realm of declarations. At the August 2007 summit of the Shanghai Cooperation Organization (SCO), Lavrov stated that, while Moscow and Beijing were "analyzing the U.S. global missile defense plans targeting Europe and the East," both governments were addressing the issue independently, and in parallel, and had not yet considered formally cooperating on BMD. Such collaboration could presumably range from simply exchanging intelligence assessments to undertaking joint research and development programs for shared anti-BMD technologies. Lavrov merely affirmed that Beijing and Moscow "share a vision of how to provide security."[127] In contrast to this limited missile defense cooperation between Moscow and Beijing, the United States and its NATO allies have launched several multinational BMD development programs. Unlike their Russian colleagues, who have urged NATO to collaborate with Russia in constructing a joint BMD network, Chinese government representatives have not expressed any interest in participating in a global, multinational missile defense network.

THE GEORGIAN WAR

Beijing's uneasy response to Moscow's August 2008 military intervention in Georgia also underscored the limited nature of the Russian-Chinese strategic partnership. Chinese leaders had cultivated good relations with Russia, Georgia, Europe, and the United States, and were not eager to antagonize any of these actors by siding too closely with one side. Another consideration was China's long-standing stress on the need to uphold the national autonomy and territorial integrity of existing countries. Endorsing Russian policies, especially Moscow's decision to recognize the independence of Georgia's separatist regions of Abkhazia and South Ossetia, would violate these principles and have undesirable implications for China's own separatist regions.

On August 9, 2008, a day after the war began, President Hu met visiting Russian Prime Minister Putin, who was attending the opening ceremony of the Summer Olympics.[128] Although neither president commented publicly on the conflict at this time, the following day a Chinese Foreign Ministry spokesperson expressed Beijing's "grave concern over the escalation of tension and armed conflicts." The official also urged the "relevant parties to keep restraint and to cease fire immediately to safeguard regional peace and stability."[129] The Georgia issue arose, moreover, during the August 10, 2008, discussion between Hu and visiting U.S. President George Bush in Beijing.[130]

When the Russian government on August 26, 2008, announced its formal recognition of Abkhazia's and South Ossetia's independence from Georgia, the Chinese Foreign Ministry expressed unease at the move:

> The Chinese side expresses concern for the most recent changes in the developing situation in South Ossetia and Abkhazia. We understand the complicated history and the current situation of the South Ossetia and Abkhazia issue. At the same time, based on the Chinese side's consistent principled position on this sort of issue, we hope that each of the relevant parties can satisfactorily resolve the issue through dialogue and consultation.[131]

Differences between Beijing and Moscow over Georgia were also evident at the annual leadership summit of the SCO, which occurred on August 28, 2008, in Dushanbe, the capital of Tajikistan. Before the summit, President Medvedev and other Russian leaders likely had expected that their SCO allies would endorse Russian policies regarding Georgia's breakaway regions of South Ossetia and Abkhazia—at least Moscow's original militarily intervention on behalf of the separatists, if not the more controversial subsequent decision to recognize their declarations of independence from Tbilisi. Medvedev also took care to discuss the Georgia issue in his private meetings with each SCO leader before the summit began. According to the PRC Foreign Ministry, when Medvedev briefed Hu during their bilateral meeting the day before the summit began, the Chinese President simply replied that, "China has noticed the latest developments in the region, expecting all sides concerned to properly settle the issue through dialogue and coordination."[132]

Despite Medvedev's lobbying, however, the SCO summit declaration does not blame the Georgian government for causing the war or refer to its alleged acts of "genocide" in South Ossetia, which Moscow has cited, as well as the supposed need to defend Russian citizens from Georgian military aggression, in justifying its intervention. China and the Central Asian members also noticeably declined—either in the summit statement or in other public statements—to follow or even support Russia's decision to recognize the independence declarations of the leaders of the pro-Moscow leaders of South Ossetia and Abkhazia. According to the Russian media, each of the leaders told Medvedev in their bilateral sessions that, while they personally supported Moscow's actions, they could not publicly endorse them.[133] Instead, the comprehensive political declaration issued by the SCO heads of government merely relates that the members "express their deep concern in connection with the recent tension around the issue of South Ossetia, and call on the relevant parties to resolve existing problems in a peaceful way through dialogue." Rather than endorse Moscow's military intervention and subsequent formal dismemberment of Georgia, moreover, the text simply welcomes the August 12 ceasefire and backs "the active role of Russia in promoting peace and cooperation in the region." Elsewhere, the declaration repeats standard SCO language about preserving the "unity and territorial integrity of states" and "encourage[ing] good-neighborly relations among peoples and their common development." The statement also stresses the disutility of force and warns that, "Attempts to strengthen one's own security to the prejudice of security of others do not assist the maintenance of global security and stability."[134]

China's lack of enthusiasm for Russia's military intervention in Georgia may have been partly due to pique at the war's distracting global attention from the Beijing Olympics, but other considerations were even more important given that the PRC has yet to alter its policies despite the passage of time. Although no SCO government has openly objected to Russia's original military intervention to defend the South Ossetian separatists, the leaders of China and the other SCO countries appear genuinely uneasy at Moscow's subsequent decision to use overwhelming military force to effectively redraw Eurasia's postwar boundaries by detaching South Ossetia and Abkhazia from Tbilisi's control and recognizing them as independent countries. A core principle governing China's bilateral policies towards other countries, which also features in Beijing's positions within the SCO, is to discourage these governments from supporting separatism in Xinjiang, Tibet, or Taiwan. As the events before the 2008 Summer Olympics make clear, Chinese leaders remain concerned about movements for national self-determination among the non-Han ethnic groups in Tibet and Xinjiang. From this perspective, the Georgia invasion came at a particularly inopportune time, since ethnic violence among both Buddhists and Muslims in the two minority regions had surged in the preceding months, heightening Beijing's concerns about dampening any independence aspirations in either region. Although the new Taiwanese government has shown itself less inclined to pursue controversial measures than its predecessor, Chinese officials still worry about the long-term strength of separatism on the island.

At the SCO summit, Chinese leaders simply reaffirmed these principles when they refused to endorse Russian military intervention in Georgia, and Moscow's diplomatic recognition of the independence of

Abkhazia and South Ossetia. Chinese policymakers want to discourage activists in Tibet, Xinjiang, and especially Taiwan from drawing inspiration from the successful drives for independence by South Ossetia, Abkhazia, and, earlier that year, Kosovo. Chinese leaders have also long opposed international doctrines that would sanction military intervention in a country without the consent of the host government or UNSC approval—whether on humanitarian grounds or to defend ethnic or religious groups against government repression. Russian leaders might have expected more generous backing from China, given how actively they have cultivated Beijing and how the SCO, with Moscow's presumed blessing, has endorsed the PRC's control of Taiwan and Tibet. But from Beijing's perspective, the situation in South Ossetia and Abkhazia is fundamentally different in that Russia sided with the separatists against the central government in Tbilisi. In contrast, Chinese policymakers have no qualms about endorsing Russian military operations in Chechnya because many of the insurgents are fighting to secede from Russia and establish an independent Islamic state.

So while there are many signs of partnership, even signs of strategic partnership (a highly elastic concept these days) in Sino-Russian relations, there are also significant points of discord. Since this is one of the most crucial relationships in Asia, and certainly the most important one for Russia, the continuing rise of China will not only shape just Russia's and China's prospects, but also that of the entire global order.

ENDNOTES - CHAPTER 8

1. *The National Intelligence Strategy of the United States of America*, Washington, DC: Office of the Director of National Intelligence, August 2009, p. 3.

2. Dennis C. Blair, "Media Conference Call with the Director of National Intelligence," Washington, DC: Office of the Director of National Intelligence, September 15, 2009, available from *www.dni.gov/interviews/20090915_interview.pdf*.

3. "Rossiya ne postavlyala Iranu zenitno-raketniye kompleksy C-300" ("Russia is not Delivering the S-300 Air Defense System to Iran"), *Izvestiya*, October 28, 2009, available from *www.izvestia.ru/news/news219596*.

4. Uzi Mahanimi, Mark Franchetti, and Jon Swain, "Israel Names Russians Helping Iran Build Nuclear Bomb," *The Sunday Times*, October 4, 2009, available from *www.timesonline.co.uk/tol/news/world/middle_east/article6860161.ece*.

5. Robin Wright, "Deepening China-Iran Ties Weaken Bid to Isolate Iran," *The Washington Post*, November 16, 2007, available from *www.washingtonpost.com/wp-dyn/content/article/2007/11/17/AR2007111701680.html*.

6. "Iran and China Sign Oilfield Development Contract," AFP, January 14, 2009, available from *www.energy-daily.com/reports/Iran_and_China_sign_oilfield_development_contract_999.html*.

7. "Missile Exports to Iran Alarm U.S.," BBC News, April 21, 2006, available from *news.bbc.co.uk/2/hi/middle_east/4932814.stm*.

8. Dan Blumenthal, "Providing Arms: China and the Middle East," *Middle East Quarterly*, Spring 2005, available from *www.meforum.org/article/695*.

9. Dennis C. Blair, "Annual Threat Assessment of the Intelligence Community for the Senate Committee on Intelligence," February 12, 2009, available from *www.dni.gov/testimonies/20090212_testimony.pdf*.

10. "China Defends Iran Gas Deal Talks," BBC News, January 11, 2007, available from *news.bbc.co.uk/2/hi/business/6251365.stm*.

11. See for example Fyodor Lukyanov, "Engagement With Iran? Here Are Some Likely Scenarios," February 10, 2009, available from *www.rferl.org/Content/Engagement_With_Iran_Here_Are_Some_Likely_Scenarios/1490775.html*.

12. "Intel Used by Obama Found Iran Long-Range Missile Capacity Would Take 3-5 Years Longer," FOXNews.com, September 18, 2009, available from *www.foxnews.com/politics/2009/09/18/nie-used-obama-iran-long-range-missile-capacity-years-longer/*.

13. "DoD News Briefing with Secretary Gates and Gen. Cartwright from the Pentagon," U.S. Department of Defense News Transcript, September 17, 2009, available from *www.defenselink.mil/transcripts/transcript.aspx?transcriptid=4479*.

14. Peter Baker, "Obama Offered Deal to Russia in Secret Letter," *New York Times*, March 2, 2009, available from *www.nytimes.com/2009/03/03/washington/03prexy.html*.

15. "Zayavlennie Dmitriya Medvedeva v svyaziyi s korrektirovkoy podkhodov SShA po voprosu o PRO" ("Dmitry Medvedev's Statement on Changed U.S. Approach to Missile Defense"), Russian President's Website, September 17, 2009, available from *news.kremlin.ru/transcripts/5496*.

16. *Ibid*.

17. "Press-konferentsiya po itogam sammita 'Gryppy dvadtsati" ("Press Conference on the Results of the 'Group of Twenty' Summit [G20 Summit]"), Russian President's Website, September 26, 2009, available from *kremlin.ru/transcripts/5578*.

18. "Inter'vyu shveydarskim SMI" ("Interview with Swiss Media"), Russian President's Website, September 18, 2009, available from *news.kremlin.ru/transcripts/5505*.

19. "NATO Seeks Missile-Defense Cooperation with Russia," *RIA Novosti*, September 18, 2009, available from *en.rian.ru/world/20090918/156175551.html*.

20. Sergei Venyavsky, "Russia's Putin Urges US to Scrap Trade Barriers," Associated Press, September 18, 2009, available from *www.google.com/hostednews/ap/article/ALeqM5i0xBv8Y QwWSZqAQgjd42RCvU1uEAD9APM6E00*.

21. "Zeayavlenie Prezidenta Rossii Dmitriya Medvedeva otnositel'no situatsii vokrug Irana" ("Statement of Russian President Dmitry Medvedev Regarding the Iran Situation"), Russian President's Website, September 25, 2009, available from *news.kremlin.ru/transcripts/5575*.

22. Anna Smolchenko, "Moscow Open to New Iran Sanctions: Official," AFP, September 23, 2009, available from *www.google.com/hostednews/afp/article/ALeqM5g_jxCe4ZzzEa2e8iqVPBmg4uRr-A*.

23. "Zeayavlenie Prezidenta Rossii Dmitriya Medvedeva," ("Statement of Russian President Dmitry Medvedev Regarding the Iran Situation").

24. "Press-konferentsiya po itogam sammita 'Gryppy dvadtsati," ("Press Conference on the Results of the 'Group of 20' Summit [G20 Summit]").

25. "Stenograficheskiy otchyot o vstreche so studentami i prepodavatelyami Pittsburgskogo universiteta"("Stenographic Record of Meeting with Students and Faculty of the University of Pittsburgh"), Russian President's Website, September 25, 2009, available from *news.kremlin.ru/news/5569*.

26. "Russia's Medvedev Won't Rule Out Iran Sanctions," Reuters, September 15, 2009, available from *www.rferl.org/content/Russias_Medvedev_Does_Not_Rule_Out_Iran_Sanctions/1823313.html*.

27. "Officials: Obama Shared Info on Iran Nuke Site with Russia, China," CNN, September 25, 2009, available from *www.cnn.com/2009/POLITICS/09/25/iran.diplomacy.obama/*.

28. "Russia, China Urge Iran to Cooperate With IAEA," VOA News, September 25, 2009, available from *www.voanews.com/english/2009-09-25-voa34.cfm*.

29. Information Office of China's State Council, China's National Defence in 2008, January 20, 2009, Chap. 14, available from www.china.org.cn/government/whitepaper/2009-01/21/content_17162787.htm.

30. "Interv'yu tsental'nomu televidenyiyu Kitayskoy Narodnoy Respuubliki" ("Interview with Central Television of the Chinese People's Republic"), Russian President's Website, June 15, 2009, available from kremlin.ru/transcripts/4442.

31. "Vystupleniya na torzhestvennom vechere, posvyashchyonnom 60-letiyu ustanovleniya diplomaticheskikh otnosheniy s Kitayskoy Narodnoy Respublikoy" ("Speech at Gala Evening in Honor of the 60th Anniversary of the Establishment of Diplomatic Relations with the Chinese People's Republic"), Russian President's Website, June 17, 2009, available from www.kremlin.ru/eng/speeches/2009/06/17/2100_type82914type127286_218079.shtml.

32. Ibid.

33. "Nachalo rossiysko-kitayskikh peregovorov v rasshirennom sostave" ("Beginning of Russian-Chinese Talks in Expanded Format"), Russian President's Website, June 17, 2009, available from kremlin.ru/transcripts/4485.

34. Ibid.

35. "FM Spokeswoman: China Backs Dialogue to Resolve South Ossetia Issues," Xinhua, August 10, 2009, available from english.people.com.cn/90001/90776/90883/6723420.html.

36. "Russian, Chinese Businesspeople Sign 40 Contracts worth $3 bln," RIA Novosti, June 16, 2009, available from en.rian.ru/business/20090616/155267195.html.

37. Carl Mortished, "Russia Plays Power Games While World Moves On," Times Online, June 18, 2009, available from business.timesonline.co.uk/tol/business/markets/russia/article6526099.ece.

38. Toni Vorobyova, "Russia, China to Boost Rouble, Yuan Use in Trade," Reuters, June 17, 2009, available from www.Reuters.com/article/usDollarRpt/idUSLH72167820090617.

39. "Russia, China to Promote Ruble, Yuan Use in Trade," *Taiwan News*, June 18, 2009, available from *www.etaiwannews.com/ etn/news_content.php?id=979921&lang=eng_news&cate_img=35. jpg&cate_rss=news_Business.*

40. "China, Russia Say Ties Must Flourish in Economic Crisis," AFP, June 17, 2009, available from *www.spacewar.com/reports/ China_Russia_say_ties_must_flourish_in_economic_crisis_999.html.*

41. Hu Jintao, "Zeyavleniya dlya pressy po okonchanii peregovorov s Predsedatelem KNR Hu Jintao" ("Press Statement at the Conclusion of Negotiations with Hu Jintao, President of the People's Republic of China"), Russian President's Website, June 17, 2009, available from *kremlin.ru/transcripts/4486.*

42. Ibid.

43. Lyubov Pronina and Alex Nicholson, "Russia, China to Promote Ruble, Yuan Use in Trade (Update2)," Bloomberg, June 17, 2009, available from *www.bloomberg.com/apps/ news?pid=20601087&sid=aSTmuCr.RD88.*

44. For a review see Stephen Blank, "The Russo-Chinese Energy Follies," *China Brief*, December 8, 2008, available from *www.jamestown.org/single/?no_cache=1&tx_ttnews%5Btt_news% 5D=34234*; and "News Analysis: After 14 Years of Negotiation, Russian Oil Pipeline Runs into China," *Xinhua*, May 19, 2009, available from *english.people.com.cn/90001/90776/90883/6661199. html.*

45. Rajan Menon, "The Limits of Chinese-Russian Partnership," *Survival*, Vol. 51, No. 3, June-July 2009, p. 123.

46. "Russia's Transneft Plans to Start on Chinese Pipeline Leg in 2010," *RIA Novosti*, February, 17, 2009, available from *en.rian. ru/russia/20090217/120190194.html.*

47. "News Analysis: After 14 Years of Negotiation, Russian Oil Pipeline Runs into China," *Xinhua*, May 19, 2009, available from *english.people.com.cn/90001/90776/90883/6661199.html.*

48. "Sino-Russian Ties Rise to Unprecedented High Level," *Xinhua*, September 21, 2009, available from *news.Xinhuanet.com/ english/2009-09/21/content_12086165.htm*.

49. Stephen Blank, "China's Russian Far East," *China Brief*, August 5, 2009, available from *www.jamestown.org/programs/ chinabrief/single/?tx_ttnews%5Btt_news%5D=35371&tx_ttnews%5 BbackPid%5D=25&cHash=0e5a088cb1*.

50. Hu Jintao, "Press Statement Following Talks between President of Russia Dmitry Medvedev and President of the People's Republic of China," June 17, 2009, available from *www.kremlin. ru/eng/speeches/2009/06/17/1944_type82914type82915_218069.shtml*.

51. Anatoly Medetsky, "Medvedev, Hu to Speed Up Gas Talks," *Moscow Times*, June 18, 2009, available from *www.themoscowtimes.com/article/600/42/378856.htm*.

52. "Russia Ready to Fully Meet China's Gas Needs—Deputy PM Sechin," *RIA Novosti*, June 5, 2009, available from *en.rian.ru/ business/20090605/155180338.html*.

53. "No Russian Gas for China in 2011—Gazprom," *RIA Novosti*, June 17, 2009, available from *en.rian.ru/business/20090617/155275644.html*.

54. "Interview of Russian Minister of Foreign Affairs Sergey Lavrov to the Chinese Newspaper *Keji Ribao*, March 27, 2009," available from *www.mid.ru/brp_4.nsf/e78a48070f128a7b4325699900 5bcbb3/0b097cf09ba99105c325758c001f0a35?OpenDocument*.

55. Dmitry Kosyrev, "Moscow and Beijing to Talk about Pyongyang and Obama," *RIA Novosti*, June 16, 2009, available from *en.rian.ru/analysis/20090616/155264489.html*.

56. "China, Russia Say Ties Must Flourish in Economic Crisis," AFP, June 17, 2009, available from *www.spacewar.com/reports/ China_Russia_say_ties_must_flourish_in_economic_crisis_999.html*.

57. Toni Vorobyova and Denis Dyomkin, Russia, "China Flex Muscles on Currencies, Politics," Reuters, June 17, 2009, available from *www.canada.com/Business/Russia+China+flex+muscles+ currencies+politics/1705013/story.html*.

58. Andrei Fedyashin, "Russian-Chinese Relations Hinge on Delicate Balance of Interests," *RIA Novosti*, available from *en.rian.ru/analysis/20090618/155287554.html*.

59. Hu Jintao, "Press Statement Following Talks between President of Russia Dmitry Medvedev and President of the People's Republic of China," June 17, 2009, available from *www.kremlin.ru/eng/speeches/2009/06/17/1944_type82914type82915_218069.shtml*.

60. "Russian-Chinese Su-33 Fighter Deal Collapse," *RIA Novosti*, March 10, 2009, available from *en.rian.ru/russia/20090310/120493194.html*.

61. Roger McDermott, "Sino-Russian Military Exercises Conceived as a Show of Unity," *Eurasia Daily Monitor*, May 5, 2009, available from *www.jamestown.org/single/?no_cache=1&tx_ttnews%5Btt_news%5D=34949*.

62. "China, Russia to Hold Anti-Piracy Naval Drills off Somali Coast," *RIA Novosti*, September 18, 2009, available from *en.rian.ru/mlitary_news/20090918/156169511.html*.

63. "Russia, China Conduct Anti-Piracy Exercises in Gulf of Aden," *RIA Novosti*, September 18, 2009, available from *en.rian.ru/world/20090918/156174185.html*.

64. "Mission for Peace Targets Terrorists," CCTV, July 23, 2009, available from *english.cctv.com/20090723/106704.shtml*.

65. Liu Anqi, ed., "Day 2 of China-Russia Anti-Terror Drill," CCTV, July 24, 2009, available from *www.cctv.com/program/newshour/20090724/104689.shtml*.

66. "Russian Troops go Aboard Train to Take Part in Chinese Exercises," *ITAR-TASS*, July 8, 2009, available from *www.itar-tass.com/eng/level2.html?NewsID=14127785&PageNum=23*.

67. McDermott, "Sino-Russian Military Exercises Conceived as a Show of Unity."

68. "Russia and China Hold Peace Mission Drills to Show USA Its Place," *Pravda*, June 20, 2009, available from *english. pravda.ru/russia/politics/20-07-2009/108250-russia_china-0*.

69. "Chiefs of the General Staff from both China and Russia Watch Military Drill," *People's Daily Online*, July 24, 2009, available from *english.people.com.cn/90001/90776/90883/6709677.html*; and "Russia, China to hold 2nd Joint Training at Peace Mission Exercise," ITAR-TASS, July 19, 2009, available from *www.itar-tass. com/eng/level2.html?NewsID=14159658&PageNum=0*.

70. Zhang Ning, "Chinese Army Battle Group Ready for Russia-China Joint Military Exercise," CCTV, July 20, 2009, available from *www.cctv.com/program/newshour/20090720/104771.shtml*.

71. "'Peace Mission-2009' Improves Anti-Terror Response: Chinese Military Officer," *Xinhua*, July 24, 2009, available from *news.Xinhuanet.com/english/2009-07/24/content_11765127.htm*.

72. Cited in Alexander Lukin, *The Bear Watches the Dragon: Russia's Perceptions of China and the Evolution of Russian-Chinese Relations Since the Eighteenth Century*, New York: M. E. Sharpe, 2003, p. 305.

73. "Interview of Russian Minister of Foreign Affairs Sergey Lavrov to the Chinese Newspaper Keji Ribao, March 27, 2009," Ministry of Foreign Affairs of the Russian Federation, available from *www.mid.ru/brp_4.nsf/e78a48070f128a7b43256999005bcbb3/ 0b097cf09ba99105c325758c001f0a35?OpenDocument*.

74. Charles Clover; "Russia and China Settle Border Spat," *Financial Times*, July 21 2008, available from *www.ft.com/cms/ s/0/5f846434-576b-11dd-916c-000077b07658.html?nclick_check=1*.

75. Peter Zeihan, "China And Russia's Geographic Divide," Strategic Forecasting, Inc., July 22, 2008, available from *www.1913intel.com/2008/07/22/china-and-russia%E2%80%99s-geographic-divide/*.

76. Kirill Bessonov, "Russia, China End Border Tiff," *Moscow News*, July 8, 2007, available from *mnweekly.rian.ru/ politics/20080724/55338880.html*.

77. "China, Russia Sign Border Agreement," CCTV.com, July 22, 2008, available from *www.cctv.com/english/20080722/100893.shtml*.

78. "Moscow and Beijing Agree on Borders after 80 Years," *AsiaNews.IT*, July 22, 2008, available from *www.asianews.it/index.php?l=en&art=12822&size=A*.

79. "China, Russia Sign Final Agreement on Border Demarcation," *Deutsche Presse-Agentur*, July 21, 2008, available from *www.monstersandcritics.com/news/asiapacific/news/article_1418390.php/China_Russia_sign_final_agreement_on_border_demarcation*.

80. "Russia Told to Probe Ship Sinking," BBC, February 19, 2009, available from *news.bbc.co.uk/2/hi/europe/7899662.stm*.

81. "Russia Defends Sinking Cargo Ship," BBC, February 22, 2009, available from *news.bbc.co.uk/2/hi/europe/7904484.stm*.

82. Yu Bin, "China-Russia Relations: Between Crisis and Cooperation," *Comparative Connections* Vol. 11, No. 1, China-Russia Relations, available from *csis.org/publication/comparative-connections-v11-n1-china-russia-relations-between-crisis-and-cooperation*.

83. "Russia Told to Probe Ship Sinking."

84. "China Demands Russia Investigate Sinking of Chinese Ship," *RIA Novosti*, February 19, 2009, available from *en.rian.ru/world/20090219/120221660.html*.

85. "Russia Told to Probe Ship Sinking."

86. Yu Bin, "China-Russia Relations: Between Crisis and Cooperation."

87. "China Slams Russian Attitude to Sunken Ship: Report," AFP, February 20, 2009, available from *www.spacewar.com/reports/China_slams_Russian_attitude_to_sunken_ship_report_999.html*.

88. "China Expects Russia to Share Probe Result of Cargo Ship Sinking," *Xinhua*, February 24, 2009, available from *news.Xinhuanet.com/english/2009-02/24/content_10887541.htm*.

89. China and the United States have followed the same pattern after their crises, such as over the EP-3 collision in 2001 or the disputes over U.S. maritime surveillance operations in international waters that lie within China's declared Exclusive Economic Zone.

90. Ernest Raiklin, "The Chinese Challenge to Russia in Siberia and the Russian Far East," *Journal of Social, Political and Economic Studies*, Vol. 33, No 2, Summer 2008, p. 146, available from *www.jspes.org/Sample_Raikin.pdf*.

91. Cited in Patrick Moore, "Russia: On the Margins of the Pacific Rim," Radio Free Europe/Radio Liberty, September 11, 2007, available from *www.rferl.org/featuresarticle/2007/09/6378f428-9a48-43b1-96f8-378267e1b6dc.html*.

92. Cited in Marcel de Haas, "Russia-China Security Cooperation," *Power and Interest News Report*, November 27, 2006, available from *www.pinr.com/report.php?ac=view_report&report_id =588&language_id=1*.

93. State Statistics Committee of Russia, *All-Russia Population Census 2002*, October 2002.

94. David Blair, "Why the Restless Chinese are Warming to Russia's Frozen East," *The Telegraph*, July 16, 2009, available from *www.telegraph.co.uk/comment/5845646/Why-the-restless-Chinese-are-warming-to-Russias-frozen-east.html*.

95. Ibid.

96. "Survey on Chinese in Russia's Far East," *People's Daily*, January 2, 2004, available from *english.peopledaily.com.cn/200401/01/eng20040101_131677.shtml*.

97. Raiklin, "The Chinese Challenge to Russia in Siberia and the Russian Far East."

98. *Ibid*. See also Vladimir Ovchinsky, "The 21st Century Mafia: Made in China," *Russia in Global Affairs*, January-March 2007, available from *eng.globalaffairs.ru/numbers/18/1089.html*.

99. Luke Harding, "Russia Fears Embrace of Giant Eastern Neighbour," *The Observer*, August 2, 2009, available from *www.guardian.co.uk/world/2009/aug/02/china-russia-relationship*.

100. "Fradkov Will Head Commission for Developing Far East," *ITAR-TASS*, February 16, 2007, available from *www.itar-tass.com/eng/level2.html?NewsID=11258149&PageNum=2*.

101. Cited in "Isolation of Russian Far East Threat to National Security-Putin," *RIA Novosti*, December 20, 2006, available from *en.rian.ru/russia/20061220/57396954.html*.

102. Sergei Blagov, "Putin Hopes Hosting APEC Summit Will Spur Development Around Vladivostok," *Eurasia Daily Monitor*, February 5, 2007, available from *www.jamestown.org/publications_details.php?volume_id=420&issue_id=3994&article_id=2371876*.

103. Sergei Blagov, "Russia Weighs Ambitious Plans to Develop Far East," *Eurasia Daily Monitor*, March 5, 2007, available from *www.jamestown.org/publications_details.php?volume_id=420&issue_id=4024&article_id=2371970*.

104. "Putin Tells Asia: Russia is Here to Stay," AFP, September 7, 2007, available from *afp.google.com/article/ALeqM5ifKblS-w23QumSHH6swwafZLLzGOQ*.

105. Sergei Blagov, "Russia's Far Eastern Workers Wary of Chinese Migrants," *Eurasia Daily Monitor*, December 18, 2007, available from *www.jamestown.org/single/?no_cache=1&tx_ttnews%5Btt_news%5D=33252*.

106. Vladimir Putin, "Annual Address to the Federal Assembly of the Russian Federation," Russian President's Website, May 10, 2006, available from *www.kremlin.ru/eng/speeches/2006/05/10/1823_type70029type82912_105566.shtml*.

107. Zhanna Zayonchkovskaya, "Who Needs Chinese in Russia?" *RIA Novosti*, August 23, 2006, available from *en.rian.ru/analysis/20060823/53039627.html*.

108. "Russian Quota on Foreign Workers May Result in More Markets Raids," *RIA Novosti*, January 12, 2007, available from *en.rian.ru/russia/20070112/58967497.html*.

109. "No Foreign Traders on Russian Marketplaces from April 1," *RIA Novosti*, April 1, 2007, available from *en.rian.ru/Russia/20070401/62904938.html*.

110. Henry Meyer, "Russia Set Migrant Quota," Associated Press, *The Washington Post*, January 15, 2007, available from *www.washingtonpost.com/wp-dyn/content/article/2007/01/15/AR2007011500298_pf.html*.

111. "China, Russia Reach Consensus on Closure of Market," *Xinhua*, July 25, 2009, available from *news.Xinhuanet.com/english/2009-07/25/content_11772391.htm*.

112. "China Protests Russia's Shutdown of Huge Moscow Market," *Deusche Welle*, July 25, 2009, available from *www.dw-world.de/dw/article/0,4517247,00.html*.

113. "Russia, China Vow to Block 'Gray Customs' Channels," *China Daily*, September 1, 2009, available from *www.chinadaily.com.cn/china/2009-09/01/content_8639379.htm*.

114. Moore, "Russia: On The Margins of The Pacific Rim."

115. "Putin Urges More Active Measures against Nationalism, Xenophobia," *RIA Novosti*, January 11, 2007, available from *en.rian.ru/russia/20070111/58897010.html*.

116. Chinese Ministry of Foreign Affairs, "Treaty of Good-Neighborliness and Friendly Cooperation Between the People's Republic of China and the Russian Federation," July 24, 2001, available from *www.fmprc.gov.cn/eng/wjdt/2649/t15771.htm*.

117. "Trade, Economic Cooperation Priorities for Russia, China—Putin," *RIA Novosti*, March 26, 2007, available from *en.rian.ru/russia/20070326/62647755.html*.

118. Blank, "Russo-Chinese Energy Follies."

119. "Russian President Urges Coordination with China on Regional Development," *People's Daily Online*, May 21, 2009, available from *english.people.com.cn/90001/90776/90883/6663095.html*.

120. "Rossiysko-kitayskiye otnosheniya neizmenno nosyat kharakhter strategicheskogo partnyorstva" ("Russian-Chinese Relations Invariably Have the Quality of a Strategic Partnership"), Russian President's Website, September 23, 2009, available from *news.kremlin.ru/news/5545*.

121. Ministry of Foreign Affairs of the Russian Federation, "Transcript of Remarks and Response to Media Questions by Russian Minister of Foreign Affairs Sergey Lavrov Following Talks with Chinese Minister of Foreign Affairs Yang Jiechi, Moscow, April 27, 2009," available from *www.mid.ru/brp_4.nsf/e78a48 070f128a7b43256999005bcbb3/9da17eb2ca6711d7c32575a600255d45? OpenDocument*.

122. "China, Russia Sign Five-Point Joint Statement," *Xinhua*, June 17, 2009, available from *news.Xinhuanet.com/ english/2009-06/18/content_11558133.htm*.

123. "Briefing by Russian MFA Spokesman Andrei Nesterenko, July 9, 2009," Ministry of Foreign Affairs of the Russian Federation, available from *www.mid.ru/brp_4.nsf/e78a48070f128a7b4325 6999005bcbb3/02a6e642322b0505c32575f3004ce16f?OpenDocument*.

124. Cited in "China, Russia Vow to Step up Military Ties," AFP, December 12, 2008, available from *www.wsichina.org/morningchina/article.asp?id=3885*.

125. Igor Gaidar, "Yadernyy balans: opasnye igri" ("The Nuclear Balance: Dangerous Games"), *Vedomosti*, March 30, 2006. The controversial article asserting that the U.S. strategic buildup was in the process of negating Russia's and China's nuclear deterrents was Keir A. Lieber and Daryl G. Press, "The Rise of U.S. Nuclear Primacy," *Foreign Affairs*, March/April 2006.

126. "Foreign Ministry Spokesperson Liu Jianchao's Remarks on Russia's Suspension of its Participation in the CFE Treaty," available from *capetown.chineseconsulate.org/eng/fyrth/t342466.htm*.

127. "Russia Says Iran Poses No Threat," *RIA Novosti*, August 16, 2007, available from *en.rian.ru/russia/20070816/71949222.html*.

128. M. K. Bhadrakumar, "China Seeks Caucasian Crisis Windfall," *Asia Times Online*, April 19, 2008, available from *www.atimes.com/atimes/Central_Asia/JH19Ag01.html*.

129. Ibid.

130. John J. Tkacik, Jr., "Olympic Invasion: China, the Shanghai Cooperation Organization and Russia's Aggression," Heritage Foundation WebMemo #2048, September 4, 2008, available from *www.heritage.org/Research/AsiaandthePacific/wm2048.cfm*; "Press Briefing by Press Secretary Dana Perino and Senior Director for East Asian Affairs Dennis Wilder and Deputy National Security Advisor Ambassador Jim Jeffrey," Office of the White House Press Secretary, August 10, 2008, available from *www.america.gov/st/texttrans-english/2008/August/20080811114306xjsnommis0.6726496.html*.

131. "Foreign Ministry Spokesman Qin Gang's Response to Reporter's Question about Russia's Recognition of Abkhaz and South Ossetian Independence," Chinese Ministry of Foreign Affairs, August 27, 2008, available from *www.fmprc.gov.cn/chn/xwfw/fyrth/t469157.htm*.

132. Chinese Foreign Ministry, "Hu Jintao Meets with Russian President Medvedev," August 28, 2008, available from *www.fmprc.gov.cn/eng/zxxx/t469750.htm*.

133. "Dmitry Medvedev Didn't Get the Support of the SCO Members," *Kommersant*, August 29, 2008, available from *www.kommersant.com/p1017558/r_527/SCO_refused_to_support_Russia*.

134. "Dushanbe Declaration of Heads of SCO Member States," Shanghai: Shanghai Cooperation Organization, August 28, 2009, available from *www.fmprc.gov.cn/eng/zxxx/t513027.htm*.

PUBLICATIONS BY MARY C. FITZGERALD

Chinese and Russian Asymmetrical Strategies for Space Dominance (2010-30), March 2009.

Chinese and Russian Asymmetrical Strategies for Space Dominance (2010-30), September 2008 (OSD Office of Net Assessments).

Challenging U.S. Space Superiority: China's Space "Surprise," June 2007 (OSD Office of Net Assessments).

Sino-Russian Strategies for Fighting Future Wars, September 2005 (OSD Office of Net Assessments).

"China's Evolving Military Juggernaut," in *China's New Great Leap Forward: High Technology and Military Power in the Next Half-Century*, Washington, DC: Hudson Institute, 2005.

"China Plans to Control Space and Win the Coming Information War," *Armed Forces Journal*, November 2005, pp. 40-41.

"Facing China's Quiet Juggernaut," *Defense News*, November 7, 2005.

"A Noncontact, Contact War," *Armed Forces Journal*, August 2003, pp. 26-29.

"Evolving Russian Blueprints for the New RMA: 2000-2025," in Dr. R. Matthews, ed., *Managing the RMA*, New York: St. Martin's Press, 2001.

Russian Asymmetrical Military Options for the 21st Century, 1999 (Smith Richardson Foundation).

The New Revolution in Russian Military Affairs, London, England: RUSI for Defence Studies, 1994.

"The Russian Military's Strategy for Sixth-Generation Warfare," *ORBIS*, Vol. 38, No. 3, Summer 1994.

"Russian Views on Electronic Signals and Information Warfare," *American Intelligence Journal*, Summer 1994.

"The Russian Image of Future War," *Comparative Strategy*, Vol. 13, No. 2, April-June 1994.

"Russian Views on Information Warfare," *Army Magazine*, May 1994.

"Russia's Vision of Air-Space War," *Air Force Magazine*, December 1993.

"Russia's Military Reasserts Influence," *Defense News*, November 22-28, 1993.

"New Russian Military Thinking," *American Intelligence Journal*, Summer 1993.

"Russian Military Doctrine: Program for the 1990s and Beyond," in U.S. Congress Joint Economic Committee Report: The Economies of the Former Soviet Union (May 1993).

"The Burden of Defense," *The St. Louis Post-Dispatch*, May 25, 1993.

"Russia's New Military Doctrine," *Naval War College Review*, Vol. XLVI, No. 2, Spring 1993.

"Chief of Russia's General Staff Academy Speaks Out on Moscow's New Military Doctrine," *ORBIS*, Vol. 37, No. 2, Spring 1993.

"A Russian View of Russian Interests," *Air Force Magazine*, October 1992.

"Russia's New Military Doctrine," *Air Force Magazine*, September 1992.

Ibid., *Journal of the Royal United Services Institute for Defence Studies* (RUSI), October 1992.

Ibid., *Military Intelligence Professional Journal*, October/November 1992.

"The Russian Army Asserts Itself," *The Wall Street Journal Europe*, July 24-25, 1992.

"The Evolving Post-Soviet Military Doctrine," *International Defense Review*, May 1992.

"Evolving Military Doctrine of the Post-Soviet Armed Forces," *Strategic Review*, Spring 1992.

"The New `Aerospace War' in Soviet Military Thought," in Jacob Kipp and Stephen Blank, eds., *The Soviet Military and the Future*, Westport, CT: Greenwood Publishing Group, 1992.

"The Dilemma in Moscow's Defensive Force Posture," in Will Frank and Phil Gillette, eds., *Soviet Mili-*

tary Doctrine from Lenin to Gorbachev, Westport, CT: Greenwood Publishing Group, 1992.

"Soviet Military Assessments of Operation `Desert Storm'," in Ibid.

"The Soviet Military and the New Air War in the Persian Gulf," *Airpower Journal*, Vol. V, No. 4, Winter 1991.

"The Soviet Image of Future War: 'Through the Prism of the Persian Gulf'," *Comparative Strategy*, Vol. 10, No. 4, October-December 1991.

"The Soviet Military and the New 'Technological Operation' in the Gulf," *Naval War College Review*, Vol. XLIV, No. 4, Autumn 1991.

"The Future of the Soviet Armed Forces," ed., *Defense Analysis, Special Ed.*, Vol. 7, No. 2/3, Summer/Fall 1991.

"Soviet Views on Future War: The Impact of New Technologies," *Defense Analysis*, Vol. 7, No. 2/3, Special Ed., Summer/Autumn 1991.

"The Impact of New Technologies on Soviet Military Thought," in Roy Allison, ed., *Radical Reform in Soviet Defense Policy Under Gorbachev*, London, England: The Macmillan Press Ltd., 1991.

"Iraq War Reorients Soviet Aims," *Defense News*, August 19, 1991.

"Soviet Military Doctrine: Implications of the Gulf War," *International Defense Review*, August 1991.

"Gulf War Forces Change in Soviet Defense Doctrine," *The Christian Science Monitor*, May 6, 1991.

"Early Soviet Assessments of U.S. Military Success in the Gulf War," *Strategic Review*, Spring 1991.

"Soviet Armed Forces After the Gulf War: Demise of the Defensive Doctrine?" Radio Liberty Report on the USSR, Vol. 3, No. 16, April 19, 1991.

"The Soviet Navy: Roles, Doctrine, Missions," in Barry M. Blechman, ed., *The U.S. Stake in Naval Arms Control*, Washington, DC: The Henry L. Stimson Center, 1990.

"Restructuring the Armed Forces: The Current Soviet Debate," co-author, *The Journal of Soviet Military Studies*, Volume 3, No. 2, June 1990.

"A Volunteer Red Army?" co-author, *Orbis*, Volume 34, No. 3, Summer 1990.

"Advanced Conventional Munitions and Moscow's Defensive Force Posture," *Defense Analysis*, Vol. 6, No. 2, Summer 1990.

"Is the Soviet Military Leadership Yielding on an All-Volunteer Army?" co-author, Radio Liberty Report on the USSR, Vol. 2, No. 13, March 30, 1990.

"New Thinking in Soviet Security Policy," in Carl G. Jacobsen, ed., *Strategic Power: USA/USSR*, London, UK: The MacMillan Press, Ltd., 1990.

"Gorbachev's Concept of Reasonable Sufficiency in National Defense," in George E. Hudson, ed., *Soviet National Security Policy Under Perestroika*, Boston, MA: Unwin Hyman, 1990.

"The Dilemma in Moscow's Defensive Force Posture," *Arms Control Today*, November 1989.

"The New Quality of Soviet Defense," *International Defense Review*, No. 10, 1989.

"Defensive defense: Marshal Ogarkov's view," *International Defense Review*, No. 9, 1989.

Changing Soviet Doctrine on Nuclear War, Dalhousie University, Nova Scotia, Canada: Center for Policy Studies, 1989.

"Marshal Ogarkov and the New Revolution in Soviet Military Affairs," *Defense Analysis*, Vol. 3, No.1, 1987.

"The Strategic Revolution Behind Soviet Arms Control," *Arms Control Today*, Vol. 17, No. 5, 1987.

Soviet Views on SDI, University of Pittsburgh, PA: The Carl Beck Papers in Russian and East European Studies, No. 601, 1987.

"Admiral V.N. Chernavin and the 'Stalbo Debates'," *Naval Intelligence Quarterly*, No. 3, 1986.

"Marshal Ogarkov on the Modern Theater Operation," *Naval War College Review*, Vol. XXXIX, No. 4, 1986.

"The Soviet Military on SDI," *Studies in Comparative Communism*, Vol. XIX, Nos. 3 and 4, 1986.

"The Soviet Leadership on Nuclear War," *Soviet Union*, Vol. 13, No. 3, 1986.

ABOUT THE CONTRIBUTORS

STEPHEN J. BLANK has served as the Strategic Studies Institute's expert on the Soviet bloc and the post-Soviet world since 1989. Prior to that he was Associate Professor of Soviet Studies at the Center for Aerospace Doctrine, Research, and Education, Maxwell Air Force Base, AL; and taught at the University of Texas, San Antonio; and at the University of California, Riverside. Dr. Blank is the editor of *Imperial Decline: Russia's Changing Position in Asia*, coeditor of *Soviet Military and the Future*, and author of *The Sorcerer as Apprentice: Stalin's Commissariat of Nationalities, 1917-1924*. He has also written many articles and conference papers on Russia, the Commonwealth of Independent States, and Eastern European security issues. Dr. Blank's current research deals with proliferation and the revolution in military affairs, and energy and security in Eurasia. His two most recent books are *Russo-Chinese Energy Relations: Politics in Command*, London, UK: Global Markets Briefing, 2006; and *Natural Allies?: Regional Security in Asia and Prospects for Indo-American Strategic Cooperation*, Carlisle, PA: Strategic Studies Institute, U.S. Army War College, 2005. Dr. Blank holds a B.A. in history from the University of Pennsylvania, and an M.A. and Ph.D. in history from the University of Chicago.

DANIEL GOURE is a Vice President with the Lexington Institute, a nonprofit public-policy research organization headquartered in Arlington, Virginia. Dr. Goure has held senior positions in both the private sector and the U.S. Government. Prior to joining the Lexington Institute, he was the Deputy Director, International Security Program at the Center for Strategic and International Studies. Dr. Goure spent 2 years in the U.S. Government as the director of the Office of Strategic Competitiveness in the Office of the Secretary of Defense. He also served as a senior analyst on national security and defense issues with the Center for Naval Analyses, Science Applications International Corporation, SRS Technologies, R&D Associates and System Planning Corporation. Dr. Goure holds a B.A. in government and history from Pomona College, and a master's and a Ph.D. in international relations and Russian studies from Johns Hopkins University.

DALE R. HERSPRING, a retired U.S. diplomat and Navy Captain, is a University Distinguished Professor of Political Science at Kansas State University and a member of the Council on Foreign Relations. He is the author of 12 books and more than 80 articles dealing with civil-military relations in the United States, Russia/The Soviet Union, Germany, and Eastern Europe. He is currently working on a new book to be entitled, "Military Culture and Civil-Military Relations; a Four Country Study." Using military culture as the basis of comparison, the book will look at civil-military relations in the United States, Russia, Germany, and Canada. Dr. Herspring holds an A.B. from Stanford University, a M.A. from Georgetown University, and a Ph.D. from the University of Southern California.

JACOB W. KIPP taught at Kansas State University from 1971 to 1985. In 1986, he joined the Soviet Army Studies Office (SASO) at Ft. Leavenworth, KS. In 1991, SASO became the Foreign Military Studies Office (FMSO). From 2003 to 2006, Dr. Kipp served as Director of FMSO. In 2006 he took the position of Deputy

Director of the School of Advanced Military Studies (SAMS). He retired from federal service in 2009. Dr. Kipp has written extensively on Russian and Soviet military and naval history, aviation, strategy, operational art, and military doctrine. He served as deputy editor of *Military Affairs,* as assistant editor of the *Journal of Slavic Military Studies,* as founding co-editor of *European Security,* and as a member of the editorial board of the *Modern War Studies Series* of the University Press of Kansas. He is a member of the Russian Academy of Natural Sciences. At present, he is an adjunct professor of History, and Russian and Eurasian Studies at the University of Kansas and a contributor to the Jamestown Foundation's *Eurasian Daily Monitor.* Dr. Kipp worked closely with Mary Fitzgerald on several projects relating to Soviet and Russian military affairs. Dr. Kipp holds a Ph.D. from the Pennsylvania State University.

JOSHUA B. SPERO is Associate Professor of Political Science, International Studies Program Coordinator, and Regional Economic Development Institute Director at Fitchburg State College in Massachusetts. He previously was U.S. Deputy Assistant for Europe and the USSR, Office of Secretary of Defense, Foreign Military Studies Office Liaison Officer (Ft. Leavenworth, KS), and Senior Civilian Strategic Planner (NATO Division) in the Joint Chiefs of Staff, Directorate for Strategic Plans and Policy. His research and publications focus on crisis management decisionmaking and on middle power politics and international security dilemmas. He is author of *Bridging the European Divide: Middle Power Politics and Regional Security Dilemmas* (Rowman and Littlefield, 2004). Dr. Spero holds a B.A. from Brandeis University, an M.A. from the University of Michigan, and a Ph.D. from the Johns Hopkins School of Advanced International Studies.

TIMOTHY L. THOMAS is a senior analyst at the Foreign Military Studies Office (FMSO) at Fort Leavenworth, Kansas. Mr. Thomas conducts extensive research and publishing in the areas of peacekeeping, information war, psychological operations, low intensity conflict, and political-military affairs. Mr. Thomas was a U.S. Army Foreign Area Officer who specialized in Soviet/Russian studies. His military assignments included serving as the Director of Soviet Studies at the United States Army Russian Institute (USARI) in Garmisch, Germany; as an inspector of Soviet tactical operations under the Commission on Security and Co-operation in Europe (CSCE); and as a Brigade S-2 and company commander in the 82nd Airborne Division. He has written three books on information warfare topics, focusing on recent developments in China and Russia. Mr. Thomas is an adjunct professor at the U.S. Army's Eurasian Institute; an adjunct lecturer at the U.S. Air Force Special Operations School; and a member of two Russian organizations, the Academy of International Information, and the Academy of Natural Sciences. Mr. Thomas holds a BS in engineering science from the United States Military Academy, and an M.A. in international relations from the University of Southern California.

MIKHAIL TSYPKIN is an associate professor in the Department of National Security Affairs at the Naval Postgraduate School. He served as the Salvatori Fellow in Soviet Studies at the Heritage Foundation in Washington DC. He is a member of the Scientific Board of the online journal, *The Journal Of Power Institutions*

In Post-Soviet Societies. Dr. Tsypkin has published numerous articles on Soviet and Russian military affairs. Among his recent publications are "Russian Politics and American Missile Defense," *International Affairs* (London), Vol. 85, No. 4, 2009; and "Reforming Intelligence: Russia's Failure," *Journal of Democracy*, Vol. 17, No. 3, July 2006. Dr. Tsypkin holds a Ph.D. in political science from Harvard University.

RICHARD WEITZ is Senior Fellow and Director of the Center for Political-Military Analysis at the Hudson Institute. His current research includes regional security developments relating to Europe, Eurasia, and East Asia as well as U.S. foreign, defense, homeland security, and weapons of mass destruction (WMD) nonproliferation policies. Dr. Weitz has published or edited several books and monographs, including *Global Security Watch–Russia* (Praeger Security International, 2009); a volume of *National Security Case Studies* (Project on National Security Reform, 2008); *China–Russia Security Relations* (Strategic Studies Institute, U.S. Army War College, 2008); *Kazakhstan and the New International Politics of Eurasia* (Central Asia-Caucasus Institute, 2008); *Mismanaging Mayhem: How Washington Responds to Crisis* (Praeger Security International, 2008); *The Reserve Policies of Nations: A Comparative Analysis* (Strategic Studies Institute, U.S. Army War College, 2007); and *Revitalising US–Russian Security Cooperation: Practical Measures* (The International Institute for Strategic Studies, 2005). Dr. Weitz holds a B.A. in government from Harvard College, an M.Sc. in international relations from the London School of Economics, an M.Phil. in politics from Oxford University, and a Ph.D. in political science from Harvard University.

U.S. ARMY WAR COLLEGE

Major General Gregg F. Martin
Commandant

*****

STRATEGIC STUDIES INSTITUTE

Director
Professor Douglas C. Lovelace, Jr.

Director of Research
Dr. Antulio J. Echevarria II

Editors
Dr. Stephen J. Blank
Dr. Richard Weitz

Director of Publications
Dr. James G. Pierce

Publications Assistant
Ms. Rita A. Rummel

*****

Composition
Mrs. Jennifer E. Nevil

www.ingramcontent.com/pod-product-compliance
Lightning Source LLC
Chambersburg PA
CBHW080527170426
43195CB00016B/2489